HUMAN RIGHTS, HUMAN WRONGS

HUMAN RIGHTS, HUMAN WRONGS

The Alternative Report to the United Nations Human Rights Committee

Conor Foley

for Liberty
National Council for Civil Liberties

Rivers Oram Press
London

First published in 1995 by
Rivers Oram Press
144 Hemingford Road, London N1 1DE

Published in the USA by
Paul and Company
Post Office Box 442, Concord, MA 01742

Phototypeset in 10/12 Sabon by Intype, London
and printed in Great Britain
by T.J. Press (Padstow) Ltd, Padstow, Cornwall

Designed by Lesley Stewart

British Library Cataloguing in Publication Data
A catalogue record for this book is available from the British Library

ISBN 1–85489–076–X
ISBN 1–85489–077–8 pbk

CONTENTS

Contents

Contents

FOREWORD

In the 50 years since the end of the Second World War and the establishment of the United Nations, human rights has become one of the most important issues in world politics. The experience of the Second World War and the Holocaust forced nation states to confront the problem of how respect for human values could be guaranteed in different societies. By 1945 the optimism that had greeted the dawning of the twentieth century had gone: over 100 million people had been killed in conflicts between states and, in an attempt to exterminate the entire Jewish population of occupied Europe by the Nazis, as well as other groups regarded as 'inferior', millions more had died in labour camps or concentration camps. The shock of these events forced the community of states to consider a new approach to regulating conduct and to introduce human rights standards. States would sign international treaties, setting out entitlements which all human beings would be able to claim, and would be obliged to observe those standards.

The concept of a human right was not new. The US introduced a Bill of Rights in 1791 and the French Declaration of Rights of 1789 had been a valuable historic document. But these proclamations were national documents that applied to citizens and from which whole categories of people could be excluded (for example slaves in the early history of the US) and were, therefore, limited; during the Second World War, the US Bill of Rights failed to provide protection for those Japanese-Americans who were interned during the conflict. After the war a new approach was adopted: human rights standards were applied to *all* citizens of *all* countries, and they were to be guaranteed by international treaty.

Of course there were compromises. During the establishment of the United Nations, part of the world was dividing into two hostile camps. At the insistence of the dominant Western camp, the concept of human rights was divided into two categories: civil and political rights (covering those areas of social and political life traditionally guaranteed by 'Western' democracies such as the right to assemble, the right to free speech, the right to associate and so on), and social and economic rights (such as rights to health care, to education, to housing and work). This split has been a feature of human rights ever since. Poorer countries have objected to the West's insistence on upholding civil and political rights to the exclusion of social and economic rights. Others have argued that the counter position of two sets of rights has no intellectual or political justification and point out that the right to be free from discrimination does not fit well into either category.

There were also political problems in trying to establish basic human rights standards. For a several years, the Soviet Union was reluctant to sign such treaties, seeing them as a way of legitimising 'Western' interference in their internal affairs. Other countries shared these concerns. However, despite these diplomatic obstacles, progress was made. The UN founding document is the Universal Declaration of Human Rights which laid down minimum standards for the treatment of all. These fundamental principles are embodied in the International Bill of Rights which consists of three documents: the Universal Declaration of Human Rights (UDHR); the International Covenant on Civil and Political Rights (ICCPR) with an optional protocol; and the International Covenant on Social and Economic Rights (ICSER).

For much of the post-war period, work at an international level has concentrated on developing human rights standards. A number of major conventions has been agreed. In addition to the International Bill of Rights, there are for example specific conventions dealing with the elimination of all forms of discrimination against women, conventions dealing with racism and genocide, with protection for the rights of the child. Although UN human rights arrangements are often chaotic and can be difficult to understand, a great deal of work at international level has developed a comprehensive set of human rights standards. There is now broad international agreement as to what constitutes the human rights we should all possess.

The international community has had less success in finding ways of enforcing human rights standards, as it requires first that the actions of states are monitored by reputable and independent international bodies who can measure the implementation of these standards in each country and the development of such mechanisms has been very uneven. The Conference on Security and Co-operation in Europe (CSCE) – formalised at Helsinki – established a 'human rights basket' of issues that were discussed at a series of conferences in the 1970s and 1980s. From these international conferences grew a network of 'Helsinki Watch' committees. Initially these were US-based and appeared to many to be functioning as a tacit arm of US foreign policy – a means to criticise the Soviet Union and its satellite states. However, inspired by the Helsinki process, a network of human rights watch committees developed inside the old Soviet bloc – activists who pioneered the struggle for democracy that eventually culminated in the collapse of the Soviet system at the end of the 1980s. The watch committees have also proved an embarrassing thorn in the flesh of Western governments by, for example, criticising the British government's human rights abuses in Northern Ireland. It has been a good example of how effective international treaties can be if there are powerful non-government organisations (NGOs) willing to monitor them.

Other international standards have had little effect. Some governments in particular have refused to be bound by human rights treaties, notably the US which is ready to condemn human rights abuses in other countries but reluctant to accept the application of those standards to its own conduct. One of the most significant advances of the Clinton administration has been the ratification of many international human rights treaties. The British government has prided itself on its human rights record and has been one of the most vigorous critics of the records of other countries. Like the US it is unused to, and uncomfortable with, international criticism.

The United Nations Covenant on Civil and Political Rights is a legally binding treaty. The UK government has signed the treaty, but not the optional protocol which permits individuals to make representations to the UN directly. (See Appendix 2.) Each signatory country is obliged to report every five years to a special Human Rights Committee established by the UN. This committee, which is made up of international jurists from signatory countries, has the right to examine and to question the human rights record of the signatory country over the period in question measured against the standards set out in the ICCPR. Although the committee has no power to compel states to respond to its concerns, its reports can be severely embarrassing for the recipient country. So-called mature democracies, who tend to be complacent about their human rights record, are particularly concerned to ensure a good report from the Committee.

No such committee, whatever the qualifications of its individual members, can be expected to understand fully the human rights position in every signatory country. States, in their reports to the Committee, inevitably will dwell on their achievements, not their failures. Often the only alternative source of information available to the Committee is the submissions made by NGOs from the country concerned. The effectiveness and role of such organisations will be a crucial factor in determining the effectiveness of the committee's work and in creating pressure on the relevant country to improve its human rights practice.

It is perhaps inevitable, therefore, that in parallel with the development of international human rights standards there has been a substantial growth in the number of NGOs concerned with human rights throughout the world. Amnesty International is probably the most well known, but there are many other international and national groups whose experience and work is vital to the effective functioning of the Human Rights Committee. Unfortunately, in past years British based NGOs have not provided the Human Rights Committee with the best possible briefing on human rights problems in the UK, resulting in the British government having a relatively easy ride at the Human Rights Committee. Consequently, in 1993, Liberty set out to produce a series of detailed reports which sought to analyse potential abuses of human rights against the standards set out in the Civil and Political Covenant. We do not pretend the chapters in this book are a comprehensive survey of all the human rights issues, nor do we claim they form a balanced assessment – such a judgment is for the Human Rights Committee to make. The chapters set out a wide range of concerns and constitute a *prima facie* case against the UK government.

The focus of these chapters is England and Wales. There is a separate legal system in Scotland and a separate political situation in Northern Ireland, both of which would require separate sets of reports. Each will be the subject of submissions to the Human Rights Committee. However, we have set out the human rights abuses arising from the conflict in Northern Ireland. Despite these limitations, we believe that the chapters constitute one of the broadest analyses of human rights practice carried out in any country in recent years.

Liberty is well equipped to carry out the analysis of human rights issues. Since its foundation in 1934, Liberty has been concerned with protecting civil liberties and human rights within the UK, and has long recognised the importance of international human rights standards. At the time of the founding meeting of the UN in London, Liberty organised a parallel conference of NGOs from around the world. In the absence of domestically enforceable rights, Liberty has used international instruments such as the European Convention on Human Rights and taken more cases to the European Commission and Court at Strasbourg than any other individual or organisation in Britain.

It was not appropriate for Liberty to produce this analysis alone. Each chapter was researched and written in partnership with an organisation which has specialist or direct knowledge of the relevant issue. In some cases Liberty was already familiar with the human rights concerns highlighted by the report and, in other cases, the experience was an education. The analysis here does not simply reflect Liberty's view of the problem but form the broad-ranging concerns of expert organisations in the field. They are not academic documents – they are the views of people whose concern is not merely to analyse the problems but to do something about them.

The process of working with other organisations in partnership is important to Liberty since human rights protection cannot be achieved by individuals or groups working alone. One of the biggest problems facing any society is how to deal with the myriad issues that spring from the inequalities, discrimination and structural problems such societies will inevitably possess. It is easy for groups with particular concerns to feel they are in competition with others for legislative time or public resources. The human rights approach offers something quite different. It is based upon a universal set of entitlements that each human being should possess. It recognises that every human experience is distinct – that endurance of racism, for example, cannot be compared with the sense of exclusion encountered by disabled people. The human rights approach does not seek to elevate one group above another: it identifies what people share (their entitlement) rather than that which they cannot share (their experience). In so doing it establishes a bond between different groups, because you cannot argue for your own entitlements without recognising those of others.

It is this recognition that lies at the heart of human rights – and it illuminates every chapter of this book. We are seeking not to catalogue abuses, but to help lay the foundations for a human rights movement in this country. One of the startling features of British life is the absence of significant human rights entitlements in British law. With certain exceptions, such as rights contained in the Race Relations Act and Sex Discrimination legislation, British law is silent about our rights and fundamental freedoms. Our laws broadly tell us what we cannot do, and it is assumed that we are free to do anything which is not prohibited. Governments defend this historic state of affairs as providing a satisfactory method of protecting human rights, although most countries in the world no longer regard such an approach as adequate. This book tells another story. The chapters set out human rights abuses, but also identify that there is no means of redress for such abuses: there is no effective mechanism in British society to provide protection for human rights. This is the reason for the growing debate about the need for an enforceable Bill of Rights.

There are usually four reasons given for supporting a Bill of Rights. First, the existence of a Bill of Rights means that rights can be taught in schools and colleges and, as a result, a much greater awareness of rights is created. This awareness itself is empowering. People who understand that they have rights are more likely to take action to challenge abuses of those rights. Second, a Bill of Rights enforceable by the courts gives legal redress to individuals against public officials. If your rights are abused by a police officer, a customs official, a local authority worker, you have recourse to a court, either to seek an injunction to prevent the abuse, or to seek damages in compensation. The knowledge that you have recourse in such circumstances can also have a powerful impact on official culture: people who know they may end up in court are likely to think more carefully about their behaviour. It may not matter whether these powers are used, they help create a different culture. Third, a Bill of Rights can be entrenched (that is, made fundamental law protected by special voting procedures) so that it can only be amended by a large majority (say two-thirds of parliament). The effect is that parliament, instead of being free to legislate (as in theory it now is) is forced to ensure that its own laws comply with the Bill of Rights. This is the position in many countries which have written constitutions and Bills of Rights. They are 'founding' documents and act as a brake upon parliament. They also apply to the government either acting through parliament or using prerogative powers if it tries to breach those fundamental rights. This is a controversial power in our democracy which has always held parliament to be sovereign and not capable of being bound by anybody else, although in practice British participation in the European Union has begun to erode absolute parliamentary sovereignty. The British parliament, as well as the British legal system, is bound in certain circumstances to abide by judgments made by the European Court at Luxembourg. The growth of international institutions (not least the international money market) has already placed a question mark against the concept of national sovereignty. Nevertheless, as any contemporary newspaper will show, this issue arouses the greatest passions amongst members of parliament.

The fourth argument used to support a Bill of Rights is the protection it can afford to vulnerable minorities. Any democratic society will develop institutions which seek to reflect the views of the dominant majority. In most cases this will not be a problem, but in some societies minorities exist who are regarded antagonistically and, as a result, face persecution and hostility, Travellers for example. Being in a majority does not necessarily make you right: throughout history there are many examples of majority opinions leading to the suppression of important truths. At the same time, no democratically elected politician can afford to neglect the force of majority opinion. It has proved difficult for politicians to champion the rights of lesbians and gay men or the interests of the black community or other minority groups who have experienced prejudice, hostility and discrimination. A Bill of Rights can afford such protection and (in that protection is provided through the courts) can be free from the pressures of the majority, often evident in a democracy. It may well be impossible to assemble a political majority to take positive steps to uphold the rights of unpopular minorities, but such rights could be won through legal action in the courts using the non-discrimination principles of a Bill of Rights as a basis for the argument.

Yet, there is powerful opposition to the introduction of a Bill of Rights. Some argue it is not necessary: the sovereignty of parliament is the best guarantor of rights because if parliament makes a mistake, it can undo it with a subsequent piece of legislation. Such arguments are hard to reconcile with the human rights abuses set out in these chapters. It is also argued that common law provides a more solid basis for freedom, as it is flexible, open-ended and capable of responding to new circumstances. Again, the evidence from the chapters undermines this argument. Others argue that were a Bill of Rights to be introduced, too many important decisions would be placed in the hands of judges and that the scope for judicial involvement in the way governments operate would be increased. Some believe this would be undemocratic and point to the possibility of a government seeking to introduce legislation which commands overwhelming support and then being told by the courts that it cannot introduce the legislation because it contradicts the Bill of Rights. This, they believe, is an unacceptable restriction of democracy.

The issue is complex, because Bills of Rights cannot set out every contingency – they are sets of basic principles: the right to life, the right to freedom of expression, the right to freedom of information, the right to assembly – and these principles have to be interpreted in the light of circumstances. Moreover, rights are rarely absolute – the exercise of one right has to be balanced by the degree to which it conflicts with the rights and freedoms of others. This produces many dilemmas and there are those who argue that it is inappropriate for the courts to make decisions on behalf of society about such dilemmas – that they should be properly referred to parliament for a decision.

There is some force in these arguments. Courts should not be expected to take 'political' decisions. In Britain, for example, we have always regarded issues such as the legal entitlement to abortion as being properly decided by parliament rather than by the courts. However, it is possible to devise a means of enforcing a Bill of Rights which respects parliamentarians' rights to make the decisions it is proper for them to take – such as rulings on where the balance of rights might lie in various cases. Although a Bill of Rights has to be enforced by the courts, it would be possible to create a parliamentary procedure which examined how proposed government legislation matched up to the existing Bill of Rights. A parliamentary committee, perhaps elected by proportional representation so that it was without a government majority, could be asked to rule as to whether the proposed legislation was consistent with a Bill of Rights. If the committee felt that the proposed legislation contravened the Bill, then either that legislation would fall, or it would require an enhanced majority (again, say two-thirds) to pass. This model, developed by Liberty, could be called 'a democratically entrenched Bill of Rights' (see Appendix 1). It presents no great constitutional problems and it deals with many of the substantial objections from those opposed to a traditional judicially entrenched Bill.

What is certain is that any Bill of Rights would act as a constraint upon government. Its most useful function would be to inspire ordinary people to take action themselves. The US Bill of Rights was a defunct instrument for 150 years and the two most important judgments arrived at by the US Supreme Court in the nineteenth century were both hostile to human rights principles. It was only the foundation of the National Association for the Advancement of Colored Peoples and the American Civil Liberties Union that led to the serious attempt to bring human rights cases to the courts. The examples from the more recent history of international human rights law support this thesis – where there are strong, independent, monitoring bodies, human rights standards are more likely to be upheld. It is a demonstration that while a domestic Bill of Rights and powerful international human rights treaties are important and indeed a necessary legal framework for the protection of human rights, they are worthless unless people are willing and able to use them. The most important guarantee of our freedoms is the willingness of people to defend them. We hope this publication helps the readers claim their rights.

Andrew Puddephatt
General Secretary
Liberty
(National Council for Civil Liberties)

1 DEMOCRACY AND HUMAN RIGHTS IN THE UNITED KINGDOM

SOME ARGUMENTS FOR CONSTITUTIONAL CHANGE

In the general election of April 1992, the British Conservative Party was re-elected for an unprecedented fourth term. Only 41.9 per cent of the electorate, or just over two out of every five voters, voted for the governing party.[1] Britain's first-past-the-post voting system means that governments are usually elected on a minority of the popular vote.[2]

The lack of a written constitution or Bill of Rights, and the doctrine of the absolute sovereignty of the Crown in Parliament mean that the British government[3] can exercise its powers without formal domestic constitutional restraint.[4] Moreover, the British legislature contains a House of Lords whose unelected members hold seats mainly owing to hereditary peerages.[5] The House of Lords, which has the power to scrutinise and delay legislation, is dominated by Conservative Peers.[6]

Over the last 15 years, the government has extended and concentrated the powers of the State. The rights of people to organise and to demonstrate have been considerably constrained; the media censored, the powers of the police extended and the rights of defendants diminished. Basic human rights have been denied to people on the grounds of national security; local democracy has been weakened and unelected quangos are now responsible for spending more public money than elected local councillors are.

Britain's system of democracy has particular implications for the people of Scotland, Wales and Northern Ireland. The United Kingdom of Great Britain and Northern Ireland is not a single country but a multi-nation State. The present government has consistently rejected proposals for self-government or greater democratic control in Scotland and Wales.[7] The British and Irish

1

governments published a joint framework document in February 1995 and Northern Ireland's long-term constitutional position remains the subject of delicate negotiations.[8]

Moves towards a unified Europe

The national sovereignty debate in Britain has been given a new relevance by the moves towards a unified Europe.[9] Jacques Delors, a former President of the European Commission, has estimated that, by 1998, 80 per cent of all legislation concerning the economic, social and taxation decisions of the European Union's member States will originate from the Council of Ministers and European Commission.[10] Yet the Commission is an unelected and unaccountable body.

The elected European Parliament is unable effectively to monitor the work of either the European Commission or the Council of Ministers. The Council of Ministers, on which all member States of the European Union are represented, deliberates in secret and does not publish its minutes. The president of the European Commission is not directly elected by the people of Europe nor, as yet, is his or her appointment subject to confirmation by the European Parliament.[11] Individual Commissioners are similarly unaccountable to the European Parliament. The European Parliament cannot supervise the European Union's budget.[12]

The European Union has its own Court of Justice, based in Luxembourg. However, neither the Commission nor any other European Union institution is accountable to the European Court of Human Rights for breaches of the European Convention on Human Rights (ECHR).

There is also a growing number of transnational European institutions that exercise an increasing influence over the lives of the people of Europe. These include:

☐ the Trevi Group, which consists of Europe's Ministers of the Interior, has a semi-permanent secretariat and deals with terrorism and international crime

☐ the Pompidou Group which deals with drug trafficking

☐ the Ad Hoc Working Group on Immigration and the Co-ordinators Group, both of which deal with migrants and movement of people.

Although they are not formally part of the European Union, these groups are associated with the process of greater political and economic convergence. Much of their work intrudes on national sovereignty and has implications for the protection of human rights, yet there is little democratic control or scrutiny of their actions and they conduct much of their business in secret.

THE BRITISH GOVERNMENT'S RECORD

In its *Third Periodic Report* to the UN Human Rights Committee the British government stated:

The right to self-determination in the United Kingdom is exercised primarily through the electoral system. A general election, for all seats in the House of Commons, takes place at least every five years, but a Parliament may be, and often is, dissolved by the Sovereign, acting on the Prime Minister's advice, before the end of the full legal term . . . Referenda have been held on Scottish and Welsh devolution, and membership of the European Community. Whether the people of Northern Ireland want to remain part of the United Kingdom was tested in a border poll in 1973 with a positive result.[13]

In its *Fourth Periodic Report*, which was published in October 1994, the government concentrated on the political developments in Northern Ireland leading up to the ceasefire. It quoted from paragraph four of the joint declaration issued by the British and Irish governments the previous year stating that 'it is for the people on the island of Ireland alone, by agreements between the two parts respectively, to exercise their right to self-determination on the basis of consent, freely and concurrently given, North and South, to bring about a united Ireland if that is their wish.'[14]

In its introduction to the *Third Report*, the government outlined the doctrine of parliamentary sovereignty, the lack of a Bill of Rights and the case against the incorporation of the ECHR into domestic law. It stated that:

The country has not during this period felt the need for a written constitution or a comprehensive Bill of Rights: the principle has been that the rights and freedoms recognised in other countries' constitutions are inherent in this country's legal system and are protected by it and by Parliament unless they

3

are removed or restricted by statute . . . The case for more comprehensive Human Rights legislation has been argued at various times during the past 15 years. The incorporation of the European Convention into the United Kingdom domestic law has been the solution most often favoured; but neither of the two largest political parties has adopted it as their policy . . . injustice or unfairness of the kind which such a Bill would be designed to correct could in the United Kingdom context be more suitably and effectively challenged in Parliament.[15]

In its *Fourth Periodic Report* the British government reiterated this opposition but stated that 'judgments of the House of Lords have made clear that such obligations are part of the legal context in which the judges themselves operate.'[16] The government also rejected ratification of the Optional Protocol of the International Covenant on Civil and Political Rights (ICCPR) which would enable individuals to bring cases of alleged human rights violations to the UN Human Rights Committee for consideration.[17]

Despite the government's opposition, there is increasing support for entrenching human rights in some form of Bill of Rights in the UK. Both the main opposition parties in Britain have adopted policies favouring the incorporation of the ECHR into domestic law; and all the main nationalist and Unionist parties in Scotland, Wales and Northern Ireland favour the adoption of some form of Bill of Rights. There has been more debate about whether and how a Bill of Rights could be constitutionally entrenched, and a number of organisations, including Liberty, have published draft Bills for discussion.[18] Non party-political groups campaigning for constitutional reform, like Charter 88, have attracted increasing support.

The Royal Prerogative

At the centre of the UK's unwritten constitution are the powers of the Crown, referred to as the Royal Prerogative, which the Sovereign exercises on the advice of the government. After an election it is the Sovereign's duty to summon a leader from one of the political parties and to invite him or her to attempt to form a government.[19] By convention the Sovereign invites the leader of the party with the most seats, although if no party had an overall majority the Sovereign might have some discretionary power.[20]

Acting on the Prime Minister's advice, the Sovereign can dissolve Parliament and call elections, declare war, conclude foreign treaties and recognise new foreign governments without first informing Parliament.[21] Although many matters regarding the armed forces are regulated by statute, their control, organisation and disposition are within the prerogative and cannot be questioned in a court.[22] The Sovereign also appoints ministers, judges, magistrates and a variety of other holders of public office on the Prime Minister's advice, and is the only person empowered to award honours and create Peers to the House of Lords.[23] The Prime Minister cannot be questioned by MPs about the advice that he or she may have given to the Sovereign regarding the grant of honours.[24]

Ministers are still responsible to Parliament when exercising prerogative powers and governments usually recognise the importance of gaining parliamentary approval for their actions. However, ministers do not always have to report their actions to Parliament. Alan Clark, the former Trade and Defence Minister, told the inquiry headed by Lord Justice Scott into the government's policy on weapons exports to Iraq that ministers were reluctant to announce a change in policy publicly because: 'the House of Commons is very volatile and you get all sorts of rows and ooo-er. They are a bit of a nuisance . . . You try not to invite too much intrusion.'[25]

Governments are also free to use their prerogative powers to bind the United Kingdom into treaties under international law or to declare war on other countries—prior to, in the absence of, or even in spite of the expressed wishes of Parliament.[26] Ministers can sign a treaty using their prerogative powers but such a treaty cannot alter the law without Parliament's approval.[27] It can be argued that the use of prerogative powers would cause a constitutional crisis if Parliament subsequently refused to approve ministers' actions. Though convention and practice play a major part in the British constitutional tradition,[28] they are imprecise, not subject to jurisdiction but are subject to change.[29] It is in moments of crisis that decision-making processes depart from convention and practice, and precisely then that the absence of formal checks on the executive are most worrying.

For instance, the House of Commons did not formally debate and approve British participation in the Gulf conflict until 21 January 1991, four days after hostilities had commenced.[30] Although there were three adjournment debates[31] before this date, at which Parliament had approved the government's actions by large majorities, the substantive discussion took place only after resources had been committed to the conflict.[32]

During the debate on ratification of the Maastricht Treaty on European Monetary and Political Union in the spring of 1993 the government said that it was willing to defy the wishes of Parliament. Faced with a challenge from the opposition political parties and a rebellion in its own ranks, the government risked defeat in attempting to ratify the Treaty *without* the Social Chapter. The government secured the legal opinion of the Attorney-General that Parliament could not insist on the Social Chapter being incorporated. The Foreign Secretary, Douglas Hurd, told the House of Commons that the government would not incorporate the Social Chapter of the Treaty even if the House passed an amendment calling for it to do so.[33] He said that he would bring the whole Bill back to Parliament for approval, but did not deny statements from supporters and opponents that he was not constitutionally required to do so, as the government was free to ratify the Treaty using the Royal Prerogative.[34]

In July 1993 the government lost a resolution to bring the Treaty into force without the Social Chapter, but then won a motion which stated that 'this House has confidence in the policy of Her Majesty's Government on the adoption of the Protocol on Social Policy.'[35] The defeat of this motion would have brought down the government, so the Conservative rebels supported it, although they had voted against the government on the incorporation of the Social Chapter.

In the same month the courts rejected a legal challenge to the Maastricht Treaty. This included the objection that the government, by ratifying the Treaty, would be transferring some of the powers of the Royal Prerogative (those which enabled the government to conduct foreign and security policy) to the European Union, which it did not have the authority to do.[36]

The Royal Prerogative is also routinely used by the executive to secure narrow political advantage for the governing party. The government can, and does, use its power to dissolve Parliament before the end of its maximum five-year lifetime to ensure that general elections take place when the governing party's chances of re-election are at their best. Governing parties have occasionally benefited electorally from foreign policy successes and victories in wars, which makes the lack of full democratic scrutiny in the area disturbing. For example, the Conservative government, previously at record levels of unpopularity in the opinion polls, won a land-slide victory in a general election held in 1983, nine months after the end of the Falklands conflict. The first fatalities occurred when the British Navy sank an Argentine battleship, outside the British declared exclusion zone, with the loss of 368 lives. A senior civil servant, Clive Ponting, was tried under the Official Secrets Act (and acquitted) after he leaked information that 'ministers had gravely misled Parliament' about the details of the incident.[37] The conflict itself was characterised by excessive censorship and news-management.[38]

The monarchy

There is a distinction between the prerogative powers themselves and the fact that these powers currently reside in a hereditary monarchy. The main objection to having a monarch as head of State is that hereditary power, exercised in a symbolic way through the Royal Prerogative, is contrary to the principle that everyone should have free and equal rights to political participation and the conduct of public affairs. The institution of the Crown in Parliament and the dominance of the second chamber by hereditary Peers contradict the principle that governments should be representative of, and accountable to, the people. This principle finds expression in Article 25 of the ICCPR.

It has been argued that it is important to have a head of State who is seen to be above party political controversy and that this would not be possible without the hereditary principle. Lord Hailsham, a former Lord Chancellor, for example, has commented on:

> the contrast to be marked in those countries where a strutting and bemedalled figure, even if elected, claims at once to exercise more or less unbridled power, and at the same time to act as the apex and focus of political loyalty to the State and the symbol of national tradition, continuity and pride. An equally striking contrast may be drawn between our own institution and the other kind of republican presidency where a wholly uncontentious, but usually decrepit and superannuated nonentity is selected or elected as nominal head of State precisely because he or she is harmless and innocuous . . . Those who, in one capacity or another, have served in public offices . . . testify to the immense dedication to

duty and diplomacy which all members of the royal circle bring
to their respective public and private activities.[39]

Another Conservative commentator, Ferdinand Mount, has argued
that a virtue of the monarchy has been its distance from political
controversy, achieved through the tradition of silence.[40] By keeping
their opinions private, he argues, monarchs were previously seen
to be above the partisan nature of party politics and therefore
able to represent the entire nation as head of State. However, he
has pointed out that this tradition is increasingly breaking down.[41]
As members of the royal family have voiced political opinions,
they have been drawn into political controversy.[42] No head of State
could avoid all controversy, but the exalted position the royal
family enjoys in the British constitution places its individual members under intense scrutiny. As the symbol of the State and head
of the established Church, the monarch is expected to exercise
standards of discretion and behaviour, in both public and private
activities, which appear increasingly unrealistic.[43]

It is dangerous for an institution that is, by its very nature,
unelected, unaccountable and exclusive, to act as a symbol for the
State, because this negates the principle that the authority of
the State derives from the will of the people. The former intelligence
services officer, Peter Wright, for instance, has claimed that sections
of MI5 conspired against the Labour Prime Minister, Harold
Wilson, during the 1970s because they believed that their duty to
the Crown overrode their duty to the head of government.[44]

One final objection to the monarchy's current constitutional
position is that the rules of succession are discriminatory. The
principle of primogeniture, by which the right of succession passes
to the eldest son, and the specification in the Act of Settlement
1700 disqualifying Catholics from the monarchy and prohibiting
the monarch from marrying outside the Church of England are
discriminatory on the basis of both gender and religion, contrary
to Articles 3 and 26 of the ICCPR. In most other European constitutional monarchies legislation has been enacted to ensure that
rights of succession are not discriminatory. The British government
was forced to enter a reservation when it ratified the Convention
on the Elimination of All Forms of Discrimination Against Women
in 1986 because of the practice of primogeniture.[45]

The Church of England

The Church of England, as the Established Church in England, has a privileged place in the British constitution. The Church has direct and unelected representation in the British Parliament, exercised by 26 senior bishops in the House of Lords.[46] Since the monarch is also the head of the Church of England, this places restrictions on who can become King or Queen. It is only comparatively recently that the bar has been removed on Roman Catholics holding the offices of Lord High Chancellor, Chief Judicial Officer and the Head of the Judiciary.[47]

The Church is empowered to pass measures governing its forms of worship, rites and ceremonies which, if approved by the Parliament, become the law of England. Decrees of its ecclesiastical courts can also be enforced by the State.[48] Neither the Church of Scotland nor the Church of Ireland enjoys the same privileges, and no other church or religion has a comparable position.

There have been disputes, too, about Britain's blasphemy laws, which relate to Christianity but not to other religions.[49] Disestablishment of the Church of England would remove a British constitutional practice which is archaic and discriminatory in a multicultural society.

The House of Lords

The existence of an unelected second chamber to Parliament, the House of Lords, is a serious democratic anomaly. Its members are unaccountable and unrepresentative of society. They are overwhelmingly male and largely drawn from a narrow social class which often has a particular and partisan political outlook. Women are directly excluded from hereditary peerages through the principle of primogeniture, by which the right of succession passes through the male line, and make up only 7 per cent of Peers.[50] There are 775 hereditary Peers, who sit solely by virtue of their ancestry, out of a total of 1,223.[51] Only 13 hereditary Peers take the Labour Whip.[52] There are also 382 life Peers, 26 Church of England Bishops and 11 Law Lords.[53] The Lord Chancellor also sits in the Lords where the office combines the functions of member of the legislature, of the executive and of the judiciary.[54]

The House of Lords has the power to scrutinise, amend and delay non-financial legislation, although ultimate authority remains with the House of Commons.[55] Members of the Lords are aware that, without a democratic mandate, their role is strictly limited.[56] There is widespread acceptance that a second chamber is useful for scrutinising legislation and protecting fundamental human rights – but one of the arguments against that chamber being the House of Lords is that its undemocratic nature makes it unable to perform these constitutional functions adequately. Both the main opposition parties are opposed to the continuance of the House of Lords in its current form.[57]

Parliamentary scrutiny

There is concern that the government's increasing use of delegated legislation (which cannot be amended) and guillotines to curtail the parliamentary timetable has reduced Parliament's ability to scrutinise and debate legislation. In December 1993 the main opposition party announced that it was withdrawing co-operation over the conduct of parliamentary business in protest at the government's use of guillotines to prevent discussion of two clauses in the Finance Bill which arose from the Budget.[58] Between 1979 and 1989 the present government used the guillotine 47 times, more than all other post-war British governments combined up to 1979.[59] The use of guillotines on Finance Bills is virtually unprecedented: with only two occasions this century.[60]

Delegated legislation takes the form of statutory instruments which are supposed to 'fill in the gaps' of full Acts of Parliament.[61] Unlike Acts of Parliament, statutory instruments cannot be amended, only voted down, and so they are not subject to the same detailed scrutiny and debate. In 1986 the Joint Committee on Statutory Instruments reported that the volume and complexity of these instruments had increased to the point where 'instead of simply implementing the "nuts and bolts" of government policy, statutory instruments have increasingly been used to change policy, sometimes in ways that were not envisaged when the enabling primary legislation was passed.'[62]

Representation of women in public office

Women remain seriously under-represented in British political and public life. Only 9.2 per cent of members of the House of Commons are women.[63] The anti-social hours during which the House sits make it virtually impossible for women – or men – with child care responsibilities to be MPs without major disruption to their home lives, and crèche facilities in Parliament are minimal. Only 14 per cent of life Peers are women,[64] and since 1945 only 34 women have become government ministers.[65] There are no female Lords Spiritual, that is Bishops in the House of Lords,[66] and although the Church of England's synod voted to allow the ordination of women in 1994, it will take some time before any of them reach sufficient seniority to be appointed.[67]

Women hold only 26 per cent of public appointments,[68] and the proportion of women in the upper levels of appointments is even smaller. Although nearly half of all civil servants are women, they make up only 8.6 per cent of those in the top three grades, who are primarily responsible for advising ministers and implementing policy.[69] There are only two women at management level in the 40 quangos with the largest budgets.[70] There is only one woman Lord Justice out of 27, one High Court judge out of 82 and 16 circuit judges out of 421.[71]

Exercising the right to vote

The former Conservative Prime Minister, Margaret Thatcher, has been quoted as claiming that the Community Charge, or Poll Tax, had won the 1992 election for the Conservatives by removing a million people, who were mainly Labour supporters, from the electoral roll,[72] exacerbating a longer term trend of people to omit themselves from the electoral register, either because of apathy or a desire to escape the attention of the authorities.

The number one million derives from figures released by the Office of Population Censuses Surveys (part of the Government Statistical Service) and are based on preliminary returns from the 1991 census,[73] which show a substantial drop in the number of names on the 1991 electoral register compared to the previous register.[74] Non-registration was highest amongst young people, and ethnic minorities were up to four times as likely to be unregistered as white people.[75] The register of those liable to pay the Poll Tax was separate from the electoral register. However, electoral registration officers were required to supply information to the Community Charge Registration Officer.[76] Many of those who refused to pay withheld their names from the electoral register to make it more difficult for the authorities to obtain their names, either for financial reasons, or as political protest.

The Association of London Authorities has noted that the fall in the numbers on the electoral register was heavily concentrated in inner-city and metropolitan areas.[77] In some parts of London up to 10 per cent of the electorate 'disappeared'.[78] One detailed analysis of the impact of the Poll Tax on the numbers on the electoral register concluded that it probably accounted for slightly over one third of the reduction in numbers in England and Wales and for a higher proportion of the reduction in Scotland.[79] It also concluded that the great majority of those who did not register to vote, either because of their hostility to the Poll Tax, or their inability to pay it, would have voted against the government.[80] Assuming these votes were split proportionately across the parliamentary constituencies, Labour would have won as many as 13 more seats in the election, and the Liberal Democrats one more, depriving the Conservatives of their overall majority by seven seats. A more cautious estimate was that the effect saved the Conservatives eight seats which they otherwise would have lost, and consequently they would have had an overall majority of five.[81]

In addition to those unable to vote because they are unregistered, four million people face specific difficulties in exercising their right to vote. The Spastics Society (now called Scope) has pointed out that only 12 per cent of polling stations in the last election were fully accessible to disabled people and that as a result many disabled people experienced problems in voting.[82] The Royal National Institute for the Blind has estimated that about half of the one million partially sighted people living in Britain need help to register for or cast their vote and they often do not receive that help.[83]

CHAR, the Housing Campaign for Single People, has warned that many thousands of homeless people are disenfranchised from local, general and European elections because they are unable to put their names on the electoral register.[84] The campaign warns that the electoral register's requirement of permanency of residence discriminates against homeless people who are sleeping rough or staying in temporary accommodation.[85]

Eligibility to vote in British elections is subject to the vagaries of Britain's nationality and citizenship laws. Before 1948 all people born within the UK or a British colony or dependency had the status of 'British subject', and the same rights of entry, residence and political participation.[86] Immigration and nationality Acts have since restricted many of these rights.[87] But the Representation of the People Act 1983 discriminates between people living in Britain according to their country of origin. For instance, people from Poland or Colombia who have lived in this country for 20 years are not eligible to vote, while people from India or Nigeria, which are in the British Commonwealth, and the Republic of Ireland, which is not a member, can vote immediately.[88]

Local democracy

Between 1979 and 1992 the British government introduced 144 separate Acts of Parliament which affect the powers of local government. The main effect of these has been to transfer power and resources from democratically elected local councils, to unelected quangos or to central government. The London Regional Transport Act 1984 transferred control of transport from the Greater London Council to the Secretary of State for Transport. The Local Government Act 1985 abolished the Greater London Council and the Metropolitan County Councils, making London one of the few capital cities not to have an elected authority. The Education Act 1986, the Education Reform Act 1988, the Further and Higher Education Act 1992 and the Education (Schools) Act 1992 all reduced the powers of local education authorities to scrutinise schools and colleges in their area.[89]

Further Education colleges and grant-maintained schools have been removed from local authority control and State schools are also being encouraged to 'opt out'.[90] The Trade Union Reform and Employment Rights Act 1993 transferred responsibility for the provision of a careers service from local education authorities to the Secretary of State for Employment. The Local Government Planning and Land Act 1990 and the Leasehold Reform, Housing and Urban Development Act 1993 transferred responsibilities for planning and economic development from democratic local government to unelected quangos.[91]

Unelected quangos have grown in size and importance. In 1991-2 they oversaw the spending of £47.1 billion of public money, including National Health Service expenditure.[92] The Audit Commission has warned that inexperienced governing boards and managers are being handed millions of pounds of public money with too few safeguards against fraud and mismanagement, and inadequate mechanisms for independent scrutiny.[93] Members of quango boards with executive powers are often paid for part-time work and there is some evidence that the government has used its powers of patronage to reward its political supporters.[94] Some of those appointed have been involved in businesses which have made financial contributions to the Conservative Party.[95] Baroness Denton, a government minister, has been quoted as saying 'I can't remember knowingly appointing a Labour supporter' to a quango.[96]

While the rest of Europe is moving towards a devolution of power and a strengthening of local democracy, the British government is centralising power and weakening local accountability.[97] This became apparent during the debate on ratification of the Maastricht Treaty over the question of how Britain would nominate members to the Committee of the Regions. In most other countries, representatives are directly elected members of regional parliaments, but Britain has no regional parliaments. The government initially proposed that it should have total discretion over the nomination of representatives. But an amendment to the Bill was eventually carried specifying that all British nominees must be elected members of regional or local authorities.[98] The British government has also failed to ratify the European Charter of Local Self-Government which enshrines the political, administrative and financial independence of local authorities.[99]

In 1978-9 local government raised 60 per cent of all the money it spent through local taxation.[100] Now it only raises 19 per cent.[101] The rest comes from central government and can be withheld or cut if government disagrees with the spending priorities of particular local authorities. In 1993 the Audit Commission stated that local authorities were being left with cosmetic accountability for decisions largely made by central government.[102] Local authorities have also lost their right to representation on health authorities and on local Training and Enterprise Committees, all of which allocate considerable sums of public money.[103]

The lack of independence of local government has reduced interest in local politics. This is indicated by the fact that the turnout for local elections, about 40 per cent of the electorate, is well below that of most other European countries.[104]

ISSUES SPECIFIC TO WALES

The problems of centralisation and poor democratic accountability are more acute in Wales; a separate nation within the UK,[105] it already has considerably more administrative devolution than the regions of England – but this bureaucracy is not subject to sufficient democratic control by the people of Wales.

Wales is far more politically and legally assimilated with England in the UK than Scotland and Northern Ireland.[106] In the period after the Welsh Act of Union, there were very few Acts of Parliament which applied exclusively to Wales.[107] However, Welsh national identity enjoyed a revival from the mid-nineteenth century onwards,[108] a process which has continued under the present government.[109] Welsh is spoken as a first language by 20 per cent of the population of Wales[110] and there has been a long-running campaign by Welsh speakers to ensure that the British government takes adequate measures to protect and promote the Welsh language. This obligation is set out in Article 27 of the ICCPR.

Government and accountability

Two Acts of Parliament were introduced in 1978 to create separate assemblies for Scotland and Wales. The Welsh assembly was envisaged as having fewer powers than the Scottish assembly because of Wales's greater integration with England. However, the Welsh voted by a large majority against the proposal for devolution, effectively ending the Welsh movement for home rule for over a decade.[111]

The beginning of the 1990s witnessed a renewed interest in the devolution of political power to Wales.[112] There is now a consensus on the need for a Welsh assembly amongst the Welsh Labour Party, the Welsh Liberal Democrats and Plaid Cymru who, between them, won 70 per cent of the Welsh vote in the 1992 general election.[113] The Conservatives only secured 28.6 per cent of the vote in Wales[114] and have only five out of 38 Welsh MPs at Westminster.[115] The Labour Party has 27 seats, with 49.5 per cent of the vote, the Liberal Democrats have one seat and the nationalist Plaid Cymru has four.[116] The contrast is even more marked at a local government level. The Conservatives have 34 county councillors compared to 270 Labour, 41 Plaid Cymru and 34 Liberal Democrats.[117]

Government from Westminster has resulted in the growth of a large Welsh bureaucratic State structure which is not under democratic control. Two commentators have argued that:

Wales is a useful 'laboratory' in which to examine the issues of governance, patronage and accountability . . . At the heart of the problem of governance in Wales today is the fact that the devolution process has been prosecuted without reference to democratic accountability.[118]

The number of quangos in Wales has doubled since 1979, at the expense of democratic local government.[119] Eighty per cent of public expenditure in Wales, around £6 billion annually, is now channelled through the Welsh Office and its related appointed bodies or quangos.[120] A commentator has said that Wales is ruled by a new governing élite of hand-picked salaried and non-salaried nominees of the Secretary of State for Wales.[121] The opposition parties have accused the government of packing the quangos with Conservative Party supporters.[122] Some of these quango post-holders have more power and influence than junior ministers in the Welsh Office.[123]

There has been a series of financial irregularities involving several of these senior managers in two of the largest and most important Welsh quangos: the Development Board for Northern Wales (DBNW) and the Welsh Development Agency (WDA).[124] In December 1992 a parliamentary inquiry into the running of the WDA discovered evidence of widespread fraud and financial mismanagement involving several million pounds, including the appointment of a convicted fraudster to the position of Marketing Director without checking his references.[125] In the same year the Public Accounts Committee produced a damning report into financial irregularities and inadequate supervision of the DBNW.[126] The Welsh Office's monitoring procedures were criticised in both reports.

There is cause for concern about the ability of the Parliament at Westminster to oversee Welsh affairs effectively. The House of Commons only provides MPs with eight opportunities a year, each lasting about 30 minutes, in which to scrutinise and debate the activities of civil servants in the Welsh Office. There is one Welsh day debate a year[127] and no more than four sittings of the Welsh Grand Committee.[128] There is a Select Committee on Welsh Affairs but its debates tend to be wide ranging and superficial. This gives civil servants considerable scope for activity free from democratic control.[129]

ISSUES SPECIFIC TO SCOTLAND

The British government has refused to consult the Scottish people about their constitutional position since 1979, when a majority voted in favour of devolution.[130] It has also ignored the overwhelming support expressed in opinion polls and at the ballot box for a Scottish Parliament to deal exclusively with Scottish affairs.[131] At present Scotland is integrated into the UK. The legal basis for this integration is a Treaty of Union, signed in 1707 after Acts of Union were passed by the English and Scottish Parliaments. A new Parliament was created by the Act of Union and the two separate Parliaments went into adjournment.[132] The terms of the treaty allowed for the recall of the Scottish Parliament to deal exclusively with Scottish affairs.

More than 20 bills advocating some form of Scottish home rule have been introduced to the House of Commons this century.[133] Some have been passed but none enacted.[134] In 1979 the Scottish people voted in a referendum in favour of creating this assembly[135] – in effect recalling their own Parliament. However, a clause had been inserted into the Scotland Act 1978, which would have provided for the creation of this Parliament, specifying that at least 40 per cent of those on the electoral register must vote in favour of the proposal for it to be approved.[136] This condition is without precedent in British electoral law and practice. In the event, 52 per cent of the voters were in favour of the proposal and 48 per cent against; but on a 63.6 per cent turnout, the result fell foul of the new 40 per cent rule. The Scotland Act was repealed by the Westminster Parliament. (It can be noted that Britain's membership of the European Community, which arguably involved greater constitutional change, was ratified in 1975, although this was backed by a smaller percentage of the Scottish population than that which voted in favour of a Scottish assembly.[137])

Since 1979 the Scottish people have been ruled by a government which has never secured 40 per cent of the votes of the electorate as a whole or 52 per cent of those who have voted in a general election. In 1990 the Scottish Constitutional Convention was formed, consisting of the main opposition political parties in Scotland (except the Scottish National Party), together with churches, local authorities, voluntary organisations and trade unions. This Convention published detailed proposals for a home rule Parliament for Scotland within the UK, elected by proportional representation and respecting 'the principle of equal representation of women.'[138] The Scottish National Party also favours the establishment of a Scottish Parliament, elected by proportional representation, but believes that Scotland should negotiate its independence from the UK and enter the European Community as a separate State.[139]

Increasing European co-operation and moves towards integration have effectively narrowed the difference between these two positions.[140] It is now generally accepted that the nation States of Europe are interdependent in areas of foreign policy, defence and economic policy, and that governments can no longer use the argument of national sovereignty to prevent scrutiny of their domestic social and human rights policies.[141]

In the 1992 general election, parties committed to the establishment of some form of Scottish Parliament received between them 75 per cent of the vote.[142] The Conservative Party, the only main political party opposed to the establishment of a Scottish Parliament, received 25 per cent of the vote and won 11 parliamentary seats out of 72.[143] The Conservatives placed defence of the constitutional *status quo* at the centre of their manifesto and, while their share of the vote increased slightly compared to the 1987 result, they were resoundingly beaten by the parties committed to constitutional change. After the election the main opposition parties together demanded that the British government call a referendum in Scotland and put the options of no change, independence or devolution directly to the Scottish people.[144] The British government has not yet done so.

Scotland's legal system

The 1707 Act of Union guaranteed the continuance of Scottish private law[145] and the Scottish courts,[146] while Acts to maintain a distinct Scottish Church and educational system were also incorporated into the 1707 Treaty of Union. In response to growing pressure for some form of home rule from the end of the nineteenth century onwards, a Scottish Office was developed as the department responsible for administering Scotland.[147]

Scotland's constitutional tradition is also distinct from England's. The Lord President of the Court of Session, Scotland's supreme civil court, has ruled that: 'The principle of the unlimited

sovereignty of Parliament is a distinctly English prin[
has no counterpart in Scottish constitutional law.'[148]
Scotland is one of the few countries that possesses a
body of law which is not scrutinised by its own legislature. S[
laws are often made for Scotland but these have to be fitte[
Westminster's programme, and the Scottish legal system somet[
suffers because of this.[149] Because the government at Westmins[
has been unrepresentative of Scottish political opinion for the la[
16 years, this means that laws have been introduced in Scotland
against the wishes of the majority of Scottish people. The unpopular and now discredited 'Poll Tax' was introduced in Scotland a
year before it was imposed in England and Wales, despite the
opposition of the vast majority of Scottish people.[150] Other controversial measures, such as the compulsory testing of school children,
have been similarly imposed earlier in Scotland, leading to allegations that the country is being used a 'testing ground'.[151]

Although Scotland has one of the richest economies in the
European Community in terms of energy production, its unemployment rate was well above the UK average throughout the 1980s.[152]
Scotland's population also fell rapidly and consistently during the
decade 1981 to 1991 mainly because of emigration.[153]

Scotland produces 80 per cent of the oil and gas produced in
the European Community and is rich with other sources of
energy.[154] However, the government used much of this revenue to
fund cuts in income tax which mainly benefited the better off, who
are concentrated, geographically, in the south-east of England.[155]
Gas from Scotland's territorial waters in the North Sea is piped
directly to England which encourages industries such as steel to
relocate in the south.[156] Steel production has collapsed in Scotland
over the last 10 years but has risen in the rest of the UK.[157] There
have also been allegations that lucrative defence contracts, such as
the refitting of Britain's Trident submarines, have been awarded to
English rather than Scottish shipyards because of vigorous political
lobbying by English yards.[158]

Cultural minorities

It could be argued that the Scots are not a people but an 'ethnic,
religious or linguistic minority', and are therefore not entitled to
self-determination, but only to freedom from discrimination and
the right to enjoy their own culture. However, the people of Scot-

defined as an ethnic minority within their own
;h the British government concedes some of the
onhood to Scotland, and recognises that the Scots
ople entitled to pursue a separate economic, social
elopment, it denies them the right to self-govern-
breach of Article 1 of the ICCPR.

HUMAN RIGHTS IN THE EUROPEAN UNION

As the power of the European Union (EU) and other pan-European
institutions has grown, concern has increased about their lack of
accountability to democratic structures and effective human rights
monitoring.[159] The Treaty of Rome 1957, which established what
has become the European Union, created four main bodies: a
European Parliament, a Council of Ministers, a Commission and
a Court. The Single European Act 1986 and the Treaty on European Union 1992 (the Maastricht Treaty) amended some of their
powers and functions.

The Council is the legislative body which includes one government minister from every member State. Who those ministers are
varies according to the subject under discussion. The presidency of
the Council rotates amongst countries every six months. Most
decisions of the Council have to be unanimous, although an
increasing number take place by majority voting, using a weighted
system to reflect the different size and influence of member States.

The Commission is the executive body. It consists of 17 members from all 12 member States – appointed by agreement between
the governments. The president and six vice-presidents are chosen
from the members of the Commission by agreement between the
member States. The Commission initiates legislative proposals for
the Council to consider and implements the policies on which the
Council decides. The Parliament is essentially a consultative body
although it has powers to change or veto the European Union's
budget. It can also make representation to the Commission. The
Court, based in Luxembourg, consists of 13 judges assisted by six
advocates-general. It is the final arbiter on interpretation of the
Treaty of Rome and EU Directives. There are four other EU institutions: the Court of Auditors, the Economic and Social Committee, the Committee of the Regions, and the European Investment
Bank. It is proposed to create a European Central Bank in 1997.

In 1992 a new treaty on economic, monetary and politic union was signed by the members of the European Communit (EC) at Maastricht. The treaty transformed the European Community into the European Union and seeks to establish common citizenship of the European Union, a common European currency and, eventually, joint defence and foreign policies. This treaty was ratified by all the member States during 1993 and the European Union formally came into existence in November 1993.[160]

Since its creation by the Treaty of Rome in 1957, EC law has had supremacy over the domestic laws of member States.[161] Consequently all member States surrendered some of their legislative power to the EC on accession. The EC also has powers to make various international agreements and treaties with other international organisations, States or unions of States.[162] Once adopted, new treaties are binding on all member States. They may contain provisions that are directly effective; that is, they are not conditional on the parliamentary approval of member States, and member States' Parliaments are obliged to introduce legislation to implement them. The British government may conclude treaties using its prerogative powers, but these do not have direct domestic legislative effect without parliamentary approval. EU treaties, by contrast, directly bind each member State even if they have *not* been approved by the State's own Parliament.[163]

It is a basic principle of international law, enshrined in Article 1 of the ICCPR and elsewhere,[164] that if nation States freely choose to pursue their economic, social and cultural development in association with other independent States, then any new institutions created should be subject to some form of democratic control. The precise form that it should take is a political question which falls outside the scope of human rights organisations. All pan-European institutions should respect fundamental human rights and freedoms and be subject to regular scrutiny of their human rights records. The Treaty of Rome, which created the European Community (now the EU), contained no mention of fundamental and universal human rights.[165] Paradoxically, however, the EC did in theory grant a variety of social and economic rights to the citizens of its member States in order to bring about greater economic and political integration. The EC has upheld the rights of freedom of movement and the right to broadcast across frontiers, both of which are logical components of moves to bring down frontiers across Europe. The EC has also set minimum standards of social pro-ion, in order to stop member States gaining competitive advantage in the internal market through low wages and minimal protection for their workforce.

In 1987 the Single European Act extended the scope for imposing minimum social standards throughout Europe[166] and in 1989 a new draft Social Charter was published which was eventually incorporated into the Social Chapter of the Maastricht Treaty. EC (and now EU) Directives in a number of areas – such as health and safety, conditions at work and women's rights – have put pressure on the present British government to grant more rights to its citizens. However, these protections usually apply only to EC nationals and not to all individuals within the territorial jurisdiction of the member States. The European Parliament has four committees which draw up reports and resolutions on human rights, but these do not often result in effective action. Members of the European Parliament often find that issues they have attempted to raise, such as telephone-tapping and conscientious objection to military service, are ruled as outside the scope of the Community's competence.[167]

Governments argue that national representatives are answerable for their actions to their own national Parliaments. However, because there is no requirement from the EU itself for member States to have meaningful consultation with their own Parliaments, levels of accountability vary significantly from country to country. In 1992 a House of Lords Select Committee said that in the UK in practice 'the influence of Parliament over treaties is marginal.'[168]

Civil and political rights

The European Court of Justice, based at Luxembourg, is charged with ensuring respect for EU law. Until the mid-1970s it saw human rights as the responsibility of member States. More recently, the Court has made a series of judgments which have affirmed the existence of fundamental human rights inferred from the common constitutional traditions of member States and from international treaties ratified by them.[169] However, the Court has ruled that such inferences can only provide a 'guideline' in making judgments and are secondary to the EU's own structures and objectives:

> The protection of such rights whilst inspired by the
> constitutional traditions common to member States, must be

ensured within the framework of the structure and objectives of the Community.[170]

The most important influence on the EU's Court in Luxembourg has been the Convention for the Protection of Human Rights and Fundamental Freedoms – usually known as the European Convention on Human Rights (ECHR). All member States of the EU have now ratified the ECHR,[171] although the EU itself has not. The ECHR allows individuals, where permitted by their governments, to take petitions about alleged human rights violations to a European Commission of Human Rights. This Commission can refer individual cases to the European Court of Human Rights, based in Strasbourg, whose decisions are regarded as binding on States party to the ECHR.

Ratification of the ECHR by the EU would allow individuals to petition the Court over alleged breaches of the ECHR by the EU.[172] The EU has a vast and growing bureaucratic apparatus, is a major employer and initiates legislation which is binding on member States. Ratification would give individuals a mechanism by which they could bring the institutions of the EU to account. The ECHR has many weaknesses: it does not address freedom of information and data protection, its anti-discrimination provision is limited in both scope and protection and its exemptions, on grounds of national security and public morality, are too wide-ranging. Nevertheless, ratification would provide individuals with more protection than they currently enjoy.

The British government, which has not incorporated the ECHR into its own domestic law, is one of the principal opponents of ratification of the ECHR within the European Union.[173] It has also opposed giving greater powers of scrutiny and control over the European Union to the European Parliament, on the basis that this would mean surrendering powers from national Parliaments. As a Foreign Affairs Committee report stated:

> We do not believe national Parliaments should become subordinate to the European Parliament. Nor do we wish to see a strict hierarchy of responsibility established.[174]

It went on to state that national Parliaments should 'get a better grip on their own ministers' actions in the Community' and be brought into the decision-making process of the inter-governmental pillars but did not spell out how this could be accomplished.[175]

Most EU legislation concerns social and economic matters and exists in the form of Directives. Some issues, such as employment and welfare rights, are within the scope of the ECHR. Ratification of the ECHR would offer the possibility of introducing an individual petition system.[176] Because EU Directives take precedence over the law of member States and the EU has not ratified the ECHR, it is currently theoretically possible that member States could be required by EU legislation to implement a law which is contrary to the provisions of the ECHR, if it passes the hurdle of the EU's own Court at Luxembourg.[177] This anomaly would be removed if the EU ratified the ECHR.

The European Union

The Maastricht Treaty proposes greater co-operation between member States in the areas of justice, asylum policy, external border controls, immigration policy, control of third country nationals, combatting drug smuggling, combatting international fraud, judicial co-operation, customs co-operation and police co-operation. It formulates a system for adopting joint action on the initiative of either a member State or the European Commission (the executive body of the EU). The Council of Ministers can decide on some issues by qualified majority[178] rather than consensus, and can draw up inter-governmental conventions.

Because the areas outlined in the Maastricht Treaty supposedly only involve closer co-operation between member States, and no extension of the EU's competence, any agreements on them arrived at by member States are not subject to challenge or scrutiny by the European Parliament.[179] However, the Council of Ministers can stipulate that the Court of Justice shall have jurisdiction over some inter-governmental conventions. Clearly both the Council of Ministers and the Commission have a formal role here, and it can be argued that any agreement between member States represent acts for which the EU should be held responsible in law.[180] However, what seems likely is that these agreements will lead to the creation of EU-wide administrative and possibly executive bodies which are not under the control of any one member State nor subject to EU law. The lack of democratic scrutiny and control is becoming a more acute problem.

2 CRIMINAL JUSTICE AND HUMAN RIGHTS

JUSTICE IN CRISIS

British justice is in crisis. Since 1989, scores of people have been released by the Appeal Court in recognition of the fact that their convictions were unsafe. The system that gaoled them is in urgent need of reform.

In March 1991, following the quashing of the convictions of six Irish men who had been gaoled for the bombing of two public houses in Birmingham in 1974, the government announced the establishment of a Royal Commission on Criminal Justice.[1] The bombings, the biggest mass murder in British criminal history, caused the deaths of 21 people and the crime remains unsolved. An Electrostatic Document Analysis (ESDA) test showed that the men's 'confessions' had been altered by police officers while the forensic evidence, which purported to show that they had handled explosives, gave the same result after contact with playing cards, cigarette smoke and cleaning fluids. The six men alleged that after the police learned the results of the test, they were beaten to make them sign false confessions.[2]

The release of the men – the Birmingham Six – followed a series of cases where convictions were quashed either because of police malpractice or following the exposure of flaws within the criminal justice system. In October 1989 three Irish men and an English woman (the Guildford Four) who had been gaoled for IRA bombings in Guildford and Woolwich in 1974 had their convictions quashed after it emerged that the police had falsified notes regarding the interviews they conducted, suppressed an alibi statement for one of the defendants and altered notes concerning the times of interviews.[3]

In December 1991, the convictions of three men gaoled for the killing of a police officer during a riot in north London (the

Tottenham Three) were overturned.[4] An analysis of their confession statements, the only evidence against them, indicated that they had not been written contemporaneously and that police officers had lied under oath regarding the circumstances of the interrogations. The three were denied access to a solicitor and claim that they were threatened and abused.[5]

In February 1992 a court quashed the conviction of Stefan Kizsko who spent 16 years in prison for the sex killing of an 11-year-old girl in 1976.[6] He alleged that he had been coerced into signing a false confession by the police. He was freed after forensic evidence showed he could not have carried out the killing but this evidence was withheld from the defence at the original trial.[7]

In December 1992, the convictions of three men who had been gaoled for the murder of a prostitute in Cardiff in 1990 (the Cardiff Three) were overturned after it emerged that the police had coerced one of them into signing a false confession.[8] In the same month an English woman, Judy Ward, was released after spending 18 years in prison for an IRA coach bombing in 1974.[9] She had been convicted on the basis of an unsound forensic test and a statement she made to the police while she was undergoing a nervous breakdown. The prosecution had also failed to disclose material evidence to the defence during her original trial.

These are only amongst the most high-profile cases of miscarriages of justice. Liberty has compiled a dossier of over 200 cases in which we believe the safety of the convictions is in doubt.[10] These cases have exposed considerable flaws in the British legal system: on occasion police officers fabricate evidence and extract false confessions under duress; supposedly expert scientific evidence is flawed; prosecutors fail to disclose evidence material to the defence; access to solicitors is delayed; Legal Aid is inadequate and the legal advice provided is often poor; convictions are based upon unsound identification evidence; prejudicial references to previous convictions disclosed during the trial are allowed in court proceedings; summing up by judges is often biased; and breaches of the Police and Criminal Evidence Act (PACE) codes of conduct occur throughout investigation and during the arrest, detention and questioning of suspects.

In July 1993, the Royal Commission on Criminal Justice published its report with 352 recommendations for reform.[11] Many of the Commission's proposals were condemned by campaigners for reform of the criminal justice system.[12] The Commission proposed extending the time when the police could continue questioning suspects after they had been charged,[13] extending the police's powers to take intimate samples from suspects,[14] limiting a defendant's right to jury trial,[15] the introduction of open-ended plea bargaining[16] and a requirement on the defence to disclose its evidence in advance.[17]

In the British government's *Fourth Periodic Report to the United Nations Human Rights Committee*, it stated that the government had accepted, in principle, 128 of the Royal Commission's recommendations and was still considering 165 recommendations addressed to it.[18] However, most of the recommendations that it has endorsed are likely to make miscarriages of justice more likely. The gaoling of innocent people contradicts the British government's claims to be upholding Articles 9 and 14 of the International Covenant on Civil and Political Rights (ICCPR) which protect people from arbitrary arrest and detention and ensure their right to a fair trial. The conditions in which many people are held in custody violate Articles 7 and 10 of the ICCPR which protect people from cruel, inhuman and degrading treatment and uphold their right to be treated with respect for the inherent dignity of the human person.

Liberty, along with many other organisations, has campaigned for a fundamental reform of the criminal justice system, in particular for a strengthening of the right of silence, the outlawing of convictions based solely on confessions and the establishment of a new body with the power and resources to review all alleged miscarriages of justice. We have also called for the following reforms:

☐ Those arrested should have immediate access to independent legal advice from qualified solicitors

☐ The maximum period of detention should be reduced to 24 hours

☐ The prosecution and police should have a statutory duty to disclose all evidence to the defence

☐ The accused should have the same access to forensic expertise as the prosecution

☐ Black defendants should not have to face all-white juries

☐ Defendants should have an unqualified right to challenge

prosecution witnesses and judges should not comment on
the evidence at trials.[19]

While the Commission's proposals fell far short of these reforms,
it did reach some welcome conclusions. It proposed the establishment of a new authority to review possible miscarriages of justice
and refer them to the Court of Appeal, removing this power from
the Home Secretary.[20] It also argued for the retention of the right
of silence for suspects and defendants.[21]

The Home Secretary responded, at the Conservative Party's
conference in October 1993, by announcing that the government
was abolishing the right of silence as part of a new package of
punitive measures.[22] In December 1993 it published these proposals
in the Criminal Justice and Public Order Bill.[23]

The Criminal Justice and Public Order Act 1994

The Criminal Justice and Public Order Act became law in November 1994.[24] The right of silence was abolished in April 1995, and
the police issued a new caution:

> You do not have to say anything. But it may harm your defence
> if you do not mention when questioned something which you
> later rely on in court. Anything you do say may be given in
> evidence.[25]

The Act also contains other proposals which are likely to lead to
innocent people being wrongfully convicted. It limits the right
to jury trials[26] and abolishes the requirement that judges should
warn juries in criminal trials that the evidence of accomplices –
which is notoriously unreliable – should be considered as potentially unsafe.[27] It creates two new offences under the Prevention of
Terrorism Act 1989, possession of information likely to be of use
to terrorists and possession of articles which might be used by
terrorists.[28] These are sweepingly defined and the onus of proof is
reversed in the charges. The Act extends the police's powers to
stop and search people[29] and criminalises a variety of other previously civil activities, mainly in relation to trespass.[30]

The Act creates a sentencing power that allows young people,
aged 12 to 14, to be detained in new institutions called secure
training centres.[31] It extends the police's powers to take samples
of body tissue, allowing the use of 'reasonable force' in some
circumstances and to store information extracted from samples,

on a national DNA database.[32] Liberty accepts that DNA profiling is useful for the detection of particular types of crime, such as rape and other crimes of violence, where the perpetrator is unknown to the victim. However, there are problems with the use of DNA evidence in court, which have resulted in the overturning of some cases.[33] Unlike fingerprinting, DNA profiling is not unique and the evidence must be backed by a statistical evaluation of its probability. Research for the Royal Commission on Criminal Justice highlighted the problems defendants can experience in being able to challenge DNA evidence.[34]

The Royal Commission also considered the role of forensic science evidence in criminal proceedings.[35] This has been a key feature of a number of notorious miscarriage of justice cases.[36] Most forensic scientists work for laboratories established by the Home Office or the police. This poses problems for the defence, compounded by problems with Legal Aid, of obtaining information about, and access to, forensic scientists and make it almost impossible to challenge forensic scientists' findings in criminal cases.[37] The forensic evidence against the Birmingham Six was first shown to be flawed, not in a court room but by the makers of a television documentary.[38]

The right of silence

The right of silence is a centuries-old safeguard against wrongful conviction,[39] based on the principle that anyone who is charged with a criminal offence should be presumed innocent until proven guilty beyond all reasonable doubt. The prosecution must prove guilt: it is not for the defendant to establish his/her innocence.[40] A suspect in police custody or a defendant in a trial should therefore have the right to remain silent without the prosecution commenting on this at a trial and without the court drawing any inferences from that silence.[41]

Abolition of the right of silence will allow the court to draw adverse inferences if a defendant has:

- failed fully to answer all police questions
- failed fully to account for real or forensic evidence found on arrest
- failed fully to mention any fact when first arrested on which he or she later relied as part of the defence

- failed to give evidence in court
- failed to account for being found in a particular place.[42]

The British criminal justice system is based on the adversarial model.[43] However, there is an inequality between the police and the prosecution on the one hand and the suspect on the other.[44] The prosecution has the power to interview witnesses, take samples from the defendant, conduct forensic tests, search premises, seize documents, arrest and question other suspects and co-defendants, probe alibis, and seek out additional evidence to present against the defendant in court.[45] The defence has none of these advantages and the right of silence and presumption of innocence help correct the balance.

Under the new law, a suspect is under pressure to disclose the details of his or her defence to the police and prosecution before the trial. Advance warning of the defence case will enable the prosecution to adjust its own case accordingly. Given the recent evidence of police and prosecution malpractice, as well as the problems that some defendants have experienced obtaining adequate legal representation, this is particularly worrying.

Removing the right of silence in the police station will also increase the pressure on people to make false confessions. According to a study for the Lord Chancellor's Office, the police have developed up to 22 ploys to dissuade people from exercising their right to silence and very few people do so.[46] Research for the Royal Commission on Criminal Justice showed that over 70 per cent of suspects in its study answered all of the police's questions while only 2.5 per cent remained absolutely silent during police interrogation.[47] Rather than separate the innocent from the guilty, abolition will benefit the strong-willed, smart and linguistically competent and discriminate against the weak, unintelligent, inarticulate and vulnerable.

In June 1994, the European Commission on Human Rights declared admissible a challenge to the abolition of the right of silence in Northern Ireland in 1988, on which the proposals in the Criminal Justice and Public Order Act 1994 are based.[48] The UK Commissioner noted, in a dissenting opinion, that it would be more difficult in a court with a jury to ensure that proper inferences were drawn from a defendant's silence than in a non-jury court such as those that exist in Northern Ireland.[49]

Stop and search

Section 60 of the Criminal Justice and Public Order Act 1994 gives a police officer of the rank of Superintendent or above the power to authorise uniformed officers, within a specified area, to stop and search pedestrians and anything they are carrying for offensive weapons or dangerous articles. The police officer will not need to have reasonable suspicion that the person being stopped and searched has committed a crime. It also enables them to stop and search vehicles and their occupants for such articles, where the authorising officer has reasonable grounds for believing that serious incidents of violence may take place within the area, and it is expedient to authorise the exercise of the powers in order to stop such incidents occurring. The authorising officer can exercise this power for a period of up to 24 hours, with the possibility of an extension of six hours.

These powers allow the police to stop and search people at random and there is considerable concern that they will be used in a discriminatory way. Even before they were introduced there was considerable evidence that ethnic minorities were far more likely to be stopped and searched than white people. In December 1994, the government gave an ethnic breakdown for stop and searches carried out by the police during 1993-4. In almost every area of the country the stop and searches against ethnic minorities far exceeded their proportion in the population and the contrast was even greater in inner-city areas.[50] Indiscriminate stop and search is a breach of Article 9 of the ICCPR which safeguards against arbitrary arrest.

Arrests and detentions

Arrests and detentions are regulated by the Police and Criminal Evidence Act (PACE).[51] People can be arrested without warrant under PACE, if they have committed an 'arrestable offence.'[52] One police officer's subjective judgment may determine whether an offence is 'serious, arrestable' and this creates different consequences for the same actions.[53] Police are entitled to keep suspects in custody without charge for 24 hours for ordinary offences and for 36 hours for serious, arrestable offences. After 36 hours the detention may be extended up to a total of 96 hours if authorised by a magistrate.[54]

Police behaviour is also regulated by codes of practice issued under the Act. They not enshrined in primary legislation and breaches will not subject the violator to civil or criminal proceedings.[55] Evidence obtained through abuse of procedures is often admissible at trial because breaches do not automatically lead to exclusion of evidence. Breaches of the code and other malpractices can be dealt with using the police complaints system.[56] But this is inadequate because the investigation of allegations is carried out by other police officers, often from the same force.[57] Furthermore, the procedures and secrecy of the process, and the fact that the standard of proof in such cases is the higher one of 'beyond all reasonable doubt', results in many people not pursuing complaints.

In May 1993 it was revealed that the Metropolitan Police had paid out nearly £2 million in out-of-court settlements and £758,000 in court awards, largely arising out of civil actions alleging assault, false imprisonment and malicious prosecution over the last five years. In 59 cases the awards were for over £10,000 but disciplinary action was only taken against officers involved in one out of five cases.[58] In February 1995 the Police Complaints Authority announced that it was investigating 30 deaths that had occurred in police custody, 27 of which had taken place in the previous six months.[59]

Legal representation

Under PACE a person can be arrested and detained in custody for 36 hours without being allowed to contact a solicitor, friend or family member.[60] Studies have shown that police still employ tactics to avoid the presence of a solicitor at the police station; the most frequently used ploy is telling the suspect his or her rights too quickly for the suspect to understand.[61] Research for the Royal Commission on Criminal Justice highlighted claims that the police sometimes fail to provide the suspect with a leaflet explaining these rights.[62]

The lack of adequate funding and the under-funding of the advice and assistance at police stations scheme result in people being advised by untrained and inexperienced clerks.[63] In a study conducted for the Royal Commission, for three-quarters of the cases in the sample, suspects who requested a solicitor were actually seen instead by a non-qualified representative. These often lack training in police station advisory work, are unconfident in confronting the police and 'exhibited serious role conflict, or were prone to reliance upon and over-identification with the police.'[64] These problems may be exacerbated by the Lord Chancellor's decision, in the 1995 Green Paper, to reduce Legal Aid.[65] Currently, a court will grant criminal Legal Aid upon assessment of income and savings, and if it decides that it is in the 'interest of justice' the accused should have legal representation.[66] Generally, to qualify for criminal Legal Aid, the case must be sufficiently serious that the accused might be sent to prison or lose his/her job. Whether or not a defendant will be awarded Legal Aid to obtain representation is dependent upon the particular court's attitude toward certain defendants or certain crimes.

The government has also introduced a new system of payment for Legal Aid lawyers. For the majority of criminal cases the lawyer will be paid a standard fee instead of recompensed for the amount of work done. This will not encourage the improvement of often poor standards of legal work, rather it might encourage lawyers to cut corners.[67]

Disclosure

In the course of investigation the prosecution often collects vast numbers of documents and witness statements which, in the past, were not declared to the defence. The failure to disclose evidence played a crucial role in the conviction of the Guildford Four and Judy Ward.[68] While the situation improved following Judy Ward's acquittal,[69] the Court of Appeal has now backtracked, inventing a system that allows the prosecution to apply to the judge in secret for authority not to reveal specific documents, or even the existence of a document or category of documents.[70] Such hearings, without the defence present, allow the prosecution too much scope. The rules for such disclosures are not contained in statutory form but are merely set out in a code produced by the Attorney-General, the political head of the Prosecution Service. It is only since November 1994 that the prosecution has been required to disclose these documents, including prosecution witness statements.[71]

Magistrates courts and sentencing

Magistrates courts still deal with more than 90 per cent of all criminal cases adjudicated each year in England and Wales, even in contested cases. The principle of English justice, 'equality before the law', implies an even-handed administration of legal processes.

However, research has shown that the possibility of receiving a custodial sentence also depends on where the trial takes place.

Adult male offenders are more than two-and-a-half times more likely to be sent straight to prison by magistrates in the far south-west of England than in the far south-west of Wales.[72] Although this may be due in part to the difference in types of crimes in these areas, there is no overall statistical correlation between rates of crime and rates of imprisonment in specific areas.[73] Imprisonment is used twice as frequently in Greater Manchester as in Merseyside. A study on race and sentencing noted that a Crown Court in Birmingham which tried offences of high seriousness sent 46 per cent of convicted defendants to prison while a Crown Court in Coventry which tried offences of medium seriousness imprisoned 61 per cent of convicted defendants.[74]

Right to appeal

The current system of last resort for miscarriages of justice – referral to the Court of Appeal by the Home Secretary – is inadequate. Preparation of cases to submit to the Home Secretary is inadequately funded by Legal Aid. Moreover, the 'political' role of the Home Secretary has resulted in a blurring of the powers of the executive and judiciary. The Court of Appeal spends most of its time reviewing appeals against sentence and trial judge determinations on points of law.[75] The Court of Appeal rarely reviews trial verdicts on the basis of new evidence. Fewer than 10 per cent of all appeals against conviction are 'fresh evidence' appeals and fewer than 17 per cent of these cases succeed in overturning convictions.[76] When the Court does review these cases, it can only receive evidence not received at the original trial which is likely to be believed and which was not entered at the trial for a credible reason.[77] As a result, it is difficult for the accused to obtain a review based on scientific evidence, evidence that was omitted owing to counsel's error, or evidence that did not appear significant at the time of the trial.[78]

Not only is there a lack of any basic right to appeal, the scope of review is insufficient to ensure justice. The Appeal Court has access to the transcripts of the original trial and only calls live witnesses to hear fresh evidence. It is not in a position to weigh up the evidence as a whole and is therefore unable to put itself in the position of the original trial jury. The British system of justice is based on the importance of the role of the jury and this role should not be usurped by the Appeal Courts. Moreover, no Legal Aid is available to investigate and mount an appeal unless leave is secured. If no leave is granted, or if the accused's appeal is unsuccessful, no further aid is available for subsequent investigation. As a result, those without independent resources are dependent upon support organisations or lawyers who will work without fees to challenge wrongful convictions. Defendants who renew their application for leave to appeal to the full court rarely have legal representation and, if in custody, will not be able to put their arguments themselves. Inevitably those without Legal Aid are much less likely to succeed in their appeals.[79]

The flaws in the present system are highlighted by the case of the Birmingham Six who had their convictions upheld twice by the Court of Appeal, in 1976 and 1988, despite the growing evidence of their innocence. The courts also blocked another attempt by the men to expose the fact that they were brutalised into signing false confessions. In 1976, a group of prison warders were acquitted of assaulting the six men after claiming that the horrific injuries which everyone accepted they had sustained in custody had all been inflicted on them before they arrived at the prison. The six men then initiated a civil action against the police officers who they alleged had beaten them up. After a series of legal wrangles the Court of Appeal finally blocked the case in 1980. Lord Denning, Master of the Rolls, senior justice, explained their reasons:

> Just consider the course of events if this case is allowed to proceed to trial. If the six men fail it will mean much time and money will have been expended by many people for no good purpose. If the six men win, it will mean that the police were guilty of violence and threats, that the confessions were involuntary and were improperly admitted in evidence and that the convictions were erroneous. That would mean that the Home Secretary would either have to recommend they be pardoned or he would have to remit the case to the Court of Appeal. This is such an appalling vista that every sensible person in the land would say: It can not be right that these actions should go further.[80]

The Home Secretary's role in deciding referrals provides a further obstacle for convicted persons seeking leave to a higher tribunal. The Home Secretary's current power to refer cases to the Court of

Appeal is discretionary and therefore subject to political pressures.[81] The Home Secretary did not refer the case of the Guildford Four to the Court of Appeal until a week after the Conservative Party conference in 1989 despite prior knowledge that the convictions could not be sustained.[82] Given the sharp criticism at Conservative Party conferences for supposed leniency on law and order issues, there is suspicion that the Home Secretary's announcement was deliberately delayed to spare him embarrassment.

The government has stated that it accepts the proposal for an independent Criminal Cases Review Authority but it did not include this measure in the Criminal Justice and Public Order Bill. It was not until February 1995 that the government published a Bill for the establishment of this body and Liberty is concerned that the Authority will have insufficient powers or resources to perform its task adequately.[83] It will rely on the police to conduct its investigations, complainants will not have an automatic right to access to all documents about them which the Authority holds and the Bill contains a provision which allows documents from previous cases and appeals to be kept from the complainant and from the Authority.[84] There is no provision in the Bill for access to Legal Aid for the legal work that needs to be done prior to the case being referred to the Authority and, in some cases, the right of appeal has been reduced by the Bill.[85]

PRISONERS AND PRISONS

British prisons have been the subject of repeated criticism by a variety of official inquiries, which have stated that they are overcrowded, dilapidated, badly equipped and badly managed.[86] The buildings in which many prisoners are housed are unfit for habitation. Prisoners are often forced to spend up to 23 hours each day in their cells which are frequently overcrowded, insanitary, and even dangerous. These conditions are dehumanising and constitute a denial of some of the prisoners' basic human rights. In 1991, an official report into prison disturbances in Strangeways, Manchester, and into five other prisons and remand centres across the country, stated that the conditions were one of the underlying factors behind the riots.[87] In November 1991, the European Committee for the Prevention of Torture and Inhuman or Degrading Treatment (CTP) published its report based on a study of three prisons in the UK in 1990. It concluded that, 'the cumulative effect of overcrowding, lack of integral sanitation and adequate regimes amounts to inhuman and degrading treatment.'[88]

A report published in February 1995 by the Chief Inspector of Prisons, Judge Stephen Tumin, finds the conditions in one of the prisons condemned by the CTP Report 'an affront to human dignity' and concludes that 'it is abundantly clear that little has changed since our 1989 inspection.'[89] The UK imprisons a considerably higher proportion of its population than any other European country[90] and the number is rapidly rising. In its *Fourth Periodic Report*, the government stated that in 1993 the UK had an average prison population of about 52,100 (90 per 100,000 of the population as a whole),[91] on 1 September 1993, 53,400[92] and by February 1995 over 58,000.[93]

The prison population in England and Wales fell by about 4,000 between 1989 and 1993[94] largely thanks to the effects of the Criminal Justice Act 1991, which encouraged courts to award fewer custodial sentences. Central sections of the Act have since been amended or repealed by the government.[95] Between March 1993 and March 1994 the prison population rose by 13 per cent, an average increase of 465 new prisoners per month.[96] The rise has been attributed to the increasing numbers imprisoned for fine default and the tighter restrictions on the granting of bail.[97]

In its *Fourth Periodic Report*, the government stated it was 'committed to providing decent conditions for prisoners and eliminating overcrowding' and that it had completed 'the largest prison building programme in England and Wales since Victorian times' with the construction of 21 new prisons since 1985.[98] The *Report* noted that the number of prisoners being held two to a cell designed for one had halved from 17,800 in January 1987 to 8,500 in March 1994.[99] Although the spate of rioting in 1990 was the most serious prison disturbance since the 1970s, the number (defined as 'any action by two or more prisoners against the smooth running of the prison') has been rising steadily since the mid-1980s, from 38 in the year 1985-6 to 147 in the year 1993-4.[100] The relatively high suicide rate in British prisons, also increasing, is another indicator of the appalling conditions in which many prisoners are held. There were 102 suicides of prisoners between 1982 and 1986, and 171 between 1988 and 1991.[101]

After the 1990 disturbances, the government accepted the need for wide-ranging reform and implemented some of the central recommendations of a report drawn up under the chairmanship of Lord Justice Woolf, into the causes of the riots. Since 1993, government penal policy has reverted to an emphasis on security, punishment and austerity.[102] At the Conservative Party's conference in October 1994, the Home Secretary, Michael Howard, stated that:

> Last year, I said something controversial. I said 'prison works'. What an outcry that provoked from the woolly-headed brigade . . . The courts have the power to send violent and persistent offenders to prison. They are using those powers increasingly. And they must continue to use them whenever that is what justice requires.[103]

In January 1995, following some widely publicised prison escapes, the Home Office drafted a corporate plan which stressed the need 'to set security as the overriding priority' and to ensure that the 'facilities in prisons must not be excessive or out of keeping with the public's expectations of what imprisonment should be like.'[104]

Increasing numbers of prisoners are being held long distances from their homes. This, combined with limited visiting hours, makes the maintenance of contacts with families extremely difficult.[105] Prisoners are entitled to two half-hour visits every 28 days, unless the Home Secretary directs that this should be reduced to one half-hour. The *Woolf Report* recognised that this was not sufficient for the maintenance of family ties and should be increased.[106] In its *Fourth Periodic Report*, the government states that 'every prison in England and Wales now offers prisoners the opportunity to exceed the minimum visiting entitlements set out in the Prison Rules.'[107] However, without statutory guarantees, extensions to visiting times remain arbitrary and within the discretion of prison authorities. In December 1994 an Irish Republican prisoner, Dr Felim OhAdhmaill, had a visit terminated because he attempted to speak to his wife in Irish. He has been unable to communicate with his two children in Irish, their first language, and has been charged with breaking prison regulations for attempting to do so.[108] Following a European Court ruling,[109] Prison Rule 37A was amended to allow for all legal correspondence to be treated as confidential. This amendment is routinely abused by prison staff[110] and prisoners have no right to compensation for such abuses.

Prisoners are among the only groups to be denied access to the National Health Service (NHS). The Health Care Service for

Prisons (HCSP) is not part of the NHS and its staff are not answerable to the Regional Health Authority. Since a government recommendation in 1990 the HCSP has adopted NHS standards. However, fears remain that courts continue to accept lower standards of medical care from prison authorities as they have ruled that the standard of care in prisons must be assessed relative to resources available.[111]

The average length of time that remand prisoners are held before trial has increased: in 1981 the average length of remand for men was 38 days, and 25 days for women. By 1991 the average length of remand was 51 days for men and 40 days for women.[112] On 30 September 1994 there were 1,920 prisoners on remand for between 3 and 6 months; 1,270 between 6 and 12 months; 300 between 12 and 18 months; and 220 for over 18 months.[113] The effects of being on remand can be extremely stressful and prison suicides[114] are much more likely to occur among remand prisoners.[115] In 1991, 58 per cent of those on remand were not returned to prison after being sentenced.[116]

In its annual report for 1993, the Wandsworth Prisons Board of Visitors stated that conditions in A and B Wings which are used exclusively for remand prisoners:

> simply do not meet any civilised standards of accommodation. The physical conditions on A Wing are extremely poor: slopping out, flooding in recesses, lack of showers, continuing cockroach infestation, inadequate equipment for association – are all unacceptable for any prisoners; for unconvicted prisoners they are intolerable.[117]

Prison Rules and complaints

The *Woolf Report* recognised that prisoners are particularly vulnerable to 'arbitrary and unlawful action'[118] and it is therefore essential that prisoners have legal recognition to enable them to assert realistically their rights. Although the number and effectiveness of domestic channels of redress have improved, there is still no comprehensive mechanism for the definition and protection of prisoners' rights.[119]

Prison law in Britain has developed in a piecemeal and haphazard fashion.[120] The primary pieces of legislation governing prisons are the Prison Act 1952 and the Prison Rules 1964. The Prison Act laid down the basic framework for the running of the prison system but gave no comprehensive statement of the rights and duties of authorities or inmates. It also vested considerable discretionary powers with prison authorities and the Home Secretary. The Prison Rules offer a more comprehensive formulation for the treatment, regulation and management of prisons and are supplemented by Standing Orders (SO) which are non-statutory administrative guidelines. The Prison Rules do not represent a code of directly enforceable rights. As Lord Denning has stated:

> The Prison Rules are regulatory directions only. Even if they are not observed, they do not give rise to a cause of action.[121]

The Prison Rules are not 'actionable' in that they cannot give rise to a claim for breach of statutory duty, but they are 'justiciable' in that they may give rise to a public law remedy.[122] Prisoners have no effective means of ensuring that the authorities comply with the Prison Rules and the inconsistency and lack of accountability has been a cause of resentment among prisoners and of concern among internal and external prison bodies.[123]

Because of the courts' attitude to the Prison Rules, prisoners have tried to use the torts of false imprisonment and breach of statutory duty to challenge the lawfulness of their conditions. In 1991 the House of Lords rejected the claims of two prisoners. One had been held in solitary confinement for 28 days, the other had been beaten up by prison staff and left naked in a strip cell overnight. Although these practices breached Prison Rules, the Lords decided that they did not amount either to a breach of statutory duty or to a case of false imprisonment.[124] However, the Home Office did subsequently issue Circular Instruction 37/90[125] which incorporated virtually all the procedural safeguards for which the plaintiffs had been arguing.[126] The *Woolf Report* stated that 'A system without an independent element is not a system which accords with proper standards of justice.'[127] British prison law had no such independent element until 1994 and the complaints procedure and available remedies remain largely inadequate.[128]

In September 1990 new complaints procedures were introduced to replace the old system.[129] This gave prisoners the right to:

- confidential access to governors, area managers and Boards of Visitors
- written replies to complaints within a fixed time limit
- access to reasons for decisions made by prison authorities.

The Chief Inspector of Prisons' *Report* 1991-2 suggested the new complaints system was not working smoothly, with delays in responses and excessive legality in replies.[130] In April 1994, a Prisons Ombudsman was appointed as an independent adjudicator on grievances, to review complaints once all internal procedures have been exhausted. However, the Ombudsman is not empowered to review substantive decisions made by the Parole Board and its powers are purely advisory.

Until recently the structure of the prison disciplinary system was unfair. The requirement laid down in Article 14 of the ICCPR that everyone facing a criminal charge 'is entitled to a fair and public hearing within a reasonable time by an independent and impartial tribunal established by law' was side-stepped by British law which stated that punishments administered in prisons were internal matters and not subject to criminal law. In 1985 a judgment by the European Court of Human Rights showed that prison disciplinary hearings *could* amount to 'criminal proceedings' and so breach the ECHR's guarantees of the right to a fair trial.[131] The European Court held that the Board of Visitors could not be viewed as an 'independent tribunal' and that the inability of the applicants to consult a lawyer before and be legally represented at the Boards' hearing constituted a violation of the ECHR.

In 1992 reforms were finally achieved under the Prison (Amendment) Rules,[132] stripping the Board of Visitors, who, held a dual role as watchdog and adjudicator, of its disciplinary functions. The Rules introduced a distinction between disciplinary and criminal sentences: normal disciplinary cases were left in the hands of the prison governor whilst serious offences were dealt with by outside courts, thus ensuring the prisoner normal procedural protection. The maximum punishment available for disciplinary officers to impose was reduced in 1989 from loss of 120 days' remission[133] to 28 additional days.[134]

The procedural standards in governors' hearings are inadequate. Prisoners are not permitted legal representation and evidential and procedural standards are so poor that approximately 40 per cent of adjudications which come under review are quashed.[135] The dual managerial and judicial role of prison governors is cause for concern. The close relationship between the governor and prison officers who lay the charges and upon whose loyalty the governor relies, means that the judgments are not always impartial.[136] In September 1994 six prisoners attempted to escape from

Whitemoor prison. A prison officer was injured during the escape and the prisoners claim they were assaulted after being recaptured. The prisoners are suing the prison authorities and are subject to disciplinary hearings. Nevertheless the prisoners were kept at Whitemoor, in segregation units, with the challenges pending.[137]

Under Prison Rule 43, prison governors are given the power to remove prisoners from association in the interests of 'good order and discipline.' Prisoners are not given the right to any form of hearing before they are segregated and are often not given any reasons for their segregation.[138] A Circular Instruction in 1990 states that 'inmates have no entitlement to be given the reasons for their segregation under rule 43' but encourages reasons to be given nonetheless.[139]

Prisoners are often segregated in punishment cells where they have no access to any recreational facilities or they are taken to local prisons. Standing Order 3D provides that the governor can only authorise segregation for up to three days and thereafter it must be approved by the Board of Visitors. According to the Prisoners Advice Service, there are no known instances where the Board of Visitors has refused to authorise segregation.[140] Being segregated makes it extremely difficult for a prisoner facing a hearing to prepare his or her case and amounts to a form of punishment before trial.

Sentencing and parole

Following criticisms by the European Court of Human Rights, the Criminal Justice Act 1991 introduced changes to the system of release on licence or 'parole'. Parole procedures have been improved but the process remains discretional and inefficient.[141] Prisoners see their dossier and are granted an oral hearing with a member of the Parole Board and given reasons for the decisions made regarding their eligibility for parole.

The legal position on setting parole for prisoners serving life sentences has recently changed, most notably for discretionary lifers. In two cases, one of which was brought by Liberty,[142] the European Court of Human Rights ruled that the British government was in breach of the ECHR.[143] These cases established that the lawfulness of discretionary life-sentence prisoners' continued detention after the punitive element of the sentence was completed should be considered by an independent body with the power to order their release.

The Criminal Justice Act 1991 led to the tariff period for discretionary lifers being fixed openly and the option of going to the Parole Board after that time. Prisoners sentenced to life imprisonment at the discretion of the courts, who are appearing before the Parole Board, are now entitled to see and comment on the dossier that is submitted to the panel as evidence. They are also entitled to attend the hearing with legal representation, call and question witnesses and receive the panel's decision and reasons for it within seven days of the hearing.[144] Although a prisoner still does not have the right to have his or her case heard in court, the Parole Board has the power to order the release of discretionary lifers if satisfied 'that it is no longer necessary for the protection of the public that the prisoner be confined.'[145] This still leaves the burden of proof with the prisoner.

Recommendations by the Parole Board other than for release (for example, early reviews) are not binding on the Home Secretary. An application by a prisoner alleging that the procedure for setting the timing of the subsequent reviews is in breach of the ECHR is currently being considered by the European Commission on Human Rights.[146]

Mandatory life-sentence prisoners can still only be released by the Home Secretary. The Parole Board can make recommendations for release but the Home Secretary is not required to accept these, nor the judicial recommendation on tariff. Although mandatory life-sentence prisoners are permitted to see their parole dossier and make representations before it is considered by the Parole Board, they have no right to an oral hearing. The procedures implemented by the Home Office, designed to enable mandatory life-sentence prisoners to be informed of the judicial recommendations as to the tariff and the decisions made by the Home Secretary,[147] have been judged unsatisfactory in that they fail to provide sufficient information for a lifer to make representations.[148]

In English law a person on parole remains a prisoner and can be recalled to prison at any time. This means a life-sentence prisoner who is paroled is subject to recall for the rest of his or her life. People have frequently been recalled for minor offences which would not normally warrant imprisonment.[149] The recall decision[150] is an executive decision with no recourse to independent judicial control. The European Court has ruled it essential to give a person on parole an opportunity for a judicial hearing over recall just as for a release decision.[151] However, the British government has refused to act on this judgment.

Minors who are sentenced to be detained at Her Majesty's Pleasure are treated in the same way as mandatory life-sentence prisoners and are subject to that system of review. The European Commission on Human Rights ruled that this was in breach of the ECHR, but the British government has failed to take any action.[152]

HIV and AIDS in prison

Between 1985 and 1990, the Prison Medical Service recorded 314 prisoners who were HIV-positive, and seven prisoners died of AIDS-related diseases.[153] It is estimated that there are between 50 and 65 prisoners who are HIV-positive in prison at any one time.[154] Although the government has produced a training pack on the spread of HIV within prisons, a survey conducted in 1992 showed that over half the ex-prisoners questioned had not seen it.[155] Another study found that fewer than one-third of prisoners tested for HIV received counselling, either before or after they were tested.[156] Many prisons have kept those who are HIV-positive or are awaiting HIV-test results in a prison hospital, in the mistaken belief that HIV may be transmitted during the course of day-to-day activities. Some prisons have even isolated prisoners they judged to belong to a 'high-risk group', such as gay men, until they agreed to be tested and a negative test result was returned.[157]

DISCRIMINATION IN THE CRIMINAL JUSTICE SYSTEM

Racism

In the UK's *Third Periodic Report to the UN Human Rights Committee*, the government noted that:

> concern has been expressed at the fact that members of ethnic minority groups are over represented in the prison population of England and Wales . . . The proportion of those of Afro-Caribbean origin is steadily increasing.[158]

Afro-Caribbean men comprise 10 per cent of the male sentenced population, between eight and nine times their proportion in the population.[159] Afro-Caribbean women account for nearly one-quarter of all female prisoners.[160] Even if the numbers of foreign women serving sentences for importing drugs are omitted, the number of black women prisoners comprises 13 per cent of the total.[161]

The *Third Periodic Report* stated that government research has found no evidence of discrimination in sentencing by the Crown Courts but concedes that 'there is however evidence that ethnic minority people are more likely to be stopped by the police, to be refused bail if they are arrested and charged, to plead not guilty, and to opt for trial by jury where the choice is open to them'.[162] In its *Fourth Periodic Report*, the government stated it had stepped up its monitoring and was reviewing its training on race issues.[163] The claim that there is no evidence for discrimination in sentencing patterns has been challenged by studies which indicate that black people are more likely to receive immediate custodial sentences or suspended sentences than their white counterparts. One concluded that black defendants were 5-8 per cent more likely than whites to receive a custodial sentence for an offence of medium seriousness and that black and Asian people received longer sentences than white people. It noted differing patterns of disposal of cases. Although it estimated that 80 per cent of the over-representation of black males in custody could be accounted for by the greater number of black offenders who appeared before the Crown Court for sentencing, the remaining 20 per cent was attributed to this differing treatment. One-third of the latter category appeared to be sentenced more harshly owing to their race while two-thirds were subject to harsher sentences because they had pleaded not guilty.[164]

The government's report also concedes that black people are more likely to plead not guilty and opt for trial by jury, thereby increasing their chances of receiving a longer custodial sentence if they are convicted, because they lack confidence in the British criminal justice system.[165] Black people are over-represented not only among the prison population, but also in Liberty's dossier of unsafe convictions: 23 per cent of those listed are black.[166]

Black people are more likely to face problems of faulty identification evidence. The police acknowledge this problem, claiming that because of difficulties in assembling black line-ups, they frequently use confrontations instead.[167] The lack of adequate translation facilities during interrogation and trials further frustrates equal access to justice.[168] Afro-Caribbean juveniles are more likely to be sent to court than cautioned.[169] Area studies have shown that one-half of black suspects are prosecuted, compared to one-third of white suspects.[170] A 1989 study by the National Association for the Care and Rehabilitation of Offenders (NACRO) concluded that 'the proportion of young black men going into custody is twice as high as the proportion of young white men, this means that nearly one in ten of the young men in the black community will have been locked up by his twenty-first birthday.'[171] Because black defendants are more likely to be refused bail than their white counterparts, more black people remanded in custody are subsequently acquitted of the charges made against them.[172]

Black people also spend longer in prison than their white counterparts. In response to a parliamentary question in November 1991 the Home Office revealed that the average length of sentence served by Afro-Caribbean men was eight months longer than for their white counterparts, while Afro-Caribbean women faced average sentences more than twice as long as those of their white counterparts.[173] Adult white men received average sentences of 17.7 months compared to 25.5 months for adult Afro-Caribbean men. Adult white women received average sentences of 12.4 months compared to 25.6 months for Afro-Caribbean women.[174]

Black people are significantly under-represented within the police force. Many officers display overtly racist attitudes. In August 1992 it was reported that police in Bristol had advised their Neighbourhood Watch Scheme to call 999 if they noticed black people in the area.[175] In the Newham area of East London in 1992 a monitoring project dealt with 165 cases of police harassment against the black community which included physical assaults, verbal abuse, systematic use of stop-and-search powers and raids on people's homes.[176]

Discrimination against disabled people

Suspects suffering from mental health problems are vulnerable to pressure during police interrogations which has sometimes led to false confessions. The Court of Appeal has ruled that confessions made by mentally vulnerable suspects, in the absence of a solicitor or appropriate adult, should not be automatically rejected as unreliable.[177] The guidelines for judges, advising on which confessions should be rejected and which cases withdrawn, are extremely narrow, and would not have prevented such miscarriages of justice as the cases of Judith Ward[178] and Stefan Kizsko.[179]

According to the Council for the Advancement of Communication with Deaf People, there are only 92 fully qualified interpreters who perform all the interpreting duties for deaf people in the legal system.[180] Deaf people have to pay for their own interpreters in domestic disputes and on average their legal costs are higher than those of non-deaf people because their cases last longer.[181] The difficulties in finding interpreters mean that deaf people are likely to spend longer in police custody and may be questioned without either having one present or being forced to use one who is not properly trained. Unqualified interpreters often make errors because they are usually not well versed in police jargon or not used to acting as strictly objective two-way channels. Small uncorrected errors can lead to major miscarriages of justice.

In February 1994 a court heard how two deaf teenagers had been arrested on suspicion of breaking into a house, attempting to retrieve a ball from the garden. They were interrogated in the absence of a translator or solicitor and, it was claimed, the officers concocted a false confession.[182] Such abuses of justice occur despite the code of practice in the Police and Criminal Evidence Act 1984 which says that a deaf or speech-handicapped person must not be interviewed without an interpreter unless he or she agrees in writing. This is reinforced by a European Court of Human Rights decision which stresses that the authorities have responsibility for the interpreter's competence. However, suspects do not have a right to insist on a qualified interpreter and, even if they did, there is no recognised qualification of legal expertise for interpreters.

Perversely, in some circumstances the courts do recognise the potential dangers of subjective translations – for example, many judges bar deaf people from jury service if they need to be accompanied by an interpreter, even though there is no law or ruling which prevents this.[183] The declaration requiring people to attend jury service specifies that people may be discharged 'if there is doubt as to your capacity to serve on a jury because of physical disability or insufficient understanding of English.' Such decisions rest with individual judges and this can lead to disabled people being excluded from juries through prejudice or ignorance. In January 1994 a woman due to become Britain's first deaf juror was banned from sitting despite the availability of equipment to enable her to read evidence from a computer screen.[184]

The right of people who are arrested and facing criminal charges to be informed of their rights and the charges against them in a language that they understand is recognised as a fundamental part of the protection offered by Articles 9 and 14 of the ICCPR against arbitrary detentions or wrongful convictions. However, the British criminal justice system does not make these rights fully available to deaf people. Trial by a jury of peers is a corner-stone of the British criminal justice system which can be denied to disabled people.

Discrimination against women

A study of sentencing in 1984 found that almost one in four women who had been sentenced to imprisonment had no previous convictions compared to one in 17 men.[185] However, crime is predominantly committed by males. Women make up less than 4 per cent of the prison population[186] – there were only 1,189 women prisoners in Britain in 1991, 133 of whom were juveniles.[187] Women commit fewer crimes than men and are less likely to be repeat offenders.[188] Proportionately more women than men who appear in court will therefore have no previous convictions.

The offences that women do commit tend to be less serious than those by men and, while it does not appear that the courts sentence women more harshly than men, some decisions are erratic and the system as a whole is discriminatory towards women. Women lawyers have complained that male judges often unself-consciously give sentences according to pre-conceived ideas about what constitutes 'good' and 'bad' behaviour in women.[189] Some judges have sent women to prison because they have children, considering them unsuitable for community service.[190]

Over 70 per cent of all cautioned or convicted women in 1989 had committed theft-related offences,[191] a figure conforming to a broad pattern apparent between 1981 and 1991.[192] The proportion of convicted men who had committed similar offences is much lower – 45 per cent – while the proportion of convicted men who had committed offences involving violence – 18 per cent – is much higher than that for women – just 9 per cent.[193] One analysis of court records indicates that most thefts by women involve shop-lifting, usually of goods of small value,[194] while between one-third and one-quarter of all women in prison are convicted for non-payment of fines.[195]

Many women are held on remand, rather than under sentence, and a high proportion of those remanded in custody and then released are women. It is a violation of Article 9 of the ICCPR to keep people awaiting trial in custody as a 'general rule' and it is clearly discriminatory for more women than men to be treated in this way. In 1992, a total of 383 women were held on remand, of whom 22 per cent were acquitted of the charges against them and 52 per cent received non-custodial sentences. Only 26 per cent of the women who had been held on remand were sentenced to imprisonment by the courts.[196]

The proportion of women held on remand and subsequently given non-custodial sentences appears to be higher than that for men.[197] While the criteria for making remand and sentencing decisions are separate, if the effect of the practice is discriminatory it is a violation of Articles 2, 3, and 9 of the ICCPR. There is no evidence that women, even those facing serious charges, are more likely to abscond, commit further offences or interfere with the course of justice than men.

Prison

Because of insufficient prison accommodation for women, female prisoners are often held at great distances from their homes.[198] A report in April 1993 by the Chief Inspector of Prisons stated that women who had been sentenced for relatively minor offences were being sent to the maximum security H-wing of Durham prison simply to justify keeping it open to house two Irish Republican women prisoners.[199] The two women concerned campaigned for many years to be allowed to serve their sentences in Northern Ireland, where they would be closer to their families,[200] and the British government finally agreed to allow this in 1994.[201] However, many Irish Republican prisoners remain in English jails.[202] This violates the rights of people in custody to be treated with dignity and respect, as set out in Article 10 of the ICCPR, and breaches the government's own stated policy of holding prisoners as close to their families as possible.[203]

About half of all female prisoners have two or more children[204] and many women choose to serve their sentences with their babies. However, only three out of 12 women's prisons have facilities for mothers with babies – two of these in closed prisons. This shortage of mother-and-baby units in prisons increases the likelihood that even small babies will be taken away from offenders.[205] Some women may have to transfer to prisons far away from their homes in order to have their children with them, a particular problem for remand prisoners.[206] Education facilities for women in prison are inadequate and, on the whole, worse than those for men. A study conducted by the Women's National Commission showed that women are often treated more harshly for violations of prison discipline than men and that more petty restrictions are placed on inmates in women's prisons than in men's.[207] Studies also indicate that far more drugs are prescribed to women prisoners than to men.[208]

In September 1993, there were 255 foreign women prisoners in Britain, 70 on remand and 185 serving sentences.[209] Foreign women prisoners are often kept in isolation and their children, if in the UK, are usually taken into local authority care.[210] The majority are from the Caribbean, Latin America and Africa[211] and are convicted for fraud or drug-trafficking offences, usually after being arrested at ports of entry into the UK.

A study of the experiences of people detained under the Prevention of Terrorism Act in Britain showed that women appear to be disproportionately likely to be subjected to strip-searches.[212] It showed that women detainees found the placement of their children in care during their detentions traumatic. A number reported that, during interrogations, they were threatened with never being allowed to see their children again.[213]

Strip-searching

Strip-searching, whether of women or men in prisons, police stations and ports of entry into the UK is an intrusive, unnecessary, humiliating and degrading practice. It offends against some religions[214] and continues in the UK despite the government's recognition that alternatives exist and that strip-searching has a low success rate.[215] There is considerable anecdotal evidence that women are subjected to strip-searches during police interrogation in a discriminatory way and that black and Irish people are sometimes singled out for strip-searches by the police and by authorities at ports and airports.[216]

In June 1993 the government stated it could not collect information on the number of people strip-searched each year, other than those convicted and on remand.[217] However, between July

1987 and March 1988, 16,023 people were strip-searched at ports of entry into the UK.[218] Drugs were recovered in 586 searches, dutiable goods in 180 cases and other prohibited or restricted goods in 57 instances.[219] There were 71 appeals against the strip-search being carried out and 17 of these appeals were upheld.[220]

Prostitution

The civil and political rights of prostitutes[221] are routinely violated in Britain. Being a prostitute is not illegal but it is an offence for a 'common prostitute' to solicit for trade.[222] The police have the power to caution women for soliciting and such cautions are put on to a central register. The police do not need to have any independent evidence before issuing a caution. After a woman has been cautioned twice she is defined as 'a common prostitute' and can be charged and convicted of soliciting or loitering. Only women prostitutes are dealt with in this way. This legal procedure violates the rights of alleged prostitutes to privacy, a fair trial and protection from arbitrary arrest. Prostitutes often complain that the police use their discretionary powers in an arbitrary and draconian way.[223] Police sometimes search women whom they suspect to be prostitutes to find out if they are carrying condoms and use this as supporting evidence in court.[224] In July 1993, following a campaign by the English Collective of Prostitutes, the Metropolitan Police Force announced that it would stop using this dangerous practice but there is no authority to ensure other police forces will do likewise.[225] If a prostitute shares a flat with a friend she can be convicted for running a brothel.[226] If she lives with a man and pays her share of the rent or housekeeping, he can be charged with living off immoral earnings.[227] If two prostitutes live together they can be prosecuted for both offences. There is evidence of discriminatory practices on the part of the police and the Crown Prosecution Service (CPS) towards prostitutes who are victims of rape and other forms of violence.[228] Prostitutes who allege rape or assault often complain that the police are reluctant to pursue their cases.[229]

Lesbians and gay men

Lesbians and the law

Lesbian sex is not recognised in law. A proposal to create the offence of 'gross indecency between female persons' was rejected by the House of Lords in 1921, because the Lords were concerned not to bring the 'horror' of lesbianism 'to the notice of women who had never heard of it, never thought of it.'[230] There is no explicit age of consent for lesbian sex, although the legal position that a woman under the age of 16 is not deemed able to give her consent to a sexual act effectively establishes one. The legal definitions of rape and buggery mean that women cannot be charged with these offences. In general, lesbians face discrimination in the criminal justice system because of their gender rather than their sexual orientation.

The Sexual Offences Acts

Same-sex activity between men was outlawed in all circumstances in Britain from 1885 until 1967. These restrictions were consolidated in the Sexual Offences Act 1956 which prohibited anal intercourse[231] and any other form of sexual activity between men.[232] The Sexual Offences Act 1967 created one exception to this in England and Wales only, which was consensual sexual activity between two men, both of whom were aged 21 or over, that took place in private.[233] The age limit was reduced to 18 by the Criminal Justice and Public Order Act 1994.[234]

Gay men are only allowed to have consensual sex within strictly defined circumstances – it must be in private and no more than two people may be present. If more than two people are present during homosexual sex the law does not regard it as 'in private' and, accordingly, gay men can be prosecuted for buggery or gross indecency. It could, in theory, be possible to prosecute two gay men who had sex in one room of a private flat or house while other people were in other rooms.[235] The police have raided gay private parties and arrested people for gross indecency on this basis – although charges are not usually brought.[236] Saunas, health spas and even member-only clubs are not classified as private and, if sex between men takes place on the premises, their managers can be charged under the Disorderly House Act 1751.[237] In April 1994, for example, the police raided a gay club in Manchester, arresting 13 men for alleged 'gross indecency' in a pitch black back room.[238] The raid was carried out by officers wearing rubber gloves and demanding to know 'what diseases' those arrested were suffering from.[239]

In March 1993 the House of Lords upheld the convictions of

15 men who had been given prison sentences of up to four-and-a-half years for engaging in consensual sado-masochistic sex.[240] The men were convicted of causing each other actual bodily harm even though the court accepted that what had taken place, in private, was entirely consensual.[241] After these convictions there were further police raids on gay clubs and parties.[242] Liberty has submitted, with others, applications to the European Commission on Human Rights on behalf of a number of people who may be affected by this ruling. The case was declared admissible in January 1995.[243]

Public indecency

The police often operate extensive and costly surveillance and entrapment operations to catch gay and bisexual men engaging in sexual activities in secluded places such as parks, parked cars or public lavatories. These locations are relatively private yet the legal definition of 'in private' makes prosecutions possible.[244] It would be virtually inconceivable for the police to commit the same level of resources as they regularly expend on gay men – including video cameras and *agents provocateurs* – to a surveillance operation on a heterosexual 'lovers' lane'.

The prosecution does not need to present evidence that a member of the public was offended to secure a conviction for the exclusively gay offence of gross indecency between men. It is also unnecessary for them to show that anyone, other than the police, actually saw and was affected in any way by the alleged indecency.[245] It is also no defence to a charge that the crime was actively instigated by police or police undercover agents.[246]

Heterosexuals are occasionally prosecuted for public order offences[247] or for outraging public decency. However, such prosecutions are extremely rare and sentences are much lighter. In August 1992, a man and woman were fined £50 each, with costs of £25, for having sex in the crowded second-class compartment of a British Rail train.[248] By contrast, in the previous year the police in Surrey embarked on an extensive undercover operation in an obscure area of dense woodlands, which resulted in the arrest of 28 gay and bisexual men who were fined up to £1,000 for first offences.[249]

The police use a number of other indecency clauses of local authority and public transport bye-laws to bring prosecutions against gay men. These clauses allow the prosecution to deny defendants the right to trial by jury. In 1989, 226 men were arrested for breaching British Rail's bye-law 17 which prohibits indecent behaviour on railway premises. In the same year 150 men were charged with remaining in a public toilet 'longer than is necessary', which contravenes a bye-law in the London Borough of Richmond.[250] The law is also used to criminalise public displays of affection between same-sex couples. People have been convicted under the public order laws for kissing in public[251] and threatened with prosecution for walking hand-in-hand.[252] In 1989 one man was convicted of behaviour likely to cause a breach of the peace after he was arrested when wearing women's clothing.[253]

Even where a homosexual act itself is legal, steps taken to arrange it, by one of the participants or by a third party, may be against the law. It is a crime for a man 'persistently to solicit or importune another man in a public place for immoral purposes.'[254] The courts have ruled that 'immoral purposes' covers any sexual activity between men, including between two men, in private, who are both over 21 years of age.[255] It is also an offence for a man to 'procure' or bring about either 'an act of buggery' or any other act of sexual activity between two men.[256] The term 'public place' can mean anywhere other than a private dwelling and the terms 'soliciting' and 'importuning' can mean chatting up, or any word or gesture which conveys a sexual intent.[257]

Policing and sentencing

Research for the Home Office showed that between 1967, when homosexuality was decriminalised, and 1979 the number of convictions for 'homosexual offences' quadrupled in England and Wales.[258] This upward trend accelerated during the late 1980s partly because of the homophobic atmosphere in which section 28 of the Local Government Act 1988 was enacted.[259] Four times as many men were convicted of indecency between males in 1989 as in 1966 – the year before some homosexual acts were decriminalised.[260] In the 10 years 1980 to 1989 (inclusive), an estimated 25,000 men were convicted of the mainly gay consensual offences of buggery, indecency, soliciting and procuring. Of these, at least 2,500 were imprisoned. About half received prison sentences of between six months and three years. The estimated cost of these prosecutions and imprisonments was £160 million.[261]

Between 1990 and 1992, 2,913 men were prosecuted for indecency between males.[262] In 842 of the cases the charge involved indecency between a man aged over 21 and another man aged under 21. A total of 2,249 men were convicted and 30 were sentenced to immediate custody. Between 1989 and 1992, 2,258 men were prosecuted for buggery,[263] 860 were convicted and 610 were sentenced to immediate custody.[264] A total of 2,233 men were prosecuted for procuring or soliciting during this period,[265] 1,573 were convicted[266] and 14 were sentenced to immediate custody.[267] In 1992, the last year for which figures are available, 997 men were convicted of the predominantly gay and victimless offences of buggery, indecency, soliciting and procuring, and 159 received terms of imprisonment.[268]

An estimated 70 per cent of buggery convictions relate to consensual under-age sexual activity.[269] The police are more likely to press charges for buggery than for indecency when one of the partners to sex is under 21. Where one partner is under 16 the maximum sentence for buggery is life imprisonment for the older partner and two years for the younger partner. Where one partner is aged between 16 and 21 and the other is aged over 21 the maximum sentence is five years' imprisonment.[270] Where both are aged between 16 and 21 the maximum sentence is two years' imprisonment.[271] The myth of the predatory gay male as a threat to children is one of the main negative stereotypes that gay men have to face. Discriminatory policing and sentencing practices reinforce this. In fact paedophiles are far more likely to be heterosexual men. Home Office research has found that about 75 per cent of men convicted of sexual offences with children under 10 years old are heterosexual.[272]

It is police practice not to investigate most consensual under age heterosexual sexual activity. They often caution rather than charge heterosexual male offenders, unless there is a large age discrepancy or the girl is under 14 years old.[273] They virtually never bring indecent assault charges against a man 'petting' an underage girl but will do so against a man 'petting' a boy. The maximum sentence for sexual intercourse with a girl aged between 13 and 16 is two years' imprisonment while men accused of buggery with someone under the age of 16 face life sentences. In fact 30 per cent of *all* convictions for sexual offences are for consensual gay behaviour, which accounts for only 13 per cent of recorded sex offences.[274] Men who commit consenting homosexual offences are four times more likely to be convicted than men who commit heterosexual and violent sex offences.[275] Hundreds of gay male teenagers have been criminalised and dozens imprisoned in the last five years. In 1989, for example, 185 teenagers were convicted, 147 cautioned and 23 were imprisoned for the predominantly gay consensual offences of buggery, soliciting, indecency and procuring.[276]

The maximum penalty (in the crown courts) for indecency between males – both of whom are aged 21 or over or both of whom are aged under 21 – in a non-private place is two years' imprisonment, possibly accompanied by a fine of no fixed limit.[277] If one of the men is aged between 16 and 21 and the other is 21 or over, this can be raised to up to five years' imprisonment.[278] Publicity about a man's conviction for gay sex, even when the acts involved are totally victimless, can be extremely damaging. There were six reported suicides of men arrested for gay sex offences in 1989.[279]

Homophobia in the police and criminal justice system

The criminalisation of much gay sexual activity has reinforced the discriminatory attitudes of sections of the police.[280] Officers taught to regard gay men as a category of criminal suspect may be less sympathetic in their dealings with people whom they believe to be gay. One survey conducted in part of south-east London in 1992 claimed that the police were to blame for 21 per cent of the incidents of abuse suffered by gay men.[281] Gay police officers have been driven out of their jobs by discrimination and harassment[282] and there has been unfair treatment of lesbian and gay victims of crime by police officers. In March 1994 it was reported that a 19-year-old gay man who had been raped was driven to attempt suicide as a result of insensitive treatment by the police. He claimed that the police were careless and indifferent and their questioning amounted to an interrogation about his sexuality. In their statements to the media the police appeared to blame the victim and their comments compromised both the likelihood and effectiveness of any possible prosecution.[283] The victim waited before he reported the incident, for fear that he would be prosecuted because he was younger than the age of consent at that time.[284] In another well-publicised case, in March 1993, a Chief Superintendent in the Metropolitan Police described a group of women delegates, at a domestic violence conference in a police training college, as 'a bunch of lezzies. There is not a normal one amongst them.' Although he was initially suspended and required to resign, in May 1994 he was reinstated to his post.[285]

Lesbian and gay prisoners

Lesbian, gay and bisexual prisoners frequently face hostility, harassment and assaults from other prisoners and from prison guards.[286] Because of this many gay prisoners opt to serve their sentences in segregation from other prisoners, under Rule 43, although this can mean solitary confinement in appalling conditions for 23 hours a day. Rule 43 offers segregation for those prisoners suffering persecution from other inmates. It is normally applied to sex offenders – such as rapists and paedophiles – and ex-police or ex-prison officers, and it carries a high level of stigma. Segregated prisoners are still likely to face abuse from prison guards and other prisoners, and a number of gay prisoners held in segregation have been killed during prison riots.[287]

Gay prisoners are often held under far tighter security than is justified by the offences for which they have been imprisoned. It has been claimed that some lesbian and gay prisoners have been denied transfer to lower security prisons, because they have dormitory accommodation.[288] Lesbian and gay prisoners also face intrusions into their privacy. Mail is frequently censored under Standing Order 4 of Prison Rules,[289] which allows magazines and newspapers to be withheld from prisoners if their contents 'present a threat to good order and discipline' or could have 'an adverse effect on the inmate from a medical point of view'. Soft-core heterosexual pornography is freely available in prisons but equivalent same-sex material is routinely withheld. Even publications such as *Gay Times*, which contain no sexually explicit material, have been banned from prisons on some occasions.[290]

3 RACISM IN ENGLAND AND WALES

THE CONTEXT TODAY

On 14 January 1991 Malkjit Singh Natt was arrested at his work-place, a factory in east London.[1] He immediately telephoned his solicitor and arranged to meet him at Plaistow police station. Mr Natt was placed in an unmarked police car by two women officers and then transferred into a marked car where he recognised two male officers who had previously arrested and assaulted him on a number of occasions. Fearing a repetition Natt turned on a tape recorder which he had been carrying in his pocket and recorded the following conversation:

Mr Natt	Why am I being arrested?
PC	Yer just a pain in the arse, ain't yer?
Mr Natt	Oh God.
PC	Why don't you go and set fire to yourself, or something?
Mr Natt	You carry on arresting me – you carry on arresting me with no reason. Why carry on? I don't know why.
PC	Eh?
Mr Natt	Why? Why do you [unintelligible] to me like that?
PC	'Cos you're a shit.
Mr Natt	Eh?
PC	Behave yourself.
Mr Natt	Last time you arrest me without any reason. You try and arrest me again and again – why?
PC	It often happens in your country don't it?
Mr Natt	Eh?

PC	It happens at home where your lot come from.
Mr Natt	Yes – what happens over here it would never happen like that.
PC	Yes it does. Worse than that.
Mr Natt	What?
PC	They'd go out and shoot yer, or something.
Mr Natt	What?
PC	That's what we should do – fucking shoot yer.
Mr Natt	You shoot me?
PC	Yes I would.
Mr Natt	What for?
PC	Well . . . wanker.
Mr Natt	What? That's no good for police officer doing that thing, you know. You know that? Eh?
PC	Why don't you go home?
Mr Natt	What's go home?
PC	Go home – you know – to India or Pakistan, or wherever you fucking come from.

The verbal abuse continued during the seven-minute journey to the police station and the sound of Mr Natt being assaulted was recorded. When he arrived at the station the tape was discovered and confiscated. However, Mr Natt's solicitor insisted on it being played and, after a protracted legal battle, obtained a court order for it to be released. Mr Natt was charged with threatening behaviour, assaulting a police officer and attempting to escape. It was alleged that he had punched one of the women police officers and fled from them before being recaptured and placed in a police car with the male officers.

Despite the evidence on the tape – Mr Natt continually asks why he is being arrested and no reference is made to his alleged assault or escape attempt – and despite the fact that he had previously arranged to meet his solicitor at the police station, Mr Natt was convicted by a magistrates court of assault and threatening behaviour, a conviction which was overturned on appeal.

After the tape recording was played at a press conference, and its contents extensively reported, the police set up an internal inquiry which 'disciplined' the officers by docking them a day's pay. Although both Sir Peter Imbert, then the Commissioner of the Metropolitan Police, and Kenneth Clarke, then Home Secretary, have distanced themselves from the remarks and expressed regret at the leniency of the punishment, no further action has been taken against the officers by the authorities and they remain on duty in east London.

The Police Federation, which represents police officers, defended the men. In August 1992, *Police Review* magazine said in its editorial that Sir Peter Imbert's criticism of the officers had 'overstepped the bounds of natural justice'. While conceding that the officers were 'abusive, impatient and certainly prejudiced' against Mr Natt, the editorial noted that 'despite being urged to remain silent' by the officers he had 'kept up a running complaint against both of them.'[2]

The incident highlights the progress still needed before the British government can claim to be upholding the rights of ethnic minorities[3] to freedom from discrimination, equal protection of the law, outlawing of incitement to racial hatred and respect for the cultural rights of ethnic minorities. The deteriorating state of race relations in Britain was further highlighted in September 1993 when the far-right British National Party (BNP) won a local authority council seat in the East End of London.[4] It was the party's first ever electoral victory and the first time in nearly 20 years that an openly racist party had won a council seat in Britain.[5] Although the BNP lost the seat in the subsequent local election, in June 1994, their candidate, Derek Beackon, increased his vote to over 2,000 which represented over 10 per cent of the total poll.[6]

It is now almost 20 years since the Race Relations Act 1976. Despite this legislation, levels of discrimination and disadvantage remain alarmingly high. Ethnic minorities have a much greater unemployment rate than white people, which cannot be explained by differences in age or qualifications.[7] Ethnic minorities remain over-represented amongst the homeless and the socially disadvantaged. Ethnic minorities also bear the burden of poor housing and health, education and welfare cuts. In recent years the number and proportion of young black people forcibly detained in mental health institutions has increased.

Ethnic minorities continue to experience high levels of harassment, abuse and physical violence. The police force often fails to provide sufficient protection to victims of racial violence. It is itself often guilty of racist practices, abusing ethnic minorities, using discriminatory policing practices towards them and subjecting them to arbitrary arrests and wrongful detentions.

THE BRITISH GOVERNMENT'S RECORD

In its *Fourth Periodic Report to the UN Human Rights Committee*, the British government stated that three million residents of Great Britain belonged to ethnic groups other than white, making them 5.5 per cent of the population.[8] These figures were based on the 1991 census[9] which showed that the ethnic minority population was growing. In the government's *Third Periodic Report* (1989), it stated that the ethnic minority population of Great Britain constituted about 2.5 million people (4.5 per cent of the total population)[10] and that it was:

> fully committed to the elimination of discrimination and the development of a fair and just society in which all individuals, whatever their race or colour, have equal rights, responsibilities and opportunities. The government seeks to ensure that its general policies and programmes, including the special initiatives it is taking in inner cities, benefit all sections of society. The government also supports legislation, institutions and programmes which are targeted directly at tackling racial discrimination and promoting equality of opportunity.[11]

In its *Fourth Report* the government stated that it 'seeks to ensure that its policies and programmes benefit all sections of society and supports legislation, institutions and policies directed at tackling discrimination and promoting equality of opportunity.'[12] It outlined a number of monitoring and training initiatives that had been undertaken, particularly in the criminal justice system, and highlighted the continuing problem of racial violence directed at ethnic minorities. The *Report* noted that the Race Relations (Remedies) Act 1994 had removed the ceiling of £11,000 in compensation that can be awarded by industrial tribunals in cases of racial discrimination. A parallel change has been made for sex discrimination cases. Both have been forced upon the government by a ruling of the European Court of Justice.[13]

The *Report* noted that the Criminal Justice and Public Order Act 1994 creates a new offence of intentional harassment which carries with it powers of arrest and 'is aimed at providing higher penalties for the most serious cases of harassment, particularly those which are persistent and racially motivated.'[14] The Act defines intentional harassment as occurring when someone uses words, displays or behaviour with the intention of causing alarm or distress.[15] However, the government rejected proposals to make racial harassment a specific crime.

The Race Relations Act 1976

The Race Relations Act 1976 replaced the earlier Acts of 1965 and 1968, covering discrimination in employment and training,[16] education,[17] housing,[18] and the provision of goods and services[19] and outlawing both direct and indirect discrimination.[20] The 1965 Act created the criminal offence of incitement to racial hatred, which made it an offence to use speech, written words or illustrations in public which were either abusive, threatening or insulting, or were likely to stir up racial hatred. The 1976 Act transferred this offence to the Public Order Act 1936, now contained in the Public Order Act 1986.[21] The 1976 Act established the Commission for Racial Equality (CRE) whose goal is to work towards the elimination of discrimination. The CRE has the power to:

- investigate organisations that it thinks may be practising racial discrimination
- aid individuals making complaints
- issue codes of practice to assist in eliminating discrimination in the workplace
- promote equal opportunity and good race relations[22]

In addition, the CRE keeps the workings of the Act under review, and may, either when required by the Secretary of State or when it thinks it necessary, draw up and submit proposals for amendments to the Act.[23] The government stated that in 1993 the CRE received 1,630 individual applications for assistance following alleged discrimination of which 1,160 were employment related. In the same year the Commission's legal committee provided assistance in 1,175 cases and legal representation for 250 cases. Of the cases which the CRE supported in 1993, which included some cases from the previous year, 100 were successful after a hearing, 110 were settled on agreed terms and 26 were dismissed after hearing.[24]

In its *Third Periodic Report*, the British government noted that the Act had been amended by the Housing and Planning Act 1986, the Housing Act 1988 and the Education Reform Act 1988,[25] that the law on incitement to racial hatred had been strengthened by an amendment to the Public Order Act 1986, which made it an offence to use threatening, abusive or insulting words or behaviour either where racial hatred was likely to be stirred up or where the person intended such hatred to be stirred up.[26] The *Report* further stated that the government believed the Race Relations Act to be 'generally working well' but that 'the government remains ready to fill any gaps where they think this is necessary and where the opportunity arises.'[27] This assessment is in stark contrast to the CRE's view, expressed in the Chair's foreword to a consultation paper which led to a 1992 review of the Act:

> The report of the Commission's first review of the Act was submitted in 1985 and we remain disappointed that there was no formal response from the government. Since then, the Commission has sought to ensure that some of its recommendations are incorporated into specific legislation, and we acknowledge that in this way a few of our concerns have been met. We were given the power to issue codes of practice in housing, but we are still arguing for the power to issue similar codes in other non-employment areas such as education and health . . . The continuing evidence of widespread discrimination on racial grounds exposes the complacency of those who contend that the Act is fulfilling its intention . . . Though effective legislation is not the only antidote to discrimination, it provides crucial sanctions and makes an explicit declaration of principle. Those individuals and institutions who strive to combat the injustice of discrimination on grounds of race deserve a stronger legal framework to support their efforts.[28]

The CRE has noted numerous areas of weakness in the Act; for example, the definition of discrimination is too narrow. According to the terms of the Act, direct discrimination occurs where a person treats another less favourably on racial grounds.[29] Indirect discrimination occurs when all persons are apparently treated equally, but a requirement or condition is applied with which a considerably smaller proportion of one racial group can comply.[30] However, it is lawful to use unnecessary requirements or conditions, which *do* disadvantage ethnic minorities and which cannot be shown to be justifiable or necessary, provided that they are not an absolute barrier but merely express a preference. Similarly, conditions may be imposed which are not necessary, only justifiable in the circumstances.[31] The Courts have ruled that if several criteria are used, a criterion that disadvantages black people, but may be overcome if compensatory qualities exist, is lawful.[32] The phrases 'requirement or condition', 'considerably smaller' and 'justifiable' have likewise been interpreted to make racial discrimination easier. If a requirement or condition rules out all of one racial group then, as none of that group could comply and as none is not a proportion, the considerably smaller test could not be implemented.[33]

The CRE has complained that protection against victimisation for invoking the Act is too narrow. Proof is difficult and the law only covers victimisation and harassment 'in circumstances relevant for the purposes of any provision of this Act.'[34] The CRE has called for a remedy for victimisation to protect a person suffering any detriment as a result of becoming involved in allegations or proceedings.[35] The CRE also maintains that formal investigation procedures are too cumbersome, time-consuming and limited in their scope and that industrial tribunals as they are currently constituted provide inadequate protection against racism in the workplace.[36] In its 1992 review of the Act, the CRE called for the following changes:

□ employers should have a statutory obligation to carry out ethnic monitoring

□ employers should develop equality targets

□ all public authorities should ensure that all their contractors are equal opportunity employers

□ the CRE should be able to act like an inspectorate to examine major areas for racial inequality

□ a special division of industrial tribunals should be developed, to handle discrimination cases

□ legal aid should be extended to cover racial discrimination cases

□ compensation levels should be raised for victims of discrimination.

The Commission also pointed to the Fair Employment (Northern Ireland) Act 1989 as an example of the stronger methods of monitoring and affirmative action programmes which could be introduced.[37]

Exemptions to the Race Relations Act 1976

Section 20 of the Act, which prohibits discrimination in provision of goods, facilities or services, has been held to apply to the government only in the context of matters analogous to those provided by private undertakings.[38] Activities such as immigration control, prison and police services and planning control are specifically rendered outside the scope of the Act.

The Act also has subordinate status in relation to some other laws, so can be overruled by them. Because the UK has no Bill of Rights to enshrine such fundamental freedoms as the right not to be discriminated against, it is impossible to protect individuals from discriminatory practices when they are sanctioned by Parliament. Normally where two statutes conflict, in British constitutional law, the later one prevails. However, section 41(1) of the 1976 Act protects discriminatory practices on the following grounds:

☐   in pursuance of any enactment or Order in Council; or

☐   in pursuance of any instrument made under any enactment by a Minister of the Crown; or

☐   in order to comply with any condition or requirement imposed by a Minister of the Crown (whether before or after the passing of this Act) by virtue of any enactment.

Section 41(2) extends this to government circulars and to ministerial pronouncements, where they concern matters of nationality and residence.[39] Since all of these can be made without the approval of Parliament, the government can discriminate by decree.

The CRE has pointed out that subordinate legislation rarely receives detailed parliamentary scrutiny and includes pronouncements that may receive no parliamentary scrutiny at all. In its review of the Act, the CRE argued that:

> The Act should assume the normal status of an Act of
> Parliament superior to all earlier Acts and all subordinate
> legislation. If discrimination is required in any area as a matter
> of policy, it should be provided expressly in the statute. This
> would have the valuable effect of requiring each particular
> discriminatory policy to be examined critically and then
> defended publicly if it is to be retained.[40]

Section 75(5) of the Act exempts certain discriminatory employment procedures of the Crown Service and other public bodies.[41]

This section protects discrimination by public organisations on grounds of birth, nationality, descent and origin. In practice, much civil service employment is restricted by nationality.[42] The restriction even extends to clerical workers and the CRE has condemned the use of exemptions from the Act by bodies such as the Bank of England, the British Council and the National Army Museum.[43]

DISCRIMINATION IN EMPLOYMENT, HOUSING AND OTHER SERVICES

According to the CRE there are tens of thousands of acts of racial discrimination in job recruitment each year.[44] Most cases are not brought to industrial tribunals because the candidate does not know that such discrimination has occurred. One study conducted in the mid-1980s, covering three major English cities, showed that over one-third of employers who advertised vacancies in the press discriminated against black candidates.[45] This research provided a measure of the extent only of direct discrimination, rather than broader indirect discrimination and only covered the first stage of recruitment.[46]

In a 1995 survey of the race equality programmes of large firms in Britain, who between them employ more than four million people, the CRE concluded that 'the most striking finding of the investigation was the gap between promise and practice.'[47] While 88 per cent of the companies surveyed said they had a policy specifically covering racial equality, for many this did not go beyond a formal statement and only half the companies were making any systematic effort to put their programme into practice.[48] The CRE commented:

> The companies concerned are all leaders in their respective industries, for whom, by their own admission, the financial costs of delivering racial equality are no problem. Moreover, they are all companies that are already likely to have sophisticated personnel systems dedicated to good practice; extensive, even global, experience of strategic management and monitoring of company policy; and routine reporting procedures at all levels.[49]

The CRE has also warned that one provision in the government's Deregulation Act 1994, an ending of the licensing of private job agencies, may make it more difficult to promote race equality policies. Recruitment through private job agencies is increasingly important in the British economy. The CRE has conducted several formal investigations into their hiring programmes and was working to build equal opportunities policies into their licensing agreements.

The CRE believes that the complaints reaching industrial tribunals are only 'the tip of the iceberg' although it notes that the numbers have increased significantly over the last decade.[50] The CRE has repeatedly criticised the fact that Legal Aid is not available for people pursuing claims in industrial tribunals, pointing out that the procedures[51] in race discrimination cases are particularly complex and claimants often require expert legal help.[52]

In a 1993 report, the Policy Studies Institute (PSI) found that the overall unemployment rate amongst ethnic minorities was almost double that amongst white people – 13 per cent compared to 7 per cent – and that there was a higher concentration of black and ethnic minority people in low-paid and casual work.[53] Twenty per cent of ethnic minorities were likely to be engaged in shift work, compared with 15 per cent of white workers. The over-representation was even greater in some groups, such as Pakistanis, 33 per cent of whom were engaged in shift work.[54] While there is a lack of up-to-date information on comparable pay levels, a 1982 PSI study found that Afro-Caribbean and South Asian men earned 15 per cent less than white men and that even when comparisons were made within job levels and age groups, a gap remained.[55] An analysis of the Labour Force Survey conducted by the Trades Union Congress in 1994 showed that the gap between the unemployment rates of white and ethnic minority workers is now significantly greater than it was 10 years ago and is continuing to widen.[56]

The PSI's 1993 report showed considerable differences in the levels of disadvantage experienced by different ethnic minority groups and a sharp contrast between the position of women and men.[57] A 1994 report published jointly by the CRE and Equal Opportunities Commission (EOC) showed that ethnic minority women experienced a 16 per cent unemployment rate, compared with 6 per cent for white women, while ethnic minority men experienced a 20 per cent unemployment rate, compared with 11 per cent for white men.[58]

Britain's ethnic minority population is increasingly a British born one and so may no longer be hampered by many of the problems facing new arrivals in a foreign country. Therefore, racial discrimination is likely to become an increasingly important factor in explaining the disadvantages suffered by Britain's ethnic minorities.

Housing

A CRE report published in 1990 found that one-fifth of housing accommodation agencies in England, Scotland and Wales discriminated against ethnic minority applicants.[59] However, the Minister of Housing has rejected recommendations by the CRE that accommodation agencies be licensed.

Local authority housing is often subject to racist policies and practices. The CRE has found that:

☐ In the London Borough of Southwark the local authority has systematically awarded new and improved properties to white tenants.[60]

☐ White residents in Liverpool are four times as likely to be allocated new houses as black residents, while Glasgow's points system favours white people.[61]

☐ Although over half the local authorities in London have adopted formal policies on combatting racial harassment, only 10 have ever taken court action in a total of only 25 cases.[62]

☐ In the London Borough of Tower Hamlets, East London, Bangladeshis have been consistently awarded the worst housing, placed in the poorest temporary bed and breakfast accommodation, waited longer than white people to be allocated housing and waited longer for emergency housing than white people. Of three estates examined, the two with the poorest quality housing had five times the number of Asian tenants than the Asian proportion of the local population.[63]

Councils have been accused of forcing Asian families to move into estates where they are more likely to suffer racial attacks. In Tower Hamlets the local Law Centre recorded 228 racial incidents in 1992 on a single estate housing fewer than 30 families, and where Asian families were regularly placed.[64] Liberal Democrat councillors in Tower Hamlets, where the British National Party won a council by-election in September 1993, have been accused of deliberately inflaming racial tensions and have been formally criticised by their own national party. In 1990 they admitted producing and distributing bogus Labour Party leaflets which promised preferential treatment to Bangladeshis. Leaflets and newsletters have since accused the Labour Party of favouring Asian residents over white residents, boasted about the Council's defiance of the CRE and attacked a move to make a council donation to famine relief, with the headline 'Bangladeshi Shocker.'[65]

In April 1993 the Court of Appeal upheld the right of Tower Hamlets Council to investigate the immigration status of all those who apply for housing in the borough. The Court ruled that the Department of the Environment's guidance on housing the homeless was 'wrong and misleading'. The guidance says that everyone admitted into Britain is entitled to equal treatment under the law and that information on an applicant's immigration status should be considered confidential. The Appeal Court overturned the decision of the High Court that immigration control was a function of the Home Office only and not of local authorities.[66]

The Asylum and Immigration Appeals Act, which came into force in July 1993, imposes responsibilities on local authorities which have 'reason to believe' that a person applying for housing is an asylum-seeker. The local authority is obliged to investigate the applicant's immigration status and, if it decides that the applicant is an asylum-seeker, it is only required to offer temporary accommodation.[67] In practice these measures are likely to lead to immigrants facing greater difficulties in obtaining council accommodation and to legitimise harassment by racist council officials.

Changes in government housing policy throughout the 1980s have resulted in growing numbers of homeless.[68] Racial minorities, along with the poor and single parents, are at a higher risk of becoming homeless than the general community.[69] It has been estimated that ethnic minority households are up to four times as likely to end up on the streets.[70]

Health

There is considerable evidence that the under-representation of ethnic minorities within the medical profession is thanks to discriminatory hiring practices. A CRE investigation into St George's Hospital Medical School's admission policy in 1988, for instance, showed that academics' initial selection decisions had been built into a computer programme which had created a 'score bias' against ethnic minorities.[71] A conference in July 1993 heard that a qualified and experienced doctor had been turned down for 126 jobs after winning a racial discrimination case against a hospital.[72]

A major cause for concern is the stigmatisation of much of the black community as potential HIV 'carriers'.[73] The British government has officially sanctioned the view that people from Africa are a 'high risk' group by, for example, allowing the Blood Transfusion Service to refuse to accept blood from people who have visited Africa. This policy also legitimises and encourages racism towards black people. Black health care workers, for instance, have been subject to rising abuse and hostility following a front page newspaper story in February 1993 about a black midwife who was HIV-positive.[74]

The UK Forum on HIV and Human Rights has reported that growing constraint is put on black people to take HIV tests. Pregnant women have been pressurised and babies have been tested without their mothers' consent.[75] Black people, especially those with African-sounding names, complain that they are also frequently asked 'lifestyle' questions or forced to undergo blood tests when applying for life insurances and mortgages. They report a similar level of discrimination to that experienced by gay men.[76] These are grave invasions of privacy which are being targeted against a particular racial group.

Social Security

In 1988 a new question was introduced on the form for people claiming Income Support, asking them if they have come to live in the UK within the last five years. If they have, then they are obliged to arrange a full interview to which they must bring all their travel documents and details of their immigration status. Officers from the Department of Social Security (DSS) maintain a close liaison with the Home Office and inform them about claims from people who may have come from abroad. The Home Office will often follow up the application to check the claimant's immigration status.[77]

Since 1988, all people coming to join family members have had to show that they can be supported and accommodated 'without recourse to public funds'.[78] 'Public funds' means (for immigration purposes) Income Support, Family Credit, Housing Benefit and housing under the homeless provisions of housing law *only*. Thus there is a means test on family unity; British citizens and others claiming benefits to which they are entitled may not be able to bring in family members solely on financial grounds.

In November 1991 a new screening procedure for asylum-seekers was introduced. It requires applicants to obtain an 'identity interview' at which various details are scrutinised and the asylum-seeker is given a Standard Acknowledgement Letter, a passport-type document. Increasingly, DSS officers are demanding these documents before they will issue benefits. However, delays of several months in issuing a Standard Acknowledgment Letter are not uncommon, which is leaving a growing number of asylum seekers destitute.[79]

The Asylum and Immigration Appeals Act 1993 provides for the compulsory fingerprinting of all asylum-seekers, and their dependants, on their arrival in the UK. This measure is normally only applied in the UK to those charged with a criminal offence.[80] DSS officers have been given access to these files and are empowered to take further fingerprints to check a claimant's identity.[81] These measures may deter many ethnic minority people from claiming benefits to which they are entitled. Claimants who speak little English are likely to be treated with suspicion and may face additional barriers in claiming legitimate entitlements. Many people, whose residence in the UK is entirely legal, may be intimidated into not claiming their benefits. These problems are likely to be exacerbated by the lack of translators and interpreters.[82]

Criminal law and related professions

Ethnic minorities are dramatically under-represented in the criminal justice professions. There are no black Law Lords, Court of Appeal or High Court judges, only four black Circuit Judges (0.8 per cent of the total), 11 Recorders (1.3 per cent of the total), and nine Assistant Recorders (1.3 per cent of the total).[83] In its *Fourth Periodic Report* the government states that the Lord Chancellor appoints solely on the basis of merit but that 'without prejudice to this overriding principle . . . he has repeatedly stressed, however, that he would like to see more legal practitioners from ethnic minorities appointed to the judiciary.'[84] Nevertheless in the 12 months ending June 1993 only 85 of those appointed to the lay magistracy were of ethnic minority origin: 5 per cent of the total number of appointments. This is less than the proportion of ethnic minorities in the population and does not support the government's claim that it is trying to increase the representation of ethnic minorities in the judiciary.[85]

The Law Society has produced figures that show that an alarmingly small number of ethnic minorities is eligible to join the pool from which the judiciary is drawn. In 1991, it was estimated that only 6 per cent of practising barristers and 1.5 per cent of solicitors were members of ethnic minority groups.[86] The Courts and Legal Services Act 1990 amended the Race Relations Act 1976 to make it unlawful for barristers to discriminate on racial grounds in their selection of pupils.[87] However, the Law Society has noted that the appointment system, which is heavily dependent on word-of-mouth recruitment, may lead to indirect discrimination.[88]

Ethnic minority solicitors are more likely to be found in small practices than white solicitors; 80 per cent of ethnic minority solicitors work in firms of fewer than four solicitors, compared to 56 per cent of all solicitors and 22 per cent work alone, compared to 9 per cent of all solicitors.[89] On average, ethnic minority students make twice as many applications for articles with solicitors' firms, but receive significantly fewer interviews[90] and proportionately fewer offers for employment than their white counterparts.[91] Black students generally find themselves excluded from high paying commercial law firms[92] who often seek to recruit students with an 'Oxbridge' education; which is an unspecified but clearly restrictive hiring criterion. The vast majority of barristers' chambers have no black barrister members.

In March 1993 the Council of Legal Education (CLE), which administers the Bar's Law School, commissioned an independent inquiry into allegations of race discrimination in its selection process following persistent complaints about racial discrimination, legal challenges by a number of black former students and a growing public outcry. The CLE admitted that ethnic minority students suffered nearly three times the failure rate of white students on the Bar's vocational course in 1991-2 – 44.7 per cent compared to 16 per cent – but denied that this was owing to direct discrimination.[93]

The CLE inquiry released an interim report in September 1993 which noted that while 'a part of the disparity can be explained by poorer prior academic performance' on the part of ethnic minority students, 'a substantial difference remains between the final results of white and ethnic minority students even after allowing for the effects of degree, class, university- versus polytechnic-educated, age, year of graduation, and sex.'[94] Figures released the previous month showed that while the gap had narrowed in the year 1992–3, black students were still twice as likely to fail as white students.[95]

In December 1992, 5 per cent of probation officers were recorded as belonging to an ethnic minority.[96] According to a voluntary survey carried out in 1993, only 2 per cent of prison officers and governors described their ethnic origin as other than white.[97] Only 1.5 per cent of the police force are from ethnic minorities, although the numbers are rising, and there are no ethnic minority officers above the rank of Chief Superintendent.[98] Compared to white officers, a higher proportion of black officers quit the force. In 1989, 26 of 35 new black recruits to the Metropolitan Police quit.[99] This high departure rate is not surprising. Racism is rampant within the police force. A tribunal investigating complaints of racism in the Nottinghamshire CID found that displays of racial prejudice were used to offend ethnic minority officers. Moreover, senior officers were found to be tolerant of such behaviour, making little effort to end racist actions.[100] In May 1993, for instance, an industrial tribunal awarded £25,000 agreed damages to an Asian graduate who had joined Nottinghamshire police force and had been subjected to 42 incidents of discrimination and victimisation involving 60 of his colleagues.[101]

In the past the police force has stated that the racism of a few officers is only a reflection of the fact that, as a representative body, it includes a cross section of society. While this may explain racist attitudes it does not excuse them. It would be extremely surprising to hear police spokespersons use the same arguments about police criminality.

RACISM AND IMMIGRATION

While human rights abuses against refugees, asylum-seekers and migrants deserve separate consideration, the political arguments surrounding immigration and immigration control have linked the issues of immigration and racism closely.

There is an historical pattern of media reports about influxes of migrants and refugees coinciding with rising levels of racism and racist violence, even when the stories have little factual basis. British immigration law has become increasingly restrictive, with the result that primary immigration has virtually halted. In 1990, for example, which was a record year for immigration, although 267,000 people immigrated to Britain, this was balanced by 231,000 emigrating which left a net gain of 36,000 people. By far the largest group of immigrants (106,000) were British citizens returning from stays abroad. Migration from the New Commonwealth – India, Pakistan, Africa and the Caribbean – totalled 38,000 while migration from the Old Commonwealth – Canada, Australia and New Zealand – was 32,000.[102]

The discriminatory nature of immigration legislation has caused a deep underlying resentment amongst ethnic minorities that racism is institutionalised in Britain. As one commentator has noted:

> You cannot consistently and openly discriminate in immigration control and at the same time argue that discrimination is wrong. As an employer once asked at a conference 'Why is it wrong for me to refuse to have any of these people in my firm when the government is refusing to have them come into the country? If the government does not want them, why should I want them?'[103]

The enactment of new immigration measures has also led to a deterioration of race relations as the accompanying media coverage is often racist. It has been argued that race hate and race violence do not rise and fall directly according to the numbers of new immigrants, but according to the extent to which they are encouraged by the media and mainstream politicians.[104] The late 1970s and early 1980s saw a sharp increase in reported racial violence,[105] followed by a lull in the late 1980s and by another increase in the early 1990s. The two surges did not coincide with sudden influxes of new immigration but with severe economic recessions, the passage of two Acts aimed at restricting the number of immigrants and asylum-seekers and a series of widely reported racist remarks by senior government figures.

In 1978, Margaret Thatcher was asked about her party's plans to reduce immigration. After stating that there was a problem in predicting immigration trends and implying that the Home Office figures were an underestimate, she commented:

there was a committee which looked at it and said that if we went on as we were then by the end of the century there would be four million people of the New Commonwealth or Pakistan here. Now that is an awful lot and I think it means that people are really rather afraid that this country might be rather swamped by people with a different culture and, you know, the British character has done so much for democracy, for law and done so much throughout the world that if there is any fear that it might be swamped people are going to react and be rather hostile to those coming in.[106]

In the same year eight people died in what appear to have been racist murders.[107] The following year the Conservatives were elected to government and introduced a Bill which eventually became the 1981 Nationality Act. In 1980 there were six racist murders. In 1981, 25 people died in what appear to have been racial attacks (although, as is described below, the exact circumstances of a fire which claimed 13 lives are still disputed).

In 1983 Alan Clark, then a junior minister in the Department of Employment, with responsibility for race issues, discussed ethnic monitoring at Unemployment Benefit Offices with senior civil servants. He commented that black people 'are afraid we are going to hand them over to the Immigration Services so they can send them all back to Bongo-Bongo land.'[108] Despite the publicity this remark received, he went on to hold other senior positions in the government.

After a period of relatively good race relations in Britain, racial violence began to rise again in the early 1990s. New immigration during this period was minimal but Britain experienced another recession and there was a series of inaccurate stories in the media about so-called 'bogus refugees.'[109] Race relations have been further damaged by the passage of the Asylum Bill and a number of racist remarks by senior politicians.

In May 1990 Lord [Norman] Tebbit, former Conservative Party Chairman and close advisor to Margaret Thatcher, advocated a 'cricket test' for Asian people to test their loyalty to Britain. He asked rhetorically which side they cheered for and warned that 'where you have a clash of history, a clash of religion, a clash of race, then it is all too easy for there to be an actual clash of violence.'[110] In 1993 Winston Churchill, a back-bench Conservative MP, falsely claimed that 'the population of many of our

northern cities is more than 50 per cent immigrant and Muslims
claim that there are now more than two million of their co-religion-
ists in Britain.' He went on to state that immigrants 'equivalent to
a town the size of Grantham were being brought into the country
every year.'[111] (Grantham is Margaret Thatcher's birthplace.) In a
subsequent letter to a national newspaper he warned of racial
civil war in Britain, drawing a parallel with former Yugoslavia,
complaining of a 'relentless flow of immigrants both legal and
illegal' and stating that the 'most effective way of combating racism
in Britain is not by passing more legislation, the effect of which will
only be marginal but by not adding to the scale of the problem.'[112]

Such comments, as well as being offensive to ethnic minorities,
encourage and legitimate discrimination and violence. One commentator has summarised the impact that the debate about immigration can have on race relations:

> The argument about numbers is unwinnable because however
> many you decide upon there will always be someone to
> campaign for less [sic] and others for whom one is too many.
> Since you have admitted that black people are a problem in
> themselves it is impossible to resist the argument for less [sic]
> of them. Even if new migrants are reduced to nil, the argument
> can be shifted to numbers of dependants; when they are reduced
> it can be shifted to the question of illegal immigrants; when
> these are shown to be few in number it can be argued that the
> government is cooking the books. In the last analysis if you play
> the numbers game then black people already here and every
> black child born here is a problem and the discussion shifts
> to the question of deportation.[113]

RACIAL VIOLENCE

In its *Fourth Periodic Report* the government stated that it was
'fully committed to developing policies that address the continuing
problem of racial violence and harassment in the United Kingdom.'[114] The *Report* stated that there were 7,734 incidents in which
racial motivation was suspected in 1992, compared to 7,882 in
1991 and 4,383 in 1988.[115] However, it is widely accepted that
this is a significant under-estimate as so many incidents go unreported. In July 1993, the Minister of State at the Home Office told

a Home Affairs Select Committee on racial violence that there might be 130,000 to 140,000 racial attacks a year, and that the 'true figure' could be as high as 330,000.[116]

The Select Committee criticised the government for its failure to provide statistics which accurately reflected the nature and extent of racial attacks in Britain.[117] The Select Committee expressed concern that the problem of racial violence was 'at least as bad now, and probably worse, than at the time of our last report in 1989.'[118] It urged that the police should give a greater priority to tackling the problem,[119] that greater efforts should be made to tackle racism within the police force[120] and that a new offence of racially motivated violence should be created.[121]

In its submission to the Select Committee, the Campaign Against Racism and Fascism (CARF) stated that Britain experienced the second highest incidence of reported racially inspired murders anywhere in Europe, surpassed only by Germany.[122] The Association of London Authorities has pointed out that monitoring by local authorities has revealed extremely high levels of under-reporting to the police in particular. In one borough during 1991-2 only 34 of a total of 190 incidents reported to the local authorities had been reported to the police.[123]

Racial harassment is an everyday experience for the majority of black people in Britain. In a general survey on violence against women in the London area in 1984, 84 per cent of black respondents said that they had suffered verbal abuse because they were black while 40 per cent said they had been assaulted for this reason.[124] Even if the exact numbers are impossible to calculate, they appear to be escalating at an alarming rate. In 1992, 10 people died as a result of what are believed to have been racially motivated murders[125] and many only narrowly escaped death after racist attacks. Two of the men killed had fled from political violence in their own countries.[126] Reports from monitoring groups, advice centres and legal officers for 1992 told of increasing racist vandalism, graffiti, and personal abuse in the streets, estates and schools. They detailed incidents of black people being forced to leave their homes and businesses because of racist abuse, of families living under self-imposed curfews, and of so-called 'reception committees' springing up to vandalise or deface houses allocated to black families and turn out in force to greet the new tenants.[127]

Anti-racist organisations complain that such practices are often condoned or encouraged by council tenants' associations and their social clubs. It is common for social clubs to have a requirement that new members must be proposed and seconded by existing members, a practice used to exclude non-white members.[128] In January 1992 a Birmingham court upheld a finding by the CRE that this indirectly discriminated against potential ethnic minority members. The court heard that six white applicants and six black applicants had separately attempted to join a 1,500-strong club and received markedly different responses.[129] Despite the ruling, the Club and Institute Union, the national federation of social clubs, announced it has no plans to change its rules. Several thousand social clubs, including many that operate under the auspices of local authorities, effectively continue to operate colour bars.

All-white drinking clubs are often the scene of violent confrontations. Many have been attacked during disturbances between black youths and the police as it is often alleged that they are used by racists as a base from which to launch attacks. The Hanborough Tavern in Southall, west London, was burnt to the ground in 1981 at the start of the most widespread riots ever seen in Britain. The pub had hosted a 'skinhead' concert attended by a large number of neo-Nazis in a predominantly Asian area.[130] In 1992 and 1993 pubs and social clubs in the Plumstead area of south-east London were attacked following protests about the murders of local black youths.[131]

Official denials of racial motivation

There is a long history of denial of racial motivation for attacks. In 1981, Satwinder Singh was attacked in Southall, west London, and had the initials 'NF' carved in his chest (the National Front was then the biggest far-right organisation). The police at first denied there was any racial motivation to the attack and later charged Mr Singh with wasting police time. He was convicted at a magistrates court but this was overturned on appeal.[132]

The biggest single killing of black people in Britain in recent years occurred in early 1981, when 13 young black people died at a party after a house was set on fire. The exact circumstances of the deaths are still disputed. A police inquiry alleged that the fire was caused by gate-crashers while the families of those killed remain convinced that the motive was racial. The perception that the authorities were covering up a racial attack was encouraged by the authorities' apparent initial indifference to the tragedy. It took five weeks for Margaret Thatcher, then Prime Minister, to send a letter of condolence and, when she did so, it was to a community worker in the area rather than to the families.[133]

Similar official insensitivity was highlighted after Nelson Mandela, the South African President, met the family of the murdered black teenager Stephen Lawrence in May 1993. Stephen's mother, Doreen Lawrence, complained that no similar gesture had been made by the British authorities. She said that 'people from abroad are more concerned about the death of black children than the Prime Minister from our own country, the Queen and all the ministers.'[134]

A blatant example of the failure to highlight racial motivation was shown at the trial of Mark Jarvis, accused of murdering Ashiq Hussein in September 1992. Despite clear evidence, including the stated view of prison officers that Jarvis was a 'known racist' who had 'assaulted an Asian inmate in 1985,'[135] the prosecution failed to argue that racial motivation was a factor. Jarvis was found guilty of manslaughter and given a five-year prison sentence. The Anti-Racist Alliance wrote a special addendum to its submission to the Home Affairs Select Committee on this case and wrote to the Attorney-General arguing for a review of the sentence.[136] In August 1993 it was announced that the sentence would be reviewed. The Anti-Racist Alliance has pointed out that this is only the latest of a number of cases where prosecuting barristers have failed to respect Crown Prosecution Service guidelines, issued in 1987, that racial motivation should be considered an aggravating factor.[137] There are some signs that the police force is taking the issue of racial violence more seriously.[138] However, many officers deny that crimes have a racial motivation, despite the insistence of the victim and refuse to consider racist, attacks they regard as neighbourhood disputes:

☐   In its submission to the Home Affairs Committee on Racially Motivated Harassment and Violence, CARF criticised the failure of the police to intervene in a number of cases where mounting racial harassment in particular neighbourhoods eventually resulted in serious assaults and, in some cases, murders.[139]

☐   The police said they were 'keeping an open mind' about the motive for the murder of an Asian taxi driver in March

1993, despite reports that the two men charged had boasted of 'killing a Paki'.[140]

☐ In October 1992 an Asian market-stall trader, Sher Sagoo, was beaten to death in east London by a group of youths who had been regularly abusing black people in the area.[141]

The government rejected the proposal from the Home Affairs Select Committee to introduce specific crimes of racial harassment and racial violence. The Criminal Justice and Public Order Act 1994 instead creates the new offence of intentional harassment.[142] Not only does this fail to address the central problem of racial harassment, the requirement that it must be proved that the person carrying out the harassment *intended* to cause alarm or distress may be very difficult to satisfy.

Incitement to racial hatred

The British government has been condemned by the UN Committee on the Elimination of All Forms of Racial Discrimination (CERD), for not taking stronger action to stop racial violence. CERD has called for the proscription of far-right racist organisations, the extension of the Race Relations Act to Northern Ireland and more training for police officers to enable them to deal with race attacks.[143]

Liberty recognises that an appropriate response must be found which balances the preservation of freedom of speech and association with the protection of the rights of minorities. We do not believe that there is an absolute right to free speech. As the UN Human Rights Committee has noted, freedom of expression carries with it special responsibilities including respect for the rights of others. Current race relations and public order legislation does not recognise this, and instead focuses on the threat to public order that racist organisations, publications and events might pose. In its *Third Periodic Report*, the British government stated:

> The Committee has in the past criticised the existence in the United Kingdom of neo-fascist organisations. While the government does not approve of the views of such organisations, they do not have a significant influence on the life of the country or represent a threat which cannot be dealt with by other means, and provided they act within the law the government sees no need to introduce new legislation to

proscribe them. Different considerations apply to organisations concerned in terrorism.[144]

The report declared that since 1979 there have been 44 prosecutions for incitement to racial hatred.[145] Although the law on incitement was strengthened by amendments to the Public Order Act 1986, by May 1994 there had only been 15 prosecutions brought under that section of the Act.[146] There was one prosecution in 1990, four in 1991 and one in 1992.[147]

Verbal abuse of ethnic minorities, which can be proven to incite violence, has been a common law offence in the UK for centuries. However, the principal concern has not been the direct impact of such attacks on the groups themselves but the possibility that such attacks might provoke disorder. The law of seditious libel, for instance, which prohibits vilification of the Crown or government or the raising of 'discontent or disaffection amongst Her Majesty's subjects' proved unsuccessful in prosecuting an anti-Semite publisher shortly after the Second World War, on the grounds that his attacks on Jews were not likely to provoke violence.[148]

Similar considerations have applied in other prosecutions brought under the various Public Order Acts. The Public Order Act 1936, which was introduced after clashes between anti-fascists and Oswald Mosely's blackshirts, made it an offence to wear political uniforms. However, only one prosecution has been brought under this section of the Act since 1945.[149] In its justification for keeping the offence of sedition on the statute, the government claims:

> The offence is not a restriction on the freedom of speech as it bites only where the language used exceeds the bounds of fair and temperate discussion. Case law suggests that an intention to cause violence must also be proved.[150]

In its *Third Periodic Report* the British government concedes that its principal concern in restricting free speech is the maintenance of public order. The primary aims are not, therefore, the protection of ethnic minorities from 'incitement to discrimination and hostility', as guaranteed under Article 20 of the ICCPR, or the respect for rights of ethnic minorities 'to enjoy their own culture' as enshrined in Article 27. Critics of the government's approach claim that the provisions on incitement to racial hatred do not recognise the pain and suffering endured by members of ethnic minorities as worthy of legislative action. One commentator has explained how this affects people from ethnic minority groups:

> Drafters and backers of anti-incitement legislation assumed that white people are the main target audience of the racists and fascists. However, there is a great deal of evidence to suggest racists and fascists are at least as interested in targeting ethnic minorities. Racist speech and literature is employed as a form of intimidation. It can be a form of racial harassment, an abuse of the right to freedom of expression with the aim of intimidating and restricting target groups in the enjoyment of their rights. Racial harassment in the workplace, in the home and in the street may restrict members of target groups in their freedom of movement, expression, association and assembly, and in their right to practise their own religion.[151]

Terrorism and racist violence

The government's failure to protect the right of ethnic minorities to live free from fear of racial attacks is starkly illustrated by a comparison with the array of measures deployed against terrorist organisations in Britain. The current definition of terrorism could be used to cover the activities of many neo-Nazi organisations, particularly those on the violent fringe.[152] While not all racial violence can be directly attributed to the activities of the far right, the connection has been well documented. In 1985 *Searchlight* magazine published a report that documented 400 cases of known fascists being convicted of offences, including 12 cases of murder, 14 of unlawful possession of weapons, several convictions for bombing, arson and armed robbery and over 60 cases of violent assaults.[153] John Tyndall, the leader of the British National Party, has a series of convictions and has served three prison sentences for a variety of offences, including the possession of offensive weapons and a shotgun.[154]

The activities of the far right have often led to violence. Neo-Nazi groups sometimes claim responsibility for racial attacks and demonstrations. There is also a clear correlation between the activities of far-right and neo-Nazi organisations in certain areas and increases in reported levels of racist violence. In the Plumstead area of south-east London, there has been a reported increase in racist violence of 140 per cent since the far-right British National Party established its headquarters in the area in 1991.[155] Four young black people have died as a result of racist murders in the area since that date.[156]

In the *Third Periodic Report*, the government distinguished between the activities of organisations which may be regarded as 'offensive', whose activities should not be subject to any restrictions, and those concerned with 'terrorism', which it reserves the right to proscribe and in other ways curtail. Terrorism is defined under the Prevention of Terrorism Act (PTA) as 'the use of violence for political ends and includes any use of violence for the purpose of putting the public or any section of the public in fear.'[157] Although the 1984 Act widened the scope of its powers to include international terrorism, the main focus of the PTA remains terrorism related to Northern Ireland.

All known Irish Republican paramilitary organisations have been proscribed as have, more recently, some Loyalist paramilitary organisations.[158] It is an offence to belong to a proscribed organisation, to solicit support, to arrange meetings or to display support in public for a proscribed organisation.[159] Between 1988 and 1994 television and radio stations were banned from broadcasting the words of representatives of eight proscribed organisations and three legal groups.[160]

The problems of political violence in Northern Ireland have had a spill-over effect into Great Britain. Between 1981 and 1993, 49 people died in Britain as a result of the conflict in Northern Ireland.[161] During the same period as many as 55 people may have lost their lives as a result of racist violence.[162] The two problems cannot of course be equated, but the vastly different responses of the State deserve some comment. The following example provides a useful illustration.

In November 1986 an Old Bailey jury at the Central Criminal Court found an Irishman, Patrick McLaughlin, guilty of conspiring to cause explosions. He was gaoled for life.[163] Two days later, another Old Bailey jury convicted self-confessed fascist Anthony Lecomber, of making and possessing explosives. He was sentenced to three years' imprisonment.[164] The alleged offences were extremely similar.

In the McLaughlin case, the Irish National Liberation Army (a fringe Republican paramilitary grouping) claimed responsibility for planting a bag of crude explosives outside Chelsea barracks in London. The bombing attempt made front-page headlines[165] and

13 people were arrested under the PTA, following armed dawn raids by police in London[166] – though none was subsequently charged. There were complaints that the police had carried out trawling raids.[167] McLaughlin was arrested some weeks later, remanded in custody, locked up for 23 hours a day and held in isolation for nearly a year before he appeared in court. The case against him was weak and circumstantial. Part of the prosecution's evidence suggested that he had, at most, been a passive spectator to the alleged conspiracy. He received a life sentence.[168]

Anthony Mark Lecomber was an active member of the far-right British National Party (BNP), and a bodyguard for its leader. He had a number of previous convictions and had been questioned earlier that year about the murder of an Asian woman and her three children.[169] He was also known to have organised an attempted attack, using hand grenades, on an anti-racist conference.[170] Lecomber was arrested when a bomb exploded in his car, which was parked near the headquarters of a left-wing political party. The explosion, ten days before the attempted bombing of Chelsea barracks, made the inside pages of some newspapers.[171] A police search of Lecomber's home revealed a cache of hand grenades and detonators, and an apparent 'hit-list' of liberal and left-wing people and organisations.

Lecomber was charged with making explosives and endangering lives. Another neo-Nazi, Philip Kersey, who had connections with far-right terrorist organisations,[172] was charged with aiding and abetting Lecomber to cause explosions. Both men were granted unconditional bail. At the trial Kersey admitted helping Lecomber make the bomb but said they disagreed about how it should be used. He was acquitted. Lecomber said his bomb-making was merely a hobby, and it was coincidence that he had been near another political group's headquarters when the bomb exploded.[173] He was released after serving one and a half years of his three-year prison sentence. He is now the BNP's Propaganda Officer, and subsequently served a prison sentence for a violent assault on a young Jewish teacher.[174]

The similarities between the two cases are striking. What distinguishes them is the vastly different responses of the police, the press and the judiciary, which seem to have determined the markedly different outcomes of the trials.

Anti-Semitism

Jewish people experience racial violence and discrimination. They are particularly threatened by the rise of far-right, neo-Nazi organisations, many of whose members have a history of attacking synagogues, desecrating Jewish cemeteries and carrying out violent attacks on Jewish people, their homes and workplaces.

According to the Institute of Jewish Affairs, the number of reported anti-Semitic incidents in 1992 increased by 9 per cent compared to 1991, indicating a continuing upward trend.[175] The increased dissemination of anti-Semitic literature has been notable in recent years, but in 1992 there was also an increase in the number of violent assaults, particularly on young Jewish people.[176]

Anti-Semitism rarely surfaces in mainstream British political life, but the failure of the government to take action against anti-Semitic literature, and in particular against publications denying that the Holocaust took place, is a serious concern.[177] Holocaust denial is primarily limited to the political fringes. However, in 1992 one leading exponent of this 'revisionist' view, the far-right historian David Irving, was widely considered to have been given an inappropriate platform: the *Sunday Times* used him as an advisor in its publication of Goebbels' diaries. During the same year, Irving was banned from entering a number of countries because of his views and activities.[178]

Anti-Irish racism

The discrimination suffered by Irish people is qualitatively different from that suffered by black ethnic minorities. However, in the absence of detailed research, its nature and extent are difficult to prove. The Irish are not recognised as an ethnic minority in Britain. Irish was not included as a separate category on the 1991 census and, although the CRE has recently supported a number of cases of Irish people which have proved discrimination on the grounds of race, there has been little research on the experiences of the Irish community in Britain.[179] Nevertheless, the existing evidence suggests that Irish people living in Britain experience substantial disadvantage.

The 1991 census showed that there were 837,464 people born in the Irish Republic resident in Britain, which indicated that the overall size of the population had stabilised. This may have been a slight under-estimate.[180] Estimates of the number of people of

Irish descent vary between two and eight million. The last influx of Irish people occurred during the 1980s while immigration from elsewhere in the world had virtually halted.

The Irish now have the highest standard mortality rate of any ethnic minority in Britain; it became higher than the rate for people from the African sub-continent in the 1980s. Irish people in Britain are more than 50 per cent more likely to die young than their English counterparts and the Irish are the only ethnic minority whose life expectancy decreases on their arrival in Britain.[181] Irish people are also more than twice as likely to be admitted to mental hospitals as English people and 50 per cent more likely than Afro-Caribbeans, the next most over-represented group.[182]

The Irish are over-represented amongst the homeless population and concentrated in the worst housing.[183] They are concentrated in low-paid and insecure employment,[184] suffer from negative stereotyping in the media and may be subject to a number of discriminatory practices. In June 1994 the CRE won a case of unfair dismissal against a firm who sacked a worker after he objected to anti-Irish abuse.[185] A sample of prisoners in 1991 found that 2.8 per cent had been born in either the north or south of Ireland.[186] However, this may be an under-estimate. According to the 1992 Annual Census of Religious Registration in Prisons, 19.4 per cent of the prison population in England and Wales are Catholic which greatly exceeds their proportion of the population as a whole and may be indicative of the fact that the Irish community is disproportionately represented.[187]

Irish people also suffer day-to-day discrimination within the British criminal justice system. Research indicates that Irish people, when charged, are less likely to be offered bail because they are considered more likely to abscond and they are more likely to have their houses searched if they have been arrested. Irish defendants receive sentences most adversely removed from the recommendations in their probation reports and are 20 per cent more likely to receive gaol sentences than their white, European counterparts.[188]

The conflict in Northern Ireland generated hostility towards Irish people in Britain, much of which was encouraged by indiscriminate policing, irresponsible media coverage and provocative remarks by politicians.[189] In July 1993, for example, Lord Tebbit said in an interview that the Irish would only be persuaded to alter their constitution when Dublin began to experience the same sort of bomb attacks that London and Belfast had suffered. The Prime

Minister refused to disassociate himself from these remarks when challenged in the House of Commons.[190] They were made a few weeks after the broadcast of a television documentary which alleged that no-warning bombs, planted in Dublin and Monaghan in 1974 killing 33 civilians, may have been planted with the connivance of British intelligence operatives.[191] On the same night that Lord Tebbit spoke, Loyalist paramilitaries bombed the homes of three members of the moderate nationalist Social Democratic and Labour Party in Northern Ireland, including one of their Members of Parliament.

Discrimination against Gypsies and other Travellers

Gypsies have enjoyed the protection of the Race Relations Act 1976 since a 1988 Court of Appeal ruling that they shared sufficient common history and geographical origin, and were regarded as a sufficiently distinctive group by others, as to constitute a racial group within the meaning of the Act.[192] However, newer groups of Travellers are not covered by this protection and both Gypsies and other Travellers continue to suffer from considerable discrimination, police harassment and public prejudice and considerable social and economic disadvantage.[193]

Travellers have historically experienced considerable problems obtaining adequate private-site provision, because of official restrictions which often make it illegal for them to settle on their own land or on land where they have obtained the owner's permission to settle.[194] In addition, the vast majority of local authorities breached statutory obligations to provide an adequate number of authorised council encampments.[195] Many Travellers are therefore forced to camp illegally or on sub-standard sites. This often poses a threat to their health and usually results in a deterioration of education and employment prospects. The Safe Childbirth for Travellers Campaign estimates that long-term Travellers are forced to move on average 20 times a year, while they would probably choose to move only four or five times a year.[196]

The government's failure to use its powers under the Caravan Sites Act 1968 has effectively sanctioned this breach of their statutory obligations by many local authorities. Travellers forced to camp illegally have faced pressure and hostility from the settled population.

The Criminal Justice and Public Order Act 1994 repeals the

Caravan Sites Act 1968, which places a duty on local authorities to make provision for Travellers, and makes trespass and unauthorised camping a criminal rather than civil offence. Travelling has been criminalised as a way of life. During the debates which preceded the Bill's enactment, there were calls in Parliament for the mass deportation of Irish Travellers.[197] Liberty believes that these proposals are draconian and likely to be counter-productive, and is also concerned that they violate Article 27 of the ICCPR.

4 NORTHERN IRELAND: HUMAN RIGHTS AND THE PEACE DIVIDEND

On 31 August 1994 the Irish Republican Army announced the cessation of its campaign of military violence.[1] On 13 October 1994 the Combined Loyalist Military Command, representing the Ulster Volunteer Force and the Ulster Defence Association, announced that it was also ending its campaign.[2] On 21 October the British government said it was making a working assumption that the IRA's cessation was intended to be permanent and that this would lead to the beginning of exploratory talks with Sinn Fein before the end of the year.[3] The British government has met representatives of Sinn Fein and Loyalist groups, and discussions are continuing at the time of this chapter's publication.

The government has stated that if this demilitarisation leads to a lasting peace, it believes many new opportunities for political advances will arise. The potential dividend of peace in Northern Ireland has four main aspects:

- ☐ Financial: money previously spent on security measures could potentially be used to combat unemployment and poverty.

- ☐ Political: it is easier to conduct the dialogue and compromises which are the business of politics when people are not killing each other.

- ☐ Civil liberties: the government could reasonably be expected to repeal emergency laws and the use of emergency measures as it becomes clear the conflict is over.

- ☐ Constitutional: there is a need for new structures of government on the island of Ireland which give democratic expression to the wishes of its people and which safeguard majority and minority rights.

The political and economic peace dividends are not within the scope of this chapter. We focus on the connected constitutional and civil liberties aspects of the peace dividend.

In a letter to Liberty from the British Prime Minister's office in November 1994 the government stated:

> Once it becomes established that terrorism has genuinely ended, there will be significant consequences for the maintenance of law and order and for the administration of justice, particularly in Northern Ireland but also in Great Britain. The government has always made it clear that the exceptional provisions in the Prevention of Terrorism Act and the Northern Ireland (Emergency Provisions) Act will remain in place only for so long as they are required by the police and courts in order to combat terrorist violence. The government will, however, need first to be satisfied that the threat which terrorism has presented to the people of the United Kingdom for the past 25 years has ended for good before taking steps to lower the nation's defences against terrorist crime.[4]

Northern Ireland has been in a state of emergency since its inception in 1922. Many of the measures in the Prevention of Terrorism Act 1989 and the Emergency Provisions Act 1991 were on the statute (in other laws) long before the conflict of the past 25 years. Other emergency laws and practices, originally introduced in response to crises, have found a wider application or have been incorporated into ordinary law.

Liberty does not believe that the threat of violence justified many of the emergency laws and practices which were implemented during the period of the conflict. They made little contribution to reducing violence and may even have helped to perpetuate it, by adding to the sense of grievance of some sections of the community. It is not an acceptable response to political violence to deny individuals their civil rights, to erode due process in the administration of justice or to provide the authorities with powers which are unchallengeable in the courts.

Liberty is concerned that whatever constitutional settlement results, it should have at its heart the protection of human rights. We believe that State violations of internationally accepted human rights standards exacerbated the Northern Ireland conflict. Between 1959 and 1990, the British government was taken to the European Court of Human Rights more frequently than any other signatory to the European Convention on Human Rights (the ECHR), and found to be in breach of its provisions on more occasions than any other signatory.[5] Many of these violations have arisen in relation to the conflict in Northern Ireland. Britain has been found guilty of using inhuman and degrading treatment,[6] arbitrary arrest[7] and failure to bring suspects promptly before a judge.[8]

Liberty supports the enactment of a British Bill of Rights. We believe that people need legally enforceable rights as protection against possible government abuses.[9] Human rights violations arising from the Northern Ireland conflict highlight the need for such entrenched protection. However, there are other ways in which the centralism and unaccountability of the British State have eroded human rights or reduced the opportunities for redress of abuses of rights. The constitutional settlement on which the United Kingdom is based is archaic and in urgent need of reform.

HOW EMERGENCY RULE HAS ERODED CIVIL RIGHTS

There are three basic concerns about the administration of justice in Northern Ireland:

- the powers given to the repressive State apparatus are arbitrary and excessive
- the safeguards to protect the individual are inadequate
- the apparatus is not accountable to or representative of the whole community.[10]

The presence of soldiers on the streets and the absence of juries in court rooms provide stark illustrations of the consequences of attempting to uphold the rule of law in the absence of consent about the legitimacy of the State. But there are other consequences in the denial of many basic human rights regarding Northern Ireland's inquest system[11] and police-complaints procedure:[12] dissatisfaction at the treatment of sentenced and remand prisoners, including complaints by prisoners about the way their sentences are reviewed.[13] These concerns are all the more serious in this context: the legitimacy of the State itself is contested by a substantial proportion of the population. The ceasefire provides an opportunity for a fundamental overhaul of the State apparatus in order to protect human rights.

Northern Ireland was created by the Government of Ireland Act 1920. This partitioned the island of Ireland and created two legislatures, both of which were intended to be subordinate to the Westminster Parliament.[14] The Act passed control for policing in Northern Ireland to a subordinate Parliament at Stormont in Northern Ireland. A Royal Ulster Constabulary (RUC) was established. The force was armed and given wide-ranging powers under the Special Powers Act 1922.[15] It was supplemented by an auxiliary police force, popularly known as the B-Specials. Both forces were overwhelmingly Protestant in their composition.[16]

The Civil Authorities (Special Powers) Act 1922 was based on previous British coercion acts.[17] Initially designed to be temporary, it was renewed annually and later given a five-year lifespan. In 1933 it was made permanent. The Act provided for arrest without warrant or charge and detention for 48 hours, indefinite internment without trial, house raids without warrant, flogging and execution, deportation, the destruction or requisition of property, the blocking of roads, curfews, the prohibition of inquests and the banning of organisations, meetings and publications.[18] The Home Secretary was also empowered to introduce additional regulations, by decree, if the government considered them necessary for the preservation of law and order.[19]

The security forces

In 1969 British troops were redeployed on the streets of Northern Ireland, for the first time since the 1920s. In August 1971 internment without trial was reintroduced, having previously been used intermittently by the police. In 1972 Northern Ireland's Stormont Parliament was discontinued during a general outcry after soldiers of the Parachute Regiment shot dead 14 civil rights protesters in Derry.[20] From 1972, Northern Ireland has been governed directly from Westminster.

Government policy since the mid-1970s has been to place primary responsibility for security in the hands of the police and to expand the roles of the Royal Ulster Constabulary (RUC) and the Ulster Defence Regiment (UDR). However, the British army still has a highly visible presence in west Belfast, Derry city, parts of Tyrone and south Armagh. Their presence remains a source of frequent tensions and conflict.[21] Since the ceasefire this presence has been scaled down but it is still noticeable. The behaviour of soldiers has led to many other complaints, particularly against members of the Parachute Regiment.[22]

Problems also exist in relation to the police force. In March 1969 the government's Cameron Commission conducted an inquiry into policing in Northern Ireland.[23] Its report led to the establishment of the Hunt Committee which made a series of recommendations for reforms: the disbanding of the B-Specials and the creation of a new part-time reserve force, the disarming of the RUC, the establishment of a Police Authority and the repeal of much of the Special Powers Act.[24]

The attempt to create a civilianised police force lasted until November 1971, when the RUC was rearmed. The B-Specials were abolished in April 1970 and replaced with the Ulster Defence Regiment (UDR). This was integrated into the regular army and it was hoped that it would live down the sectarian reputation of its predecessor. However, the proportion of Catholics in the UDR declined rapidly, from around 20 per cent in 1970 to less than 3 per cent by the 1980s.[25] In 1992 the UDR was merged into the Royal Irish Rangers (RIR). But, even after the merger, the new regiment's composition is still less than 6 per cent Catholic.[26]

Allegations of shoot-to-kill and collusion

A recurring problem during the conflict was the allegation that special units within both the police and army operated an unofficial shoot-to-kill policy. Over 330 people were killed by the security forces during the conflict.[27] A survey by international lawyers in 1985 concluded that in 155 of the 269 deaths it investigated the people killed had no paramilitary connections.[28] In some other cases it has been alleged that the security forces killed people when they could have arrested them or killed people after first wounding them.[29] Article 6 of the International Covenant on Civil and Political Rights (ICCPR) states that no one should be arbitrarily deprived of the right to life. Article 2 of the ECHR specifies that a deprivation of life is only justifiable when it is 'absolutely necessary' in strictly defined circumstances.[30] However, in Northern Ireland the security forces may use lethal force 'as is reasonable in the circumstances'.[31]

Only four soldiers have been convicted of murder while on duty in Northern Ireland. One of them, Ian Thain,[32] who killed a civilian in 1985, spent two years and three months in prison before he was released and allowed to rejoin his regiment. The conviction of the other soldier, Lee Clegg, who killed a teenage woman joy rider in 1990 has been the subject of a vigorous lobbying campaign.[33] In February 1995 two soldiers were sentenced to life imprisonment for the murder of a Belfast teenager in 1992.[34] In the same month a soldier, Andrew Clarke, fired 20 bullets into a crowd of mourners outside a dead IRA member's house. He hit one person twice, who was wounded but not killed. Clarke received a 10-year prison sentence.[35]

International attention was focused on the alleged shoot-to-kill policy by the SAS which resulted in the deaths of three unarmed IRA members in Gibraltar in 1988,[36] and six fatal shootings carried out by an RUC special unit in Armagh in 1982 which was followed by an inquiry headed by Manchester police officer, John Stalker. He encountered obstruction and deceit involving senior RUC and MI5 officers before his dramatic removal from the investigation on disciplinary charges, later proved to be fabricated.[37] The report's findings, concluded by another police officer, have never been made public and the inquests into the deaths have had to be abandoned.[38]

There have also been numerous complaints about the behaviour of the UDR, both on patrol and in relation to alleged collusion between some of its members and Loyalist paramilitaries.[39] Nationalist politicians have demanded that the regiment be disbanded.[40] In 1989 the Deputy Chief Constable of Cambridgeshire, John Stevens, conducted an inquiry following claims made by the Ulster Defence Association (UDA) and Ulster Volunteer Force (UVF), in the same year, that they were receiving high quality information from military, police and intelligence sources enabling them to murder suspected Republicans.[41] The inquiry concluded that information, passed by members of the security forces to Loyalist paramilitaries, had been used in planning or carrying out attacks. It also concluded that the passing of such information was neither widespread nor institutionalised, although leakages of information may never be completely eliminated.[42]

These conclusions have been rejected by some observers. One study looked into 99 killings by Loyalist paramilitaries between March 1990 and 1992. It concluded that 88 had either a political or sectarian motive and in 48 cases there was some evidence of collusion with the security forces.[43] At least two Loyalist paramilitaries, Albert Baker and Brian Nelson, have claimed that they worked under the direction of military intelligence. In Nelson's case the British army has admitted that he was one of their agents, but denies that it used him to set up targets for assassination. He did, however, hold a senior position within the UDA, was involved in arranging a massive shipment of arms to Loyalists from South Africa and would have had prior knowledge of many of the UDA's murder plans.[44]

The extent to which the authorities may have tolerated or promoted collusion remains debatable. One of the most controversial incidents was the murder of a defence solicitor in Belfast in 1989 after a highly publicised accusation by a government minister that members of the legal profession were colluding with terrorists. In January 1989 a parliamentary committee debated the amendments to the Prevention of Terrorism Bill, in which the government was seeking to overturn the normal confidentiality between solicitors and their clients. Government Minister, Douglas Hogg, declared that:

> I have to state as a fact, but with great regret, that there are in Northern Ireland a number of solicitors who are unduly sympathetic to the cause of the IRA. [interruption] I repeat that there are in the Province a number of solicitors who are unduly sympathetic to the cause of the IRA. One has to bear that in mind.[45]

He was immediately challenged by a Nationalist MP, Seamus Mallon, who said that Douglas Hogg's remarks threatened the entire legal profession in Northern Ireland, and that 'it will be on the head of the Minister and government if the assassin's bullet decides to do, by deed, what this government has done by word.'[46] Hogg refused to retract or substantiate his remarks but repeated the allegation several times, in virtually identical language, claiming that he had received guidance from 'people who are dealing in these matters.'[47] Less than a month later a well-known Catholic solicitor, Patrick Finucane, who specialised in criminal defence work, was murdered by Loyalist paramilitaries.[48] Finucane had represented both Loyalist and Republican suspects but had come to public attention during a number of high-profile cases involving Republicans. He represented a man who was injured during one of the shootings John Stalker investigated. Stalker was criticised by an RUC Sergeant for attempting to talk to Finucane during his investigation. The Sergeant told Stalker '[Finucane] is an IRA man – any man who represents IRA men is worse than an IRA man. His brother is an IRA man also and I have to say that I believe a senior policeman of your rank should not be seen speaking to the likes of either of them.'[49] One of Finucane's brothers had received a prison sentence for IRA activities, but there is no evidence that Finucane was himself involved in the IRA. However, the RUC clearly disliked him intensely. There were a number of reports of the RUC naming him and other solicitors as IRA men to people whom they were interrogating.[50]

Strip-searching

Systematic strip-searching of Irish women prisoners was introduced in the early 1980s against women remand prisoners in Armagh gaol.[51] Nothing of any security value was found on these women, who were stripped naked twice a day. Many complained that the anguish they suffered on their way to and from court appearances affected their ability to prepare for their trials.[52] In 1983 the authorities announced that they were abandoning routine strip-searching, but would still carry out random strip-searching.[53]

In March 1992 the authorities carried out a mass forcible strip-search of women prisoners in Maghaberry gaol, conducted by officers in riot gear. Twenty-one prisoners who resisted were forcibly stripped, with up to six prison officers holding down individual women. Nothing of security value was found in a search lasting 10 hours.[54]

There have been continued protests that strip-searching constitutes inhuman and degrading treatment and violates the right of people held in detention to be treated with respect for the inherent dignity of the person. Women prisoners who have been granted compassionate leave to attend the funeral of a family member have been strip-searched on their way into and out of prison.[55] Women detained under the Prevention of Terrorism Act, most of whom never face charges, are also often strip-searched.[56]

The use of plastic bullets

Seventeen people have been killed by plastic and rubber bullets in Northern Ireland.[57] Hundreds have sustained serious injuries. Eight of those killed have been children.[58] The use of plastic bullets has been condemned by politicians from both communities in Northern Ireland. A resolution calling for them to be banned was overwhelmingly carried by the European Parliament in 1982.[59] A plastic bullet is as heavy as a cricket ball but harder and leaves the gun at 160 miles per hour. It is designed for crowd dispersal and the security forces maintain that most of those who have been killed were rioters.[60] Fourteen people have been killed by plastic bullets.[61] In 11 cases the police's claim that the victim was rioting has been contested by witnesses or by the judge or coroner at the inquest into their deaths.[62] Only one RUC officer has been prosecuted for causing a death. He was acquitted even though it emerged at his trial that the bullet was fired in contravention of the rules.[63] In 1988 Standard Fireworks, then the principal supplier of plastic bullets to the Ministry of Defence, announced that it would cease production, after a meeting with relatives of people killed and injured by the bullets.[64]

There have been no fatalities from plastic bullets since 1989, but they have caused many horrific injuries. The security forces have continued to use plastic bullets since the ceasefire. In October 1994 in Belfast, one man had to be placed on a life-support machine after his skull was fractured by a plastic bullet fired from a distance of about 10 yards.[65] The bullet was fired after a confrontation between a group of youths and a joint RUC and army patrol, during which, the security forces claim, they came under attack. In the same month a man was hit on the leg by a plastic bullet in Cookstown during a mini riot outside a hotel. It was claimed that the RUC fired into the crowd indiscriminately.[66] The continued use of plastic bullets since the ceasefire sets a dangerous precedent for public order policing. Liberty believes that the use of plastic bullets should be banned.

THE PREVENTION OF TERRORISM ACT

The Prevention of Terrorism (Temporary Provisions) Act (the PTA) was introduced to Parliament on 25 November 1974, four days after bombs in Birmingham pubs killed 21 people. The Home Secretary acknowledged the Act's powers were so draconian as to be 'unprecedented in peacetime'. During the debate, it was estimated that the Act would be in force for about six months.[67] The Act was passed in 42 hours, virtually without amendment or dissent. Over 20 years later, the Act is still on the statute book, having been re-enacted in 1979, 1984 and 1989. Some of its provisions have been modified, but its basic powers remain largely unchanged.

According to the government's statistics, the Act does little to combat terrorism. More than 7,000 people have been detained in

Britain under the Act, but the vast majority have been released without charge. Three per cent have been charged with offences under its provisions, between 5 and 6 per cent have been charged with other offences and 4 per cent have been excluded or deported.[68] Almost without exception the people who were charged with terrorist-related offences could have been arrested under ordinary criminal law.[69]

In his memoirs, Sir Robert Mark, who was Chief of the Metropolitan Police when the PTA was enacted, stressed that at the time the police regarded the Act as primarily a political measure:

> It was introduced by the Home Secretary because he felt a need to reassure the public of the willingness of the government to take firm measures in the face of Irish terrorism. The police were largely indifferent. The NCCL were quite right in assuming that we would not let any legal niceties prevent us from dealing with terrorism and that we were therefore not all that interested in what we thought was essentially a propaganda measure. In fact the real beneficiaries were the one and a half million decent Irish people living and working in this country who were overnight relieved of the embarrassing spectacle of their intellectually subnormal compatriots collecting money for the IRA or indulging in childish melodramatics on their behalf. That was about the only real benefit afforded by the Act, but I have no doubt the Irish minority were grateful for it ... The new Act was undoubtedly helpful in that it curbed the activities of the civil libertarians who are always so anxious to bomb, to maim and to kill.[70]

Arrests and detentions

From 1990 to 1993 inclusive, the numbers of people arrested and charged under the PTA in Britain were as follows:[71]

year	arrested	charged				excluded/ deported	not charged	not charged % of arrests
		offences under PTA	'terrorist' offences[72]	theft	other			
1990	193	6			22	16	163	84
1991	153	4			3	11	144	94
1992	160	9	7	4	18	3	124	77
1993	152	5	17	1	9	4	120	79

These figures give rise to serious concern. The majority of charges brought under the PTA are for offences such as refusing to co-operate with an examination, breaching an exclusion order or withholding information. None of these offences is serious.

Of the people who face charges brought under other Acts, only a minority faces charges that can be reasonably considered to be terrorist-related – murder, possession of firearms or explosives, conspiracy to commit murder, explosions or arson. Most face charges for other offences, such as possession of cannabis, possession of stolen goods, and social security fraud offences. While these are crimes, they hardly justify the retention of the PTA's draconian provisions.

Police powers

Under Section 14(1) of the PTA the police may arrest without a warrant any person 'who is or has been concerned in the commission, preparation or instigation of acts of terrorism.' This involvement can be 'active' or 'passive'.

Section 14(1) is a major departure from ordinary criminal law. Generally, a warrantless arrest may only take place if the police have reasonable suspicion that a specific arrestable offence has been committed and that the individual they are arresting committed this offence. Because no crime has to be specified under Section 14(1), the police have been given greatly increased powers of arrest. Individuals being questioned or facing criminal charges, and their lawyers, may not know the specific crime of which they are suspected.

Arrests usually take place either at ports of entry into the country or following police raids. Often these are carried out in high-profile and dramatic fashion. People have had their front door smashed in during the early hours of the morning and have been dragged from their bed at gunpoint.[73] Such raids employ excessive and unreasonable force, they stigmatise the person being arrested and ensure that people are frightened and disorientated when they arrive at the police station. These objections are compounded by the fact that ordinary criminal law is quite sufficient to deal with situations where the police have reasonable suspicion that the person they are arresting is armed and dangerous.

Liberty is concerned that arrests can be made without evidence that the arrested individual has committed a specific crime. The experience of the raid is likely to be traumatic for the person, and damaging to their reputation with friends, neighbours and colleagues. Such arrests can lead to the loss of jobs and homes and it is not uncommon for individuals to suffer abuse or assaults after detention. Some detainees have experienced long-term psychological traumas after their release and there are cases of suicides being linked to detentions.[74] If charges are brought, the person's chances of receiving a fair trial may be prejudiced by such a high-profile arrest. We emphasise that, overwhelmingly, most people arrested under the PTA are innocent of terrorist involvement. Liberty has documented many cases in which people have been arrested in these circumstances, often after terrorist attacks, only to be released without charge, explanation or apology.[75] In summer 1993 Liberty made British legal history when it extracted an apology from the Metropolitan Police and compensation for wrongfully arresting a group of young people.[76]

Under Section 18 of the PTA it is a criminal offence to withhold from the police information about terrorism and terrorists. This offence erodes the right of silence, since the police can threaten to charge people if they refuse to answer all of the police's questions. Charges under this section have been infrequent and it has been suggested that it has been used mainly against people whom the police suspect – with little evidence – to be involved in terrorist activity.[77] However, there have been complaints that it has been used to intimidate relatives of people whom the police suspect of involvement in terrorist activity.[78] In a review of the operation of the PTA, Lord Shackleton commented:

> There are genuine doubts about its implications in principle and about the way it might be used in the course of interviewing someone . . . it has an unpleasant ring about it in terms of civil liberties.[79]

Section 18 of the PTA has also been used to force the media to hand over footage and information relating to terrorist activities.[80] There have been few prosecutions, but in 1992 Box Productions and Channel 4 Television were fined £75,000, for refusing to comply with an order to identify a source for allegations in a programme about collusion between members of the security forces and Loyalist paramilitaries.[81]

Examinations

Schedule 5 of the PTA confers powers of detention at ports of entry in Britain and Northern Ireland on police, immigration officers and customs officials. An individual may be questioned for up to 12 hours if the officer has no suspicion about the individual, and up to 24 hours if the officer has reasonable suspicion as defined under Section 14. After the first hour of the examination the detaining officer must record that the individual is being detained, inform him or her in writing of his or her right to contact a lawyer, and notify a relative.

In determining whom to examine, the police and port authorities routinely screen millions of travelling people every year. In a review of the PTA, Lord Colville estimated that approximately one million people were stopped at ports of entry each year and questioned briefly by an officer, or made to fill out an embarkation card detailing their name and address, occupation, nationality, purpose of travelling and details of where they would be staying.[82] The Act allows the police and other officers to hold people at ports for up to an hour without having to record this fact. During this time people can be subjected to intrusive and intimidatory questioning and miss a connecting train, boat or plane, without this fact being recorded anywhere.

Conditions of custody

The first people arrested under the Act were three young Irish men and a teenage English woman who all signed statements, after extended periods of detention, confessing to other pub bombings earlier that year.[83] The Guildford Four, as they became known, served 15 years before their convictions were quashed.

People detained under Section 14 of the PTA can be held in 24-hour solitary confinement for up to seven days without access to a court. The Home Secretary, or the Secretary of State for Northern Ireland in the case of detentions in Northern Ireland, must authorise the extension of a detention beyond the first 48 hours. Detentions of seven days are in breach of Article 5 of the European Convention on Human Rights and the British government has been forced to derogate from this Article (that is, set it aside, because the UK cannot ensure the protections it specifies).[84] This derogation was supported by the European Court of Human Rights in May 1993, on the grounds that an emergency existed in

101

Northern Ireland which was sufficiently serious to justify the denial of these rights.[85] It is doubtful whether the European Court would accept that grounds for derogation still exist, now that the ceasefire has come into effect. Extended detentions clearly breach the spirit of international law.

In England and Wales the custodial regime for a person detained under the PTA is expressly tied to the Code of Practice for the Detention, Treatment and Questioning of Persons by the Police, which is contained in the Police and Criminal Evidence Act 1984.[86] Similar rules operate in Scotland via police force orders. There is also a Code of Practice made under the Emergency Provisions Act 1991 (the EPA), which governs the treatment of detainees in custody in Northern Ireland. Because the PTA allows extended detentions, issues of diet, bedding and exercise take on an added importance. A detained individual is unlikely to see natural light or to exercise for up to seven days. There have been many complaints from individuals who allege that their sleep was interrupted, they lost track of whether it was day or night, their cells were too hot or cold, their food inedible, they were denied washing facilities and reading or writing material.[87]

Following the release of the Guildford Four in 1989, more police forces in Britain are recording interviews on tape.[88] However, the government refuses to make it a requirement to video- and tape-record all interrogations of individuals detained under the PTA in Britain and Northern Ireland, in spite of persistent complaints from detainees of threats, physical abuse and fabrication of evidence.[89]

Detained individuals can be denied access to a solicitor for the first 48 hours of their detention and may be questioned in the absence of one. A 1993 study by the Home Office into PTA detentions in Britain found that access to legal advice was delayed in over one-quarter of all cases in which detainees asked for it, and that in some cases no grounds were given for this delay.[90] Only 19 per cent of all foreign nationals were informed of their right to communicate with their embassy.[91]

In Northern Ireland it is particularly difficult for solicitors to gain access to their clients. The police can also refuse to notify a detainee's friend or relative for 48 hours. The PTA enables the police to use 'reasonable force' to photograph and fingerprint detainees without a court order and without their consent. Files on detainees can be kept even if they are released without charge.[92]

Banning and prohibition

Under Section 1(2)(a) of the PTA, the Secretary of State may proscribe any organisation which 'appears to him to be concerned in, or in promoting or encouraging terrorism occurring in the United Kingdom and connected with the affairs of Northern Ireland.' The power to proscribe is entirely at the discretion of the Secretary of State. No evidence need be produced and no appeal is permissible. The Secretary of State does not need to refer the matter to Parliament before proscribing an organisation. The organisations currently proscribed under the PTA are the Irish Republican Army and the Irish National Liberation Army.[93] Membership of a proscribed organisation is an offence under Section 2 of the Act, punishable by up to 10 years' imprisonment.[94] Supporting a proscribed organisation is also an offence under Section 3.[95] Proscription makes very little difference to the activities of paramilitary organisations, which by their nature operate in a clandestine fashion. The powers of proscription are far more likely to be used against political supporters of Republicanism or Loyalism than against those involved in paramilitary activity, though these are rarely employed.[96]

The argument against proscription is that terrorist actions should be (and are) criminalised, not involvement in political organisations. Government advisors have accepted that proscription makes very little contribution to combating terrorism, and have rejected adding other organisations to the list of groups proscribed under the PTA.[97]

Exclusion orders

Section 5(1) of the PTA empowers the Home Secretary to make an exclusion order if it appears to him or her that an individual 'is or has been involved in the commission, preparation or instigation of acts of terrorism to which this Part of the Act applies . . .' The terms 'preparation' or 'instigation' are vague, and can include planning, encouragement, or direct involvement. The terms of the Act allow an exclusion to be made if the individual may have been involved in terrorism in the past or could have an intention to be involved in terrorism in the future.

British citizens cannot be excluded from the United Kingdom entirely but can be restricted to living in Britain or Northern Ireland. This Section effectively creates a system of internal exile.

Irish citizens who do not have British citizenship can be excluded from the whole of the UK. It is a criminal offence, punishable by up to six months' imprisonment, to break an exclusion order.[98]

Exclusion orders are made entirely at the discretion of the Home Secretary, who acts on the advice of the police. The order includes no explanation of why it is being served. Exclusion orders are based on secret evidence, often in the form of uncorroborated statements, whose accuracy is impossible to judge. A person subject to an exclusion order has no right to know the evidence on which it was made, no right to examine that evidence, to offer a defence or to have the case heard in public but may appeal by requesting an oral hearing before an adviser appointed by government, under Schedule 2 paragraph 3(1). The excluded individual has no right to legal representation. The Home Secretary has a duty to take into account the report of this adviser, but has no obligation to inform the individual of the reasons for the success or failure of the appeal.

The majority of people excluded from Britain still live and move freely in Northern Ireland, which has led to complaints that the area has been turned into a 'dumping ground'. Unionist politicians believe it repugnant that the government believes some people too dangerous to allow into Britain, yet places no restrictions on their movement in Northern Ireland. [99]

People subject to exclusion orders are stigmatised as terrorists without appearing in court on formal charges and having the opportunity to clear their name. In October 1993 John Matthews was rearrested and served with an exclusion order, *after* terrorist-related charges against him had been withdrawn.[100] Liberty has also received complaints from individuals who have attempted to leave Northern Ireland to escape problems of political violence, only to be served with exclusion orders obliging them to remain there.[101]

The UK cannot ratify Protocol 4 of the European Convention on Human Rights, which provides for freedom of movement and settlement within one's own country, because of exclusion orders. The UK is the only country in Europe to have a system of imposing internal exile on its own citizens.[102] The UK has also had to enter a reservation on the application of Article 12 of the ICCPR (which sets out the right to freedom of movement), to the effect that the right of freedom of movement shall apply separately to each of the territories of the UK.[103] This means that people have the right to move within England, Scotland, Wales and Northern Ireland but not necessarily between these territories.

On 4 March 1993 a person subject to an exclusion order was granted leave for a judicial review in the Court of Appeal, challenging exclusion orders as a breach of Article 6 of the ECHR (the right to a fair trial), and of European law on the free movement of labour.[104] In July 1994 Liberty won a referral to the European Court of Justice in Luxembourg, of a case brought on behalf of Sinn Fein's president, Gerry Adams. The grounds for referral were that exclusion orders may violate the right of freedom of movement contained in European Union law.[105] Since the ceasefire, exclusion orders served on Gerry Adams and other leading Irish Republicans have also been lifted.[106] However, the power of exclusion remains and continues to offend against international human rights standards. On 29 November 1994 the government announced that 61 exclusion orders remain in force and stated that:

the government hope that the day is approaching when exclusion orders will no longer be needed but we are not prepared to lower our guard prematurely.[107]

Liberty believes that the continued use of exclusion orders is no longer justified.

THE EMERGENCY PROVISIONS ACT

The Northern Ireland (Emergency Provisions) Act 1973 (known as the EPA) was enacted following the report of a commission chaired by Lord Diplock. It was established to consider 'what arrangements could be made in order to deal more effectively with terrorist organisations . . . otherwise than by internment.'[108] Most of the commission's recommendations were enacted in the EPA, in spite of criticism that its examination had been cursory and overly dependent on the British army's assessment of the situation.[109]

The EPA's provisions only apply in Northern Ireland. The EPA was amended in 1975 and re-enacted in 1978 and 1987. Before 1987 most emergency arrests in Northern Ireland took place under the EPA, but since then the security forces have relied upon the powers contained in the PTA.[110] Internment was gradually phased out in 1975 as the authorities made more use of the new powers in the PTA and EPA, although the power to order internment remains in the EPA. In 1961 the European Court of Human Rights clearly stated that it is a breach of the ECHR to hold someone in detention to prevent them committing criminal offences without bringing the accused before a court, and without the intention to hold a trial.[111] A further challenge to internment was upheld by the European Court in 1978.[112]

A new EPA was passed in 1991 which repealed the previous legislation but re-enacted most of its provisions and incorporated the powers of the PTA that only applied to Northern Ireland. It also created two new offences: going equipped for terrorism and possession of information likely to be of use to terrorists.

The 1991 EPA re-enacted other provisions contained in the Special Powers Act giving the security forces extended powers to stop, search, question, arrest and detain people and to block roads.[113] The EPA gives soldiers the power (unique in UK law) to arrest and detain people for up to four hours.[114] The EPA also gives the Secretary of State for Northern Ireland the power to ban organisations,[115] though there are few prosecutions for membership or support of proscribed organisations.[116]

The Diplock Courts

The EPA creates a separate legal regime for people arrested on suspicion of committing what are known as 'scheduled offences' – principally crimes of violence, attacks on property, explosives and firearms offences, theft, intimidation, blackmail and membership of a proscribed organisation.[117] There are special provisions governing notification of arrest and access to solicitors. If people are charged with these offences they are tried in what are known as Diplock Courts. These have no juries, there are special rules governing the admissibility of some evidence and the burden of proof is reversed in some charges (that is, innocence is not presumed and must be proved).[118] Originally these courts were envisaged as a temporary measure to deal with the problem of intimidation of jurors and perverse jury verdicts (that is, usually, verdicts in which the jury acquits in spite of the evidence). However, this original justification was at the time vigorously challenged.[119]

Most significantly, the EPA lowers the standard for the admissibility of confessions which may have been obtained through improper means. While under the Police and Criminal Evidence Act 1984 confessions must automatically be excluded if they have been obtained 'by oppression of the person who made it,'[120] under the EPA they remain admissible provided that they have not been obtained through torture or inhuman or degrading treatment or violence or the threat of violence.[121] Judges in Northern Ireland retain some discretion to exclude confessions which have been improperly obtained but it is unclear what other physical ill-treatment a suspect could have to undergo before any statement would be ruled inadmissible.

Between 1976 and 1979 the Diplock Courts achieved a 94 per cent conviction rate. The vast majority of these convictions rested wholly or mainly on confessions signed by suspects while in police custody.[122] Concern about the treatment of detainees grew after it was revealed that a selected group of the first internees in 1971 had been subjected to special interrogation techniques. These included being made to stand spread-eagled against a wall, hooded, subjected to continuous noise and being deprived of food and sleep for days on end. In 1976 the European Commission on Human Rights found that Britain had tortured these 'hooded men'. A ruling by the European Court of Human Rights in 1978 amended the verdict to that of using inhuman and degrading treatment.[123]

By the late-1970s a number of human rights groups registered concern about alleged ill-treatment suffered by detainees in attempts to force them to sign confessions while they were in police custody. In 1978 Amnesty International published a damning report.[124] The British government responded by setting up its own inquiry, chaired by Lord Bennett. It reported that a number of detainees suffered injuries which could not have been self-inflicted.[125] After 1979, the number of complaints about ill-treatment fell but rose again at the end of the 1980s and the start of the 1990s. A 1991 Amnesty report stated that 'existing procedures and safeguards are inadequate to prevent the ill-treatment of detainees.'[126] In 1991 Amnesty International issued an urgent action notice over ill-treatment of a 17-year-old youth in Castlereagh. The United Nations Committee on Torture has expressed its concern about the regimes operating in Northern Ireland's holding centres.[127] The Strasbourg-based Committee for the Prevention of Torture, set up by the Council of Europe, has accused the British government of permitting psychological and physical ill-treatment of detainees, including assaults and death threats, during police questioning.[128]

There are also clear difficulties in a system which has a judge, in a court with no jury, considering the admissibility of evidence and also deciding what weight should be attached to that evidence. These difficulties have been highlighted by the RUC's reliance on confession and accomplice evidence. In cases involving these types of evidence, it is usual for a judge to warn the jury about the reliability it should attach to such testimony. In the absence of a jury, Diplock Courts sometimes witness the bizarre spectacle of a judge stating that he is warning himself that the evidence he is about to consider may be unreliable.[129]

During the early 1980s several hundred people were charged in Northern Ireland on the basis of uncorroborated statements by alleged accomplices. A series of mass trials in the Diplock Courts occurred in what became known as the 'supergrass' system.[130] The supergrasses (informers) were all former paramilitaries and in most cases had been induced to testify by promises of a shorter sentence for their own crimes or payments of up to £100,000. Many were shown to have a history of perjury or psychotic behaviour. In 1984 and 1985 a number of supergrass trials collapsed and other convictions were overturned in the Court of Appeal. Some supergrasses admitted they had been put under pressure to supply as many names as possible, that they had named people they had never even met, had substituted names and had simply signed statements drawn up by the police.[131]

Judges became more sceptical of supergrass evidence and fewer supergrasses became willing to give evidence. Some observers concluded that a policy decision had been taken to abandon the 'system'. The existence of a system was denied by the authorities, who have always insisted that the emergence of people they preferred to call 'converted terrorists' had been spontaneous. However, some supergrasses who retracted their evidence claimed they had been threatened with long prison sentences on falsified charges or that the security forces would set them up to be murdered.[132] The emergence of the 'supergrass system' highlighted serious concerns about the criminal justice system in Northern Ireland, pointing to the need for thorough reform.

The abolition of the right of silence

On 20 October 1988 the Secretary of State for Northern Ireland, Tom King, announced that he would bring forward measures to

108

abolish the right of silence for people arrested in connection with scheduled offences in Northern Ireland.[133] He claimed that this right was regularly being abused by hardened terrorists to frustrate the police and prosecuting authorities. He alluded to a trial which was taking place at the time in Britain in which he himself was the alleged victim of a terrorist conspiracy.[134] The day before this announcement the three defendants in this trial had chosen not to give evidence. There has been speculation that the announcement's timing was deliberately designed to influence the trial's outcome.[135] All three defendants were convicted but in 1991 these convictions were quashed on the grounds that King's announcement had infringed their right to a fair trial.[136]

In November 1988 the House of Commons approved the Criminal Evidence (Northern Ireland) Order. This removed the right of suspects in Northern Ireland to remain silent under police questioning and at trial without adverse inferences being drawn.[137] Tom King referred to 'the acknowledged difficulties faced by the police and prosecuting authorities in bringing to justice hardened, professional criminals – often assisted by able legal advisors.'[138] The Criminal Evidence (Northern Ireland) Order was an Order in Council, a type of 'delegated legislation', which can only be accepted or rejected by Parliament and is not open to amendment. This use was criticised at the time by the Conservative MP Ian Gow and subsequently by the Standing Advisory Commission on Human Rights, amongst others, because of its inadequate opportunity for parliamentary scrutiny and debate.[139]

The right of silence is a centuries-old safeguard against wrongful convictions and oppressive questioning.[140] The new law permits a judge, jury or magistrate to draw such inferences as they think fit from a suspect's failure to mention, at the earliest possible moment under police questioning, facts which are material to their defence, or from their failure to account for anything else which might connect them with a crime.[141] The law also requires courts to call on defendants to give evidence at trials and gives the courts the power to draw adverse inferences from defendants' failure to do so.[142] Silence may also be treated as corroborative evidence against the accused.[143]

Abolition of the right of silence has increased the concern felt by many criminal justice practitioners and human rights activists in Northern Ireland about the risk of wrongful convictions.[144] It is of particular concern because of the legal regime governing the arrest, detention, interrogation and trial of people accused of scheduled offences in Northern Ireland. A person arrested in connection with a scheduled offence in Northern Ireland may be denied access to legal representation for 48 hours. Solicitors cannot sit in on interviews and interviews are not tape-recorded. In one case the courts ruled that adverse inferences can be drawn from the failure of a suspect to answer questions, even if he or she has requested legal advice before making a statement.[145]

In 1994 a challenge to this ruling was declared admissible by the European Commission on Human Rights, on the grounds that it breached the ECHR.[146] The Commission decided that the denial of access to a solicitor was a breach of the ECHR. It also decided that in this instance, the fact that adverse inferences could be drawn when he failed to answer the police's questions or give evidence at his trial, did not mean that the complainant had been denied the right to a fair trial; however, this fact had to be seen in the context of the strength of the case against him as a whole. In the circumstances of this particular trial the Commission decided that the loss of the right to silence did not constitute a breach of the ECHR, but Convention case law makes clear that all the facts and circumstances of each case have to be considered in order to decide whether an applicant has had a fair trial. The UK Commissioner noted, in his opinion on the decision, that it would be more difficult in a non-jury court to guarantee that there were adequate safeguards to ensure proper inferences were drawn from a defendant's silence, than it would be in courts in which a judge had to direct a jury.[147]

The Committee on the Administration of Justice (CAJ) has documented a number of cases in Northern Ireland in which it believes the safety of the conviction is in doubt. In these cases, either adverse inference was drawn from the silence of the defendant, or the defendants may have been induced to make false confessions because they feared that their refusal to answer all the police's questions would be held against them at their trial.[148] Vulnerable and naive suspects are believed to be particularly at risk of miscarriages of justice because of the abolition of the right of silence. A new caution warns people of the consequences of their responses to police questioning, but there is concern that it is little understood and widely misinterpreted, and that it has placed undue pressure to speak on suspects.

A study was carried out in 1994 by CAJ and Justice, the British section of the International Commission of Jurists, to inform the debate about the proposal in the Criminal Justice and Public Order Act 1994 to abolish the right of silence in England and Wales. It confirmed these concerns and also found that the abolition of the right of silence has not reduced crime or improved charge and conviction rates.[149] The government's figures show that the proportions of people caught and convicted of recorded crimes have actually dropped since the abolition of the right of silence. 'Clearup' rates for crimes (that is, the percentage of crimes reported for which someone is charged with an offence) peaked at a record high of 45 per cent in 1988, but fell in each successive year after the abolition of the right of silence. They were 11 per cent lower in 1992 than before abolition of the right of silence.[150] Conviction rates also dropped. They were 3 to 4 per cent lower in the four years after the abolition of the right of silence than in the four years before it.[151]

The CAJ and Justice study noted that judges initially showed considerable caution about how much weight they gave to the defendant's remaining silent in police custody or during the trial. However, it noted a 'real and pronounced' shift in the burden of proof which judges were requiring when applying the Criminal Evidence (Northern Ireland) Order, 'which almost takes silence as presumptive of guilt.'[152] The study concluded that the Order 'offends the principles of self-incrimination and presumption of innocence' and 'raises serious considerations on whether the provisions of the Order can be compatible with the right to a fair trial enshrined in Article 6 of the European Convention on Human Rights.' [153] However, it also stated that:

> The government's main argument for change [in England and Wales], in 1994 as in 1988, rests on the likelihood of charging and convicting more people, particularly serious and habitual criminals. The available evidence from Northern Ireland gives no ground for supposing that has been the case there, or will be in England and Wales. On the contrary, the statistics support the opposing views advanced during the debate, and supported by all the research evidence into the actual effect of silence in the United Kingdom: that as a weapon in the fight against crime, the abolition of the right of silence is of little use.[154]

THE CRIMINAL JUSTICE AND PUBLIC ORDER ACT

On 3 November 1994 the Criminal Justice and Public Order Bill became law.[155] The Act abolishes the right of silence in England and Wales for anyone accused of any criminal offence. It increases the powers of the police in a variety of situations, reduces the rights of defendants and it creates a number of new criminal offences.

The Act confers stop and detention powers on the police in Britain which are similar to those the police and army currently possess under the Northern Ireland (Emergency Provisions) Act 1991. Under Section 81 of the Act, a police officer of Commander rank can authorise the stopping and searching of people in a particular location for a period of up to 28 days, 'where it appears' to him or her 'that it is expedient to do so in order to prevent acts of terrorism.' This became law after the Republicans and Loyalists had both declared their ceasefires. The police can also stop any vehicle and search it, as well as its driver and passengers, and stop and search any pedestrian for 'articles of a kind which could be used for a purpose connected with the commission, preparation or instigation of acts of terrorism.'[156] The Act specifies that 'A constable may, in the exercise of those powers, stop any vehicle or person and make any search he thinks fit whether or not he has any grounds for suspecting that the vehicle or person is carrying articles of that kind.'[157] The Act makes it a criminal offence to refuse to co-operate with a stop and search.

Once an operation has been authorised, the police do not need to have any suspicion, reasonable or otherwise, that the person that they are stopping has any involvement with terrorist activity or is guilty of any specific crime. There is no objective test of a just cause for the detention. Instead, if it 'appears' to a police commander 'that it is expedient to do so', all police officers in a given area will be given the power to stop and search people, on the grounds that they are 'preventing terrorism'.

Before the enactment of the Criminal Justice and Public Order Bill, the City of London police had established road blocks around the City of London, in July 1993, and were carrying out random checks on motorists. They claimed to be acting under powers contained within the Road Traffic Act,[158] but Liberty believes they were in fact exceeding their powers. Liberty received complaints from people who objected to being stopped, and has gathered anecdotal evidence that some people were arrested for technical motoring offences and that black people were frequently being detained.[159] In response to a complaint from a member of the public, the Acting Commander of the City of London wrote:

> I note your comments about black people being stopped. Many members of the public who are stopped may not necessarily fit the current profile of a terrorist, however, terrorist tactics are constantly changing and we must be alert to all possibilities.[160]

In November 1994 the police issued statistics for the number of vehicles stopped for which details are recorded (which is significantly fewer than the total number of vehicles stopped).[161] The figures show that the overall number of stops has fallen, but the proportion of black people being stopped has risen sharply. Between 1 July 1993 and 31 December 1993, 4,595 drivers had their details recorded, of whom 82 were black: 1.7 per cent of the total. Between 1 January 1994 and 31 July 1994, 3,949 drivers had their details recorded, of whom 254 were black: 6.4 per cent of the total. Between 1 August 1994 and 31 October 1994, 1,446 drivers had their details recorded, of whom 159 were black: 10.8 per cent of the total.[162] These figures illustrate how intended 'anti-terrorist' measures erode civil rights, and can disproportionately affect particular groups in society.

Section 82 of the Act creates two new offences. A person is guilty of an offence if he or she is in possession of an article 'in circumstances giving rise to a reasonable suspicion' that it is intended 'for a purpose connected with the commission, instigation or preparation of acts of terrorism.'[163] A person is also guilty of an offence if he or she is found to be collecting or possessing, without authorisation, 'any information which is of such a nature that it is likely to be useful to terrorists.'[164] Both of these offences carry a maximum sentence of ten years. There is no requirement that the person who has material intends to use it for terrorist purposes. This new offence is likely to be of particular concern to campaigners, journalists and other researchers, who might in certain circumstances have to prove that information they were collecting *could not* be of use to terrorists. This would be a formidable legal challenge.

THE SECRET SERVICES AND ACCOUNTABILITY

The Northern Ireland ceasefire provides an opportunity for reviewing the role and accountability of the UK's Secret Services. With the end of the Cold War and in the absence of a conflict in Northern Ireland, the Security Services might extend their remit into ordinary criminal investigations without being subject to adequate democratic scrutiny and control.[165]

During 1994, Stella Rimmington, head of the internal Security Service MI5, conducted a public lobbying campaign to gain support for extension of the organisation's role. In an annual lecture in June 1994 she set out her view of the organisation's future after the Cold War and the 'dramatic' diminishing of the 'threat of subversion'. In the past, Rimmington said, MI5's principal task had been to counter the espionage of the Soviet Union and its allies. MI5 had also 'set out to identify all the members of these subversive groups (Trotskyists and Communists) and to investigate their activities.'[166] But now, she said, less than 5 per cent of the organisation's time is spent on monitoring political subversion. MI5's most important task, which takes up nearly half its resources, is now 'mounting intelligence operations to counter the threat from Irish terrorism.'[167]

The second largest area of MI5 operations, international terrorism, accounts for 26 per cent of its work and has been mostly concerned with the Middle East. She said that 'the threat to British interests from terrorism of international origin is lower than it was in the 1980s' but believed it remained a significant threat, singling out 'extremists from North Africa and also Kurdish groups' as posing an increasing threat.[168] This could signal the start of operations by the Secret Services against some ethnic minorities, particularly the Kurdish community which has been targeted for special surveillance.[169] The lack of accountability in the way MI5 operates, and its track record in combating Irish terrorism, are serious causes for concern.

In November 1994, following the ceasefire by the IRA and Loyalist paramilitaries, Rimmington said, in a speech to a police-officers' conference, that MI5 would be taking an increasingly active part in criminal prosecutions. She said that she saw no reason for any overall reduction in its activities. She said that MI5's 'distinctive role' was:

the way that we use secret sources and techniques to find out what those who we are investigating are at pains to conceal . . . [T]he immediacy of the terrorist threat in recent years has focused attention on the potential for integrating secret intelligence into the judicial process . . . The question now arises about what role the Security Service should play in the prosecution of such crimes.[170]

Stella Rimmington also admitted that: 'It is almost inevitable that national security intelligence work, which is based on the use of covert sources and techniques will involve some infringement of the civil liberties of those who are under investigation.'[171] In 1992 MI5 was given primary responsibility for Northern Ireland counter-terrorism within Britain which had previously been the preserve of the Special Branch.[172]

MI5 did have notable successes between 1992 and 1994 but some of their techniques were controversial. In the first case that came to trial in which MI5 had been involved, it was revealed that MI5 operatives had set up and largely financed a bogus terrorist operation.[173] Inert explosives had been placed in a quarry in Somerset by an MI5 operative after he had been approached by the Irish National Liberation Army (INLA), two of whose members were subsequently arrested attempting to break into the quarry in order to steal the explosives. The cars, a safe house and metal-cutting equipment used in the operation were all supplied by MI5. In another trial it was alleged that MI5 operatives had allowed bombs to go off in London and the bombers to escape back to Ireland although they were constantly under surveillance during the time they were in Britain.[174]

The trials were marked by the appearance of MI5 agents in court as anonymous witnesses and the use of Public Interest Immunity (PII) certificates (certificates that the Home Secretary signs, advising the trial judge that certain information is too sensitive to be disclosed to the defence). Liberty believes that, despite the safeguards that exist, the use of secret intelligence and anonymous witnesses during criminal trials infringes the right of defendants to a fair and public hearing. The use of PII certificates, in all trials in which MI5 are involved, is a particular concern.

In August 1994 the Court of Appeal upheld the right of defendants to see and know the identity of their accusers, including witnesses for the prosecution.[175] However, the court ruled that this right could be set aside in exceptional circumstances at the judge's discretion.[176] This could pave the way for increasing involvement by secret agents in criminal prosecutions, leading to an increased number of criminal trials with agents giving evidence from behind screens. In December 1994 MI5 officers gave evidence at another trial involving suspected IRA members. They were completely obscured from the press and public gallery by screens, brown paper and masking tape. [177]

MI5 is barred from disclosing to anyone any of the material or intelligence that it has gathered on individuals. The Security Services Act 1989, which placed MI5 under statutory control, permitted one exception to this ban. It specified:

> that there are arrangements for securing that no information is obtained by the Service except so far as necessary for the proper discharge of its functions or disclosed by it except so far as necessary for that purpose or for the purpose of detecting serious crime.[178]

The Intelligence Services Act 1994 extended this and enabled disclosure 'for the purpose of any criminal proceedings.'[179] This signalled MI5's increased willingness to involve itself in criminal prosecutions, including allowing its operatives to appear as prosecution witnesses. In October 1994 it was reported that MI5 had taken control of all investigations into computer hacking and computer abuse in Whitehall.[180] This action, taken without reference to Parliament, gives the Secret Service formal access to all Whitehall computers, including the Police National Computer (PNC) and personal information about millions of people.

In her November 1994 lecture Rimmington also said that the relationship between MI5 and Special Branch was 'closer than ever', and she referred to guidelines published by the Home Office in the same week on relations between the two organisations. These specified that the Special Branch had a duty to gather 'accurate assessments of the public order implications of events such as demonstrations' and suggested that the force should monitor the activities of people who might cause violence at such events.[181] The Special Branch is sometimes described as 'the eyes and ears of MI5'.[182] The two forces perform similar functions although, unlike MI5 operatives, Special Branch officers have powers of arrest.

The Special Branch operates with minimal accountability or public scrutiny. MI5 and the Special Branch have their own liaison officers in different parts of the country and it is normal practice for these to deal directly with each other and to bypass the local chief constable.[183] A Special Branch commander has told a Home Affairs Select Committee that he 'did not think it in the public interest' to reveal how many files they kept on people[184] but it is estimated that between them MI5 and the Special Branch hold about three million personal records on computer.[185] A former police Chief Constable, John Alderson, has said that about half the files retained by the Special Branch in his area should not have been held.[186] Considerable concern has been expressed about people being labelled as 'subversive' and continuing to have their movements monitored simply because they took part in a perfectly legitimate protest 10 years previously.[187]

In the context of the Northern Ireland conflict it is understandable why the authorities keep many operational details confidential, although the government's refusal to divulge even how many Special Branch officers there are in Northern Ireland seems difficult to justify.[188] However, the use of an internal secret police force to enforce ordinary criminal law raises a number of civil liberty concerns.

The scrutiny and democratic accountability of the Secret Services in particular are totally inadequate and its agents are not subject to statutory rules of conduct and evidence. The existence of MI5 was not even officially acknowledged until 1989 when the Security Service Act placed it on a statutory footing. Stella Rimmington is the first head of the organisation to appear in public and it was not until July 1993 that the service published a booklet setting out its structure.[189]

The Security Services are not accountable to Parliament or to the public. There is a Commissioner who reviews their operations but parts of his reports are never made public.[190] A tribunal to deal with individual complaints has never upheld a single one and can never give reasons about its decisions or reveal anything to the complainant about the case.[191] The Intelligence Services Act 1994 created, for the first time, a parliamentary committee with limited scrutiny powers over the operation of MI5, MI6 and GCHQ. However, it cannot examine operations, it can be denied access to 'sensitive' material, and it reports to the Prime Minister rather than to Parliament. Its members are also appointed and can be dismissed by the Prime Minister.[192]

The Northern Ireland ceasefire provides an opportunity for

scaling down this unaccountable security work. However, there is a danger that these practices will simply be extended into the criminal justice system or used against legitimate political protesters.

CONSTITUTIONAL ISSUES

The fundamental cause of the Northern Ireland conflict has been the conflicting views of its inhabitants about the territory's constitutional status. Liberty does not take a view on Northern Ireland's long-term constitutional status. However, we do believe that discussion about how the territory is governed should be informed by a human rights perspective and that there are important lessons from Northern Ireland's experiences about the protection of human rights.

From a negative point of view, Northern Ireland's experiences show the failure of the existing British constitutional arrangements to protect fundamental human rights and freedoms. Since its inception, Northern Ireland has failed to uphold the rights of all its population to equal treatment before the law. Emergency laws and practices have violated international human rights standards. There has been widespread social, economic, cultural and political discrimination against Northern Ireland's minority Catholic community.[193]

Between 1922 and 1972 Northern Ireland was governed by a devolved Parliament at Stormont,[194] although ultimate sovereignty remained with the Crown in Parliament at Westminster. Certain subjects were reserved for the UK, including treaties and foreign relations, the armed forces and defence, nationality, postal services, customs and excise and income tax.[195] It has been argued that Northern Ireland's experience of devolved government sharply illustrated the limitations of the Westminster model of government. The system was characterised by majoritarianism – that is, the mistreatment of the minority (Catholic in this case) by the (Protestant) majority – which was facilitated by a strong executive unchecked by safeguards for minority rights.[196]

Since 1972, the Secretary of State for Northern Ireland, who sits in the British Cabinet is, like the Welsh and Scottish Secretaries, not accountable to the people he or she governs. The Secretary of State has direction and control of virtually all the powers of decision-making relating to Northern Ireland. Most laws made for Northern Ireland take the form of Orders in Council. These are introduced by the Secretary of State, as a type of what is known as 'delegated legislation'. They must be accepted or rejected in their entirety because they cannot be amended by Parliament.[197] And many powers, which are the responsibility of local authorities in the rest of the United Kingdom, are vested in unelected quangos in Northern Ireland. Northern Ireland has 161 appointed executive quangos and concern has been expressed at their lack of openness and their varying degrees of accountability.[198]

In 1985 the Hillsborough Agreement granted the Irish government a consultative role in running the affairs of Northern Ireland. This has provided a mechanism for airing the grievances of the minority community as well as providing institutional recognition of the constitutional aspirations of the minority community in Northern Ireland. In December 1993 the British and Irish governments agreed a declaration which stated that:

> It is for the people of Ireland alone, by agreement between the two parts respectively, to exercise their right to self-determination on the basis of consent, freely and concurrently given, North and South, to bring about a united Ireland, if that is their wish ... It would be wrong to attempt to impose a united Ireland, in the absence of the freely given consent of a majority of the people of Northern Ireland. ... the democratic right of self-determination by the people of Ireland as a whole must be exercised with and subject to the agreement and consent of a majority of people of Northern Ireland.[199]

Following the IRA and Loyalist ceasefires the governments and political parties are seeking agreement on new proposals within the next two years which will then be put to a referendum. The framework document published by the UK and Irish governments proposes:

- ☐ a devolved assembly for Northern Ireland, elected by proportional representation

- ☐ a new North/South body of elected representatives of the Northern Ireland assembly and the Irish Parliament

- ☐ a parliamentary forum of representatives of the Northern Ireland assembly and the Irish Parliament to hold wider discussions

☐   amendments to the British and Irish constitutional claims over Northern Ireland to incorporate the principle that any change in its constitutional status can only come about with the consent of its people increased co-operation between the British and Irish governments through the inter-governmental conference established by the Hillsborough Accord

☐   guarantees by both governments to protect the civil, political, social and economic rights of the people of Northern Ireland.[200]

These proposals are likely to be the subject of lengthy discussions and will eventually be put to the people of Ireland in two separate referenda, both of which will require majority support.

Northern Ireland can also offer some positive lessons in rights for British society. One legacy of the civil rights movement is that there is a highly developed rights culture in Northern Ireland.[201] All the political parties in Northern Ireland support the introduction of a Bill of Rights and most believe that merely incorporating the ECHR into domestic law would not itself provide adequate protection.[202] Northern Ireland also contains bodies such as the Standing Advisory Committee on Human Rights[203] and the Fair Employment Commission which could act as potential models for a new Human Rights Commission in Britain with enhanced powers to promote human rights. Increased co-operation between the British and Irish governments and the possible creation of new institutions covering the whole of Ireland may also mean that an all Ireland human rights organisation will be needed, to scrutinise their activities.

CONCLUSION

The history of Britain's involvement in Ireland shows that temporary measures have become entrenched, exceptional powers have been normalised and laws and institutions originally introduced to deal with Irish insurgencies have subsequently found wider applications.

The British government's record before the European Court of Human Rights shows that many of the measures introduced in relation to Northern Ireland would probably have breached a British Bill of Rights had there been one. One lesson from the conflict is that the doctrine of parliamentary sovereignty has failed to protect human rights during crises. Any new settlement must respect the differing aspirations of the peoples on the island of Ireland and have at its heart the protection of legally enforceable rights against government abuse.

On 9 December 1994, the following organisations adopted a *Declaration on Human Rights, the Northern Ireland Conflict, and the Peace Process*: the Committee on the Administration of Justice, Irish Council for Civil Liberties, Liberty, Scottish Council for Civil Liberties and British Irish Human Rights Watch. The text of this declaration is as follows.

Declaration on human rights, the Northern Ireland conflict, and the peace process

Firm and effective legal protection of human rights and civil liberties, and the creation of a culture in which everyone's human rights are respected, are crucial if the peace process is to succeed.

For too long human rights abuses have been regarded as normal in Northern Ireland and increasingly in the neighbouring jurisdictions as well. The failure of the legal and political systems to address such abuses has left its mark on the conflict, creating a climate of abuse, oppression and fear. At this historic moment, there is a unique opportunity to put in place new structures which will defend and promote human rights.

The effects of the conflict have not been confined to Northern Ireland but have also led to the introduction of draconian legislation and practices in the Republic of Ireland, England, Scotland and Wales. In order to dismantle oppressive laws and practices, the following minimum changes are urgently required in all these jurisdictions:

☐ emergency legislation must be repealed

☐ special courts must be abolished

☐ the right to silence must be restored

☐ political censorship must be ended for good and the legislation which allowed it repealed

☐ all forms of discrimination must end and comprehensive anti-discrimination legislation must be introduced

☐ military personnel should play no further part in policing and all forms of covert operations must be ended

☐ Castlereagh and other holding centres for persons detained under emergency legislation must be closed and extended detention periods ended

☐ an urgent review must be conducted in partnership with local communities into all security barriers and surveillance installations

☐ there must be a planned review of the sentences of all those imprisoned under emergency legislation.

All those involved in negotiating a new political framework for Northern Ireland must recognise the central role of human rights and civil liberties if there is to be a just and lasting peace in the longer term. New systems of justice are required which will address the injustices of the past and ensure rights for the future.

In particular:

☐ A broadly based and fully representative Commission on Policing must be instituted to examine the nature, structure and methods of policing in Northern Ireland with a view to producing a model of policing which is representative of and has the confidence of all sections of the community and which is impartial, just and fully accountable.

☐ A fully independent system for investigating complaints against the police must be established.

☐ A Bill of Rights must be enacted which protects the rights and liberties of everyone.

☐ The criminal justice system in Northern Ireland should be thoroughly and independently reviewed and, where necessary, changed.

☐ An independent Commission of Investigation must be instituted in order to investigate human rights abuses arising from the emergency legislation.

☐ Human rights education and awareness must become an integral part of every school curriculum and training programme.

Respect for human rights and civil liberties must be made an integral part of any political settlement and the political process must include all the communities in Northern Ireland. Everyone there is entitled to be engaged and involved in the peace process and to have his or her rights guaranteed as part of any new political settlement.

Just as the conflict in Northern Ireland has led to emergency laws and assaults on democratic rights and freedoms in all the jurisdictions in these islands, so the opportunity must now be taken not just to dismantle this apparatus of repression, but to put in place safeguards which will prevent any similar erosion of human rights and civil liberties in any of these jurisdictions in the future. To that end, we will work to ensure the adherence of the two governments to all relevant international human rights conventions and standards.

Human rights belong to everyone, being universal and inalienable. Our societies, our legal systems, and our political processes should affirm and guarantee that guiding principle.

5 WOMEN'S RIGHTS, HUMAN RIGHTS

THE BRITISH GOVERNMENT'S RECORD

In its *Third Periodic Report to the UN Human Rights Committee*, the British government stated that sex discrimination is outlawed in employment, education and training, the provision of goods, facilities and services, and in the disposal of and management of premises.[1] It stated that legislation is supported by extensive enforcement provisions, through the work of the Equal Opportunities Commission (EOC), and that anyone who felt they had been the victim of unlawful discrimination in these areas had direct access to the courts or to an industrial tribunal. The report also noted that the government had amended its immigration legislation after provisions about marriage partners were found to be discriminatory by the European Court of Human Rights.[2]

In its *Fourth Periodic Report* the government stated that the EOC received 302 requests for legal assistance in Britain in 1993 of which 199 were granted and which resulted in 39 cases being heard in that year.[3] Of these, 14 cases were settled on terms, 12 were successful after a tribunal or court hearing and 13 were dismissed after a hearing.[4] Following a ruling by the European Court of Justice in the case of *Marshall* v. *Southampton and South West Hampshire Health Authority,* the government has removed the ceiling of £11,000 compensation which can be awarded by tribunals in cases of sex discrimination with the passage of the Equal Pay (Remedies) Regulations 1993.[5] The case of *Porcelli* v. *Strathclyde Regional Council* established that sexual harassment can, in certain circumstances, amount to sex discrimination and the government has taken steps to protect the anonymity of complainants.[6]

The Trade Union Reform and Employment Rights Act 1993 extends the maternity rights of pregnant workers.[7] In November

1991 the government agreed to a European Council Declaration on the protection of the dignity of women and men at work and in March 1992 the government issued a guidance booklet on sexual harassment which has been widely distributed.[8] In May 1992 a cabinet minister was given responsibility for women's issues and a Women's Issues Working Group was established as a Cabinet sub-committee to review and develop policy on women's rights and oversee its implementation.[9]

The British government ratified the UN Convention on the Elimination of all forms of Discrimination Against Women (CEDAW) in 1986. The second of its reports was considered by CEDAW between May 1991 and January 1993.[10] However, it maintains a number of reservations, including one to Article 2, which outlines the fundamental obligation on governments to remove discrimination against women.

In March 1991 the government and a number of leading business people launched Opportunity 2000, a campaign which aimed to 'increase the quality and quantity of women's participation in the workforce.'[11] Within two years it had won the endorsement of 200 organisations representing 6 million workers – one-quarter of the waged workforce. It claims to have made progress in the areas of flexible working and family-friendly policies but has been hampered by the recession and management resistance.[12]

DISCRIMINATION AGAINST WOMEN IN PUBLIC LIFE

Women in public office

Women in Britain hold fewer positions in public life than in most other member states of the European Union.[13] Women constitute only 9.2 per cent of the total number of members in the House of Commons,[14] 6 per cent of the House of Lords and 8 per cent of senior civil servants.[15] There has been one female Prime Minister or leader of a major political party in British history and 34 women have reached ministerial level in the last 50 years.[16] It is estimated that, in 1994, 22 per cent of councillors on local authorities were women and of the 40 councils affiliated to the National Association of Local Government Women's Committees three had female council leaders.[17]

Women are directly discriminated against in entering the House of Lords by the rule of primogeniture, which means that titles usually pass to male heirs. The same rule applies to succession to the throne.[18] Only 16 per cent of life peers are women because they are under-represented amongst the social groups from which such peers are appointed.[19] Women are under-represented in the senior ranks of the judiciary, academia, private industry, the trade union movement and the other areas from where such appointments tend to be made.[20]

In the 1992 general election, 318 women stood as candidates for the three main parties and 60 were elected because most had been selected to fight seats considered unwinnable.[21] In addition, out of six black MPs in total, there is only one black woman.[22] Women MPs often complain that the atmosphere in the House of Commons resembles that of an all-male club.[23] Childcare facilities are minimal and the anachronistic hours that MPs in the House are forced to work indirectly discriminates against women and men with childcare responsibilities.

Women in the media

Women are under-represented in all aspects of broadcasting: as employees, as members of decision-making bodies and as figures portrayed on screen and on air. Although the Broadcasting Act 1990[24] included an equal opportunities provision, its effects have been limited. Equal opportunities officers are now in place, but none of these officers is appointed at senior level and they are all under-resourced.[25] Within the British Broadcasting Corporation (BBC) only 12 per cent of senior executives and 24 per cent of senior producers and middle managers are women.[26]

Sexism in the police force

The police service is an overwhelmingly male-dominated institution with women comprising 12 per cent of the service.[27] Women are over-represented in posts such as community relations and juvenile liaison and seriously under-represented in the CID, traffic and training.[28] In March 1993 it was reported that the police in Derbyshire had admitted operating a 'quota system' to restrict the appointment of policewomen to the CID, while a study issued at the same time by the Inspectorate of Constabulary revealed that breaches of equal opportunities are often 'instigated or defended' by chief officers.[29] In February 1993 the findings of a leaked Home

Office study showed that 80 per cent of policewomen had experienced sexual harassment from their colleagues, ranging from assaults to sexually explicit comments to the display of hard core pornography in police stations.[30]

In May 1990 Assistant Chief Superintendent, Alison Halford, the most senior female police officer in the country, took Merseyside police force to an industrial tribunal claiming that she had been discriminated against in being barred from promotion on nine occasions.[31] The case was eventually settled by an out of court payment after considerable controversy and claims that Halford had been the victim of a smear campaign within the force.[32]

DISCRIMINATION AGAINST WOMEN IN EMPLOYMENT

Sex discrimination law and employment

The Sex Discrimination Act 1975 provides protection from direct and indirect discrimination on the basis of sex[33] or marital status[34] in employment, training, education, in the provision of goods and services and in the disposal and management of premises. It also protects against the victimisation of employees who bring complaints, or give evidence, under the Act's provisions.[35] It covers discrimination by trade unions and employment agencies, and, following pressure from the European Courts, it has been widened to cover any aspect of a collective agreement which is discriminatory.[36]

An employer is defined as discriminating directly against a woman employee if she is treated 'less favourably' than a man and as discriminating indirectly where a 'requirement or condition' is in operation which, although it applies equally to men and women, has a disproportionate effect and a detrimental impact on one gender.[37] A complainant does not need to prove that the employer intended to discriminate, only that this was the outcome.[38]

Those excluded from the Act include people providing a personal service in private households, those working in situations where privacy and decency require a specified gender and those working in single-sex institutions.[39] It does not cover situations where an employer can show that there is a 'genuine occupational qualification' for hiring an employee of a particular sex.[40]

The EOC was established by the Act to work towards the elimination of discrimination and to promote equality of opportunity between men and women. The EOC consists of 12 government-appointed Commissioners and performs similar functions to the Commission for Racial Equality (CRE),[41] commissioning research, issuing codes of practice and investigating organisations that may be practising discrimination. It can also provide legal and financial assistance to individuals making complaints.

However, the EOC may only investigate an organisation if it has reason to believe that the law is being broken. Although it can promote good practice, it cannot directly intervene without first issuing a non-discrimination order.[42] The EOC's budget, £5.7 million a year, is about one-third of the CRE's.[43] There is also concern at the secrecy which surrounds the appointment of EOC Commissioners by the government.[44]

The Sex Discrimination Act 1975 was introduced to reinforce the provisions of the Equal Pay Act 1970 which prohibited pay discrimination on the basis of gender. This said that a woman could claim equal pay for the 'same or broadly similar work'[45] as a man, or for work which has been 'rated as being equal'[46] by a job evaluation scheme.

However, the Equal Pay Act did not come into force for five years, and this gap gave some employers the opportunity to minimise its effects by changing the content of men's and women's jobs and so avoid like-work comparisons.[47] Grading systems were restructured so that women stayed at the bottom of the new mixed-sex grades, regardless of their skill, as job evaluation factors were altered to give more weight to skills usually acquired by men. Despite these two pieces of legislation there is evidence that sex segregation in employment increased in some respects in the late 1970s and early 1980s.[48]

Following the introduction of the Equal Pay Act, women's pay rose relative to men's from 63.1 per cent in 1970 to 75.5 per cent in 1977, although it has been claimed that this was more a result of the incomes restraint policy of the government of the time which curbed men's pay more than women's.[49] However, for most of the 1980s the gap between male and female earnings remained constant. It has narrowed slightly in the 1990s, from 76.5 per cent in 1990 to 78.8 per cent in 1992, but this period also coincided with a recession and a fall in the real value of many people's wages.[50]

The Equal Pay Act also gives a woman the right to go to a

tribunal to enforce equal pay for work of equal value. However, an equal value claim can be defended if a job evaluation scheme has rated two jobs as not equivalent[51] and employers often implement such schemes when they are faced with a claim. Disputes about the objectivity and impartiality of job evaluations have been the subject of a number of legal challenges in the UK[52] and at the European Union's Court of Justice.[53] Both the EOC and the European Commission have commented on the need for clarification of the important factors, and their relative weight, and the need for more training for tribunal members.[54]

Because the nature of discrimination makes it very difficult to prove, the EOC has recommended that the burden of proof should be shifted from the applicant to the employer.[55] The EOC has also argued that, in order to comply properly with European directives and court judgments, the government should make effective collective remedies for sex discrimination.[56]

In 1982 the European Community's Court of Justice ruled that the British government was in breach of the EC Equal Pay Directive[57] and this ruling forced the government to amend the Equal Pay Act. It did so by introducing subordinate legislation which could only be approved or rejected by parliament, not amended. The new measures were criticised in parliament for being 'complex and badly written', 'legal gobbledegook', 'an algebraic mystery', 'a waste of time' and were said to have been drafted with the sole object of deterring 'the maximum number of applications from those seeking remedy and to provide the greatest possible resistance to those who persist.'[58]

In more than ten years since the 'equal pay for work of equal value' legislation was introduced, there have only been 23 successful cases, some of which took more than six years to complete.[59] The most significant are still proceeding after seven years and are expected to last several more.[60] The EOC has described the process as tortuous, time-consuming and unworkable,[61] while in 1990 the President of an Employment Appeals Tribunal described them as 'scandalous' and amounting to 'a denial of justice'.[62]

Cases can cost applicants up to £50,000 and Legal Aid is not available to those making claims, despite the complexity of the process and the limited financial assistance available from the EOC.[63] The EOC has said that delays of this magnitude are probably in breach of Article 6 of the ECHR, which guarantees effective access to civil courts and a fair hearing within a reasonable time period. These provisions are echoed in Article 14 of the ICCPR. The EOC has proposed various amendments to Britain's equal value legislation and has challenged the government, unsuccessfully, over its refusal to introduce them. In July 1993 the British government formally rejected the EOC's main proposals for amending the legislation[64] and the EOC requested the European Commission to commence legal proceedings against the government.[65]

Women in the workforce

There were about 12 million women in the waged labour market in Britain in the summer of 1993.[66] Women constitute 45 per cent of people in waged employment[67] and the number of women in the workforce is steadily rising.[68] However, the British workforce is conspicuously segregated by gender.

Despite laws prohibiting discrimination in employment and pay, there is a substantial gap in average gross hourly earnings between men and women. For every £1 that an average man earned per hour in 1992 the average woman in manual employment earned 71.5p and the average woman in non-manual employment earned 63.4p.[69] Britain has the highest earnings gap between men and women of all the major countries in the European Union.[70] Almost half the female workforce work part-time[71] – with lower pay and fewer rights and benefits – and this percentage is growing.[72]

There are only two women employed at management level in the top 40 quangos with the largest budgets.[73] Only 2.3 per cent of the 1,300 directors of companies quoted in the FT-SE 100 index and 7 per cent of the membership of the Institute of Directors are women.[74] By contrast, 70 per cent of clerks, 77 per cent of workers in the catering and related service industries, 81 per cent of cleaners, 98 per cent of secretaries and typists and 76 per cent of clerical assistants in the civil service are women.[75] Segregation also occurs within other sectors of the economy. In the National Health Service, for example, women make up 80 per cent of the total number of employees but only 17 per cent of unit general managers, 4 per cent of district and regional general managers and 1 per cent of consultant general surgeons.[76]

Merit pay

Merit pay schemes that link pay or promotion prospects to subjective judgments by supervisors or managers run the risk of directly discriminating against women.[77] A 1992 report by the Institute of Manpower Studies, on the effect of performance evaluation on women's earnings and opportunities, found that managers, who are mainly male, valued different attributes in men than in women and this often reinforced gender stereotypes.[78] It also showed that proportionately more women underestimate their own skills and therefore are more likely than men to lose out in merit pay systems. The report found evidence that some women received lower pay increases than men even when performance ratings were equal, and that they were less likely to be offered promotion and training opportunities.[79]

Merit pay schemes may also discriminate indirectly if the awards are limited to sections of the workforce – such as full-time employees – where women are under-represented, or if they are only available after an extended period of work for one employer which women are less likely to have served.[80] In addition, the appraisal and merit pay procedures usually do not include a right of appeal.[81]

Training

Women are given fewer opportunities for employment training than men and are offered narrower choices. One in four male employees aged between 16-19 receives job-related training compared with one in five women.[82] Despite a theoretical commitment to equal opportunities in training, through the Training and Enterprise Councils (TECs), a survey of unemployed women training to return to work showed that fewer than four out of 100 trainees on government-funded programmes run by TECs received help with childcare costs.[83] A formal investigation by the EOC, carried out between November 1991 and January 1993, found that many TECs had abandoned training programmes for women who wish to return to work after having children and that the vast majority of TECs 'were either unwilling or unable' to provide information on the gender make-up of course participants.[84]

Women are ineligible for many other training courses because they are not classified as long-term unemployed. The EOC has also expressed concern that the composition of the TECs is unrepresentative because two-thirds of TEC Directors are from the private sector, where women are even further under-represented.[85]

Older women and pensions

There are seven million women in Britain aged over 60, the official retirement age.[86] Only 17 per cent retire on a full basic State pension and the average retirement income for women is much lower than for men.[87] Men's average occupational pension is £61 per week compared with £30 per week for women.[88] More than half of all pensioners live on or near the poverty level, but, on average, older women are poorer than older men.[89]

Because women earn less than men, their occupational pension schemes are reduced and therefore their reliance on the State pension is greater. Before 1978 women did not have the automatic right to join occupational pension schemes. Even now, part-time workers (disproportionately female), are still denied the right to join some schemes.[90] Women are sometimes required to make greater contributions than men for the same pension on the basis that they are likely to live longer.

Occupational pensions, including the State Earnings Related Pension, tend to be based on traditional working patterns of continuous employment for approximately 40 years. These make no provision for the fact that many women take career breaks, or work part-time in order to care for children and sick or elderly relatives, nor that some women interrupt their careers because their husband moves to work elsewhere. It has been argued that women would benefit if pensions were based instead on a person's best 20 years' earnings.[91] Women can claim Home Responsibilities Protection against their National Insurance contributions for years spent at home caring for children or dependants, but only if they make a complete break from work. Women who work part-time lose this protection.[92]

Sexual harassment in the workplace

A 1993 survey by the Labour Research Department showed that one in three women had experienced sexual harassment at work although less than half had reported it.[93] Another survey by the Industrial Society showed that 54 per cent of women suffer workplace harassment while about half of all employers receive complaints of sexual harassment each year.[94] It is widely reported that sexual harassment can have an extremely damaging emotional effect and can lead to women losing their jobs or being dismissed for absenteeism.[95]

Although the British government has issued guidelines on the subject, in line with an EC recommendation,[96] it considers existing law adequate for tackling the problem. However, it has encouraged employers to combat sexual harassment at work and to be pro-active in creating a harassment-free working environment.[97] The rising number of cases being reported to the EOC, from 150 in 1988 to over 400 in 1991, may reflect a greater willingness of employees to report such a problem.

Indirect discrimination against women in employment

Part-time workers

Eighty-seven per cent of Britain's 5.5 million part-time workers are women.[98] Almost 50 per cent of women employees work part-time, compared with only 6 per cent of working men. Part-time workers have fewer rights than their full-time counterparts because the majority of statutory employment rights are dependent on an individual's length of service and hours of work. The majority of women part-timers are married and work part-time so that they can look after dependants. Almost all male part-timers are over 60 years old.[99] About 90 per cent of part-time employment is in the service sector which tends to be low paid, low skilled and low status.[100] Women working part-time earn 59 per cent of the average hourly earnings of men working full-time,[101] while 80 per cent of women part-time workers earn wages below the Council of Europe's decency threshold.[102]

In March 1994 the House of Lords ruled that employees who worked for less than 16 but more than eight hours a week should be entitled to protection from unfair dismissal, to pro-rata redundancy pay and to notice of dismissal.[103] The Lords ruled that the previous measures, that part-time workers were not entitled to these rights until they had been in employment for five years continuously, constituted a form of indirect discrimination against women.

This decision rested on an interpretation of the jurisdiction of European Union law. The case, taken by the EOC, could open the door for further challenges to government policies in British courts.[104] The ruling is likely to affect about 640,000 workers who work between eight and 16 hours a week and who will now only have to work for two years in continuous employment before qualifying.[105]

The most important pressure to improve the rights of part-time workers in recent years has come from cases in the European Court of Justice. These have established the rights of part-time workers to equal access to pension schemes,[106] the right to equal sick pay benefits,[107] the right to equal severance payments[108] and the right to pay increases for seniority.

The government has reluctantly and minimally agreed to the adoption of new European Community directives. The Trade Union Reform and Employment Rights Act 1993 entitles part-time employees to receive a written statement of the main terms and conditions of employment.[109] Their maternity rights have also been improved.[110] However, the Act only extends the right to a statement to those who are employed for eight hours or more a week, thus excluding 700,000 employees – most of them women.[111]

Low pay

The Trade Union Reform and Employment Rights Act 1993 has curbed trade union rights and abolished the Wages Councils[112] which had previously fixed statutory minimum wages for Britain's two million lowest paid workers. This will have a disproportionate impact on women, since they constitute about 80 per cent of workers in industries which were previously regulated by Wages Councils.[113] It will also disproportionately affect black workers – male and female – who are also concentrated in these industries. Black and ethnic minority women earn just 77 per cent of white women's pay and work in poorer conditions with fewer fringe benefits.

The British government is obliged by European law to provide 'effective mechanisms' to ensure equal pay. One such mechanism was the Wages Councils system. In all other countries in the European Union the right to equal pay is underpinned by a national minimum wage enforced by a labour inspectorate or by legally binding collective agreements.[114] Britain is now almost alone in the European Union in not providing employees with a minimum wage.[115] Article 3 of the ICCPR also requires 'effective action' from governments to ensure that all individuals enjoy equal protection under the Covenant.[116] While the Equal Pay Act 1970 provides a theoretical remedy for unequal pay, in practice it is not effective.

Britain is a comparatively low waged economy[117] and high levels of male unemployment in recent years have meant that women are often the main or sole wage earners in the family. The government recognises that the abolition of Wages Councils will have an adverse effect on women's pay.[118] However, it attempted to justify the abolition by claiming that 'most workers in Wages Council trades are part-timers, many of them contributing a second income to the home.'[119] In 1992 a minister stated that the end of Wages Councils would mainly affect married or cohabiting women.[120]

This argument is a direct contradiction of the government's professed commitment to equal pay. It is incompatible to pay people strictly according to merit on the one hand, and to maintain a wage structure based on assumptions about 'family need' and second earners on the other. The argument is sexist, discriminatory and based on incorrect assumptions about earnings and spending within the family.[121]

Childcare

Statutory provision for childcare in Britain is minimal and facilities are very poor relative to other European countries.[122] For example, Britain has one of the lowest levels of publicly funded care for children under three years old in the European Union – 2 per cent are provided for, whereas Denmark has places for 50 per cent.[123] Britain's provision of daycare facilities for children from three years to school age is also way behind other EU states, with countries such as France and Belgium providing places for more than twice the number that are provided for in Britain.[124] The impact of inadequate provision compounds the discrimination that women face in employment because they usually have primary responsibility for childcare. It is also estimated that the lack of adequate childcare provision in Britain keeps 500,000 children in poverty because their mothers cannot take paid work.[125]

Maternity and sick leave

The Trade Union Reform and Employment Rights Act 1993 gives all pregnant women the right to 14 weeks' paid maternity leave, to protection against dismissal on grounds of pregnancy or child birth, to demand written reasons for dismissal during the pregnancy or maternity leave, to protection of employment status and other contractual rights, to specific health and safety protection and to suitable alternative employment if made redundant whilst on maternity leave.[126]

The most important element of these measures, which were imposed on the British government by pressure from the European Union, is that they extend rights of maternity leave to part-time workers and those who have not worked continuously for the same employer for a certain period. The present government had previously reduced the numbers of women entitled to maternity leave by extending the necessary qualifying period of continuous employment from six months to a year in 1979, and then to two years in 1985. However, considerable problems remain which the government has not addressed.[127] Most women in Britain take 30 weeks' maternity leave and will receive no maternity pay at all for the 12 weeks of this time, nor protection against the loss of their jobs. The EOC has stated that it considers 14 weeks' leave for maternity much too short, especially as part of this time must necessarily be taken before the birth, meaning that most women will have to return to work when the baby is two to three months old.

There is concern that the Act does not specify what contractual rights are to be protected while women are on maternity leave and it has been suggested that pension and other entitlements may not be included. The recommended level of pay to pregnant women set out in the Act is the minimum amount that complies with the European Union's Pregnancy Directive and is less than 20 per cent of women's average earnings.

Employers are increasingly using sickness as a reason for dismissing employees. Women are statistically more likely to need sickness absence than men, primarily due to the existence of female-specific illnesses such as pre-menstrual tension, period pains, pregnancy-related illnesses and menopausal complaints.[128] In 1992 an industrial tribunal ruled that the dismissal of a woman who had taken time off work to have a hysterectomy constituted sex discrimination.[129]

Overseas domestic workers and slavery

Women domestic workers can face specific exploitation. Several thousand domestic workers in Britain come from overseas.[130] British immigration law does not recognise private domestic servants in their own right and so they have no effective legal protection. Often they enter as the 'chattels' of foreign employers and are forced to stay with that employer for fear of losing their residency rights. They are also forced to live with their employer, which can increase their isolation and vulnerability. There is evidence that many suffer abuse and exploitation, including beatings, imprisonment in the home, degrading treatment and the denial of food, but cannot escape because British immigration laws state that those who leave their employers are liable to deportation.

It was not until 1992 that the government was able to produce any figures on the numbers of women who might be affected in this way.[131] It was acknowledged at the time that 439 'concessionary visas' had been issued over an eight-month period, but Kalayaan, a support organisation working with migrant domestic workers, documented 247 cases of domestic workers who had sought help after fleeing abusive employers during the same period. The Commission for Filipino Migrant Workers has estimated that there are at least 4,500 migrant domestic workers in Britain, the vast majority of whom are women.[132]

The government has revealed that between January 1991 and August 1993, 20,000 entry clearances were issued for resident domestic servants and during this time 234 people were given extensions to stay in the country on the basis that they were employed as domestic servants.[133] The government justifies these practices by claiming that it is necessary to appease potential foreign investors. Speaking during a parliamentary debate, in 1990, Lord Reay claimed:

> If wealthy investors, skilled workers and others with the potential to benefit our economy were unable to be accompanied by their domestic staff they might not come here at all but take their money and skills to other countries.[134]

Although the Home Office also announced new measures to minimise abuse in 1990, these were condemned as inadequate by the Joint Council for the Welfare of Immigrants and by Anti-Slavery International, among others.[135] However, in May 1993 the government announced that it had no plans to carry out a further review of arrangements for foreign domestic workers.[136] Such continued tolerance of abuses of domestic workers by the British government places it in breach of Article 8 of the ICCPR, which outlaws slavery.

DISCRIMINATION AGAINST WOMEN IN EDUCATION, WELFARE AND HEALTH

Education

The education system plays a major role in socialising women into accepting particular roles in later life.[137] Girls' education often contains implicit preparation for domesticity and boys for entry into the labour force.[138] There are roughly the same number of male and female teachers. However, male teachers have higher paid and more senior jobs.[139] For example, although 48 per cent of secondary school teachers are women, they account for 20 per cent of head teachers.[140] Men are more likely to be employed at higher grades than women in primary, secondary and tertiary education.[141]

Welfare and social security

The British government spends a lower proportion of its Gross Domestic Product (GDP) on social protection – social security, pensions, unemployment and housing – than any other state in the European Union apart from Greece, Spain and Portugal[142] and the size of the workforce outside the social insurance net is greater in Britain than in most other European countries.[143] A greater proportion of women than men are affected by the shortcomings of Britain's welfare state because 50 per cent more women are dependent on State benefits than men.[144]

The social security system in the UK also discriminates against women in many of its basic assumptions.[145] For example, in linking entitlements solely to labour market participation, it ignores the unpaid work of women who interrupt their working lives to raise families and care for other dependants. To qualify for unemployment benefit people must prove that they are available for and actively seeking work, a condition which makes many women with children or other dependants ineligible. An analysis of the 1992 Labour Force Survey by the Child Poverty Action Group found that although there are 631,000 women officially unemployed – 23 per cent of the total number of claimants – a modified interpretation of the 'actively seeking work' qualification would mean that 1,464,000 women are really available for and wanting to work.[146]

Health

Women can be subjected to medical procedures which are discriminatory and violate their right to privacy and freedom of conscience. For example, in September 1993 a gynaecologist carried out an abortion on a woman, without her consent, after discovering that she was pregnant while he was doing a hysterectomy operation.[147] When she complained, he claimed that this was 'usual practice' – although he later said that with the benefit of hindsight he might have acted differently.[148] Although the woman concerned is now pursuing a civil action against the doctor, this is unlikely to succeed because the courts rarely challenge a medical decision made in good faith.[149] It is also unlikely that they will find the doctor negligent if 'he has acted in accordance with a practice accepted as proper by a responsible body of medical men [sic] skilled in that particular art.'[150]

In 1992 a court authorised a blood transfusion to a woman recovering from an emergency Caesarean operation even though she had informed her doctors, in writing, that she objected to this on religious grounds.[151] In October 1993 a court ruled that a Caesarean could be performed even if the woman had refused to have one on religious grounds.[152] Family courts reserve the right to override the wishes of teenagers – even when they are old enough to understand and decide their own fates, for example, courts have authorised the force feeding of an anorexic teenager[153] and forced medication on a girl described as 'defiant', although she was not diagnosed as sufficiently mentally ill to warrant a compulsory detention.[154] Courts have also authorised the compulsory 'therapeutic' sterilisations of patients with learning disabilities.[155]

Women are twice as much at risk of infection by Human Immunodeficiency Virus (HIV) through heterosexual intercourse as men.[156] There are far more men than women with Acquired Immune Deficiency Syndrome (AIDS) but during 1992 and 1993 there was a 51 per cent increase of female AIDS cases compared with a 5 per cent increase of reported male cases.[157] However, most research and publicity about the disease has concentrated on how men are at risk from the virus and few drug trials incorporate women with HIV.[158] There has been little research into how women pass the virus to each other or how the virus operates specifically in women.[159] Some women from ethnic minorities have complained about feeling pressurised to allow their children to be used in HIV-related tests, or to take part in tests themselves, so as not to jeopardise their residency in the UK.[160]

There is evidence that female genital mutilation, although illegal in the UK, is carried out secretly in some private clinics, while some young women from ethnic minorities have been sent to their home countries to be mutilated.[161] There has also been some criticism of the medical profession and local authorities for ignoring the issue and failing to provide adequate support to young women, due to the reluctance of medical authorities to interfere in the 'cultural practices' of ethnic minorities.[162]

VIOLENCE AGAINST WOMEN

Violence against women is widespread throughout British society. While both men and women are at risk from violence in public, their perceptions and experiences of such violence often differ.[163] Fear of violence has a pervasive influence on the lives of many women. Studies have shown that one-half of all women feel afraid when they go out alone during the day and up to 92 per cent of women do not feel safe outside at night and restrict their movements accordingly.[164] Another survey showed that one-fifth of women never feel safe anywhere, including in their own homes.[165]

The British government is failing in its duty to provide women with equal protection from violence through the law. It is also failing to promote initiatives which will raise public awareness of violence against women as a crime. In 1993, the Edinburgh District Council launched a campaign entitled Zero Tolerance of All Violence Against Women. It aims to highlight the need for:

☐ public awareness campaigns about violence against women

☐ changes to the criminal justice system and policing to protect women from violence

☐ adequate provision of refuges and places of safety for the victims of such violence.

A similar campaign was launched in London in 1994 by the Association of London Authorities with the support of the Metropolitan Police and a variety of other organisations.[166] These campaigns aim to use posters and publicity to increase awareness of the problem of violence against women. In particular, campaigners have called for greater emphasis on awareness training for people in the police and criminal justice system. Such campaigns have not been matched by the government which is still significantly failing in its duty to provide women with adequate protection.

Rape

The rate of convictions of men accused of rape is significantly lower than the rate for other serious crimes and it appears to be falling while the incidence of reported rape is rising.[167] It is also believed that the proportion of rapes reported is extremely low.[168] In British law, a man commits rape if:

☐ he has unlawful sexual intercourse with a woman who at the time of intercourse does not consent to it

☐ at that time he knows that she does not consent to the intercourse or he is reckless as to whether she consents to it[169]

The Criminal Justice and Public Order Act 1994 widened the scope of this offence to include male rape.[170] The use of the word 'unlawful' in this definition has been successfully used in the defence of men who were accused of raping their wives because, prior to March 1991, rape within marriage was not a crime in England and Wales.[171] Up until that date husbands could only be prosecuted for aiding and abetting rape by allowing other men to rape their wives.[172] The House of Lords has now ruled that, in certain circumstances, rape within marriage should be regarded as a crime. This ruling came from a particular case involving a man who had separated from his wife but broke into her parents' home, where she was staying, and assaulted and attempted to rape her.[173] The government has not incorporated this ruling into statutory law[174] and it seems likely that other cases of men who rape their wives might not lead to prosecution.

The use of common law to widen the scope of a criminal offence breaches Article 15(1) of the ICCPR and a number of men convicted on this basis have made successful complaints to the European Commission on Human Rights, claiming violations of Article 7 of the ECHR.[175] There have been widespread calls for the word 'unlawful' to be removed from the definition of that which constitutes rape.[176]

There has been one prosecution case against a married man who was cohabiting with the woman he was alleged to have raped.[177] In this case the man was acquitted after the judge directed the jury that they should 'not confuse lack of consent with a wife not wanting it, not enjoying it or not feeling like it but letting it happen. Many a wife submits, not through fear of violence, but because that is what she is used to doing.'[178] In March 1994 a man was acquitted at Southwark Crown Court of raping his wife and received a 12-month conditional discharge for assaulting her. A few days later, in their back garden and in front of their children, he beat her to death with a metal tyre wrench. He also knocked unconscious a neighbour who intervened, breaking her nose. Accepting his plea of manslaughter on the grounds of diminished responsibility, rather than murder, Judge Gerald Butler QC said: 'This was a terrible killing. I bear in mind the history of this case, particularly the false allegation of rape made against you.'[179]

The majority of rape cases hinge on the man's subjective understanding of the woman's consent to the act of sexual intercourse. This creates enormous difficulties in proving rape. The distinction between submission (allowing it to happen) and consent (wanting it to happen) is often blurred. Yet without proof of physical resistance, courts remain reluctant to convict. Also, the current definition does not cover cases where consent is obtained through threats of violence to be carried out at some time in the future.

A Home Office study published in 1992 found that one in four incidents of rape reported to the police resulted in a conviction. One-quarter of all cases were eventually 'no-crimed', 10 per cent went undetected, 13 per cent were dropped by the prosecution, and 40 per cent of cases resulted in a conviction of some kind, of which one-quarter were for rape or attempted rape. The key factors influencing the conviction rate appeared to be the relationship between complainant and suspect, the age and marital status of the complainant, the degree of consensual contact between the complainant and suspect, the place of initial contact and the extent of injury suffered by the complainant.[180] The study also found that over two-thirds of the defendants who knew their alleged victims were acquitted of the principal charge. In these cases defences almost always hinged on the defendant's perception of the woman's behaviour.[181] It is here that subjective interpretations of the word 'consent' become crucial.

In rape cases, as in any other criminal trial, the defendant's right to a fair trial necessarily involves the right to bring forward relevant information and to cross-examine witnesses. The law currently allows the defendant's legal representatives, with the judge's permission, to cross-examine the woman about previous sexual experiences and bring this evidence to court.[182] The defendant merely has to satisfy the judge that 'it would be unfair to the defendant to refuse' a request to question the woman about her experience with men other than the defendant.

Judges' interpretations of this section of the law vary considerably and can allow irrelevant and objectionable questions to be put to victims during cross-examination and inappropriate evidence to be brought to court.[183] For example, in November 1993 a court was told that a female student and alleged victim of rape had been voted 'slut of the year' by a group of male students.[184] The comment, widely reported in the media, should not have been allowed as evidence as it had no bearing on the particular circumstances surrounding the alleged offence. The male student accused of rape was acquitted.

Prior to 1994, in all offences of a sexual nature, judges were obliged to warn juries of the dangers of convicting solely on the basis of the victim's testimony and to look for supporting evidence.[185] This is the only type of crime where such warnings are issued, crimes in which the vast majority of victims are women. The 'rape warning' was abolished in the Criminal Justice Public Order Act 1994[186] which also revised the definition of rape so as to make rape by a man of another man an offence.[187] Liberty supports these measures.

The 'rape warning' was particularly significant because the courts often do not treat evidence backing the testimony of the victim as corroborative, nor evidence about the mental and physical state of the victim at the time that she reported the offence.[188] Judges are also allowed to exert excessive influence over the outcome of trials when summing up. The under-representation of women in the judiciary, and the prevalence of sexist attitudes, can lead to particularly prejudicial comments on rape trials. In 1990, for example, Judge Raymond Dean QC said, during his summing up of a case at the Old Bailey: 'When a woman says no she doesn't always mean no. Men can't turn their emotions on and off as some women can.'[189] The defendant was acquitted. In 1992 a judge described the rape of a young girl by two teenage boys as 'a prank'.[190]

In 1986, the Lord Chief Justice, Lord Lane, laid down guidelines to bring about increased sentences.[191] The minimum sentence for rape should now be five years' imprisonment, with eight years to life for rapes committed with additional violence and for gang rapes. The only mitigation which can reduce the sentence below five years is if the woman's behaviour is thought to have given the defendant reason to believe that she had consented to sex. Only in wholly exceptional circumstances should a rapist not be imprisoned.

However, research has shown that these guidelines are not being adhered to and that there are considerable variations in sentencing patterns in different regions of the country.[192] In England and Wales as a whole during 1991, 41 per cent of convicted rapists received sentences of under five years' imprisonment, 50 per cent received sentences of between five and 10 years and 9 per cent received sentences of over 10 years or life.[193] Judges in Britain who are required to preside over rape trials receive just one day's training about the psychological effect of rape on its victims.[194]

All of the factors which weigh against convictions in rape cases are likely to deter women victims of rape from reporting their experiences to the police. Police discourage women from pursuing rape complaints if they have not been reported immediately because of the difficulty in getting a conviction.[195] Although many police forces do try to ensure that women who have been raped are questioned by female officers and examined by female doctors, this does not always happen and there have been many complaints of insensitive questioning.[196]

Domestic violence

Domestic violence against women is a serious violation of women's rights. The majority of adult victims of domestic violence are women and the majority of perpetrators are men.[197] While specific changes to the law are needed to ensure that women can be adequately protected from rape, the issue of domestic violence raises broader concerns.

One-third of all reported crimes against women result from domestic violence. Seventy-five per cent of assaults on women take place in either the victim's or the suspect's home.[198] According to a government-sponsored national inter-agency working party, domestic violence is more frequent than violence in the street, the pub or the workplace and its victims are overwhelmingly either adult women or children.[199]

Domestic violence accounts for nearly one-quarter of all reported violent crimes.[200] Almost one-half of the homicides of women are committed by partners or ex-partners. One in five of all murder victims, of either sex, are women killed by their partners. In 1990, in London alone, the police received an average of 1,000 calls each week for assistance in domestic violence incidents, but incidents are believed to be significantly under-reported so the true picture of the extent of domestic violence is likely to be even worse than the statistics show.

There is a growing awareness about the nature and extent of domestic violence in Britain.[201] A House of Commons Select Committee noted that three police organisations which had submitted evidence to it – the Police Federation, the Association of Chief Police Officers and the Police Superintendents' Association – reported that known domestic violence was 'only the tip of the iceberg'.[202]

According to one survey conducted in London in 1993, one in ten women had been assaulted by their partners in the previous 12 months and 8 per cent had suffered physical injury as a result.[203] Over one-quarter had suffered some physical injury from their partners during their relationship, including 6 per cent who had suffered broken bones.[204] The survey also showed that 6 per cent of women had been raped by their partners during the previous 12 months, nearly one-half of these cases involving additional physical violence.[205] The survey found that 19 per cent of men had admitted hitting their partners and only 37 per cent of men said they would never act violently to a partner.[206]

The housing charity, Shelter, has stated that domestic violence causes between 10 and 20 per cent of all its homelessness case-work.[207] The Women's Aid Federation in England, who co-ordinate refuge provision, receives approximately 130,000 calls about domestic violence at its refuges every year.[208]

There are some encouraging signs of changing attitudes to domestic violence by the public authorities. Evidence submitted by the Home Office to the Home Affairs Select Committee on Domestic Violence in 1992 said:

> Against a background of traditionally poor responses from criminal justice agencies to incidents of domestic violence – and,

indeed, a tradition of responding to the problem, if at all, in terms of the health, social and accommodation needs of the women and children rather than the criminal behaviour of violent men – there has been strong emphasis in recent years on domestic violence as a crime . . . The objective is to identify and promote practices which will reduce violence and suffering while not departing from the principle that violent offenders must be punished and their violent behaviour condemned.[209]

All police forces in England and Wales have adopted policies on domestic violence and reported improvements in their responses to incidents, following a Home Office circular in 1990.[210] However, the reported comments of a police Chief Superintendent in 1988 reflected a deep-rooted attitude in the police force and wider society:

Police practice has always been based on the assumption that, other than in extreme circumstances, what happened in a male-female relationship was essentially a private matter between the parties concerned.[211]

In general, violence in the home is still given a low priority because it has a low visibility and occurs within a sphere traditionally considered private.[212] Although the establishment of Domestic Violence Units (DVUs) by the police has generally been successful, standards vary widely. The police also still appear prepared to put women's safety at risk while attempting reconciliations. For example, in April 1991 Vandana Patel was killed inside the DVU at Stoke Newington police station where she had been left alone with her violent husband.[213] In November 1991, Carolyn McLaughlin was beaten to death at her home in Manchester, where she had gone to collect her belongings, while two police officers left her alone with her violent husband.[214]

There is also concern that victims are provided with insufficient protection and support during prosecutions and that some may withdraw their complaints due to intimidation. The fact that victims and defendants often have to wait together in the same part of the court building, without police protection, demonstrates the pressures that they face.[215]

Changes to the housing benefit and social security legislation, cutbacks in local authority spending and a lack of adequate public housing provision have made it difficult for women to leave violent partners. While refuge and hostel provision is totally inadequate, many local authorities still take the view that a woman who has fled her home to escape domestic violence has made herself intentionally homeless and so deserves no priority on housing waiting lists. The Home Affairs Select Committee has pointed out that these local authorities are acting illegally and has recommended that they 'should be advised in the strongest possible terms to put an end to [this] nonsense.'[216] It is estimated that, in London, of all the women escaping violent relationships, ten times as many have to rely on informal contacts as can find places in refuges.[217] The refuges which women do find are often underfunded, cramped and unsuitable for long-term stays. The Select Committee has recommended that 'the first priority for government action on domestic violence should be the establishment of a central, co-ordinated policy of refuge provision throughout the country.'[218]

Violence against black women

Women from ethnic minorities are especially vulnerable to sexual violence because they are also targets of racial violence which often involves sexual harassment and abuse. Inadequate interpreting facilities at police stations for women whose first language is not English, and the possibility of facing questions about their immigration status, often deter these women from reporting incidents of violence.[219] There have been complaints that the police are often prepared to rely on the children of the abused woman or even the alleged perpetrator of the abuse to act as interpreter.[220]

In addition, the police often appear unwilling to intervene in domestic disputes within ethnic minority families due to a perception that the community has self-policing mechanisms.[221] Southall Black Sisters (SBS), who are based in an area of London with a majority Asian population, say that the police's interpretation of multi-culturalism includes an assumption that Asian women have 'higher tolerance levels' of domestic violence.[222] They also note that the Police Complaints Authority has dismissed every complaint brought against the police by SBS or the women that they have assisted.[223]

147

Domestic violence and civil law

It has been argued that the law's treatment of domestic violence as a civil rather than a criminal offence trivialises women's experiences of violence within the home.[224] For example, it is common practice in county courts for judges to accept a sworn undertaking from a woman's aggressor as a substitute for a court order.[225] Such undertakings theoretically have the same force as a court order, and may occasionally be more appropriate, but they can be made by a man without accepting that he is in any way at fault and, in practice, can sometimes be regarded as not legally binding.[226]

The standard legal remedy open to a woman experiencing domestic violence is to gain a court injunction, either in the form of a 'non-molestation order', forbidding her partner from pestering her, or an 'ouster', evicting him from the home. Certain categories of women who are experiencing abuse fall outside the criteria of existing legislation – some former spouses, ex-cohabitants and those who have never lived with the abuser.[227] Such injunctions are limited both in terms of whom they apply to and what they can specify. For example, there is no tort of invasion of privacy nor any statutory tort of harassment.[228]

The problems that women face in attempting to use civil law as a remedy for domestic abuse are compounded by delays in obtaining orders, the inadequacy of Legal Aid, a lack of trained and sympathetic solicitors, a confusing overlap between the powers of different courts and inadequate facilities in the court rooms.[229]

The main problem for women who use civil law is in ensuring that injunctions and protection orders are enforced. Courts remain reluctant to add powers of arrest to court orders and the police are reluctant to intervene where powers of arrest have not been added. Campaigners against domestic violence often complain that the police ignore calls from women who complain that former partners are breaking injunctions. The overwhelming majority of police officers have expressed the view that orders without powers of arrest are 'not worth the paper that they are printed on.'[230] The Women's Aid Federation has argued that powers of arrest should be added to all orders whenever actual bodily harm has been committed, that this should apply to all clauses of an injunction and that the police should exercise their powers of arrest when an injunction has been broken. These conclusions have been endorsed by the Domestic Violence National Inter-Agency Working Party.[231]

Provocation and self-defence

Murder carries a mandatory life sentence in Britain, whatever the circumstances of the killing. Studies on violent crime have shown that women rarely kill and, when they do, it is often as a result of experiencing violence and abuse within an intimate or familial relationship.[232] Almost one-half of the women who have been convicted of homicide in Britain have killed a member of their own family.[233] However, the two legal provisions which can be used to reduce murder to manslaughter, provocation and diminished responsibility,[234] do not take account of the different experiences of women and men.

Abused women living in fear of their partners can plead for their crime to be reduced to manslaughter, on the grounds of provocation, if they can satisfy a court that they responded immediately to physical abuse *and* had suffered a sudden and temporary loss of self-control.[235] They can also claim manslaughter, on the grounds of diminished responsibility, if they can prove that they had suffered a major mental impairment, but this could lead to them being sent to a special hospital. They can argue self-defence – which would lead to their acquittal – if they can show that they used reasonable force to defend themselves from attack at the time of the assault. If a woman accused of murder has not responded to physical violence immediately, because she has waited until her attacker's defences are low, she will be seen to have had time to regain control of her emotions or to have planned her attack in a calculated way.

However, in September 1992 the Appeal Court quashed the murder conviction of Kiranjit Ahluwalia, who had killed her husband as he lay asleep, after suffering years of violence and abuse.[236] This ruling acknowledged that in some cases the principle of 'immediacy' does not take into account the cumulative effect of long-term abuse on women. Nevertheless, there are a number of other women in prison – such as Sara Thornton and Sally Emery – who killed their partners after suffering long periods of abuse.[237]

Some of the women currently in prison for killing their violent partners had previously attempted to leave the relationship and been forced to come back by threats of, or actual, physical and mental violence.[238] Others had remained in an abusive relationship in an attempt to protect their children, and some had contacted the police or other agencies but failed to persuade them to take action.[239] However, even in these circumstances, if a woman commits homicide and is unable to prove substantial mental impairment at the time of the killing then she will be convicted of murder.

By contrast, men have successfully used provocation as a defence in cases with a much wider scope.[240] For example, although crimes of passion are not recognised in British law, judges often use their summing up to describe a soldier returning from war to find his wife in bed with someone else as an example of provocation.[241] Such interventions imply that murder can be excused because of the provocation of a woman's 'bad behaviour'.[242] While women can plead provocation successfully if they can prove that they were subjected to frequent violence from their partners, men may claim it merely because he suspects his partner has been unfaithful, because she has nagged him, refused his sexual advances, attempted to leave him or 'not been a good wife'.[243]

Home Office research published in October 1991 purported to show that more than one-half of the women convicted of killing their partners from 1982 to 1989 had their convictions reduced to manslaughter on the grounds of provocation.[244] However, there were a number of problems with the published figures and it has been argued that in tried cases pleas of provocation usually do not succeed and that many of the women who plead provocation should actually have pleaded self-defence, while those who plead diminished responsibility should plead provocation.[245]

WOMEN'S RIGHTS AND THE FAMILY

The UN Human Rights Committee recognises that the concept of the family may differ both between and within states and therefore that it is not possible to give a standard definition of the family. It recognises that the idea of the family can include 'nuclear' and 'extended' families, as well as unmarried couples and their children and single parents and their children. It asks governments to report on the concept and scope of the family and how it is defined within society and the legal system.[246] Article 23 of the ICCPR forbids forced marriages[247] and states that family planning policies should not be discriminatory or compulsory. It calls on governments to co-operate with each other to ensure re-unification of families separated by political, economic or similar circumstances:[248]

☐ the government does not respect the diverse forms of families that exist in British society

☐ the government does not adequately support the institution of the family, in all its forms, either administratively or financially

☐ women are not adequately protected against forced marriages.

Single mothers

Almost one-fifth of all families in Britain have a single parent, of whom 90 per cent are women.[249] About 40 per cent of single mothers are under 30 years old, and over one-half of these are under 25. About one-half of those who are separated and divorced are in their 30s.[250] The UK has the second highest divorce rate of countries in the European Union,[251] while, in 1989, 42 per cent of pregnancies were outside marriage.[252]

The Conservative government's attitude to single mothers was made clear at the party's annual conference in October 1993. Michael Howard, the Home Secretary, told a fringe meeting that many single parents failed to teach their children right from wrong, were less committed to their children, were indirectly responsible for rising crime levels, and were 'all too often' tempted to have more children to obtain greater welfare benefits.[253] At the conference, there were calls to penalise single mothers who claim benefit and to reduce their access to housing.[254] In his speech to the conference, Peter Lilley, the Secretary of State for Social Security, said:

> There are now 1.3 million lone parents . . . the fastest growing group are those who never married. Since the 1960s their numbers have risen seven-fold. Partly because throughout that period it has been 'politically incorrect' to uphold the traditional family as an ideal. Anyone who did was sneered into silence. Earlier this year I decided it was time to break that taboo.[255]

The Prime Minister, John Major, indirectly endorsed many of these comments, saying it was time to 'get back-to-basics' on social policy.[256] A document issued from the Prime Minister's office the following month condemned what he called 'woolly liberal-minded thinking' and, in particular, criticised people who practised or tolerated alternatives to the nuclear family. It said:

Going back to basics . . . means relying on the good sense of families rather than politically correct absurdities.[257]

In January 1994 the government announced that local authorities would no longer be obliged to give single young parents priority in allocating accommodation. Reports suggest that instead of being given a permanent home, many will now get temporary housing or 'spartan accommodation' only in the private sector.[258]

Arranged marriages

Some families in certain sections of the south Asian communities in Britain practise arranged marriages.[259] Marriages are usually arranged by families within regional, caste and religious communities and are contracts between two families rather than between individuals. Arranged marriages are perceived as traditional and cultural both within and outside the communities in which they are practised. However, there is evidence that some arranged marriages are forced upon one or both of the parties. There are no available statistics about the numbers of women and men forced into arranged marriages but SBS have noted that increasing numbers of Asian women are reporting to the police, social services, women's aid refuges, hostels, schools, colleges and advice centres.[260] Asian women aged between 16 and 24 years have a suicide rate three times the average of white women of a similar age and studies have concluded that pressure to enter into an arranged marriage is a major contributory factor to this phenomenon.[261]

Women are forced into arranged marriages through pressure from both the immediate family and the wider caste or religious community to which they belong. The pressure can take a number of forms.[262] Such women may face the stark choice of consenting to an arranged marriage or becoming a pariah within their community, to be denied education and career opportunities. There have even been a small number of 'honour' killings of women who have failed to submit to the will of their families.[263]

The rise of religious fundamentalism in this country has increased the pressure on many Asian women to conform to arranged marriages. SBS have noted that an increasing number of Asian male gangs and networks are being established in various parts of Britain to hunt down young, single, Asian women who have run away from their families to escape either an arranged marriage or pressure to enter into one.[264]

SBS have also criticised the authorities for failing to recognise the nature and scope of this problem. Forced arranged marriages are not recognised as an abuse of women's human rights and women are given inadequate protection against them. Perceptions of 'multi-culturalism' ignore the internal divisions within ethnic minority communities and generally uncritically accept traditions and customs which have been defined by male community and religious leaders.

In 1992 a Scottish court ruled that a forced arranged marriage which a girl had entered into in Pakistan was illegal and SBS are currently pursuing another case where a woman was coerced into a marriage by emotional pressure.[265] If successful, this case could broaden the legal definition of 'forced consent' which currently only applies where individuals are under physical threat. However, the problem also demands the attention of hostels, refuges and specialist advice centres, the funding for which is currently inadequate for this task.[266]

SUMMARY

The distinction between civil and political and social and economic rights is particularly difficult to make when considering violations of women's rights. Issues such as childcare and maternity rights sit more comfortably within the International Covenant on Social and Economic Rights (to which the UK government is also a signatory), but the abuse of these rights prevents women from enjoying their civil and political rights in equality with men. This in turn prevents women from participating fully in public life and their under-representation in public office ensures that the laws and practices which govern society are still largely drawn up and presided over by men. This is also true in the international human rights arena.

Women's lack of representation in public life is both a cause and an indication of the failure of the UK's anti-discrimination laws to ensure that everyone has the equal protection of the law. The British labour market is rigorously segregated along gender lines, where women are over-represented in low paid and low status jobs. Women earn less than men and the present government has removed some of the protections against discrimination which did exist.

The British criminal justice system also discriminates against women. Women's under-representation within the police force and criminal justice system, as well as shortcomings in the law itself, means that women are effectively denied equal protection by the law. Women are inadequately protected against male violence and the fear of violence, which consequently affects their general participation in society as a whole.

Women's campaigns for emancipation have brought some improvements for women but progress has been painfully slow. It is only in the last 100 years that women have secured the right to vote in this country and there are still vast aspects of the British political system in need of reform. Women carry the bulk of the world's labour and reap little reward. The enjoyment of full civil and political rights will necessitate – and help to achieve – greater social and economic equality.

6 LESBIANS, GAY MEN AND BISEXUALS

SEXUALITY AND THE STATE

On 21 February 1994, Parliament rejected a proposal, by 307 votes to 280, to equalise the age at which heterosexual and homosexual men may engage in consensual sexual activity. The House of Commons instead passed an amendment to the Criminal Justice and Public Order Bill, which reduced from 21 to 18 the age at which two men can lawfully engage in consensual sexual activity in private. The equivalent age for heterosexuals is 16.

The decision was portrayed by the government as a compromise. The Home Secretary, Michael Howard, claimed it was necessary to 'protect young men from activities which their lack of maturity might cause them to regret'.[1] However, he rejected advice from leading medical and social service organisations that criminalising gay teenagers would not help protect the vulnerable.[2] Edwina Currie, the Conservative MP who moved the proposal, pleaded that 'people are not entitled to insist that their prejudices are written into British law',[3] but failed to convince the House. The Home Secretary insisted that the proposal should be called 'the buggery amendment'.[4] The government's Home Affairs spokesperson in the House of Lords, Earl Ferrers, had said he would prefer the age of consent to be raised to 75.[5]

Many organisations publicly called for the age of consent to be reduced to 16. These included the British Medical Association, the British Psychological Society, the Royal College of Psychiatrists, the Health Education Authority, Barnados, the British Association of Social Workers, the Terrence Higgins Trust and the National Association of Probation Officers.[6] Supporters of an equal age of consent argued that different ages for heterosexual and homosexual sex are deeply discriminatory and send a signal of intolerance to the rest of society.[7] The British government's attitude

is significantly out of step with many other countries.[8] Before the vote, the age of consent in Britain was higher than anywhere else in Europe, except Cyprus and the few ex-Soviet and ex-Yugoslav countries where homosexuality is still illegal.[9] At 18, the British age of gay consent is still the equal highest in Europe.[10] In most other European countries the age of consent is less than 18 and does not discriminate on the basis of sexual orientation.[11] A case against Britain's age of consent laws has been submitted to the European Commission on Human Rights.[12]

Lesbians, gays and bisexuals have faced persecution and prejudice for centuries. The current majority in Parliament and much of the popular press are deeply homophobic, but the public is becoming more accepting of diversity. An opinion poll published in the *Independent* newspaper in 1992 found that 71 per cent of people questioned agreed that there should be the same laws applying to heterosexuals and homosexuals.[13]

One month before the vote a headteacher of a primary school in Hackney, east London, had turned down an offer of reduced price ballet tickets for some of her pupils, citing, amongst a number of other practical objections, her opinion that the ballet, Prokofiev's *Romeo and Juliet*, was 'blatantly heterosexual'.[14] The headteacher, Jane Brown, quickly admitted that she had made a mistake and apologised, but some sections of the media made much of the story when it emerged that she was a lesbian. They raised questions about her appointment, because her lover was a member of the school's board of governors, although they had not been in a relationship at the time of Jane Brown's selection. Smear stories led to hate mail and death threats which forced Jane Brown into hiding.[15] However, the media had misjudged the popular mood. Parents, staff and pupils rallied to Jane Brown's support. A meeting of the parent governors overwhelmingly endorsed her position as headteacher and pointed out that she had lifted educational standards at the school significantly.[16] A poster, painted by pupils at the school, appeared to sum up the feelings of the local community with its message 'Keep on keeping on Janey'.[17]

Yet lesbians, gays and bisexuals face discrimination throughout British society.[18] Discriminatory laws and measures enacted by Parliament or arising out of court judgments in recent years have eroded rights. Section 28 of the Local Government Act 1988 prohibits the 'promotion of homosexuality' by local authorities.[19] Section 31 of the Criminal Justice Act 1991 reclassifies many forms of consenting gay behaviour as 'serious' sex crimes and empowers judges to impose longer sentences.[20] The Human Fertilisation and Embryology Act 1990 includes restrictions interpreted to deny the availability of donor insemination services to lesbians.[21] In December 1990, in a trial of gay men, the courts ruled that private, consensual sado-masochistic sexual practices could be imprisonable offences, and the House of Lords confirmed this judgment in March 1993.[22]

SEXUAL ORIENTATION AND THE ICCPR

The International Covenant on Civil and Political Rights guarantees all people the right to privacy, freedom of conscience and freedom of belief. Freedom of conscience and freedom of belief are described as absolute rights. Although the ICCPR does not specifically prohibit discrimination on the basis of sexual orientation – or specify that its guarantees apply to lesbians, gays and bisexuals – its wording permits this interpretation.[23] The ICCPR contains all-encompassing prohibitions of discrimination and the Human Rights Committee has made it clear that a broad interpretation should be given to concepts such as the family and the home.

Discrimination on the grounds of sexual orientation can also be considered a human rights abuse on three grounds:

☐ sexual orientation in an immutable part of every person, like their race and gender

☐ the expression of sexual orientation entails the exercise of other fundamental human rights, such as privacy, freedom of expression and freedom of association

☐ lesbians, gays and bisexuals form a recognised and distinct group within society, and they are entitled to protection from discrimination

A debate continues about whether sexual orientation is a biologically innate characteristic or a conscious political choice.[24] Both arguments strengthen the case for anti-discrimination protection for lesbians, gays and bisexuals – similar protection to that afforded to women and ethnic minorities,[25] or protection from discrimination because of political or other opinions, as set out in the ICCPR, which also protects the right of people to enter into

relationships without suffering discrimination. The European
Court of Human Rights has upheld a number of cases against
government interference into the privacy of lesbians, gays and
bisexuals.[26]

The European Convention on Human Rights

In 1960 the European Commission on Human Rights ruled that:

the Convention does allow a High Contracting Party to punish
homosexuality since the right to respect for private life may,
in a democratic society, be subject to interference . . . for the
protection of health or morals.[27]

In 1978 the Commission ruled as admissible an application which
challenged the prohibition of homosexuality in Northern Ireland.
This led to a judgment by the European Court in 1980 that:

the legal prohibition of private sexual acts between consenting
males over 21 . . . breaches the applicant's right to respect for
private life.[28]

The Court reached similar conclusions in 1988 and 1993 in cases
brought against the Republic of Ireland[29] and Cyprus.[30] Each
decision relied heavily on the changes in laws and practices on the
issue in other member States. These judgments have in turn led to
changes in the criminal law in Northern Ireland[31] and a number
of territories for which the UK is responsible. The law was liberal-
ised in Guernsey in 1983,[32] Jersey in 1990,[33] the Isle of Man in
1992[34] and Gibraltar in 1993.[35] However, the European Human
Rights Commission has ruled in at least 15 other cases which
challenged sexual orientation discrimination – 10 of which origi-
nated in England and Wales – that there was *no* violation of
the ECHR,[36] including the discriminatory age of consent,[37] and the
prohibition of sexual activity between men 'when more than two
persons take part or are present'.[38] The conviction of the publisher
and editor of *Gay News* for 'blasphemous libel' has been upheld.[39]
The Commission has also rejected claims brought by a Belgian
lesbian teacher, dismissed for speaking on a television programme
about the discrimination that she faced because of her sexual orientation,[40] and by a gay British soldier dismissed from the army.[41]

Five European Commission decisions have upheld British
government practices which discriminate against same-sex couples,

mainly in the areas of housing and immigration.[42] The Commission has ruled that same-sex couples – whether or not they have children – are not entitled to the right to respect for family life or the right to marry as defined in the ECHR.[43] Differences in the treatment of heterosexual and same-sex couples have been found to be 'objectively and reasonably justified'[44] and not discrimination as defined in the ECHR. The European Commission and Court have shown an inclusive attitude in considering what constitutes a family when it involves heterosexual couples, but they have been restrictive when it involves same-sex relationships.[45] Immigration rules which have forced the break-up of same-sex relationships have been found not to be in violation of the ECHR's protection of the family,[46] even in cases in which the couple concerned had a child,[47] or in which one partner had previously lived in a country where homosexuality was outlawed.[48]

The Commission has only considered one case on the rights of gay, lesbian and bisexual parents,[49] where it upheld the Dutch government's refusal to grant a woman's request for joint parental authority over her female partner's child, whom she had conceived by donor insemination.[50] The ECHR does not contain an equivalent to Article 26 of the ICCPR, an autonomous anti-discrimination provision, which protects people in areas such as employment, housing and health care not covered elsewhere in the Covenant.[51] However, the Court and Commission have ruled, in principle, that some forms of discrimination can be so severe as to constitute degrading treatment, as specified in the ECHR, and that the grounds for discrimination covered by the ECHR include sexual orientation.[52]

An important factor behind these decisions has been the Commission's assessment of the degree of consensus amongst member States on each issue.[53] The Commission's change in attitude about the criminalisation of homosexual activity seems to have been motivated by the changing laws and practices of member States, and its narrower interpretation of the ECHR in other areas reflects these States' current discriminatory practices. This 'European consensus' is perhaps becoming more progressive.

European Union

Although the European Court and Commission have refused to uphold challenges under the ECHR brought by lesbians, gays and bisexuals who have experienced discrimination because of their sexual orientation, the European Parliament has called for the introduction of anti-discrimination laws.[54]

On 8 February 1994, the Parliament in Strasbourg voted (by 159 to 96 with 18 abstentions) for a resolution calling on the Commission of the European Union to draft a policy outlawing anti-gay discrimination, including discrimination in the ages of consent, public indecency laws, employment, marriage and the fostering and adoption of children.[55]

THE BRITISH GOVERNMENT'S RECORD

The British government's *Third Periodic Report* contained few references to its treatment of lesbians, gays and bisexuals. It has never been illegal in the UK to be attracted to a member of the same sex, only for men to act on that attraction by having sex with another man. However, there is no law protecting people from discrimination because they are sexually attracted to the same sex. People can be denied jobs, houses or other services and treated less favourably in a variety of other ways purely on the basis of their perceived sexual orientation. Lesbians, gays and bisexuals face discrimination in employment, training, education, housing and the provision of goods and services, against which they have no legal redress.[56]

Some protection is already written into British law against discrimination on the grounds of marital status,[57] trade union membership,[58] religion and political opinion.[59] There is no reason why such protection cannot be extended to cover sexual orientation.

Lesbians, gays and bisexuals are denied recognition under civil law, such as the rights of same-sex couples to form a family, with the following associated rights: to bring a partner into this country from overseas; to raise, foster or adopt children; in the case of lesbians, to have equal access to donor insemination services; to have next-of-kin hospital or prison visiting rights; to maintenance or an equitable division of property in the event of the break-up of a relationship; to enjoy the same National Insurance, pension, employee spousal benefits, tax and inheritance rights as heterosexual couples. Further discrimination occurs through the operation of the criminal justice system.

DISCRIMINATION IN EMPLOYMENT, HOUSING AND OTHER SERVICES

Employment

A survey was conducted in 1993 involving nearly 2,000 lesbians and gay men. The results showed that 37 per cent had either experienced discrimination at work because of their sexual orientation or suspected that they had, and 8 per cent had been sacked for this reason.[60] Nearly one-half (48 per cent) had experienced harassment, ranging from unwanted jokes and innuendo to abuse, threats and violence.[61] Almost one-quarter (24 per cent) had avoided certain jobs or careers because they feared discrimination, and 89 per cent had concealed their sexuality at some point from colleagues.[62]

Employers are free to determine the terms of employment of their workers, except where rights or protection have been specified by case law or statute.[63] There is no legislation that prohibits discrimination on the grounds of sexual orientation. It is therefore legal to discriminate against lesbians, gays and bisexuals in employment.

An individual can be denied a job – or sacked - on the grounds of their sexual orientation without any form of official redress. There is no law that prohibits other forms of homophobic discrimination, such as harassment, victimisation or denial of promotion. The laws on race and sex discrimination make provision for immediate and relatively comprehensive protection, but employees who believe they are subject to discrimination on the grounds of their sexual orientation have no other option but to resign from their job and claim 'constructive dismissal'. Such claims are extremely difficult to win.[64]

Industrial tribunals and Employment Appeal Tribunals (EAT), whose decisions create precedents which subsequent tribunals must follow, have established the following precedents regarding the lawful dismissal of lesbians, gays and bisexuals:

- because their job requires them to work in the proximity of children[65]
- because of public prejudice[66]
- because of the prejudices of co-workers[67]

Employers can dismiss a lesbian, gay or bisexual worker because they believed that public prejudice *might* have an impact on their business – and they do not have to substantiate this – although such considerations must be weighed against the specific behaviour of the employee.[68] Employers can also dismiss an individual because of the antagonism of other workers, but this must be a last resort for solving disputes. However, a tribunal has upheld the dismissal of a gay man on the grounds that his supervisor claimed to be afraid that he would 'catch AIDS'.[69]

School and college teachers and others who work with young people are often particular targets for discrimination. Dismissal often follows when a (male) teacher has been convicted of a homosexual offence (under current law) for having sex with another consenting adult. These dismissals have usually been upheld as fair by industrial tribunals.[70] Some challenges to discrimination on the grounds of sexual orientation have been brought under the Sex Discrimination Act. In June 1993 a Scottish industrial tribunal ruled, at an initial hearing, that two women who were in a relationship and worked at the same workplace might be entitled to protection under the Sex Discrimination Act 1975 on the basis that they might have been treated differently if one of them had been a man.[71] However, this case was settled out of court and there are no other precedents to show that discrimination on the basis of sexual orientation in employment constitutes a form of sex discrimination outlawed by the 1975 Act. The Equal Opportunities Commission has also succeeded in challenging an airline which had a policy of refusing to employ male stewards on the grounds that they would be likely to be gay and the airline believed they would therefore constitute a high risk of AIDS.[72]

More public sector employers are incorporating protection against sexual orientation discrimination into their equal opportunities policies. Most trade unions have policies to defend members who experience discrimination or victimisation on these grounds.[73] However, such policies are rare in the private sector, and other public sector employers – such as the Civil Service and the armed forces – have been among the most hostile to lesbians, gays and bisexuals. As Stonewall has pointed out, the lack of equal opportunities protection creates a vicious circle.[74] Because of discrimination and harassment, many lesbians, gays and bisexuals conceal their sexual orientation at work, which means that they cannot confront or complain about the harassment and discrimination, nor can they request that sexual orientation be included in equal opportunities protection.

Gay men have been most affected by HIV in the UK. Thus they are most affected by discriminatory practices towards people who are HIV-positive. There is no law which specifically outlaws discrimination in employment on the grounds of HIV-antibody status. Much fear and prejudice has manifested itself in discrimination against people who are, or are believed to be, HIV-positive. People have lost jobs based on ill-founded fears. People who are HIV-positive can be disadvantaged by conditions which require job applicants to have negative test results.[75]

The Civil Service, armed forces and merchant navy

Lesbians, gays and bisexuals have traditionally been seen as security risks (because of the perceived potential for blackmail) and have therefore been banned from the diplomatic service and sections of the security services.[76] This blanket ban was removed in 1991 when the Prime Minister, John Major, stated that:

> in the future there should be no posts . . . for which homosexuality represents an automatic bar to security clearance . . . except in the armed forces.[77]

Sexual orientation is still considered a relevant factor in the vetting process for the Civil Service. Between 1982 and 1992, half the people who lost their security clearance lost it because they were gay.[78] The stated grounds for such discrimination are that lesbians, gays and bisexuals may be open to blackmail. Openness about sexual orientation, which removes the potential for blackmail, is not accepted either. In 1987 the High Court upheld the sacking of a civil servant at the government's intelligence-gathering centre, GCHQ, who lost his security clearance after informing his employers that he was gay.[79] The High Court rejected his argument that he was not vulnerable to blackmail because he was open about his sexual orientation. The judgment stated that the courts were not entitled to review the decision, as it concerned national security, and claimed his gay lifestyle and openness about his homosexuality could make him a security risk.[80]

Lesbians, gays and bisexuals are banned from membership of the armed forces. Those who join and conceal their sexual orientation, or realise later that they are homosexual, face dismissal.

The military ban on lesbians, gays and bisexuals applies whether or not they are sexually active. Homosexual sex was, until recently, considered a criminal offence for members of the merchant navy and armed forces (even when it took place off duty and in private).[81] Before 1992 the policy of the armed forces required that anyone discovered to be lesbian, gay or bisexual should at least be 'administratively discharged', if not court-martialled, imprisoned and dismissed with disgrace. Each year before 1992 an estimated 10 military personnel were imprisoned for homosexual behaviour, and about 100 others were discharged each year because of their homosexuality.[82]

In June 1992 the Ministry of Defence announced that it would no longer bring criminal prosecutions against gay, lesbian and bisexual soldiers.[83] However, the government emphasised 'that homosexual activity remains incompatible with military service and those who engage in it must [expect] to be discharged.'[84] It does not appear, however, that decriminalisation has stopped the investigation of 'suspected homosexuals' in the armed forces with a view to obtaining evidence for their dismissal.

Health

The medical profession used to define homosexuality as a disease or disorder[85] and lesbians, gays and bisexuals still face homophobia from the medical establishment. In November 1993, the *British Medical Journal News Review* carried an article in which a doctor wrote that 'under no circumstances ought homosexuality to be regarded as anything other than a destructive habit system.'[86] Some gay doctors reported that they had contemplated suicide owing to the homophobic attitudes of colleagues.[87] In a 1989 survey about one in nine general practitioners believed that homosexuality was an illness.[88] In 1993 a survey reported that only one in two clinical medical students thought that homosexual activity could form part of an acceptable lifestyle.[89] The spread of HIV and AIDS has fuelled this homophobia.

Housing

Lesbians, gays and bisexuals face substantial discrimination when they try to rent or buy accommodation. A same-sex couple seeking accommodation is often assumed to be lesbian or gay and may be discriminated against as a result.

Public housing provision in Britain is now geared towards the needs of people with children and married couples. Therefore single people tend to seek housing in the private sector. Because there is no legal recognition of same-sex marriages, lesbians and gays are disproportionately concentrated in housing's private rented sector.[90] Some local authorities have equal opportunity policies that seek to prevent discrimination in allocations, and harassment and intimidation of tenants on the basis of their sexual orientation. In 1992 only 69 local authorities granted joint tenancies to same-sex couples.[91] However, equal treatment is much less common in the private sector.[92] The courts have upheld the rights of property owners and developers to exclude certain categories of people from houses.[93] Landlords can lawfully refuse to rent accommodation to lesbians, gays and bisexuals.

Discrimination which takes place because a tenant is – or is assumed to be – HIV-positive is not illegal under any existing housing legislation. Some private landlords, hostels and housing authorities are unwilling to offer housing to people who are HIV-positive or whom they consider to be a member of a 'high-risk' group – such as gay men or drug-injectors.[94] Life insurance companies often insist that men whom they believe are gay take an HIV test before providing cover.[95] Without life insurance it is impossible to obtain some mortgages. Some companies insist that all single men over a certain age take the test, while others ask 'lifestyle' questions or obtain the information from people's medical records. Even gay men who are not HIV-positive are often refused cover, or made to pay a higher premium, on the grounds that they are a 'high-risk' group.[96] People who are known to be HIV-positive will be denied insurance and once someone has been denied insurance by one company it is very unlikely that they will be offered it by another. This bars many people who are HIV-positive from owner-occupation.[97]

Lesbian and gay couples who live in rented accommodation or jointly own property may also experience problems if they separate or if one partner dies.[98] The law recognises the right of succession to a tenancy for members of the tenant's family. This includes unmarried heterosexual partners. However, because the law does not recognise same-sex relationships, in the absence of any written agreement, a surviving lesbian or gay partner may be evicted from the property. The courts are sometimes prepared to imply that a trust existed, which gives the partner some rights to the property, but the lack of clear statutory guidelines often makes judges unwilling to do so.[99] In January 1993 Parliament rejected an amendment to a Housing Bill, which specified that local authorities should not evict a surviving lesbian or gay man from council housing on the death of the partner holding the tenancy.[100]

FREEDOM OF EXPRESSION

The protections guaranteed under Article 19 of the ICCPR are particularly important for lesbians, gays and bisexuals. Societal pressures force many to conceal their sexual orientation, increasing the isolation and vulnerability of the whole lesbian and gay community. The freedom to advertise, publish and disseminate literature and art which has a lesbian and gay perspective is vital for the culture of the community, which in turn provides essential support for individual members. The right to freedom of expression for lesbians and gays is inadequately protected by the British government.

In any society the law has a legitimate interest in regulating aspects of sexual expression and curbing aspects of sexual freedom. Most societies have laws governing paedophilia, incest, prostitution, pornography and polygamy, which do interfere with sexual freedom but are considered necessary to protect the rights and freedoms of others.[101] However, any regulatory controls on sexual expression deemed necessary should be non-discriminatory. In Britain, these regulatory laws have been framed and are applied in a discriminatory way towards lesbians, gays and bisexuals. They criminalise certain acts for homosexuals which are legal for heterosexuals, compounded by homophobic attitudes within the police force and the legal profession. Their effect is to deny to lesbians, gays and bisexuals the right of equal treatment under the law.

The Obscene Publications laws

A variety of laws in Britain prohibits publications on the grounds that they are 'obscene', 'indecent' or 'blasphemous'. Existing legislation is based on a narrow concept of public morality, which reflects traditional heterosexual concepts of indecency. The laws are enforced by a police and customs service, and presided over by a criminal justice system, all of which are homophobic.

The Obscene Publications Act 1959 is the main legislation in England and Wales governing the production and distribution of publications which might 'offend public morality' or 'deprave and corrupt' those who see, hear or read them. Offences are tried by judge or jury or dealt with by 'forfeiture' proceedings – local magistrates can authorise the destruction of obscene articles discovered within their jurisdiction.[102] These provisions are reinforced by a number of other laws.[103] The police and courts routinely apply the powers contained within this body of legislation in a far harsher way against literature dealing with same-sex activities than that with heterosexual activities.[104]

Customs and Excise officers have more extensive powers than the police[105] and their powers of confiscation are difficult to challenge – anyone wishing to do so can face prosecution. There is evidence that lesbian and gay material is more likely to be seized than equivalent heterosexual literature. *The Joy of Sex* is widely available in Britain, stocked by most booksellers and frequently advertised in the media. However, *The Joy of Gay Sex* and *The Joy of Lesbian Sex* have been confiscated by Customs and Excise officers.[106] In September 1991, it was reported that a lesbian was warned for attempting to import two lesbian erotic videos, which were for her private use, from an overseas mail order company.[107]

In 1973 the House of Lords upheld the conviction of the publishers of the *International Times*, on a charge of conspiracy to corrupt public morals for carrying gay contact advertisements.[108] Although there has only been one similar prosecution since that date,[109] the precedent has been set and more are possible. Because prejudice often makes it difficult for people with same-sex attractions to meet each other in everyday social situations, for many lesbians, gays and bisexuals, contact advertisements are a significant means of finding prospective partners.

Section 28

Section 28 of the Local Government Act 1988 inserted a new Section 2A into the Local Government Act 1986. This states that:

(1) A local authority shall not
   a) intentionally promote homosexuality or publish material with the intention of promoting homosexuality;
   b) promote the teaching in any maintained school of the

acceptability of homosexuality as a pretended family relationship.

Section 28 is the first law enacted this century to single out lesbian and gay lifestyles for legal disapproval. It was established after a series of incidents in which some Conservative politicians and sections of the media alleged that local authorities were mounting a propaganda campaign 'to glamorise homosexuality, to make all aspects of homosexuality seem attractive . . . [to conduct] a hard sell of homosexuality.'[110]

The Section's wording does not distinguish between promoting same-sex conduct and promoting an understanding of sexual diversity. A strict interpretation of Section 28 could require local authorities to ban all council-produced or council-funded literature which portrays homosexuality in any positive manner, to deny funding to any organisation which does likewise and actively to discriminate against lesbians, gays and bisexuals in employment and training practices and in the provision of council services. Another interpretation could simply require local authorities to refrain from attempting to convince people – particularly children in schools – that they should become homosexual or experiment with homosexual relationships.[111]

The scope of Section 28's provisions has yet to be interpreted by the courts, as no proceedings have been brought against a local authority decision which rested on those provisions. Many of the examples of local authority practices, which supporters of Section 28 used to justify their arguments, were fictitious or gross distortions,[112] and so the law has not led to an increase in aggrieved litigants. Local authorities have often chosen *not* to rely on Section 28 when denying grants to lesbian, gay and bisexual organisations, in the knowledge that such decisions could be challenged by judicial review.[113] However, there have been cases where Section 28 has led to self-imposed restriction on support for local lesbian and gay organisations by councils.[114]

Liberty has received complaints which suggest that local authorities have significantly reduced support and facilities for lesbians, gays and bisexuals since the enactment of Section 28.[115] In May 1994 a local authority banned *The Pink Paper* from its libraries on the basis of Section 28. Liberty lodged an application for judicial review of this decision and in January 1995 the local authority backed down.[116]

It has been argued that Section 28 is legally meaningless.[117] Few, if any, existing local authority practices have been outlawed, because the Section was aimed at policies and practices that did not exist.[118] However, the passage of this Section of the Act was significant. Parliament expressed the view that homosexuality is undesirable and should not be 'promoted', and that same-sex relationships should be regarded as inferior to heterosexual relationships.[119] This contributed to prejudice and hostility towards lesbians, gays and bisexuals in the late-1980s. During the parliamentary debate, for example, a Conservative MP refused to condemn an arson attack on the offices of a gay newspaper, and stated that 'It is quite right that there should be an intolerance of evil.'[120]

Section 28 is a discriminatory law which inhibits lesbians, gays and bisexuals from enjoying the rights guaranteed to them in the ICCPR. It is a violation of Article 2 and should be repealed.

Education

Section 28 prohibits 'the teaching . . . of the acceptability of homosexuality as a pretended family relationship.' Some schools, colleges and local authorities adopted self-censorship because of Section 28, which may have contributed to a 'chilling effect' on discussions of lesbian, gay and bisexual issues in classrooms.[121]

The Education Act 1986 specified that sex education must encourage pupils 'to have due regard to moral considerations and the value of family life.'[122] A follow-up circular from the Department of Education and Science stated that: 'There is no place in any school in any circumstances for teaching which advocates homosexual behaviour, which presents it as the "norm" or which encourages homosexual experimentation by pupils.'[123] This was dropped after a vigorous lobbying campaign.[124]

As discussed in the section on mental health in this book, lesbian and gay teenagers often suffer from feelings of isolation, loneliness and confusion, which lead many to contemplate suicide. The British education system offers them little support and often promotes negative images. A 1994 survey into sex education and the age of consent revealed that most lesbian and gay people had experienced a hostile and oppressive environment at school.[125] Many respondents reported bullying and physical violence from other pupils as well as threats of disciplinary action, expulsion and criminal prosecution from the authorities. Such attitudes led many lesbian and gay teenagers to conceal their sexual orientation, but they still experienced the negative attitudes of pupils and staff. Teachers often displayed homophobic attitudes in the classroom – particularly in biology and religious education classes – and some respondents said they had been taught that homosexuality was contagious.[126]

Sex education at school

School governors have discretion over the content of sex education lessons and parents may remove their children from them if they wish to do so.[127] In May 1994 the government published new guidelines for teachers. The only direct reference to homosexual sex in these comes in an annexe dealing with the legal position. 'Committing buggery in private' appears within a section entitled 'other indecent conduct' which also refers to sex with animals.[128]

Stonewall's survey on sex education, based on 2,408 responses from people of all ages, showed that almost one-third had received no sex education in school.[129] Of those that had received general sex education, 82 per cent had not discussed homosexuality between men, and 89 per cent were given no information about lesbianism. Of 390 young men who had received sex education since 1987 – the year in which the government began its AIDS-awareness campaign – 41 per cent said safer sex had been discussed, but only 2.5 per cent said that there had been any discussion of safer sex for gay men or lesbians.[130]

General safer-sex education

Britain's obscenity laws and the attitudes of the British government and authorities have led to the suppression of a number of gay safer-sex publications and manuals aimed at gay and bisexual men as well as the restriction of training events.

In May 1993 police officers seized postcards advocating safer sex from a sex shop in Brighton and threatened to prosecute the owners under the obscene publication laws. The cards depicted two gay men having sexual intercourse using a condom.[131] In October 1992 customs officers seized a safer-sex video for men on the grounds that it could be obscene or indecent.[132] In 1993 a satirical lesbian and gay magazine, *F.F.*, was forced to close down after being threatened with prosecution by the Obscene Publications Squad over a safer-sex photograph which it published in one issue.[133]

In April 1994, Health Minister Brian Mawhinney ordered a sex education guide for young people by the Health Education Authority to be withdrawn from publication.[134] The Minister has also opposed giving government support to gay HIV-prevention groups.[135] In the same month a university students' union was forced to postpone a safer-sex workshop on sado-masochism after being threatened with legal action by the Education Secretary.[136]

THE RIGHT TO FORM A FAMILY

Same-sex marriages

Same-sex couples have no recognition under British law. They cannot marry,[137] there is no legal equivalent of marriage, and there is no legal recognition of cohabiting same-sex partners as there is of cohabiting heterosexual partners. The law treats lesbian and gay couples in exactly the same way as it treats two separate individuals, and Parliament has specified, through Section 28, that lesbian and gay relationships should be considered inferior to heterosexual marriages.

Heterosexual partners have the option of marriage which brings a number of benefits. These include National Insurance pensions for spouses, favourable tax treatment, inheritance rights, and recognition as next-of-kin for the purposes of visiting a partner in hospital or prison or receiving sensitive information about their medical and legal status.[138] If a husband or wife dies without leaving a will, all property is inherited by the surviving spouse and children. However, because same-sex couples cannot marry, lesbians and gay men can only ensure that their partners inherit if they leave a will. Even when a will has been made it can sometimes be successfully contested by other members of the immediate family or a former spouse. In May 1994 the Law Commission described the failure of the law to grant property rights to unmarried couples as 'unfair, uncertain and illogical'.[139]

Married people can claim a married person's tax allowance, and if the partner is working, can get earned-income relief which amounts to a single person's tax allowance.[140] A wife can claim a pension on her husband's National Insurance. Lesbian and gay partners only have pension entitlements in their own right. In addition many employers grant special benefits, such as private pensions or medical insurance, for which only married couples can apply. These benefits are directly discriminatory because they are available only to people who can comply with a criterion from which same-sex couples are legally prohibited.[141] This form of discrimination by employers against lesbians, gays and bisexuals is far more common than dismissals or refusals to hire or promote. It affects all employees with a same-sex partner, whether or not they are open about their sexual orientation.[142]

The absence of any legal recognition of lesbian and gay relationships can mean there are difficulties when a relationship ends, either through death or separation. Only married couples have the right to go to court to settle financial problems. When a same-sex relationship comes to an end there is no official legal mechanism to enable one partner to claim maintenance from the other. Even if the couple had drawn up a written 'cohabiting contract' this may not have any legal validity.[143]

British law distinguishes between the position of married couples and unmarried partners, but is increasingly recognising the rights and duties of unmarried heterosexual couples. For example, the Inheritance Provision for Family and Dependants Act 1975, the Domestic Violence and Marital Proceedings Act 1976, the Fatal Accidents Act 1976 and the Housing Act 1985 all now extend rights to unmarried couples where the relationship can be shown to be 'equivalent to a marriage'.[144]

The extent to which same-sex couples can claim similar rights remains unclear. The courts have rejected attempts by lesbian and gay couples to make use of these changes in some areas, such as the right to joint tenancies,[145] but may uphold the right of lesbians and gay men to inherit property they own jointly with their partner.[146] Under the Fatal Accidents Act 1976, lesbian and gay partners have no right to sue for compensation if the death of their partner occurred in an accident that was someone else's fault.[147] The protection offered to heterosexual cohabitants in the Domestic Violence and Marital Proceedings Act 1976 does not apply to same-sex couples. The lack of recognition given to same-sex relationships can cause serious problems if one partner falls seriously ill or becomes incapacitated.

Funeral arrangements are usually the responsibility of the next of kin. In 1990 a court clarified that a gay man could appoint executors and specify that he wanted a non-religious funeral, despite the objections of his mother. She had refused to hand over the certificate for the disposal of his body which she had obtained when registering his death.[148] If there is no will, the deceased's immediate family will have more rights and control over the funeral arrangements than his or her partner of the same sex.

Immigration

The most common grounds on which immigrants are given permission to settle in the UK are that they are coming to join a relative who is a British citizen or who has settled in the UK. This relative will most often be a spouse, fiancé, or fiancée.[149] The rules surrounding such admittances are very strict. An immigration officer must be satisfied that the primary purpose of the marriage was not merely to enable one partner to gain admittance to the country. The couple must stay together for at least 12 months and support themselves without recourse to public funds.

British immigration rules do not allow overseas lesbians, gays and bisexuals the right to enter or remain in the UK because of a same-sex relationship with a British national, a permanent resident of the UK or a European Union national living in the UK.[150] However, the Home Office does have discretionary power to grant people leave to remain, as a concession outside the immigration rules. This leave to remain has been granted on the basis of heterosexual relationships. The Home Office has commented:

> Although there is no provision within the Immigration Rules for persons to be allowed to remain in the United Kingdom on the basis of a heterosexual common-law relationship with a British citizen, or a person settled here, it is policy to consider granting leave to such persons on the same criteria as those for marriage cases. In general removal will not be enforced when a relationship appears genuine and has lasted for two years or more.[150]

By contrast, the Home Office has stated that:

> There is no provision in the Immigration Rules for a person to be granted leave to remain in the United Kingdom on the basis of a homosexual relationship . . . Ministers have indicated that such applications are very unlikely to be approved unless there are genuinely exceptional circumstances.[151]

Denmark, the Netherlands, Norway, Sweden, Australia and New Zealand all recognise same-sex partnerships for immigration purposes. In Britain such relationships are never recognised. In April 1994 a gay immigration officer was sentenced to six months' imprisonment for forging documents which would have enabled his Brazilian partner to remain in Britain.[152]

The government has argued that 'English law does not accord any legal status to homosexual relationships and our immigration practice merely reflects the general position.'[153] However, this is open to challenge. The Home Office itself has issued guidelines to its staff which recognise the existence of lesbian and gay relationships. In May 1993 the Home Office notified staff that it would consider paying transfer allowances to partners 'including same gender partnerships' of staff who were relocating.[154] The Home Office also recognises same-sex relationships for the purposes of transfers on compassionate grounds.[155]

There are a few reports of lesbians, gays and bisexuals seeking asylum in Britain on the basis that they have a well-founded fear of persecution in their country of origin because of their sexuality. No such applications have been granted, although there are reports that a handful of gay men fleeing victimisation in Iran and Argentina have been granted exceptional leave to remain.[156] In 1989 a court ruled that a Cypriot was not entitled to asylum, despite the fact that homosexuality was illegal and punishable by up to five years' imprisonment in Cyprus, on the grounds that he would not face persecution simply for his sexual orientation but only if he had a lover.[157]

Families and children

Courts are required to adjudicate on the respective rights of parents and the interests of the children, most often after the break-up of a marriage and a dispute about where the child should reside. The courts and social services are also regularly involved in deciding whether or not people can provide a suitable environment for fostering or adopting a child.[158]

No one – not even a biological parent – has an absolute right to custody over children. International law recognises that the rights of parents in this area must be subordinate to the welfare and interests of the child.[159] For the same reason, people have no automatic right to foster or adopt a child. However, in respecting the rights of people to found a family, as guaranteed under Article 23 of the ICCPR, the British government – and the courts and authorities – are under an obligation not to discriminate on any grounds, such as the sexual orientation of the parents.

Lesbian mothers and gay fathers live with the threat of losing parental rights.[160] In the event of a dissolved heterosexual marriage, the courts frequently discriminate against lesbians, gays and bisexuals when deciding with whom the children should live and have contact.[161] Sexual orientation is not usually an absolute bar to obtaining custody, but is regarded as a relevant and negative factor. It has been argued that lesbian and bisexual mothers are usually only awarded custody by default, when the father is considered totally unsuitable by the courts, or has no suitable accommodation, or when the children absolutely refuse to live with him.[162]

In deciding where the child should live, the courts' paramount consideration is the child's welfare.[163] The concept of the child's welfare has no legal definition, and it is up to the judge to consider a variety of listed factors when determining what is in the best interest of the child. Although the courts tend to presume that it is in the best interest of the child to be brought up with the mother, they also tend to presume that a heterosexual home environment is better for a child.[164]

Judges are not required to articulate a specific connection between a mother's lesbianism and its effect on her children before denying her custody. However, the courts have ruled that women who were 'advertising their lesbianism and acting in the public field in favour of promoting lesbianism' should be considered less suitable candidates.[165] Where lesbian or bisexual women have been awarded custody the courts have, on occasion, made it clear that this was with reluctance and only because there was 'no acceptable alternative form of custody'; that is, because the heterosexual father and local authority could not provide better care.[166]

Gay or bisexual fathers, who are open about their sexual orientation, are virtually never awarded custody in competition with heterosexual mothers.[167] Gay fathers often face difficulties obtaining visiting rights and some have even had all their parental rights extinguished. The House of Lords has ruled that a gay man can have his child adopted without his consent and that he should subsequently be denied any contact with that child. The reason given was that his sexual orientation 'destroys at once the main argument which is strong in normal cases that the maintenance of the tie with the possibility of parental influence is valuable to a child and should not be cut off.'[168] The ruling conceded that the father did not constitute any danger to his son, but nevertheless should be separated from him.

Judges, court welfare officers and psychiatrists often assume that a child brought up in a lesbian household will be stigmatised in social settings owing to the general homophobic prejudices of society. Some judges voice unfounded prejudices about the supposed predatory nature of lesbians, gays and bisexuals, and the possibility that their partners may attempt to abuse the children.[169] Home Office research in fact indicates that children are more at risk of molestation by heterosexual men.[170]

There have been cases of mothers being granted custody on condition that they accept draconian infringements on their civil and political liberties. Conditions, in different cases, have included women giving undertakings not to have their children in the house at the same time as their lover, not to take children on lesbian and gay rights demonstrations, not to go to meetings with other lesbians, not to continue living with their lover, not to allow lesbian, gay and bisexual friends to visit and even agreeing not to have any future contact with their lover.[171]

The Appeal Court ruled in one case that it was impractical to impose such conditions, although the judge commented that the woman's lifestyle was 'abnormal' and that it was 'simple common sense to say that the children ought to have a more normal life, in a more normal family amongst less vehemently minded people.' He stated that he hoped she would exercise 'voluntary self-restraint'.[172] However, many women who are not prepared, or unable to afford, to take their case to appeal are likely to accept such restrictions. Similar restrictions are often also applied as a condition of access to lesbian and bisexual mothers who have been denied custody of their children.[173] Concern is frequently expressed about the 'moral danger' to the children. Although the attitude of the courts is changing, there are still widespread judicial assumptions that children raised by lesbian, gay or bisexual parents will themselves grow up to be lesbian, gay or bisexual, and that this is something from which they should be protected.[174] There is no evidence to validate this argument. Research conducted by the Institute of Psychiatry in London, comparing children growing up in the households of lesbian and single female heterosexual parents, has concluded that children brought up by openly lesbian mothers suffer no detrimental effects owing to their mother's sexuality and are psychologically healthy, [175] though there is evidence that lesbian and gay children raised by heterosexual parents suffer considerable traumas if their parents are reluctant to accept their sexual orientation.[176]

Court orders are never final and either parent can go back at any time and ask for the living arrangements of the child to be altered. Those successful in these attempts have generally shown the court that important changes have occurred since the last order was made. Many lesbian, gay and bisexual parents who have custody of their children recognise this procedure as threatening, as the powers could be invoked at any time to take their children away from them.[177]

Adoption and fostering

It is extremely difficult for same-sex couples to adopt or foster a child. Until recently, the homophobia of the courts and authorities was such that lesbians and gays who were open about their sexuality were never considered suitable to foster or adopt a child.[178]

Only married couples and single people can adopt, so a same-sex couple cannot both legally become parents of a child. Local authorities are usually reluctant to allow single people to adopt. Although local authorities *are* allowing more single women to adopt,[179] gay men remain doubly disadvantaged because of their gender and because they are single. Fostering, because it is a more temporary arrangement, is a simpler process. Decisions are made by a local authority, and do not require the permission of a court.

Some politicians and sections of the media have criticised the greater willingness of the authorities to allow lesbians and gays to foster and adopt in recent years.[180] The British government attempted to insert a clause into the Statutory Guidance of the Children Act 1989 which stated that ' "Equal rights" and "gay rights" have no place in fostering services.'[181] However, this was dropped after lobbying by professional and voluntary bodies working in fostering.[182]

Artificial Insemination by Donor (AID)

Women can become pregnant without having sexual contact with a man either through self-insemination or AID at a clinic. Self-insemination is usually arranged privately. Before 1990 there was

177

no legal regulation of donor insemination. However, the Human Fertilisation and Embryology Act 1990 included some provisions to control the activities of clinics running AID 'treatment services'. There was a vigorous lobby during the passage of the Bill for an explicit ban on these services being available to single women and lesbians. As a result of this, the Act states that 'a woman shall not be provided with treatment services unless account has been taken of the welfare of any child who may be born as a result of the treatment (including the need of that child for a father).'[183]

A Code of Practice issued under the Act warns clinics against adopting policies which 'might appear arbitrary or discriminatory'. However, clinics are obliged to consider the child's 'need for a father' when single women ask for donor insemination, which implicitly discriminates against lesbians wishing to have children.[184] The Act therefore forces single women, and lesbians in particular, into private arrangements. In doing so, it is potentially encouraging interference with the right to privacy of many women, which cannot be justified as being in the interests of children. The Act specifies that donors should remain anonymous and should have no parental rights. However, this only applies to licensed clinics. Private donors are entitled to claim the right to be treated as the father of any resulting child. This means that they can apply to the courts for contact or rights of parental responsibility and residence. The court must consider such applications solely on the basis of what it considers to be in the child's best interest – regardless of the relationship between the two parents.

INCITEMENT TO HATRED AND EQUAL PROTECTION OF THE LAW

There is no law protecting lesbians, gays and bisexuals from incitement to hatred. The Press Complaints Commission is part of a voluntary self-regulatory system and its decisions are not binding. The government has announced that any law against incitement to anti-gay hatred, 'would be open to objection on grounds of eroding freedom of speech.'[185] However, some activists believe that existing laws prohibiting incitement to racial hatred could easily be extended to cover incitement to hatred on the grounds of sexual orientation without any serious practical difficulties or inhibition of freedom of expression.

In September 1992 a ragga music record was released which advocated shooting lesbians and gay men.[186] The song achieved considerable popularity in some sections of the black community. There were verbal and physical assaults on lesbians, gays and bisexuals during which the song's lyrics were shouted by the assailants.[187] The police and Crown Prosecution Service turned down requests to prosecute the record company. In July 1993, Lord Jakobovits, Britain's former Chief Rabbi, said: 'Homosexuality is a disability and if people want to have it eliminated before they have children . . . I do not see any moral objection for using genetic engineering.'[188] In May 1994 a university announced it would not take any action against a lecturer who had distributed literature that linked homosexuality with child abuse and bestiality.[189]

In May 1990 the Press Complaints Commission upheld a complaint against the *Sun* newspaper that its use of the words 'poof' and 'poofter' were 'an unnecessary crude abuse'.[190] The newspaper responded by printing the Commission's judgment alongside an editorial denouncing it and declaring that it would not change its editorial policy. In January 1991 the Commission upheld a similar complaint against the *People* newspaper.[191] In November 1991 the Commission upheld a ruling against another newspaper, the *Daily Star*, over an article entitled 'Poofters on parade' about a proposal from MPs to decriminalise homosexuality in the armed forces. The article referred to 'strident, mincing preachers of filth'.[192] This newspaper also announced that it would not change its policy. In December 1986 the Conservative leader of a local authority commented after watching a film on safe sex:

> The film said how to avoid AIDS, but it did not say specifically stop being queer. It's disgusting and diabolical. As a cure I would put 90 per cent of them in the ruddy gas chamber. Are we going to keep letting these queers trade their filth up and down the country?[193]

Because of such prejudice against their sexual orientation, lesbians, gays and bisexuals are vulnerable both to verbal harassment and to violent physical assaults.[194] Places which have a reputation as gay 'cruising areas' often become targets for those who wish to attack lesbians, gays and bisexuals.[195]

A survey carried out in London in 1991 showed that 40 per cent of gay men and 25 per cent of lesbians had experienced at least one violent assault during their lives because of their sexuality.[196] More than one-half of these had experienced an assault within the last year,[197] yet only 23 per cent of the men and 30 per cent of the women had reported the incident to the police.[198] The survey also found that 48 per cent of men and 44 per cent of women had been physically threatened, and 80 per cent of gay men and 72 per cent of lesbians had been verbally abused because of their sexuality.[199] More than one-half the respondents believed that violence against lesbians and gays was increasing.[200] While 26 per cent of the respondents who reported these incidents to the police found the police to be helpful, 35 per cent believed that they were indifferent, 16 per cent thought that they were incompetent and 22 per cent experienced harassment ranging from hostility and abuse to actual physical violence.[201]

In April 1994 the newspaper *Gay Times* published the findings of a research project, carried out in collaboration with the *Independent on Sunday* newspaper, into the handling of 129 murders in Britain over the last eight years where the victim had been identified as a gay man.[202] The survey showed that 31 of the murders – 24 per cent – had not been solved and in a further 18 cases – 14 per cent – the killer was identified but escaped murder charges. In 10 of these cases, the defendant's plea that he had been provoked by a homosexual advance was accepted, and the murder charges were dropped in favour of the lesser charge of manslaughter. In four more cases, a plea of manslaughter was accepted on the grounds that the victims had been killed either during a burglary, or during an assault motivated by their sexual orientation, but the defendant had not intended to kill them. In one other case – the lynching of a gay man accused by neighbours of child abuse – the judge commented that what the defendants had done was 'unacceptable but understandable' and the defendants were convicted of manslaughter. In another case the police closed the inquiry into the case of a man found dead with massive head injuries by claiming that he had sustained his injuries in a fall. This verdict was disputed by the man's friends, who pointed out that two months earlier he had been the victim of a homophobic assault.[203]

The courts are supposed to consider racial motivation to be an aggravating factor when dealing with cases involving crimes of violence.[204] However, there is no parallel consideration if the victim is lesbian, gay or bisexual and the motivation is homophobia. Defendants in such cases may plead, in mitigation, that their victim made a sexual advance and judges have rewarded such pleas with lighter sentences.[205] Observers have claimed that homophobia within the police and criminal justice system is such that crimes against lesbians, gays and bisexuals are treated less seriously than similar offences against heterosexuals and that victims are sometimes subject to verbal abuse by police and judges.[206] In 1988, for example, a judge described the gay victim of an assault and robbery as a 'little sodomite'.[207]

TRANSGENDERISM

Transsexuals are people (of either sex) who are born with bodies of the wrong gender. Although corrective surgery is available both privately and on the National Health Service, British law provides no corresponding legal right to have this new identity recognised. Transgenderism encompasses pre- and post-operative transsexuals and people who are not actively pursuing surgical reassignment.

Transgendered people form a distinct group from lesbians, gays and bisexuals. They may be of any sexual orientation as this is unrelated to their gender identity. However, transgendered people experience discrimination at the hands of the State and its various institutions. Because the law does not recognise the right of people to have changes to their gender recognised, many of the abuses perpetuated against transsexuals are similar to those suffered by lesbians, gays and bisexuals. This lack of legal recognition means that a transsexual's legal status will always be that of the sex entered on the birth certificate. This has wide-ranging effects on the lives of transgendered people, including denial of their right to marry or to adopt or foster children with a partner of the opposite sex as a heterosexual couple. The lack of gender acknowledgment may also present problems with custody of their children and recognition of their step-parent status with their partner's children from a previous relationship. Transsexuals seeking to bring their partners into the country may face similar problems to lesbians and gay men while those fleeing persecution because of their gender identity are unlikely to be granted asylum in this country.

The lack of general protection against discrimination means that transsexuals who have had, or are seeking to have, corrective surgery can be subject to considerable victimisation, harassment and discrimination.[208] The prejudices of members of the medical profession can deny transsexuals the right to corrective surgery and there are cases of this being denied on the grounds that a doctor disliked the attitudes, political views or even dress sense of a transsexual.[209]

The lack of a right to privacy means that transgendered people cannot prevent details about themselves being made public. They face considerable public hostility and ridicule, against which they have no redress as there is no legal prohibition of this type of incitement to hatred.

Until 1971 the law recognised post-operative transsexuals as members of their chosen sex. However, in *Corbett* v. *Corbett*[210] (a divorce case involving a male to female transsexual who had been legally married) the High Court ruled that the transsexual was still a male, and could not therefore marry a man. Many other countries do allow birth and death certificates to be amended and there have been a number of challenges to the British government's refusal to do so. Although the European Commission on Human Rights has declared some cases admissible, the Court has ruled that such arrangements are at the discretion of member States.[211] Liberty is currently taking cases on birth certificates and parenting to the European Commission.

The fact that transsexuals are denied the right to marry effectively prevents them from adopting children and makes fostering unlikely. There are a number of cases where transsexuals have been denied foster arrangements.[212] Moreover, if a woman partner of a female to male transsexual becomes pregnant by artificial insemination, because her partner is still legally female he cannot be registered as the baby's father or enjoy parental rights.[213]

Transgendered people have no protection against discrimination and may be dismissed from or denied jobs and other services solely on the basis of their gender identity.[214] However, there is an increasing amount of scientific evidence showing that gender dysphoria is a condition determined before birth – owing to hormonal factors.[215] This strengthens the case for giving the same type of anti-discrimination protection to transsexuals as that afforded to people on the grounds of race or sex, on the grounds that it is an innate biological characteristic.

The lack of a right to privacy also has a marked effect on transgendered people. They have no right to change their birth certificates and their originally recorded gender remains on all National Insurance and Benefits Agency computer records. Fear of exposure by prejudiced staff at these offices makes many transsexuals reluctant to claim benefits to which they are entitled. Prospective employers, college authorities, insurance companies and other bodies may also insist on seeing birth certificates. The originally recorded gender also appears on death certificates.

The criminal law also discriminates against transgendered people, by failing to recognise their existence. This is reinforced by the prejudice and bigotry of many members of the police, prison service and legal profession. Transgendered people who are imprisoned are often sent to prisons for the wrong gender and may be denied the hormone treatment that they need throughout their life. Both female-to-male and male-to-female transsexuals are vulnerable to assault and may choose to serve their sentence in Rule 43 conditions where they will be segregated from other prisoners. In addition, male to female transsexuals in male prisons are particularly at risk of being raped and assaulted.

7 ACCESS DENIED: HUMAN RIGHTS AND DISABLED PEOPLE

In May 1994 the Civil Rights (Disabled Persons) Bill, which sought to outlaw discrimination against disabled people in Britain, was prevented from becoming law by a series of parliamentary manoeuvres.[1] A group of back-bench Conservative MPs tabled last minute lengthy amendments, made deliberately long speeches and manipulated the quorum count to talk the Bill out of parliamentary time. Although they repeatedly denied that they were acting on the government's behalf,[2] this was shown to be untrue. The Minister with responsibility for disabled issues, Nicholas Scott MP, was forced to admit that he had misled the House of Commons,[3] while one of the MPs earned a rebuke from the Speaker of the House.[4] During ill-tempered exchanges one Conservative supporter of the Bill, Terry Dicks MP, accused one of his colleagues of 'telling a pack of lies'.[5]

These tactics caused particular outrage because the Bill had previously received unanimous all-party support in its progress through Parliament. In moving its second reading, its sponsor, Roger Berry MP, said that the measures were:

> not about charity, being paternalistic or . . . being nice to
> disabled people. It is about rights. The Bill's purpose is
> to ensure that the disabled have the same rights as everyone
> else in employment, housing, education, public transport and
> the provision of other goods and services. It is certain that the
> Bill, or something like it, will eventually reach the statute
> books. When that happens, we shall look back and wonder
> why on earth that took so long – why, in 1994, we had to
> spend time debating whether or not 6.5 million people in this
> country should have the right to protection against
> discrimination.[6]

Berry noted that one-quarter of a million postcards supporting the

Bill had been sent to MPs and that of the thousands of letters and telephone calls he had received not one opposed it.[7] The Bill also had the support of a clear majority in the House of Commons – 310 MPs signed an Early Day Motion in support of the Bill while a further 20 front-bench Members gave their approval in writing.[8] MPs from all parties spoke in favour and none in opposition. This was the sixteenth attempt to introduce some form of anti-discrimination law for disabled people and the thirteenth time such a Bill had been blocked in Parliament. Inevitably, frustration at the government's tactics is increasing,[9] especially as it ignored calls for Nicholas Scott's resignation, despite the tradition that ministers who are found to have misled the House of Commons are usually expected to relinquish their posts.[10]

Disabled people experience severe economic and social deprivation and are disadvantaged in British society in a number of ways.[11] There are higher rates of unemployment among disabled people and those out of work are likely to be unemployed for longer periods than non-disabled people. When they do find work it is often low paid, low status and in poor working conditions. They are under-represented in professional and managerial jobs, on average earn less than non-disabled people and are more likely to live in poverty. Disabled people receive inferior education, leave school with fewer qualifications and are more likely than non-disabled people to be forced into dependency on welfare benefits. The values and practices of the health and welfare system infringe the personal autonomy, privacy and independence of disabled people.[12]

In July 1994 the government published a consultation paper setting out its alternative to the Bill.[13] This proposed an extremely limited form of protection for people with 'substantial' disability against 'unjustifiable' discrimination, the abolition of the statutory quota on firms to employ a minimum of three per cent registered disabled employees, consideration of new requirements in the design of new dwellings to promote greater accessibility, a code of good practice by banks, insurers and financial groups in relation to their disabled customers and the establishment of a new advisory body, the National Disability Council.[14]

In January 1995 the government published a draft parliamentary bill and a White Paper, *Ending discrimination against disabled people*.[15] This proposed giving disabled people a 'right of access to goods and services', requiring businesses to adapt their premises where such adaptations were 'readily achievable'.[16] Businesses would be given up to 15 years to adapt their premises and between 5 and 10 per cent of their ratable value was suggested as a limit on what they would be required to spend on the adaptation. The National Disability Council would be an advisory body with no statutory powers.[17] Estimates of the cost to businesses of these measures are about £1.1 billion on physical adaptations to buildings, and about £80 million on the government anti-discrimination programme.[18] Estimates of the cost of implementing the Civil Rights (Disabled Persons) Bill are up to £17 billion. However, these costings appear to rest on a misunderstanding of the proposals.[19]

Although an official government report first recommended anti-discrimination legislation in 1982, no cost–benefit analysis of the Bill's proposals has ever been undertaken and the government has admitted that it has no idea of the costs of carrying out such measures.[20] The scarcity of research in Britain illustrates the low priority which the government gives to disabled people's rights. The misinformation circulated during the debate, the government's wrecking tactics and the disingenuousness of the minister responsible confirm this general disregard.

Disabled people are under-represented in public life and lack access to decision-making power. Disabled people's organisations have identified institutional discrimination as the main problem affecting them and are demanding legal protection against unfair treatment as part of a growing campaign for equal civil and political rights.[21] This campaign is led by disabled people and challenges the traditional philanthropic and welfarist attitudes towards people with disabilities. It favours self-organisation, self-determination, empowerment and basic human rights.[22]

THE BRITISH GOVERNMENT'S RECORD

In 1979, pressure from a variety of organisations of disabled people forced the (Labour) government to establish the Committee on Restrictions Against Disabled People (CORAD). Their report, published in 1982, is the only official publication on discrimination and disability received by the British government.[23] It examined a wide range of issues including access to public buildings and transport systems and the rights of disabled people in education, employment and entertainment. The report found discrimination to be commonplace and made a number of recommendations for improving public attitudes towards disabled people. It also endorsed the call for anti-discrimination legislation to provide disabled people with a legal mechanism for securing equal rights. However, the report's findings were dismissed by the (Conservative) government which failed to enact an anti-discrimination law.

During the 1980s two government-backed surveys have reported high levels of unemployment and poverty amongst disabled people. The Office of Population Censuses and Surveys (OPCS) produced six reports from a survey carried out between 1985 and 1988[24] and the Department of Employment commissioned a separate study by Social and Community Planning Research (SCPR) which reported in 1990.[25] Although both have been challenged for underestimating levels of disadvantage,[26] each report confirmed that disabled people have a substantially poorer quality of life than the rest of the population.

The government's argument that such disadvantage is not caused by discrimination has become threadbare in the light of growing pressure from disabled people's organisations. Vigorous civil rights campaigns in the 1980s and early 1990s have confronted discrimination directly using a range of tactics such as direct action and civil disobedience. The British Council of Organisations of Disabled People (BCODP) was formed in 1981 to harness a growing rights consciousness amongst disabled people. By 1991, it represented 75 separate organisations and about 200,000 individuals. In 1991 it published its own study examining the nature and extent of discrimination against disabled people.[27]

In 1985 a new umbrella body, the Voluntary Organisations for Anti-Discrimination Legislation committee (VOADL), was established by organisations which are representative of disabled people and those which worked with them in a more traditional manner, to press for legally enforceable equal rights. In 1994 this umbrella organisation became Rights Now.

It is estimated that in Britain by the year 2031 the size of the disabled population will have grown to about 8.2 million adults, representing an increase of 34 per cent from 1986.[28] As the populations of advanced countries are ageing, and because both the incidence and severity of disability increases with age,[29] a growing proportion of those countries' populations are likely to have physical impairments. Increasingly, therefore, countries with advanced market economies are needing to instigate specific measures to enable disabled people to enjoy equal rights and so be more economically active.[30] Denying an increasing proportion of the population access to the built environment – transport, housing, businesses and facilities – carries with it a social cost which is not only morally indefensible but economically counter-productive.

Slow progress

As the ICCPR contains no specific Articles relating to the rights of disabled people, neither the British government's *Third* or *Fourth Periodic Reports to the UN Human Rights Committee* contained any reference to its treatment of disabled people.

In 1990, the government published a consultation document which reviewed the effectiveness of the Disabled Persons (Employment) Act 1944.[31] In the same year the government revised its voluntary code of practice – first launched in 1984 – which calls on employers to encourage applications for employment from disabled people and to give greater consideration to the representation of disabled people in their workforces. The government claims that the number of companies displaying a good practice symbol of two ticks, illustrating their adherence to the code, doubled between October 1993 and March 1994.[32]

The Companies Act 1985 requires companies employing more than 250 employees to set out their policies on recruitment, training and career development for disabled workers in their annual reports, although this can be limited to a single statement and has been criticised as inadequate by the Trades Union Congress.[33] Also in 1985 the government established the Disabled Persons Transport Advisory Committee to provide 'informal advice and guidance' to the Department of Transport about making transport systems more accessible. The Disabled Persons (Services, Consultation and Representation) Act 1986 gives disabled people in hospitals or long term educational institutions the right to a statement and an assessment of their likely needs in the community. It also places a duty on local authorities to provide disabled people with information. However, much of this legislation has yet to be enforced and remains primarily a statement of intent.

In the debate on the Civil Rights (Disabled Persons) Bill in March 1994, the Minister for Disabled People, Nicholas Scott, claimed there had been 'significant recent progress in the arrangements for children with special educational needs, including those with disabilities.'[34] He said that the government would shortly be publishing a code of practice on the identification and assessment of special educational needs.[35]

However, the government's achievements must be seen in the context of:

☐ the growing campaign for civil rights by disabled people

☐ the increasing volume of evidence which details the nature and extent of discrimination against disabled people

☐ the legislative models for countering discrimination adopted by other countries.

In this light, the British government's achievements appear modest and the rate of progress frustratingly slow.

DISABLED PEOPLE AND DISCRIMINATION

According to the OPCS survey, there are just over six million disabled adults in Britain and about 14 per cent of the adult population have at least one impairment which causes disability.[36] About 400,000 disabled adults live in some kind of communal establishment.[37] The study also estimates that there are 500,000 people with hearing impairments, about one million blind people and a further two million who are partially sighted. There are an estimated four million people with mobility problems – about 500,000 people use wheelchairs on a daily basis while up to a million use wheelchairs some of the time. Around 500,000 people have a learning disability.

Additionally, there are some 21,000 people who are known to be HIV-positive – although this is probably an under-estimate – and over 8,500 are reported to have AIDS.[38] Anxiety states and depressive disorders account for the great majority of officially recognised types of mental illness. Around 2.3 million people suffer from depression and up to 2.8 million suffer from anxiety.[39] The SCPR survey estimated that 22 per cent of adults of working age had a health problem or disability.[40] These surveys are consistent with earlier studies which suggest that between 10 and 15 per cent of the general population are disabled.[41]

Defining disability

The size of the disabled population in Britain obviously depends on the definition of disability which is used[42] and much of the hostility to anti-discrimination legislation is motivated by an individualistic and medical view of disability.[43] This view seeks to explain the disadvantages experienced by disabled people as simple consequences of their individual physical and functional limitations; discrimination is rare and, where it does occur, can be justified. As one commentator put it:

> The only real remedy for a disability is a complete cure. Otherwise the best we can do is to push many small advantages the disabled person's way, in the hope that their cumulative effect will make up for the original big disadvantage. To call that 'equality', however, is to misuse the language. In place of legs we offer wheels . . . Who is to say at what point the different lifestyles of able-bodied and disabled persons are brought to a level of equivalence? How far do we have to go to avoid being accused of 'discrimination' against the disabled? . . . The truth is that the disabled [sic] cannot manage without the sympathy, indeed the protection, of the rest of society, and they have been badly misled if they think otherwise.[44]

In contrast, disabled people argue that they face unjustified discrimination[45] and that the problems they face are socially created. Disability can be defined in a different way:

> the term disability itself represents a complex system of social restrictions imposed on people with impairments by a highly discriminatory society. To be a disabled person in modern Britain means to be discriminated against.[46]

Many people who have physical impairments do not define themselves as disabled, and are not regarded as such by society, because their impairments do not lead to social exclusion. Some impairments (such as short sightedness) can be easily corrected, while others (such as colour blindness) do not prevent people from participating in most areas of society on generally equal terms. All people have different physical and mental capacities which make them more or less suited to achieving different tasks or playing different roles in life. Societies are also based on inter-dependence which does not, of itself, prevent each person realising his or her full potential as an individual. Disability by definition, therefore, is not just a functional limitation but arises from the discrimination that disabled people face.

The way that society is constructed – both the built physical environment and the dominant attitudes and expectations of its population – can lead to restrictions against certain groups which deny them equal opportunities to participate in all areas of life. This occurs either through conscious discrimination or because society has not adapted to those groups' needs. For example, people who are colour blind do not face social exclusion because, on the whole, society is not ordered and regulated by colour recognition. Similarly, social attitudes to left handed people have changed and they are no longer at risk of being burnt to death as witches – as they were during the 17th century – or forced to try and write with their right hands – which was a common practice until more recently.

It follows, then, that there are two inter-related elements to what is termed disability:[47]

☐ The physical, mental or sensory impairment of an individual

☐ The social environment, artificial barriers and attitudes which prevent the individual from playing a full part in the life of the community.

Following from this, three types of discrimination against disabled people have been identified:[48]

☐ Direct discrimination: treating people less favourably than others because of their disability

☐ Indirect discrimination: imposing a requirement or condition on a job, facility or service which makes it harder for disabled people to gain access to it

☐ Unequal burdens: failing to take reasonable steps to remove barriers in the social environment that prevent disabled people participating equally.

The first two forms of discrimination are the same as those currently outlawed in the areas of race[49] and sex[50] and could be dealt with by similar means. For example, legislation covering a wide range of activities, including employment and training, housing, education and the provision of goods and services, as well as access to the built environment, transport and communications systems, could be introduced. As with race and sex discrimination, the different aspects could be enforced using different mechanisms: industrial tribunals in the case of employment discrimination, and county courts for other forms of discrimination.

The concept of 'unequal burdens' widens the definition of discrimination in relation to disabled people. This type of discrimination exists when an artificial barrier, which could be removed by reasonable adaptation, prevents a disabled person from benefiting from an opportunity enjoyed by a non-disabled person. Enforcing measures to counter this form of discrimination may require the establishment of a new form of tribunal, although the procedures would be similar to those used in disputes about race and sex discrimination.[51]

In the case of direct or indirect discrimination an employer or service provider is committing a civil offence if they treat someone unfairly because they have an impairment. In the case of unequal burdens discrimination, the employer or service provider is committing an offence if they fail to adapt the environment to take account of an impaired person's incapacity when it would be reasonable for them to do so.

The first two forms of discrimination are defended by the argument that such discrimination is fair because the impairment in question genuinely prevents the person from performing the work or receiving the service they are excluded from. Discrimination of the third type (unequal burdens), however, is defended by the argument that the adjustments necessary to enable participation would require unreasonable expense, disruption and change, bearing in mind the size of the organisation, its financial viability and the level of hardship such adjustments would cause. It would be up to the tribunal, court or other adjudicating body to decide each case on the basis of the evidence presented by each side.

The government has opposed legislation aimed at outlawing these forms of discrimination primarily on grounds of cost. However, this argument is not convincing. Proponents of anti-discrimination law accept that it would need to be phased in over a long period and even those who argue for education and persuasion, rather than enforceable laws, as the means for change accept that these costs will have to be met eventually.

The other main argument against new legislation is that discrimination is not pervasive and, where it does occur, can be justified. In 1990 a Department of Employment consultative document stated that:

> a major difficulty is that disability, unlike race or sex, can be relevant to job performance and what to some might seem like discrimination may in reality be recruitment based on legitimate preferences and likely performance.[52]

However, there are numerous examples of direct and indirect discrimination against disabled people which are not justifiable but against which there is currently no legal redress. For example, in 1988 a worker in the advertising department at the *Daily Telegraph* newspaper was sacked because he had a mild form of controlled epilepsy.[53] Other examples include:

☐ a holiday camp which refused a week's booking from a group with cerebral palsy[54]

☐ a coach hire company which refused to carry a person in a wheelchair[55]

☐ a property owner who refused to sell to or allow occupation of land by people with a history of mental health problems[56]

☐ a landlord who banned a disabled skittles team from a public house because he believed some of its members to be 'mentally handicapped'[57]

☐ a woman who, having been accepted onto a postgraduate course, had the offer withdrawn because a doctor's report revealed that she had a history of depression. The depression was under control and, in the doctor's opinion, the woman was perfectly fit to follow the vocational course and pursue a career[58]

☐ an oil company which refused to employ people who are HIV-positive[59]

☐ a leaseholder who refused to allow a property to be converted for use as a centre for people with learning disabilities[60]

☐ an employer who refused to hire a qualified blind tele-sales person because its office was on the first floor and the employer thought that blind people could not walk up stairs.[61]

DISABLED PEOPLE IN PUBLIC LIFE

Disabled people are under-represented in all forms of public life. Disabled people's restricted access to decision-making power in society has increased their political marginalisation and compounded many of the problems that they face.

Access to political life

The British government is ignoring its obligations, contained in Article 25 of the ICCPR, to provide all people with the right to take part in public affairs on the basis of equality.

The law prevents some disabled people from registering to vote and places obstacles in the way of others who attempt to do so.[62] The physical inaccessibility of many polling stations, the difficulties in obtaining postal or proxy votes and a less than equal access to political information deny disabled people the right to make informed political choices and to enjoy political influence on equal terms with others.[63]

Some long-term hospital patients are excluded from the electoral register and, in practice, the vast majority of people in hospital with mental health problems or learning disabilities remain disenfranchised. A study by the mental health charity, MIND, found that in 1988 only 329 such hospital residents were registered from a total of 4,349.[64] MIND found widespread variations between institutions and concluded that electoral registration levels appeared to depend on the attitudes of the staff.[65]

Prior to the Representation of the People Act 1983, people living in institutions, particularly those with mental health problems or learning disabilities, were defined as patients rather than residents and were not entitled to vote. The Act gave hospital residents the right to vote but only under certain narrowly defined conditions which do not apply to similarly impaired people living in the community or to any other group in society.[66] Residents in hospitals for people with mental health problems or learning disabilities 'may' be entitled to vote but only if they have completed a 'Patient's Declaration' form by 10 October each year. They must complete the form themselves – unless they have a physical or sensory impairment which prevents them from doing so – and in the presence of a hospital staff member who is required to counter sign it. No other group in society is forced to prove that its members are capable of voting.[67] Because hospitals are not defined as residences, patients have to give an outside address in order to register to vote. This may cause problems for long-stay patients who actually live in the hospital. Other disabled people living in staffed or sheltered accommodation lose their right to vote due to ignorance and mistakes by staff.

Disabled people who are registered still face 'unequal burdens' when exercising their right to vote. There is a legal obligation on local authorities to ensure that polling stations are accessible but only 'so far as it is reasonable and practical to do so.'[68] In the 1992 general election only 12 per cent of polling stations were fully accessible to disabled people and many more were unable to reach the polling stations because of the lack of accessible public transport. Such physical difficulties persuade many disabled people not to bother registering.[69] Some presiding officers are not aware that the law allows them to give assistance to disabled people who are casting their vote[70] but the only people who are allowed assistance from someone other than the presiding officer are people with visual impairments, who may be helped by a friend or relative who meets strictly defined criteria.[71] But, because ballot forms are not available in Braille or on tape, blind people are effectively denied the right to a secret ballot.[72] Disabled people may obtain postal or proxy votes – if they have a doctor's certificate – but the procedure is complex and many find it either daunting or unnecessarily intrusive.[73]

These obstacles perpetuate the process of political marginalisation by weakening the electoral influence of disabled people. The main political parties are consequently less likely to promote issues of concern to disabled people, which decreases the relevance of mainstream politics to people with disabilities.

Disabled people who wish to play a more active role in British politics face additional problems. The Houses of Parliament are inaccessible to many disabled people while the public gallery of the House of Commons provides only four places for people in wheelchairs.[74] Although the proceedings of Parliament have been televised since 1989, these broadcasts are inaccessible to deaf people because they are not subtitled. Outside Parliament, many political meetings are held in inaccessible venues and, although the three main political parties now use signers at their annual party conferences, much of their election literature is published in forms which are inaccessible to disabled people.[75]

By contrast, in November 1993, three years after the passage of the Americans With Disabilities Act, 94 per cent of polling booths in New York were accessible to disabled people for the Mayoral elections, and every state in the USA now provides relay systems to make television accessible to deaf people.[76]

Disabled people and the media

Disabled people are under-represented at all levels in the media.[77] Disabled people have identified negative imagery in the media as a major contributory cause of the discriminatory attitudes they face in the rest of society.[78] The government's emphasis on 'education and persuasion' to help change public attitudes also acknowledges the important role that the media can play in perpetuating or reducing the discrimination that disabled people face.

Government interference with, or regulation of, the media raises serious concerns from a freedom of expression standpoint. However, the 'special responsibility' with which the UN Human Rights Committee specifies that this right must be exercised does provide potential justification for a degree of regulation in order to protect the rights and freedoms of others.

In 1990, 14.5 per cent of television programmes carried subtitles – although this is increasing. Television sets equipped to take subtitled programmes are more expensive to buy[79] and newspapers and magazines are rarely published in a form accessible to people with visual impairments. One national newspaper, the *Guardian*, is available in an accessible format on the same day as it is published. While some voluntary organisations produce taped, weekly summaries of some newspapers, visually impaired users are denied access to information of the same quality and at the same time as the non-disabled population.[80]

Disabled people are significantly under-represented in the broadcast media where negative images of disabled people are also widespread.[81] Films, plays and literature frequently portray disabled people as objects to be pitied or feared. Newspapers similarly patronise and misrepresent the experiences of disabled people. Although in 1989 the Broadcasting Standards Council stated in its Code of Practice that programmes should provide 'a fair reflection of the parts played in the everyday life of the nation by disabled people' and in 1990 the editors of the main national newspapers agreed a similar voluntary code of practice,[82] such announcements are widely regarded as 'cosmetic' by many disabled activists.[83]

The media also perpetuate a negative, stereotypical and sensationalist image of 'mental illness' which makes acceptance by the wider community more difficult.[84] An analysis by the Broadcasting Research Unit in 1988 showed that disabled people rarely figure in news and current affairs programmes except as the subjects of medical cures or treatment or as examples of the special achievements of disabled people who overcome their impairments.[85] The selection criteria of programmes with participating members of the public appeared to be discriminatory – for example, not one of the game shows examined included a disabled person.[86] The same research showed that only 1.4 per cent of the speaking characters in fictional programmes were disabled (disabled people comprise about 14 per cent of the general population) and of the characters shown, 65 per cent were male, 95 per cent were white and 50 per cent aged between 25 and 40 – which gives a misleading portrayal of the disabled population.[87]

Disabled people are more likely to be included in feature films than drama programmes but the portrayals of them are overwhelmingly negative. Of the 134 films analysed, 72 contained disabled characters. Fifty-three of these were major parts and 25 were parts in which the circumstances of the disability were an important issue. However, in 13 of these the portrayal was judged to be sentimental, while in only eight was the issue of prejudice and discrimination raised.[88] The use of negative stereotypes was frequent and disabled people were often found to be portrayed as criminals, sub-human or pathetic. The study showed that disabled people were included 'to enhance the atmosphere of a film when it needs to be one of deprivation, mystery or menace' because they are seen as 'not ordinary people'.[89]

In contrast to Britain, American television programmes are far more likely to provide positive and realistic portrayals of disabled people. In dramatic fiction disabled characters are more often portrayed as 'sociable, extrovert, moral and non-aggressive and less likely to be dependent, sad, moody or difficult to get on with'.[90] On American programmes disabled people are frequently shown having an emotional relationship and are far less likely to be portrayed as people incapable of sexual relationships or sexual activity.[91]

The politics of pity

Many disabled activists argue that their under-representation in public life, the denial of their right to equal political participation and the restrictions to their freedom of expression are reinforced by the misguided efforts of some charities.[92]

In 1990 a group of disabled activists formed the Campaign to Stop Patronage. This group demonstrated against the Telethon, an annual television fund-raising event which appeals to the public for donations to charities for disabled people and other disadvantaged groups. The images used by Telethon and those in the advertisements of some charities are seen by many activists to promote an image of disabled people which reinforces the prejudices of people in society. Disabled people are often portrayed as 'pitiable and pathetic' and such advertising has been described as 'the cynical exploitation of stereotypes'.[93]

Three types of advertising have been identified: the philanthropic, which portrays the disabled as people to be pitied; the courageous; and the 'positive', in which the 'normal' or 'able-bodied' abilities of individual disabled people are celebrated.[94] The more positive imagery is viewed as an improvement on the philanthropic approach and is one which was largely forced on the disability charities by strong lobbying against previous advertising campaigns.

However, there is still concern that such imagery does not accurately reflect the disabled community as a whole, ignoring the racial and gender divisions within it and the real differences between disabled people and the rest of the population.[95] The use of such images has also been criticised for obscuring the need for society to change. By promoting a concept of 'normality', the real differences between disabled and non-disabled people are minimised. BCODP has argued that

> there is an inherent contradiction in the assertion that disabled people are basically 'normal' but at the same time have to get others, notably non-disabled people, to beg on their behalf for the basic necessities of life.[96]

The BCODP has drawn up a code of ethics for the advertising industry and some disabled people have produced their own advertisements which use positive images and focus on the need for equal rights.[97] Disabled people are best able to speak for themselves, represent themselves and decide the ways in which they should be portrayed. These rights, which many in the rest of society take for granted, and which are underwritten in the ICCPR, are being denied to disabled people in Britain in an unjustifiable and discriminatory way.

DISCRIMINATION IN EMPLOYMENT

The Disabled Persons (Employment) Act 1944 provided a legal duty on all employers with 20 or more full-time employees to ensure that at least 3 per cent of their workforce are registered disabled people.[98] Those who fail to comply, or to keep records of their quota, are liable to a fine or imprisonment. Although employers may apply for exemption certificates to the Department of Employment, stating why they cannot meet their quota, these are issued on a discretionary basis only.

There are currently around 370,000 people registered under the Act and issued with a green card, but this is only a tiny fraction of the number of adult disabled people in the UK.[99] According to the SCPR survey, 65 per cent of unregistered disabled people saw no advantage in registering, while 21 per cent actually believed that registering would make it more difficult for them to obtain work.[100]

This cynicism is justified. The legislation requiring firms to employ a minimum quota of disabled people is widely ignored and rarely enforced. There have been only 10 attempts to prosecute employers for failing to meet their quota over the last 50 years, resulting in only seven fines, with an average value of £62.00,[101] the latest of which was in 1975. The maximum fine of £100 was set in 1944 and has never been increased and while the number of firms abiding by the quota rose until the mid 1960s (53.2 per cent in 1965), it has fallen steadily ever since (to 26.8 per cent in 1986). Since 1972 the number of employers given exemption certificates has exceeded the number complying with the scheme,[102] while an estimated 17.2 per cent of those who did not meet their quota in 1986 did not apply for exemption certificates – an indication of the low likelihood of their prosecution[103] and of the ineffectiveness of the quota system.

A succession of government reports has acknowledged that the system was largely being ignored but rejected proposals for tighter enforcement of the laws in favour of policies of 'education' and 'persuasion'.[104] The number of staff employed to enforce the legislation was cut drastically during the 1980s, while a leaked Department of Employment memorandum from 1991, obtained by BCODP, stated that 'work with disabled people is given little status and even less priority by the Employment Service'.[105]

Although the 1944 Act is not binding on government departments, they have agreed to accept the same responsibilities as other employers but are not complying with the legislation themselves. In March 1994 the Department of Health admitted that it employed 68 registered disabled people, only 1.4 per cent of the total workforce and less than one-half the legal quota.[106] Within the civil service as a whole there are 1.5 per cent registered disabled employees[107] but only 0.3 per cent work in the Home Office and none at all in the Prime Minister's office.[108] Only 0.7 per cent of employees in the private sector are registered disabled.[109]

Changes to the way in which the official unemployment statistics were recorded during the 1980s, especially an increasingly strict application of the 'actively seeking work' rule, significantly reduced the proportion of those people out of work who are registered as unemployed, which makes it difficult to make direct comparisons between the numbers of unemployed disabled and non-disabled people. However, it is estimated that disabled people are about three times more likely to be unemployed than non-disabled[110] and are also unemployed for longer periods. Those in employment are more likely to have lower paid, lower status and less secure jobs, which they are more likely to leave before the official retirement age.[111] The SCPR estimated in 1990 that 3.8 per cent of working-age adults (16-55 years for men, 16-60 years for women) who were in work or seeking work were disabled (1,272,000 people). It stated that 22 per cent of these were unemployed and 'actively seeking work' (285,000 people).[112]

These figures exclude significant numbers of disabled people who want to work but cannot be defined as 'actively seeking work'. According to the OPCS, less than one-third of disabled people of working age in the UK are actually in employment[113] and, although 34 per cent of those interviewed said that they were permanently unable to work, some of these might be able to do part-time or sheltered work if it was available.[114] Of those who were available for work, over one-half had stopped looking for it because of the difficulties they experienced[115] and of those who had stopped looking, and were therefore no longer classified as unemployed, 86 per cent of the men and 65 per cent of the women had previously taken steps to find work.[116] The OPCS also found that 31 per cent of disabled men and 16 per cent of disabled women retired early – a significantly higher proportion than in the general population.[117]

A considerably greater proportion of disabled people are employed in clerical and administrative work or in semi-skilled and personal service work than is the case for the working population as a whole,[118] whilst a much lower proportion are employed in professional or managerial positions.[119] In 1990 the government revealed that no disabled people were employed in the top seven grades of the civil service.[120]

The SCPR study found that disabled men in full-time employment earn, on average, one-quarter less per week than their non-disabled equivalents.[121] Precise information about disabled women's earnings is not available but the OPCS survey found that they earned about one-third less than male disabled people.[122] This is a smaller proportion than that of female to male earnings in the population as a whole.[123] The difference between the hourly earnings of disabled and non-disabled men is of a similar scale and, while the difference is narrower between disabled and non-disabled women, this only reflects the general disadvantage which women face in the labour market.[124]

Direct discrimination in employment

Those who argue that the under-representation of disabled people in employment is not caused by discrimination have been directly contradicted by two separate studies conducted by the Spastics Society[125] into hiring practices in the private sector.[126]

The two surveys used techniques similar to those which measure racial discrimination. Two fictitious applications were sent out in response to publicly advertised jobs. These differed only in that one purported to be from a disabled person. The studies revealed virtually identical evidence – that the non-disabled applicant was one-and-a-half times more likely to receive a positive reply, while the disabled candidate was six times more likely to receive a negative response.[127]

One-third of all people who become disabled whilst in employment and subsequently leave their jobs for health reasons are either sacked or pressurised into leaving by their employers.[128] Those with a greater length of service are more likely to retain their jobs, which indicates that the attitude of the employer has an influence as well as the nature of the impairment. Disabled employees working for large firms are also more likely to retain their jobs than those working for small firms because larger firms are more able to make reasonable adaptations to the built environment – again showing that the impairment itself is often not the decisive factor.[129]

A government study found that, while 75 per cent of a large representative sample of public and private sector employers claimed they would not discriminate against disabled people, 13 per cent said they would only employ disabled people for certain types of work and 6 per cent said that they would not employ disabled people 'under any circumstances'.[130] However, even the good intentions displayed by 75 per cent of the employers in this study do not always translate into practice and the numbers who openly admitted to discrimination may well be an under-estimation. The survey also found that 68 per cent of employers felt that the jobs in their firms would be unsuitable for disabled people, 52 per cent saying the premises would be unsuitable and 14 per cent citing transport and access problems. A total of 91 per cent of employers said that they would have problems employing a disabled person.[131] Despite the government's code of practice – which calls on employers to encourage applications from disabled people when advertising jobs – only 4 per cent of the sample said that they would positively encourage disabled people to apply for jobs.[132] The fact that 52 per cent of employers considered climbing stairs to be vital for office work[133] illustrates the report's conclusion that many of the 'so-called vital abilities (which disabled people are presumed to require) would not stand objective analysis.'[134]

The government's continued and exclusive reliance on 'education and persuasion' to overcome the disadvantages faced by disabled people is difficult to understand when its own research so conclusively demonstrates that it has been ineffective in eradicating prejudice and discrimination in employment. Discrimination is prohibited by Article 26 of the ICCPR which calls on States to ensure that all people have equal and effective protection against discrimination on any grounds. Governments are encouraged to take affirmative action to overcome the effects of discrimination and there are no circumstances under which they may derogate from these anti-discrimination obligations. The British government is comprehensively breaching Article 26 by not taking steps to eliminate discriminatory attitudes and practices against disabled people.

DISCRIMINATION IN THE WELFARE AND EDUCATION SYSTEMS

Benefits

According the OPCS survey, 75 per cent of disabled adults rely on state benefits as their main income.[135] Because disabled people are more likely to be unemployed than their non-disabled counterparts they are less likely to be eligible to entitlements from National Insurance contributions. This makes them more dependent on means-tested benefits.

The benefit system is complicated and confusing. Each benefit has a different set of eligibility criteria. For example, a person's age at the onset of the impairment, the cause of the impairment, its severity, an individual's work record, their National Insurance contributions and their country of residence all have an important influence on determining benefit levels. This can both discourage people from taking up their entitlements and lead to anomalies and discrimination. The result is that two people with identical impairments can receive benefits differing in value by over £200 per week.[136] The system directly discriminates against people who become ineligible for some benefits, such as the Disability Living Allowance, because they are over the age of retirement.[137]

Although Invalidity Benefit, a contributory benefit payable to those unable to work because of long-term sickness or disability, is payable at a higher level than unemployment benefit, in 1992 the average amount was £75.45 a week, representing only 24 per cent of gross national earnings.[138] Its successor, Incapacity Benefit, will be payable at an even lower level.

Disabled people often face higher costs as a result of their disability, such as laundry, transport, care assistance and special diets. Over one-half of those the OPCS surveyed spent more on fuel. Yet the only benefit contributing towards the costs of disability are Disability Allowance (DA) (care and mobility components) and Attendance Allowance (AA) (for people over the age of 65). In order to obtain AA or Disabled Living Allowance (DLA) (care component) a disabled person must show that he or she needs 'attention with bodily functions' or has supervision needs. Claiming is often perceived as intrusive by disabled people. In order to claim, someone must produce medical evidence from a doctor, a self assessment form and a statement from someone the claimant knows. The form asks the claimant a number of intimate questions, such as:

☐ roughly how many days/nights a week do you need help using the toilet, coping with incontinence, using a colostomy bag, changing nappies, pads or incontinence aids?

☐ roughly how long do you need help when in the bathroom?

☐ roughly how many days a week do you need someone to keep an eye on you?

☐ please tick why you need someone to keep an eye on you: you could hurt yourself, you could hurt someone else, you get confused, you could wander off.[139]

Benefit entitlement tends to be based on a medical model of disability in which the claimant presents a diagnosis and passes a test of functional impairment which focuses on what they cannot do. People with learning disabilities, sight problems, or anyone with literacy problems, will have to discuss intimate matters with someone else in order to complete the claim form. Disability activists have complained that this is demeaning and stigmatising – that it ignores the social context in which the individual is located.[140] BCODP have commented that:

> To receive financial support, applicants are encouraged to emphasise impairments and functional limitations as opposed to personal autonomy and skills. Indeed to secure the maximum economic advantage from the benefit system disabled people are forced to present themselves in the worst possible light. This has become important in recent years because of the shift away from statutory entitlements to discretionary grants.[141]

Disability and carers' organisations have for many years been united in their support for a comprehensive disability income scheme along with civil rights legislation. Such a scheme would consist of:

☐ a disablement cost allowance: tax-free, non-means tested

benefit to cover all the costs of disability, based on the
severity of the disability rather than its cause

☐   a disablement pension, payable to people who are totally or
partially unable to work because of long-term sickness
or disability, which is non-contributory and non-means tested

☐   a carer's pension.

Support services

Lack of adequate support and assistance prevents many disabled
people from participating fully in the mainstream economic and
social life of society. About 60 per cent of all disabled adults need
some form of assistance[142] and at present there is no national,
comprehensive and flexible support system for disabled people.
Around four million people, mainly women, provide informal
assistance of one kind or another to disabled relatives, friends or
neighbours.[143]

The National Health Service and Community Care Act 1990
aimed to provide a system of service providers so that long-stay
hospital patients could live at home. Home-based provision was
to be developed and expanded with a wide range of services provided both by the local authorities and private agencies. However,
lack of any additional funding has not only fragmented services
but left no clear national guidelines for provision.[144] For many
disabled people this Act has meant that institutionalisation has
been replaced by virtual imprisonment at home.

Disabled people who receive service help often experience difficulty organising their lives because of a lack of co-ordination
between the voluntary and statutory service providers and because
the services are geared to the providers' timetables.[145] They also
have little or no control over who enters their home, or what
professional helpers do once they are inside.[146] For example, in
cases where home help is provided by the local authority, the
worker can only perform those tasks approved by the local authority and cannot work to the disabled person's instructions. Regard,
an organisation of disabled lesbians and gay men, has received
numerous complaints about homophobic carers.[147]

Insufficient provision of community care support is also putting
at risk patients discharged from mental health units. Under-resourc-
ing of key workers and a shortage of hospital beds were blamed for
the deaths of two patients in Park House Unit, North Manchester

Hospital – one patient fell from a tower block and the other was found hanging in a lavatory cubicle in the hospital. A former patient of the same hospital died in a fire – he had previously told relatives that he was not getting the support he needed under care in the community.[148]

The Children Act 1989 provided a new legal framework for the provision of services to disabled children and gave a clear, positive and separate duty to local authorities to provide services to children in their area. However, the report of a national inspection of services, published by the Department of Health in 1994, showed that none of the authorities surveyed had met any of the standards required in full – only half had produced any childcare policies specifically for disabled children and none had circulated these to the relevant staff or members of the community.[149] Disabled children are particularly vulnerable to ill-treatment – such as sexual abuse – and are currently given insufficient protection against such abuse.[150] They are also more likely to be put in residential care and to be dependent on more than one carer.

Education

Disabled people receive a substantially worse education than their non-disabled counterparts. They are likely to leave school with fewer qualifications and face numerous discriminatory barriers to entering higher education.[151]

The mainstream education system is largely inaccessible to disabled people. A survey by the Spastics Society and the National Union of Teachers, published in April 1993, found that only 18 per cent of secondary schools in England and Wales considered their teaching space to be at least three-quarters accessible.[152] While 46 per cent of primary schools considered themselves to be largely accessible, the survey found that many school facilities, such as playgrounds, libraries, specialist subject areas and school toilets were inaccessible at both primary and secondary level.[153]

Disabled people are often given segregated education, which is known to be extremely socially divisive.[154] BCODP has commented that:

> school leavers are socially immature and isolated. This isolation results in passive acceptance of social discrimination, lack of skills in facing the tasks of adulthood and ignorance about the main social issues of our time.[155]

According to government estimates there are 360,000 disabled children under the age of 16 in Britain. Over one-third of these live in private households. Of those in residential homes two-thirds are educated in segregated environments.[156] Special schools appear to offer a lower standard of education than mainstream schools, although the official information about this is contradictory.[157] The government inspectorate which enforces standards in special secondary schools is different to that which operates for mainstream schools and staff at special schools do not need to have the same level of qualifications.

It is widely accepted that the best way of preventing discrimination against disabled people in education is to ensure that mainstream facilities are accessible and that disabled people can, as far as possible, be integrated into them. The government is officially committed to encourage integrated education for disabled people, yet despite the Education Act 1981, which was supposed to help achieve this, segregation remains widespread. In 1978 the Warnock Committee Report called for greater integration in education. However, between 1977 and 1989 the level of segregation fell by only 1 per cent.[158] Some local education authorities have actually increased the number of children that they send to special schools by up to 25 per cent since the passage of the 1981 Act.[159]

Although the 1981 Act made it illegal to place children in special schools unless they have been assessed and given a formal statement of their 'special educational needs', official figures show that over half the children in special schools who have been assessed have no formal statement, while 14 per cent have not been assessed at all.[160] It is also claimed that disabled children are denied places at mainstream schools because it is cheaper to segregate them.[161]

Disabled students make up only 0.3 per cent of the entire student population in higher education.[162] Most higher educational institutions are inaccessible, which restricts the choice available to potential students who are disabled. Direct discrimination in the selection process also appears to prevent qualified students obtaining places.[163]

HIV and AIDS

Gay men are the group in the UK who have been most affected by HIV and AIDS, although the incidence of AIDS is now rising more rapidly amongst heterosexuals.[164] Between 1982 and 1993 – when reporting began – 8,529 AIDS cases (7,850 male and 679 female) were reported in the UK.[165] Of those, 6,318 are recorded to be men who acquired HIV from sex with men (66 per cent gay; 12 per cent bisexual).[166] However, it is generally recognised that these figures are an under-estimate.

AIDS has highlighted various problems with the law surrounding informed consent and medical record disclosure. It is the general opinion of health authorities and the medical profession that testing without express consent is a breach of the duty of care. Although such a breach is actionable as negligence, a person bringing such a suit would have difficulty proving damage and quantifying loss.[167] There is little legislation in force specifically concerning AIDS and HIV medical record disclosure.[168] Moreover, there is no law of privacy in the UK. Although people are protected by the laws of libel and slander, these only apply to statements which are untrue. The common law duty of confidence and NHS (VD) Regulations 1974 (as amended) provide some statutory protection for patient record confidentiality. However, these regulations only apply to regional and area health authorities, and not to general practitioners or to private hospitals or clinics.[169] Although health-care teams operate under codes of professional conduct, these do not have statutory force and can be changed at any time by the General Medical Council. In November 1993 the Standards and Ethics Committee of the UK Central Council for Nursing, Midwifery and Health Visiting ruled that the HIV status of patients should be revealed to other people against their wishes in 'exceptional circumstances'.[170]

FREEDOM OF MOVEMENT AND ASSOCIATION

According to the Disabled Persons Transport Advisory Committee, between 10 and 12 per cent of the population are adversely affected by 'unfriendly features of the transport environment'.[171] The SCPR study revealed that 38 per cent of all disabled workers with jobs found the journey to work extremely tiring while another 9 per cent reported that their journey to work was more expensive because they were disabled.[172] Wheelchair users are virtually excluded from many transport services, which are supposed to be public, and people with mobility, sight or hearing impairments also find them difficult to use.

A survey by the Greater London Association for Disabled People in 1986 found that 450,000 people had difficulties using London Transport. Sixty-three per cent of these used buses only with 'difficulty or discomfort', while 20 per cent could not use them at all.[173] Little has changed since then. By the summer of 1994 the government had introduced 70 low floor buses – which are more accessible to wheelchair users – operating on five routes in London, but this is a small proportion of the total stock of more than 5,000.[174] Small buses, in common use since the deregulation of the bus services in 1987, are even more inaccessible.[175]

The problems of travelling on the underground are even worse. Wheelchair users were barred from using certain sections of the London Underground by four London Regional Transport (LRT) bye-laws until 1994.[176] They are now advised to give LRT 24 hours' notice of their time of travel and to travel off-peak, with a non-disabled companion, if they wish to use the London Underground.[177] Automatic ticket barriers, inaudible announcements and difficulties using escalators and lifts exacerbate the problems that disabled passengers face. Some more recently constructed urban railway systems – such as the Tyne-and-Wear Metro system and the London Docklands Light Railway – have overcome some of these difficulties, although problems still remain.[178] On the other hand, the comparatively recent Glasgow Underground is completely inaccessible to wheelchair users.[179]

British Rail is gradually improving its train services to disabled people and 90 per cent of its new rolling stock have wide-entry automatic doors, grab rails and some space for wheelchairs. However, even the new trains have some accessibility problems and the improvements have been concentrated on InterCity routes rather than on local services. One consumer survey pointed out that for most local and provincial train journeys 'the guard's van looms large for people who have to travel in their wheelchair'.[180]

Inaccessibility, lack of information and staff insensitivity make travelling by plane an extremely frustrating experience for many disabled people. Travel agents have to fill in forms about the medical condition of disabled people who book flights in order to prove that they are fit to travel. This frequently results in disabled people being asked highly personal or objectionable questions, such as 'does he smell?'[181] Most aircraft are not accessible to disabled travellers and staff often appear unprepared for disabled passengers even when they have been given the relevant information in advance.[182]

Despite the inaccessibility of the public transport systems, households with a disabled person are only about half as likely as other households to possess a private car.[183] Cars suitable for disabled drivers are more expensive to buy and run and insurance companies usually charge higher premiums to disabled people than to able-bodied drivers.[184] A small number of disabled people receive some assistance with the costs of motoring from government-sponsored charities, although there are problems with the type of assistance offered.[185]

Restrictions to freedom of association

Disabled people are prevented from participating in many social and leisure activities and sometimes from entering social and entertainment venues. The problems of physical access are compounded by prejudice and ignorance which frequently leads to disabled people being excluded from public houses, restaurants, museums, galleries, concert halls, cinemas, football grounds, racing grounds and other public places. BCODP has argued that some managers appear to believe that the presence of disabled people at entertainment establishments will discourage non-disabled customers or spoil their enjoyment.[186]

Some venues ban wheelchair users on the grounds that they are a safety or fire risk, while others limit their numbers or require advance notification of their attendance. Even where the venue itself is accessible, often facilities such as lavatories are not and some, such as the National Theatre in London, refuse to allow wheelchair users to enter unaccompanied.[187] According to a disabled persons' guide to London, the attitudes of staff in venues vary wildly and, while there have been some improvements, discrimination remains widespread.[188]

A report by the Arts Council in 1985 found that disabled people faced widespread discrimination within the leisure industry and that such discrimination was perpetrated by a number of organisations which it funded.[189] The report made a number of specific recommendations for change, resulting in the publication of a Consultation Paper and a Code of Practice. However, a review of progress three years later showed that little had changed[190] – the main recommendations had not been implemented and few venues receiving Arts Council funding had made appreciable efforts to improve their accessibility. In the same year the Arts Council applied for an employment exemption certificate because it could not employ the legal minimum quota of disabled people, something it repeated in 1991.[191]

DISABLED PEOPLE IN RESIDENTIAL CARE

According to the OPCS survey there are about 422,000 disabled people living in 'communal establishments' or institutions.[192] Around 20 per cent of these people are below retirement age.[193] Standards of institutional care vary. For many people, particularly elderly people, a well-kept, friendly residential institution is preferable to the isolation of home life with inadequate community support. Inevitably, however, life in an institution reduces independence, interferes with privacy and deprives people of rights and opportunities that they would otherwise take for granted 'because the routine of their life will be predetermined, to a greater or lesser extent, by the needs of the professionals in charge of the institutions.'[194]

In 1992 an official report into Ashworth Special Hospital concluded that it 'must be a prime candidate to be included as one of the establishments to be visited in the near future by the Committee for the Prevention of Torture and Inhuman and Degrading Treatment'.[195] Human rights abuses occur in many other institutions where practices breach the standards laid down in the ICCPR on privacy, respect for human dignity and protection against cruel, inhuman or degrading treatment.

In June 1994 a survey by the UK Central Council for Nursing, Midwifery and Health Visiting reported that complaints by elderly people against staff in nursing homes had doubled over a three-year period.[196] Cases highlighted in the report included:

☐ a frail and severely mentally ill woman forced to take pills by a male nurse who held his hands over her mouth so that she could not spit them out and kicked her when she struggled

☐ the forced bathing of patients, including six who were mentally confused and distressed.

211

The report revealed 'wholly inadequate' systems of drug administration, ineffective management and 'almost non-existent' training.[197]

In December 1993 the Mental Health Act Commission's fifth biennial report highlighted 'a crisis in the care of the mentally ill, particularly in psychiatric wards in the inner cities.'[198] It reported overcrowding, a shortage of beds, shortages of trained staff and inadequate management of wards, and found that patients were 'prematurely discharged from hospital often at a few hours' notice to unsupervised accommodation – to make way for more acutely disturbed patients to be admitted'.[199] It also condemned the use of police to control disturbed patients, referring to an occasion where 13 officers – some of them in riot gear – helped staff give an injection to a patient.[200] A report by the Law Commission in 1993 revealed that many people in institutions suffered compulsory physical confinement by such instruments as straps on chairs, locks and bolts on doors and electronic tagging.[201]

INTERNATIONAL COMPARISONS

A 1993 Department of Employment international comparative study identified two distinct approaches to employment policies for disabled people.[202] The first is an anti-discrimination or human rights approach, in which employment practices are included as part of an overall policy of law which recognises the rights of disabled people and seeks to eradicate discrimination against them. The second is a more compartmentalised approach in which specific government departments attempt to ensure that disabled people achieve full economic and social participation by making incremental changes to their policies. In the field of employment this second approach led to quota systems and financial incentives to encourage the employment of disabled people. It was noted that while the USA, Canada and Australia had adopted the first approach, most members of the European Union had practised the second. The report stated that policies were rapidly evolving in a number of countries as the issue of disabled people's rights gained prominence in the 1990s.[203]

European legislation

In Britain it is argued that the lack of a written constitution, or of a 'rights culture', makes the human rights approach inappropriate for this country. However, the British government is also opposed to a harmonisation of European social policy, and its record in promoting the rights of disabled people is significantly worse than that of many of its European partners in several areas.[204]

Discussions around the Social Chapter of the Maastricht Treaty led in 1991 to the publication of a draft directive on the physical and organisational barriers restricting disabled people's travel to and from work.[205] This directive is still in draft form, and there has been little progress on it since it reached the Council of Ministers in early 1992.[206] However, if it is eventually adopted, it will be the first attempt by the European Union to tackle the discrimination of disabled people in legislation rather than simply funding employment projects and relying on education and persuasion.[207]

Some European countries, such as France and Germany, have introduced anti-discrimination legislation as an 'add-on' to their existing policies.[208] The Irish government began a consultation process to consider the viability of introducing comprehensive, anti-discrimination protection in 1993 and is expected to introduce legislation in the near future. Given that the Irish legal system is closely based on Britain's, it is difficult to see why a similar solution could not be adopted in the UK.[209]

The Americans With Disabilities Act 1990 (ADA)

The most comprehensive legal protection against discrimination against disabled people is the US's ADA, which came into force in 1992. This Act prohibits discrimination against disabled people – either directly, indirectly or on the basis of unequal burdens. It guarantees equality of opportunity for people with disabilities in four main areas:

- employment
- public services, including transport
- private sector services and accommodations
- telecommunications.

Heralded as a 'Bill of Rights for the Disabled',[210] the American disabilities movement drew on the country's strong civil rights culture and the campaigning activities of many ex-service personnel who were disabled during the Vietnam War. It provided the initial impetus for the passage of the Rehabilitation Act 1973 which prohibits discrimination by the Federal government against 'handicapped persons',[211] and continued to agitate for 'rights not charity'.[212] The movement consciously modelled its tactics on the black civil rights campaign of the 1960s and the legislation it campaigned for drew on the Civil Rights Act of 1964. It also used the achievements of the Rehabilitation Act 1973 and the Education for All Handicapped Children Act 1974, which required disabled children to be placed in mainstream education institutions – where appropriate – and established individualised educational programmes for students with disabilities.

The ADA's definition of a disabled person includes anyone with a physical or intellectual impairment which substantially limits one or more major life activity, or who has a record of such an impairment or is regarded as having such an impairment. This definition is deliberately broad, covering people with a history of mental illness, people who have recovered from cancer, people who are HIV-positive and people with severe facial disfigurements. It also includes carers and people who have a known association or relationship with someone who is disabled. In general, however, people with temporary conditions are not covered.[213]

The ADA prohibits direct discrimination against disabled people in employment and bans pre-employment medical examinations (although it allows tests once a job has been offered). It also prohibits indirect discriminatory practices such as tests or selection criteria that disadvantage disabled people and are not strictly necessary for the job. It further requires employers to make 'reasonable accommodation' to enable disabled people to enter or remain in the workforce unless such accommodation would cause 'undue hardship' to the employer or is not 'readily achievable'.[214]

The term 'reasonable accommodation' was first used in the Rehabilitation Act 1973 and has an accepted legal definition. The terms 'undue hardship' and 'readily achievable' take account of the cost of the adaptation and the size and nature of the business. An employer is not required to make a particular accommodation until an applicant or employee with a particular disability needs it.[215] The ADA regulations state that 'the process of determining reasonable accommodation is an informal, interactive, problem-solving technique involving both the employer and the qualified individual with a disability.'[216]

Many of the accommodations require relatively simple adjustments to the work environment, such as changing working times, modifying machinery, making buildings accessible and providing readers and interpreters. The President's Committee on the Employment of People With Disabilities estimates that the vast majority of the accommodations necessary to make employment more accessible can be accomplished at minimal cost:

- 31 per cent can be accomplished at no cost
- 19 per cent cost between $1 and $5
- 19 per cent cost between $50 and $500
- 19 per cent cost between $500 and $1,000
- 11 per cent cost between $1,000 and $5,000
- 1 per cent cost over $5,000.[217]

Research in the USA has shown that anti-discrimination legislation is largely cost-effective as it enables disabled people to become both more economically active and more independent.[218] And although it is clear that the US disability legislation has cost some money to implement, these costs have not been anywhere near as large as opponents of the legislation had feared. Also, no companies have been made bankrupt by the legislation and some have found that making themselves more accessible has dramatically increased their profitability.[219] The costs have also been offset against significant savings to the US government's social security and social services budgets. President Bush, who signed the ADA commented that:

When you add together state, local and private funds, it costs almost $200 billion annually to support Americans with disabilities, in effect to keep them dependent.[220]

The ADA also protects the rights of all disabled people not to suffer from the discriminatory allocation of public services. Public entities must make reasonable modifications to rules, policies or practices, remove physical barriers and provide auxiliary aids so that disabled people are provided with the same range of facilities and services as those provided to the general population. Discrimination by the state or local government is prohibited and such authorities are required to make all their facilities, services and communications accessible.

215

The particular importance of transport is recognised by the ADA, which requires that:

☐ All new state and public transport facilities must be accessible and all public transport systems must provide an equal level of service to disabled people.

☐ All new vehicles for more than 16 people must be accessible and all new coaches purchased after July 1996 (1997 for smaller companies) must be accessible.

☐ New buses and rail terminals must be accessible and renovations should take account of accessibility.

☐ Key stations should be made accessible within three years, although this deadline can be extended to 20 years by the Secretary of State for Transportation.

☐ One carriage of every railway train should be accessible within five years.

Ultimately, all transportation systems are to be made fully accessible to disabled people.

The ADA also requires all telephone companies to install relay services for all persons with hearing impairments within three years and for these to be free of charge at all times. Any television public service announcement produced or funded in any way by any agency of federal government must be accessible to deaf people.

The evidence suggests that the ADA is gradually beginning to improve the lives of disabled people in the US while avoiding most of the problems anticipated by its opponents.[221] Implementation of the employment aspects of the Act has proceeded 'much better than employers had anticipated, but not as comprehensively as disability groups had hoped.'[222] The ADA has not led to a flood of litigation and its legal provisions are proving to be relatively uncomplicated to enforce.[223] While the Act is costing money, these costs are dispersed between government, companies and consumers and are offset by many increased business opportunities and savings to state welfare and social security budgets.

RIGHTS NOW

The experience of the ADA in the USA has shown that anti-discrimination legislation need not be financially prohibitive and will probably prove to be cost-effective over time. Indeed, the economic arguments are in favour of such legislation in countries like the UK which have an ageing population.

The other argument against such legislation is an ideological hostility to the concept of 'human rights'. One opponent has stated:

> As there is no general concept of 'civil rights' known to English law, the disabled would enjoy a novel and privileged status given to no one else. Whatever else that is, it is not a blow against discrimination . . . the claim to civil rights . . . aims to replace sympathy with law suits . . . The truth is that the disabled cannot manage without the sympathy, indeed the protection of the rest of society and they have been dangerously misled if they think otherwise.[224]

Such an argument ignores the fact that legislation has already been enacted prohibiting discrimination against women and members of ethnic minorities and that there is no constitutional reason why the scope of this anti-discrimination legislation could not be extended to cover disabled people. Given the extent of the discrimination perpetrated against disabled people in British society, and the government's failure to promote equality, it is a remarkable argument that this is justifiable because anti-discrimination law would amount to a 'political revolution'. The argument that preserving the structures, institutions and notions that exist at present is more important than ensuring that all people have the right to be treated with respect and allowed to realise their full creative potential is particularly perverse. Rather than justifying the British government's record, it is an indictment of the current lack of protection for the human rights of all people.

8 MENTAL HEALTH

> Such has been the low standard of much patient-care at
> Ashworth that the hospital must be a prime candidate to be
> included as one of the establishments to be visited in the near
> future by the Committee for the Prevention of Torture and
> Inhuman and Degrading Treatment.[1]

This was the conclusion of the Committee of Inquiry into Complaints about Ashworth Hospital which had been commissioned
by the Secretary of State for Health to investigate various allegations of improper care and treatment.[2] The Committee's report
(*Ashworth Report*), found that patients had been subject to
inhuman and degrading treatment in a climate of brutality, intimidation and fear, with some patients having been beaten, taunted
and provoked by their nurses.[3]

People with mental health problems or learning disabilities
are frequently subjected to human rights abuses.[4] Procedures to
safeguard their rights are ignored or inadequately enforced and the
quality of care and treatment offered to people with 'mental disorder' fall far below basic minimum standards.

The Mental Health Act 1983 established a Mental Health
Act Commission (the Commission) a multi-disciplinary agency,
responsible for overseeing the care and treatment of detained
patients and appointing psychiatrists to consider whether compulsory treatment should be authorised in cases of detained patients.
However the Commission has been hampered by insufficient
resources and legal powers[5] and its scope is also limited. Patients
who are in hospital on a voluntary basis (including those who have
been threatened with 'sectioning' if they try to leave, those receiving
treatment or care in the community or prisoners receiving care on
psychiatric wings) do not fall within the Commission's jurisdiction.
In 1990, a Code of Practice was introduced as a guide to mental

health professionals in carrying out their functions under the Act. However, there are no mechanisms for monitoring compliance with the Code, nor are its provisions mandatory, while compliance is expressly stated to depend on the availability of resources.

Perhaps the reason for these deficiencies not generating public outrage is our society's general prejudice towards (and fear of) 'mentally disordered' people. There is also a conflict between individual human rights and the demands of society for public safety. Treatment, care and supervision are currently provided to 'mentally disordered' people not according to their personal choice as consumers or clients but according to other people's views about what is in their best interests and what are the interests of society. This conflict pervades all aspects of services and legislation relating to people with 'mental disorder'.

COMPULSORY DETENTION IN HOSPITAL

Current procedures for compulsory detention under the Mental Health Act 1983 (the Act) are inadequate to protect people with 'mental disorder' from arbitrary detention.

The initial detention

Under the Act, a person can be compulsorily detained in hospital for assessment or treatment on the grounds that he or she is suffering from 'mental disorder'. The detention can be initiated by either health professionals under the 'civil' part of the Act or, if the person is involved in criminal proceedings, by the courts. People detained under the Act are often described as having been 'sectioned'.

The civil admission process of 'sectioning' is usually carried out by an Approved Social Worker[6] who makes the application supported by the recommendations of two doctors[7] (one of whom is an approved specialist).[8] A person may be admitted to hospital for up to 28 days on the grounds of his or her 'mental disorder'. The two recommending doctors must state that the person is suffering from a mental disorder of a nature or degree that warrants detention in a hospital for assessment (or for assessment followed by medical treatment) for at least 28 days and that the person ought to be detained in hospital in the interests of his or her health or safety or with a view to the protection of others.[9]

Section 3 of the Act provides for the detention of persons for up to six months. Here the two recommending doctors must agree upon the specific form of 'mental disorder' affecting the person, namely: mental illness, mental impairment, severe mental impairment or psychopathic disorder; and consider that this mental disorder is of a nature or degree that makes it appropriate for the person to be detained for medical treatment in a hospital. The section specifies that in the case of mental impairment and psychopathy it is necessary for the doctors to state that the treatment is likely to alleviate or prevent a deterioration of the condition. For every classification of mental disorder, treatment must be necessary for the health or safety of the person or for the protection of others, and this treatment can only be provided if the person is detained. The detention may be renewed for a further six months and every 12 months thereafter.

'Mental disorder' is widely defined in the Act as:

mental illness, arrested or incomplete development of mind, psychopathic disorder and any other disorder or disability of mind.[10]

'Mental illness' is not defined in the Act and the courts have declined to provide clarification, preferring to leave this for the 'ordinary sensible person' to decide in each particular case.[11] Such vague criteria leave the justification for depriving individuals of their liberty dependent on the mental health professionals' personal views of what constitutes a 'mental disorder' or 'mental illness'.

The patient is not provided with an immediate review of the decision to detain. Specially appointed officers are required to scrutinise the admission papers on the patient's arrival at the hospital, but a recent case has undermined the effectiveness of such scrutiny by holding that the detention is lawful so long as the documents 'appear to be duly made'.[12] Although the patient can apply to a Mental Health Review Tribunal (MHRT) for the grounds of the detention to be independently assessed, this could take weeks, if not months, to convene, while in the meantime the patient will be subject to the compulsory treatment provisions.[13]

In criminal proceedings a person may be detained in hospital by order of a court upon conviction or while on remand.[14] Where a person is convicted of an offence which is punishable with imprisonment[15] the court can make a Hospital Order under Section 37 of the 1983 Act if certain specified criteria are met. The court must be satisfied, on the evidence of two doctors, one of whom is an approved specialist in 'mental disorder', that the person is suffering from mental illness, psychopathic disorder, mental impairment or severe mental impairment and the disorder is of a nature or degree which makes it appropriate for the person to be detained. As with detentions under Section 3, in the case of mental impairment and psychopathic disorder, the two doctors must consider that such treatment is likely to alleviate or prevent a deterioration of the person's condition. The court must also be of the opinion, having taken into consideration all the circumstances (including the nature of the offence, the character and antecedents of the offender) that the Hospital Order is the most suitable method of dealing with the case.

In more serious cases the Crown Court may make a Restriction Order to run in conjunction with the Hospital Order. A Restriction Order can be imposed if the court believes it is necessary to protect the public from 'serious harm'. It means that the doctor responsible for that patient cannot discharge, nor grant leave of absence to, the patient nor transfer the patient to another hospital, without the Home Secretary's consent.[16] Whereas a Hospital Order without restrictions has a similar effect to detention under Section 3 and would need to be renewed for a further six months and then on a yearly basis, a Hospital Order with restrictions has no such renewal provisions. A Restriction Order is made either for a fixed period or, as is more usual, the court may order detention for an unlimited period.[17]

Lack of information upon detention

The managers of the hospital must, 'as soon as practicable' after the detention has begun, ensure patients understand under which section of the Act they have been detained and that they may apply to a MHRT to have their detention reviewed. There is, however, no statutory requirement that the patient be informed of the reasons for the detention.[18] This is in stark contrast to the rights of someone arrested and detained at a police station.

Continuing detention

Although the Act requires that two medical recommendations support the initial detention, there is no similar requirement for extending the detention. Where the Act requires the power of detention to be renewed (Section 3 and Hospital Orders) this can be achieved upon the submission of a single medical report prepared by the doctor responsible for the patient. This further detention is automatic unless the hospital managers use their powers to discharge.

There are also no objective criteria governing the exercise of the power to discharge. The Act does not expressly state when a person should cease to be detained so there is no duty on the doctor in charge of a patient to discharge that patient when the conditions which justified that person's detention no longer exist. Furthermore, if the detention is not renewed there is no statutory obligation to inform the patient that he or she may leave hospital.

Recall to hospital

Restricted patients can either be absolutely discharged from hospital or conditionally discharged. Those who are conditionally discharged can be recalled to hospital by the Home Secretary. In a case before the European Court of Human Rights[19] it was argued that the provision granting the Home Secretary this power was by its very nature arbitrary, as it allowed the Home Secretary to recall a patient without requiring even a medical report to confirm the need for re-detention. The government responded that it was implicit within the provision of the then Mental Health Act 1959 that 'unless the Home Secretary on the medical evidence available to him decides that the candidate for recall [the patient] falls within this statutory definition, no power of recall can arise'.[20]

The government's submission was accepted by the court which noted that as the 1959 Act defined a patient as 'a person suffering or appearing to be suffering from mental disorder', such a power was not arbitrary. The relevant provisions therefore remained unaltered and were included in the Mental Health Act 1983. However, the Home Secretary has since exercised the power to recall a person who had been discharged by a MHRT on the basis that he or she was not suffering from any 'mental disorder', without obtaining medical evidence to support this detention. This arbitrary action has been condoned rather than checked by the domestic courts and is currently the subject of proceedings before the European Court of Human Rights.[21]

COMPULSORY TREATMENT

Those detained under the Act may be treated for their mental disorder without their consent. Although the Act provides certain safeguards before some types of treatment can be administered compulsorily, these are restricted in scope and recent research has also shown them to be of limited value.

The use of medication

Detained patients may be forced to take medication for their mental disorder if this is required by the psychiatrist in charge of their treatment. Only if the psychiatrist wishes to continue the treatment beyond the initial three-month period and the patient either refuses or cannot give consent, is the doctor required to obtain a second opinion. The second opinion is provided by an independent, approved psychiatrist who must visit the patient and consult with various mental health professionals involved with the patient's care, before deciding whether the treatment proposed by the patient's doctor should be given.[22]

The Administration of ECT

The Act requires the same second-opinion procedure to be followed whenever ECT (electro-convulsive therapy) treatment is proposed and the patient refuses to, or cannot, give consent.

Under the Act, ECT can be compulsorily administered in emergency situations without obtaining a second opinion. Recent research into compulsory treatment cases revealed that 22 per cent of those receiving ECT did so under these emergency powers.[23] People who have received ECT can suffer problems such as memory loss, spatial disorientation and massive headaches and some have called for it to be banned.[24]

The failings of the second opinion

Anecdotal evidence suggests that this procedure is a formality – patients consider there would be little point in asking for a second opinion because the second doctor, sharing the same medical and professional outlook, would be bound to agree with the first. Recent research into second opinions and compulsory treatment found that in a study of 1,009 second opinion cases, the second doctor authorised the proposed treatment at a rate of 96 per cent.[25]

This research also highlighted the wide practice of poly-pharmacy – the use of more than one type of drug – while in many of the cases the second doctor authorised the prescribing of high doses of medication, often well above the recommended maximum.[26] The Mental Health Act Commission has estimated that in the period 1991-2, medication played an 'important role' in 9 per cent of sudden deaths of detained patients and in eight deaths reported to the Commission between 1990 and 1992, there was:

> a characteristic pattern of escalating quantities of mixed neuroleptic and other sedatives given intermuscularly every few hours, often prescribed by inexperienced staff with very little supervision.[27]

The anti-psychotic drugs commonly prescribed to treat people with a diagnosis of schizophrenia and other forms of psychosis can have seriously debilitating side effects, ranging from restlessness, dizziness and weight gain to neuroleptic malignant syndrome – a potentially fatal condition. The side effects of these drugs were described by one person as:

> your tongue lolls out, you have permanent shakes, you can be a zombie, you can have rictus – the effects are horrendous.[28]

Lack of information on treatment

In a recent survey of users of mental health services, 80 per cent of the respondents said they were not given enough information about their general treatment while 70 per cent said that not enough information had been given to them about the side effects of the medication.[29] One respondent described how information, even if sought, was not given:

> I was manipulated into saying 'yes' to a particular drug. No information was given . . . The hospital staff were reluctant

to challenge the psychiatrist about anything. I asked the nurses questions about treatment and they said that I should have asked the psychiatrist even though I had asked him.[30]

Other medical treatment for 'mental disorder'

While a second doctor must authorise the administration of ECT and medication before they can be given without consent, other treatments such as nursing and care may be given without either the patient's consent or the involvement of a second doctor, provided that they are given for the patient's 'mental disorder'. The Act should not therefore be applied to impose treatment for conditions unrelated to the patient's 'mental disorder'. However, recent decisions by the courts have extended the scope of the medical professionals' powers to treat compulsorily patients detained under the Act.

For example, in a recent case concerning a woman detained under the Act, the court held that force feeding could lawfully be carried out because it was 'ancillary' to the proposed treatment for the woman's mental disorder. The courts only require a minimal link between the mental disorder and the physical condition for the treatment for a physical condition to fall within 'medical treatment for mental disorder'.

Such compulsory treatment powers enable doctors to override a patient's clear wish not to receive treatment for the physical disorder and go far beyond the envisaged scope of the Act. They also allow for a wide range of 'treatments' to be forcibly administered to detained patients without any independent scrutiny of the decision to provide such treatment.[31]

PROPOSED CHANGES TO THE MENTAL HEALTH ACT 1983

After-care under supervision

In February 1995 the government introduced the Mental Health (Patients in the Community) Bill which, if it were to become law, would impose restrictions on the liberty of certain persons who, having been detained under the Act, are discharged from hospital subject to 'after-care under supervision'. Under this regime, a person might be required to reside in a specified place; attend at specified places and times for medical treatment, occupation, education or training and allow certain health professionals access to his or her home.

Power to convey

The proposed law would also give certain 'authorised' persons the 'power to convey' the person subject to supervised after-care to a place the person is required to reside, work, train or even receive treatment. Given that such a power authorises an individual's detention, this is effectively a power of arrest. But there are no requirements on those exercising this power to inform people why they have been arrested nor where they will be taken to, nor are there any provisions to say under what circumstances the power can be used nor for how long a person can be made subject to this power.

Compulsory treatment?

The compulsory treatment provisions under the Act do not apply to supervised after-care. However, there are no provisions to ensure that patients are told of their right to refuse treatment. Those patients who are aware they can refuse treatment may still feel obliged to accept treatment because they know that exercising this right may lead to further detention in hospital where they can be treated against their wishes.[32]

Similar issues were raised when the Health Committee considered the Royal College of Psychiatrist's proposals for 'community supervision orders' which lead the Committee to conclude that such proposals were 'unworkable' and represented an encroachment on civil liberties which the Committee was not prepared to support.[33]

The independent review of the need for supervised after-care

The Bill provides that patients may apply to a MHRT for their release from the supervised after-care. However the MHRT would only be obliged to order the applicant's release if it was satisfied that the grounds for supervised after-care had ceased to exist. Given that the grounds for this power are so wide[34] it would be very difficult for a patient to show that they no longer applied.

Thus, if 'supervised after-care' becomes law, many people could be made subject to these restrictions on their liberty for an indefinite period.

CONDITIONS OF COMPULSORY DETENTION

Special hospitals

There are three 'special hospitals' in England and Wales (Ashworth, Broadmoor and Rampton) which provide hospital care in a high security setting for over 1650 patients,[35] approximately three-quarters of whom have been detained under the Act via the criminal courts.[36]

In August 1992, following its detailed investigation, the Committee of Inquiry into Complaints about Ashworth reported that the hospital environment and culture had created an uncaring and demeaning attitude towards patients.[37]

The Committee found that patients were subject to physical bullying, violent assaults and demeaning or vicious practical jokes. Racism was rife, with propaganda by the far-right British National Party on prominent display.[38] Homosexual patients were singled out for abuse and one was made to wear a placard bearing the word 'homo'.[39] Not only did staff fail to prevent predictable suicides but their behaviour was said to have probably contributed to them.[40] Although the Inquiry was unable conclusively to uphold complaints that male staff had sexually assaulted patients, it said the accusations were 'plausible, coherent, spontaneous and internally consistent', and condemned as disgraceful the refusal of a nurse accused of an assault to give evidence.[41]

Criticisms were levelled not just at individual staff but also at management, which had abrogated its responsibility for running the hospital to the nurses' union, the Prison Officers' Association and the entire 'culture of denigration' that permeated a 'brutalising, stagnant, closed institution'.[42] One year later a report was published following an inquiry into the deaths of three Afro-Caribbean patients at Broadmoor Hospital. The report, *Big, Black and Dangerous?*, was highly critical of the regime at Broadmoor Hospital and found that there was an underlying racist attitude amongst the staff.[43]

In 1992 it was estimated that as many as half the population of the special hospitals did not need to be there.[44] The Commission has reported that as at 31 May 1993, 295 patients had been recommended for transfer or discharge and that 48 patients had been waiting over six months for their transfer or discharge.[45]

Other institutions

In December 1992 seven managers and nursing staff were disciplined at a hospital in Staffordshire following an inquiry into the death of a woman with learning difficulties. She had been tied to the inlet pipe of a toilet cistern by the cords of a bib placed around her neck while her nurses went to lunch. Her body was found by a cleaner 45 minutes later – she died as a result of the 'inhalation of vomit and suspension'. An inquiry panel found that female patients were routinely secured to a toilet cistern usually by their bra straps.[46]

Research published in 1990 revealed that over one-third of sentenced prisoners in Britain had some form of psychiatric disorder[47] and 3 per cent (over 1,000 prisoners) required immediate hospital treatment.[48] However, reports from the Chief Inspector of Prisons have highlighted the unsuitability of penal custody for people considered to be mentally ill.[49] The medical facilities and accommodation in prisons are not suitable to cater for individuals suffering from 'mental disorder'[50] and the standard of professional care is far lower than that provided in hospitals. Indeed, the requirement for the standard of care in prisons is not as high as in a hospital – in 1989 a judge ruled that a prisoner detained in prison awaiting transfer to hospital was not entitled to the same level of treatment and care as that available in a National Health Service hospital.[51]

A survey of 'mentally disordered' prisoners in 1990 found that whilst the majority of the medical officers stated that the bulk of their work was psychiatry, their level of psychiatric knowledge varied tremendously.[52] The survey concluded that as far as mentally ill prisoners were concerned, the prisons were not equipped to provide anything more than 'first-aid' care, while individuals with learning disabilities were considered one of the most disadvantaged groups in the system. In one prison, the environment in which prisoners with learning disabilities were confined was described as resembling 'the impoverished environment of the back wards of the old asylums'. The report's authors were also critical of the general state of prison hospitals:

like other parts of Victorian establishments, the prison 'hospital' is often dark, dirty, overcrowded and lacking in sanitary facilities. 'Hospital' is in many ways a misnomer for a collection of cells and dormitories pressed into a service for which they are unsuitable . . . Disabled, elderly, post-operative and even terminally ill patients are contained within the same facilities as acutely disturbed schizophrenic patients to the detriment of everyone involved.[53]

The report found that, although prison medical officers believed themselves able to cope well with many ill prisoners, when patients needed urgent transfer, they were unable to do so due to lack of available hospital beds and delays in the response to requests for an assessment to take place.[54]

SECLUSION

The *Ashworth Report* recommended that the practice of seclusion (confining a patient alone in a room, usually locked) should be phased out over a period of two to three years. Critics described the practice as a cruel and degrading way of responding to a crisis.[55] The *Ashworth Report* further stated that if this practice were to continue it should be subject to strict statutory control, requiring that a patient should not be denied human contact or prevented from leaving the room at will.[56]

Despite the deaths of a number of patients while kept in seclusion,[57] this practice is still commonplace and no legislation has been introduced to control the procedure.[58]

In 1993, the Mental Health Commission raised numerous concerns about seclusion; that it is still being used as a punishment and the length of seclusion in some cases:

There remains a worryingly high number of episodes of seclusion in excess of three days on high dependency female wards and a significant number of episodes lasting over seven days.[59]

MENTAL HEALTH REVIEW TRIBUNALS (MHRT)

A person who has been detained under the Act for reasons of 'mental disorder' can apply to a MHRT whose powers include the power to discharge him or her. The protection afforded to detained persons, however, is limited due to delays in convening tribunal hearings, the limitation on the MHRTs' powers and the ability of other authorities to override their decisions.

MHRTs are intended to provide an independent review of the need for the person's continued detention. In order to fulfil this function, MHRTs should have the power to examine the same grounds which justified the patient's original detention and consider whether they continue to exist. However, in a recent case it was held that despite the fact that one of the grounds for the detention of patients suffering from certain types of 'mental disorder' is that they are likely to benefit from medical treatment, a MHRT is not obliged to consider this point.[60] Patients who are gaining no benefit from treatment in hospital can continue to be detained even though they do not meet the conditions required for their original detention or for the detention to be renewed. Whereas most other provisions relating to an individual's liberty require the detaining authority to prove that the continuing detention is justified,[61] it is the patient who has the burden of proof and must satisfy the MHRT that conditions for detention no longer exist.[62]

In December 1992 a High Court judge ruled that a hospital could detain a mental patient even though the MHRT had ordered her release and the application for the further detention had been defective. The patient had been detained under Section 2 of the Act (for up to 28 days). She applied to a MHRT which ordered her release but her psychiatrist then arranged for a further detention under Section 3 of the Act.[63] The review function of MHRTs is rendered meaningless if loopholes in the law allow health professionals, who are neither impartial nor independent, to ignore a MHRT finding that the patient should be discharged.

Research suggests that a criminal conviction will reduce the patient's chances of obtaining a discharge[64] and that despite the clear provision that patients must be discharged if the MHRT is satisfied that they are no longer suffering from a 'mental disorder',[65] MHRTs will avoid ordering release if a patient is still seen as 'dangerous'.[66]

Patients who are subject to a restriction order have an

additional hurdle to overcome. The MHRT can only order the absolute discharge of the patient if the tribunal is satisfied that it is not appropriate for the patient to remain liable to be recalled to the hospital for further treatment. If the MHRT is not so satisfied, then the patient can only be conditionally discharged. This means that he or she can be subsequently recalled to hospital by the Home Secretary at any time and may be required to agree to certain conditions such as taking medication or living in a specified place before being released. The Court of Appeal has held that even where the MHRT finds that a patient is no longer suffering from 'mental disorder' that patient can still be subject to a conditional discharge if the MHRT believes that he or she should remain liable to recall.[67]

Those who are conditionally discharged can be subsequently recalled to hospital by the Home Secretary, who may do so without first obtaining a medical report opposing the view of the MHRT which had discharged the patient.[68] This has frequently happened at the end of a prison sentence imposed upon a person whilst conditionally discharged. For the MHRT to impose conditions when a person is not considered mentally disordered is an interference in an individual's right to privacy and any subsequent recall of a person without medical evidence to support the detention on the grounds of 'mental disorder' is an infringement of an individual's liberty.

A common practice has emerged which interferes with an individual's right to have his or her detention independently reviewed. Mental health professionals are admitting conditionally discharged patients under the civil part of the Act, rather than requesting the Home Secretary to exercise his powers of recall. Patients admitted to hospital by this route are barred under the Act from applying to a MHRT to have their detention reviewed.[69]

Delays

The Council on Tribunals, the statutory watchdog on tribunal performances and procedures, commented in its 1992 Annual Report that the time taken to arrange MHRT hearings for patients held on the longer treatment sections (Section 3 and Section 37 Hospital Orders) was up to 20 weeks, while restricted patients faced delays of up to 26 weeks. The Council urged the government to act promptly to eliminate these unacceptable delays which adversely affected the patient's rights to liberty:

> As matters currently stand, many patients are not being given the decision on the correctness of their detention until the whole or the greater part of the prescribed period authorising it has expired.[70]

The Council remains greatly concerned about delays. In its 1994 report the Council noted that the time taken for cases to reach a hearing was 'well above' the targets of 12 weeks for restricted cases and 8 weeks for unrestricted cases.[71]

THE CRIMINAL JUSTICE SYSTEM AND MENTAL HEALTH

The police station

The Royal Commission on Criminal Justice, when considering the safeguards for suspects in the police station, commented:

> The protection of suspects from unfair or unreasonable pressure is just as important to the criminal justice system as the thoroughness with which the police carry out their investigations.[72]

The Royal Commission recognised that some suspects, by reason of their mental health problems or learning disabilities, will be especially vulnerable to the psychological pressures caused by the experience of arrest, detention and interrogation. They are therefore particularly liable to make false confessions.

The Code of Practice to the Police and Criminal Evidence Act 1984 (PACE) requires that special protection be given to such a mentally vulnerable suspect:

> If an officer has any suspicion, or is told in good faith, that a person may be mentally disordered, or mentally handicapped, or mentally incapable of understanding the significance of questions or replies in an interrogation then they should be treated as mentally disordered or handicapped.[73]

The special protection envisaged by the Code is the involvement of an appropriate adult whom the police should ask to attend the police station. Anybody over the age of 18 years could be asked to act as an appropriate adult although the Code suggests that someone with experience in mental health work would be the preferred person.[74]

The role of the appropriate adult is to ensure that the suspect's rights are respected, that the suspect understands the procedures involved and that the police adhere to the Code, thereby minimalising the risk of the police obtaining unreliable evidence such as false confessions.

The appropriate adult is required to be actively involved, not simply an observer, during the police interrogation and should advise the person being interviewed, observe whether or not the interview is being conducted properly and fairly, and also 'facilitate communication with the person being interviewed'.[75] However, as this requires a knowledge and understanding of PACE and the Code of Practice to PACE a relative, would rarely be able to ensure that the suspect's rights were respected.

The major limitation on the effectiveness of the protection afforded by the appropriate adult is that it is entirely dependent upon the police recognising the suspect's mental vulnerability. Mental vulnerability covers a wide range of conditions which will not all be easily recognised. In a study carried out for the Royal Commission it was found that the police identified only 33 per cent of the persons whom the researchers had identified as being 'mentally ill' and as requiring appropriate adults.[76] The researchers also noted that identifying 'mental handicap' was a difficult task, even for trained clinicians.[77] Whereas this research suggested that one in five suspects required an appropriate adult, in a study carried out by the University of Loughborough only one in 500 suspects received appropriate adult assistance.[78]

The Royal Commission was very concerned about the problems involved with the current appropriate adult scheme and accordingly recommended that a multi-disciplinary working group be established by the Home Office to carry out a 'comprehensive review of the role, functions, qualifications, training and availability of appropriate adults'. That recommendation was made in July 1993 but the working party has not yet reported.

The courts

Under English law conviction can be based on confession alone and once made, confessions are notoriously difficult to retract. The only provision in PACE for mentally vulnerable suspects' confessions is under Section 77 which requires that the judge warn the jury of the 'special need for caution before convicting the accused in reliance on the confession' where the confession is made in the absence of 'an independent person'. But this provision offers scant protection to the mentally vulnerable suspect. First, it is limited to defendants considered to be 'mentally handicapped'. Second, the jury is likely to be greatly influenced in deciding upon its verdict by hearing the defendant's confession and the judge is not required to explain that some individuals are prone to confessing to crimes they did not commit.

Although PACE provides for the exclusion of unreliable confessions and evidence which might adversely effect the fairness of the proceedings, the courts have failed to adhere to any consistent principles when assessing the reliability of confessions made by mentally vulnerable suspects.

In the case of *R* v. *Everett*[79] the Court of Appeal indicated that the failure of the police officers involved to obtain the appropriate adult to accompany a suspect with learning disabilities was enough to make the resulting confession inadmissible owing to its potential unreliability. However, the more recent case of *R* v. *McKenzie*[80] held that the trial judge was not required automatically to exclude confessions of a mentally vulnerable suspect resulting from interrogation by the police in the absence of a solicitor and/or an appropriate adult and was entitled to conclude that such confessions were not unreliable. Although, in that case, the Court of Appeal accepted, in principle, that in certain circumstances a judge should take the initiative and withdraw the case from the jury, the court limited the circumstances to such an extent that they will only rarely apply.[81]

Prisons

A recent report carried out for the Home Office found that prisoners were not remanded on the basis of the alleged offences (indeed only a small number of the individuals studied had been charged with serious offences) but because of their need for social and psychiatric help.[82]

Very few of those remanded were subsequently sentenced to terms of imprisonment on their conviction. As the report noted:

remands in prison are an inefficient, ineffective and inhumane way of securing psychiatric assessment and treatment. Referrals to outside doctors lengthen the time spent in custodial remand and people who are adjudged sufficiently ill to require detention in hospital remain in prison for longer than those not accepted in hospital.[83]

The custodial detention of such individuals is not only arbitrary in that the detention is based on irrelevant and unjustifiable decisions, but it also discriminates against defendants suffering from 'mental disorder' who are remanded in custody in circumstances where other defendants, accused of similar offences, would be granted bail.

DISCRIMINATION

Against people with 'mental disorder'

There is no law protecting people with 'mental disorder' from unfair discrimination in employment or in the provision of goods and services. A person can be refused employment or accommodation because of a history of mental illness, learning disability or physical handicap. In 1990 the Court of Appeal upheld the right of a property developer to exclude people with a diagnosis of mental illness from its new houses.[84]

In 1994 the government blocked the passage of an anti-discrimination bill – the Civil Rights (Disabled Persons) Bill – which would provide comprehensive anti-discrimination legislation. The government's own Disability Discrimination Bill which is currently being considered by Parliament, contains such a narrow definition of 'disability' that many people suffering from mental health problems would not fall within the definition and would therefore gain no benefit from the Bill.[85]

Women and mental health

Women are far more likely to be diagnosed as suffering from 'clinical' depression than men,[86] more likely to be diagnosed by GPs as suffering from psychological problems than men, and considerably outnumber men among the 'mental health cases' of social workers.[87]

There are also more women than men admitted to psychiatric hospitals – women are admitted to psychiatric hospitals at a rate of 468 per 100,000, and for men the rate is 364 per 100,000.[88] This may be accounted for by the social problems women face, such as sexual violence and discrimination, but clinical judgments of women can be influenced by social expectations of women's behaviour.[89] The mental health charity, MIND, has commented:

> Women's experiences of emotional distress appear to be met with a medical response far more than is the case with men. And yet there is almost no evidence that the Department of Health, health authorities, NHS Trusts or other providers of mental health services are taking a close look at these figures and deciding how to address discrepancies and put an end to unfair treatment.[90]

For many women, hospitals are by no means a safe place, where abuse and harassment may range from sexual comments and jokes to unacceptable touching and rape.[91] The Mental Health Act Commission, reported on one woman's complaint that she had been indecently assaulted:

> it is unacceptable that a person should be subject to attack whilst a patient on a psychiatric ward.[92]

Women from black and other ethnic minority groups also encounter racial harassment and abuse from staff and other patients. Sometimes women who are abused find that staff fail to take the incidents seriously, and when they do, the police are often unwilling to prosecute the assailant due to the concern that the court will not accept the evidence of a 'mental patient'.[93]

The problem is particularly acute on mixed wards, where female patients may be forced to sleep in a bed next to, or share toilet and bathroom facilities with, strangers of the opposite sex, many of whom are very disturbed.[94] In December 1993, the Mental Health Act Commission stated that 'the whole policy regarding mixed wards may have to be reviewed.'[95]

Women receiving mental health treatment do not have the right to choose a woman key worker, psychiatrist or nurse; women with young children are often afraid to seek help with mental health problems because they fear that their children may be taken into care; and although caring for children increases vulnerability to depression, almost no community mental health facilities provide crèches or priority nursery places.[96]

Studies have shown that police officers are significantly more likely to refer women to hospitals than men.[97] Women appearing before a criminal court are approximately twice as likely to receive a psychiatric disposal as men.[98] In 1991 it was estimated that whereas women accounted for only 4 per cent of the prison population of England and Wales, 20 per cent of those individuals detained in special hospitals are women.[99] It is argued that this anomaly is due to the tendency to interpret the behaviour of women differently from that of men;[100] a woman deemed to be in need of control is more likely to be sent to a psychiatric hospital or secure unit whereas a man exhibiting the same behaviour is more likely to be sent to prison.[101] The Reed Committee, following its analysis of studies on this subject, concluded: 'Research tends to support the claim that women are more likely to be perceived "mad" rather than "bad".'[102]

WOMEN IN SPECIAL HOSPITALS

A disproportionate number of women are detained in special hospitals. On 1 January 1993, 284 women were detained in the three special hospitals[103] approximately 20 per cent of all patients.[104]

The Ashworth Committee received evidence upon the day-to-day experience of women detained in Ashworth Hospital[105] which was described in the Committee's report as 'compelling and disturbing':[106]

> women in Ashworth are controlled, suppressed . . . their overwhelming experience is that they are treated like children . . . It is my observation that they feel chronically frightened and . . . powerless, and that they are unable to do anything substantially to alter their lot.[107]

The Committee noted how the daily regime and culture of the hospital exacerbated the women's drive to self-harm. The regime was described as 'macho' and 'militaristic', women were subjected to abusive and offensive language and there was a general disregard for women's self-esteem.[108] Further, the Committee heard that despite the fact that a high proportion of women in Ashworth

Hospital had been sexually or violently abused by men at some point in their lives, this was an issue of which the nursing staff were never made sufficiently aware.

So far as the move towards mixed wards was concerned, the Committee came to similar conclusions to those of the Mental Health Act Commission in its *Fourth Biennial Report*: in all three special hospitals there was inadequate training of male staff in preparation for working on female wards, while the shortage of female staff meant that there were too few to attend to the personal care of women patients. The Mental Health Act Commission reported a concern expressed by some patients and staff that women are placed in mixed rehabilitation wards to 'test out whether male offenders can behave appropriately in a mixed environment'.[109]

The *Ashworth Report* concluded that the regime for women at Ashworth Hospital was 'infantalising, demeaning and anti-thera-peutic' and called for a radical change in hospital management.[110] Changes in practice and procedures in special hospitals must be implemented to ensure that women in-patients can enjoy their rights, in particular their rights to privacy, honour and reputation and to be treated with humanity and respect.

The Mental Health Act Commission noted in December 1993 that some changes had occurred as a result of the *Ashworth Report* but considered that much more work was required. Of one case in Ashworth Hospital in which a woman nearly succeeded in hanging herself, the Commission reported that it was:

> most concerned that this young woman's mental state has deteriorated whilst she has been in Ashworth and that her case is indicative of a failure to meet the needs of many of the women who are admitted.

Racial discrimination in the mental health services

Studies have shown that people from ethnic minorities are more likely than others to be removed to a 'place of safety' or forcibly detained in a hospital, special hospital or in a locked ward of a local psychiatric hospital under the 1983 Act, and to be diagnosed as suffering from schizophrenia or psychotic illness. Such treatment will often be inappropriate to their needs.[111]

Irish people living in Britain have the highest averages of first and subsequent admission to mental hospitals of any migrant group.[112] Irish people are more than twice as likely to be admitted as their English counterparts and 50 per cent more likely than Afro-Caribbeans, the next highest group.[113]

LESBIANS AND GAYS AND MENTAL HEALTH

Lesbians, gays and bisexuals with a history of mental health problems are vulnerable to discrimination both because of their health and their sexual orientation. The stress of hiding their sexuality to avoid discrimination, or of being discriminated against or harassed, can contribute significantly to mental health problems. The significant level of drug and alcohol dependency, low self-esteem, depression and attempted suicide found among some lesbians, gays and bisexuals seems to be related to personal histories of family rejection, social ostracism and prejudice as well as the psychological pressures of leading a closeted life.[114]

Users of mental health services who are lesbian or gay may face double discrimination, which may greatly reduce their chances of gaining employment, or retaining custody of their children.[115]

In February 1994 a survey of mental health counsellors showed that although all of those questioned had worked or were working with lesbian, gay or bisexual clients, none had received any specific training in issues related to counselling lesbians or gay men.[116]

Lesbian, gay and bisexual patients who are subject to compulsory detentions may, because they are being detained, be more vulnerable to homophobic abuse from staff and other patients.[117] Gay patients subject to compulsory detentions under the Mental Health Act may not have their partners recognised as their nearest relative. Staff may not recognise the special needs of lesbian, gay or bisexual patients.[118]

A survey conducted in London in 1984 found that nearly one-fifth of all lesbian and gay teenagers had attempted suicide, one in 10 had been thrown out of their home by their parents and one in seven had been sent to a psychiatrist because of their sexual orientation.[119] Gay and lesbian teenagers, who feel different from those around them, often do not have any contact with other people who are gay or lesbian. They do not often have positive homosexual role models, either at school or at home, and can consequently feel isolated, confused, anxious, and depressed.[120] Added to this stress is the knowledge that if they do 'come out', they may face ridicule, bullying, expulsion from home or school, and even criminal sanctions.[121]

COMPLAINTS

Civil action

Before a patient is entitled to sue a doctor or other person in relation to a claim arising out of the use of powers under the Act, leave must be obtained from the High Court.[122] The court will only grant leave if satisfied that the claim is worthy of investigation and raises a *prima facie* argument that the person or persons acted without reasonable care or in bad faith.[123]

By making it more difficult to commence proceedings this rule discriminates against a person with 'mental disorder' in relation to their access to the civil court system. There is no evidence to suggest that this rule is necessary in the public interest. Other rules of court and practical considerations, such as the restricted availability of Legal Aid, are sufficient to deter vexatious and groundless litigation. The bar to commencing proceedings should be abolished.

The criminal process

In relation to the most vulnerable of patients – those in special hospitals – the law of evidence which applies to their testimony[124] is unduly dismissive of patients' testimonies and thus will operate unfairly. On too many occasions the mere fact that a person is an in-patient of a special hospital and has a learning disability, or is diagnosed as mentally ill or 'psychotic', leads to the assumption that their testimony cannot be relied upon.

Weighing such evidence may be a difficult task but that is all the more reason why there should be a rule of procedure requiring the court to seek and obtain expert psychological evidence as to the reliability of such testimony before it is either relied upon or rejected. The importance of such an approach was recently emphasised in the abandonment of criminal proceedings following the death of Bryan Marsh, a patient in Rampton Special Hospital, when magistrates refused to commit nurses for trial on charges arising from that death.[125]

THE RIGHT TO PRIVACY

Correspondence and visits

In the special hospitals, hospital management has the power to censor the correspondence of patients and to withhold letters and packets from patients in certain circumstances.[126] In all hospitals, patients have no right to receive visitors, least of all in respect to conjugal rights. Visits may take place solely by permission of the medical and management staff. No legal rules exist to limit the intrusions which may occur into the patient's privacy of their person, belongings or written information about them. As a result, many patients find their privacy continually abused in numerous ways with confidential information often divulged unnecessarily.

'Supervision registers'

Interference with privacy is not confined to detained patients. Recent 'guidance' issued by the government creates a serious and unacceptable encroachment on the right of privacy of those people with mental health problems living in the community. The guidance 'requires' Health Authorities to have contracts with providers of mental health services which ensure that the providers establish 'supervision registers' of patients thought to be at risk of committing serious violence or suicide, or of serious self-neglect. The patient does not have to be informed that his or her name has been put on the register if for 'clinical reasons' it is considered inappropriate to do so and there is no mechanism for the patient to obtain an independent review of the decision to place his or her name on the register.

Whereas the general principle is that such confidential information about an individual can only be passed on to third parties in the absence of the individual's consent, in exceptional circumstances, such as in order to prevent a public danger, the guidance allows the personal details contained on the register to be disclosed to others if it is 'justified in the public interest'.[127]

The introduction of 'supervision registers' has met with widespread opposition. MIND described them as 'not only an offence against basic human rights but also a smokescreen to cover the appalling failures in the community care system' and called upon Health Authorities to spend the money which would be required to establish the registers on community care.[128] The president of the Royal College of Psychiatrists described her members' concerns:

> the broad nature of the criteria for inclusion on the register, the resource implications, the medico-legal implications associated with a decision not to include a patient, the legal position facing clinicians in the event of a violent act or suicide committed by a patient who was not included on the register, potential effects on the doctor/patient relationship, and anxieties in relation to civil liberties and confidentiality.[129]

THE RIGHT TO VOTE

Patients who are detained are deprived of their right to vote unless they are able to obtain a postal vote or are permitted to visit the polling booth to vote.[130] If detained in hospital at the time of registration they will lose their right to register and thus the right to vote. Informal patients may be registered to vote and may attend to vote.[131] Yet little effort is made to ensure that patients are registered. Moreover, a requirement that informal patients must complete a statutory declaration of the facts and give an address outside the hospital, where they can be registered in practice disenfranchises long-term patients.[132]

9 MIGRANTS, REFUGEES AND ASYLUM-SEEKERS

In November 1994 the British government stated that over 650 people seeking asylum in the UK were being held in various prisons, detention centres and police cells around the country.[1] The government estimated that the cost of holding these people was £800 per detainee per week.[2] In the same month, the Refugee Council published figures which showed that in the 18 months before the passage of the Asylum and Immigration Appeals Act 1993, 16 per cent of all asylum claims were refused, and in the 15 months since it was enacted, the rate had leapt to 75 per cent of all decisions.[3] During a period of massive global upheaval, the British government has been turning away asylum-seekers. At the same time, its treatment of those who are seeking asylum is a cause of serious concern.

The British government's treatment of refugees and asylum-seekers, and its human rights record in relation to migrants, seriously undermine any claims it may have to be a liberal, tolerant and compassionate State. Formidable legal barriers have been put up in recent years to prevent people who are escaping persecution from arriving in the UK.[4] Each year the authorities subject thousands of people (asylum-seekers and visitors) to administrative detentions, over which there is often no judicial oversight.[5] Hundreds of people are held in detention in conditions which allow them no dignity and which are sometimes cruel and degrading.[6] Many are subject to expulsions without an adequate opportunity to appeal or, if they are deported on grounds of 'national security', without an opportunity for a fair and public hearing. Some deportations are sometimes carried out with excessive force.[7]

Families are kept apart by the operation of immigration law and rules. The onus of proof is always on the applicants to satisfy an immigration official about the validity of their claim to enter the UK – and officials interpret the law differently when processing the claims of people of different countries, cultures and races.[8]

243

Children who fail to satisfy an official that they are 'related as claimed' to parents in the UK, and spouses who fail to satisfy an official that they did not marry 'primarily' for immigration reasons, are refused permission.

Some of the cases:

☐ On 27 July 1993, the House of Lords found Kenneth Baker MP guilty of contempt of court. As Home Secretary he had ordered the deportation of an asylum-seeker, in breach of an order from the High Court.[9] The asylum-seeker was returned to Zaire, where he had previously been imprisoned and tortured. His whereabouts are now uncertain.[10] Kenneth Baker has received no sentence.

☐ Between February and April 1994, over 200 asylum-seekers in detention centres and prisons across the country began hunger strikes.[11] In June 1994 police officers were used to suppress a demonstration by asylum-seekers held in Campsfield House Immigration Detention Centre.[12]

☐ In December 1993, Lejla Ibrahim, a Bosnian asylum-seeker, killed herself after losing a year-long battle with the Home Office to allow her husband into the country. Two days later her husband was granted a temporary visa on compassionate grounds because, on her death, her children had become 'unaccompanied minors'.[13]

☐ In October 1994, immigration officers attempted to deport a man who had slashed himself in detention. He was so badly injured the pilot refused to allow him on board the aircraft. He received 59 stitches to his stomach, wrists and legs.[14]

☐ On 27 April 1994, Kwande Slizba, a Zimbabwean, fell to her death from a tower block while attempting to escape from police officers. She mistakenly believed they were trying to deport her.[15]

☐ In July 1993, Joy Gardner, a Jamaican, died during a struggle with police officers who had come to her home to deport her.[16]

☐ On 14 December 1993, the Crown Prosecution Service announced that it would not prosecute six prison officers involved in the death of an asylum-seeker, Omasese Lumumba. He had been stripped and forcibly restrained in his prison cell, and an inquest jury gave the verdict that he had been killed unlawfully.[17]

☐ Three asylum-seekers have killed themselves in detention since 1987. In one case the inquest verdict was 'suicide, aggravated by official indifference and lack of care'.[18]

THE BRITISH GOVERNMENT'S RECORD

A history of immigration and asylum law and practice

This chapter is concerned with the British government's record of the last five years, but this can be seen as part of an historical trend, which is useful to describe. One commentator has observed:

> Britain's restrictions on immigration have dealt indiscriminately with whichever group the government of the day wished to exclude, subjects or aliens . . . The theoretical basis on which certain people are subject to entry controls is not that they are aliens but that they are people Parliament has decided to control. The immigration service, in concert with the Home Office, developed highly restrictive habits of thought and work practices; the notion of rights for immigrants was lost to sight, racial discrimination became entangled in the system, some British citizens came under its controls, and a large discretion for the executive became taken for granted.[19]

The first legislative regulation of immigration into Britain in the twentieth century, the Aliens Act 1905, was aimed at impecunious Jews fleeing persecution in eastern Europe.[20] They were considered undesirable aliens if it was thought they might be unable to support themselves and become a burden on the State. Further controls were introduced during and immediately after the First World War, restricting the appeal rights of those excluded, on grounds of 'national security'.

The British Nationality Act 1948 gave the same nationality to people who were British because of their connection to the UK itself or to a British colony, and all Commonwealth citizens remained British subjects. Government policies since then have restricted immigration from Britain's colonies and former colonies in covertly racist ways. Official records show Cabinet meetings in the 1950s discussed immigration on a number of occasions. They reveal that the aim was 'to keep blacks out' while 'avoiding the appearance of doing so' and avoiding 'criticism on the grounds that it would be contrary to the spirit of international declarations to which the UK government has subscribed.'[21] The Commonwealth Immigrants Act 1962 was the first Act to control the entry of people from the Commonwealth to the UK. It was supplemented by the Commonwealth Immigrants Act 1968, the Immigration Acts of 1971 and 1988, and many changes in the immigration rules (these are practice rules for immigration officers, which in fact have the force of law). Each law further restricted immigration into Britain. The appeals system, set up in 1969, has been flawed from the start. This is because all appeals are heard in the UK, but most people applying to come to the UK have to make their applications from abroad and are therefore not able to come and give evidence at their appeals.

One legacy of the British Empire was that some people from newly independent countries did not gain citizenship of these States, but remained citizens of the UK and Colonies after the creation of the Commonwealth. Some of these people had no other citizenship. The 1968 Commonwealth Immigrants Act removed the right of residence in the UK from people who did not have a parent or grandparent born in the UK. This left some groups of people effectively stateless, mainly people of Asian origin in East Africa.[22] The Immigration Act 1971 tightened these restrictions, and at the same time confirmed that people with the 'right of abode' were not subject to immigration control. People with this right included British nationals with a connection by birth or ancestry to the UK itself, and also citizens of independent Commonwealth countries who had a parent born in the UK. This meant that the descendants of settlers in former colonies would not be subject to the same immigration restrictions as the indigenous people.[23]

The 1971 Act came into force on 1 January 1973, when the UK joined what was then the Common Market, now the European Union. This gave all the citizens of European Union countries the right to travel to the UK to work. The government does not keep statistics on those who choose to do so.

Successive restrictions have ended virtually all immigration from Britain's former colonies or the Third World.[24] Practically the only people now permitted to come to live in the UK, apart from citizens of the European Union, are the close relatives of people already resident here. In July 1993 a Home Office minister stated that 'primary immigration slowed to a virtual halt years ago'.[25]

The British Nationality Act 1981 defined British nationality in terms of immigration restrictions. It divided the existing holders of UK and Colonies citizenship into three groups.[26] These are:

☐ British citizenship for those closely connected with the UK. This is acquired by birth, adoption, registration or naturalisation in the UK.

☐ British Dependent Territories citizenship (BDTC) for people with a close connection to a dependency. This is acquired by birth, adoption, registration or naturalisation in a dependency.

☐ British Overseas citizenship (BOC) for those former citizens of the UK and Colonies who do not have any of the above connections with the UK or its current dependencies.[27]

British citizens have the right of abode in the UK. Other citizens are subject to immigration controls. British Dependent Territories citizens have the right to live in a particular dependency, for example, St Helena or Hong Kong. British Overseas citizens have no right of abode anywhere in the world. They have to qualify under British immigration law to enter Britain and are liable to deportation.

Before 1983, birth in the UK entitled a person to British nationality and the right of abode. This is no longer the case; people born in the UK from 1 January 1983 are British citizens only if they have one parent who is either a British citizen or is allowed to stay permanently in the UK. When this is not the case, for example if the parents are overseas students, the children are not British citizens. The children may be stateless if they cannot inherit their parents' nationality, for example if the parents are refugees or asylum-seekers.

More recent restrictions

The Immigration Act 1988 removed the last remaining rights to family reunion in the UK, for long-settled Commonwealth citizens.[28] All family members who want to join relatives in the UK now have to show that there is adequate support and accommodation for them, without recourse to public funds. The Act also made it obligatory for anyone claiming to have the right of abode in the UK as a British citizen to have a full British passport before travelling to the UK. If a person claims to have the right of abode but is not a British citizen, she or he must have a certificate of entitlement issued through a British embassy, high commission or consulate overseas, confirming the right of abode, before she or he can travel to the UK. There is no right of appeal before removal for anyone who arrives without either a passport or a certificate.[29]

The British government has also imposed visa requirements on nationals of a number of countries.[30] This means that people must apply for entry clearance in their own country before they travel to the UK, for whatever purpose. Statistics show the rate of refusal of entry clearance is higher for applications made abroad than it is for those made at UK airports and seaports.[31] The Joint Council for the Welfare of Immigrants (JCWI) argues that the visas policy has a racial bias.[32] In 1990, one in 87 Guyanese visitors to Britain was denied a visa, compared with one in 3,600 Norwegians; applications for visitors' visas were refused at a ratio of one in eight for India, one in four for Bangladesh and one in six for Pakistan.[33]

Visas are a well-established form of immigration control, but the requirement has been imposed on different countries at different times, reflecting governments' views on immigration and asylum. Visas were imposed on India, Pakistan and Bangladesh in 1986 because of worries about family members coming to visit settled communities in the UK, and perhaps applying to stay on.[34] In more recent years, the targets have been mainly refugee-producing countries – such as Sri Lanka in 1985, Ghana in 1986, Turkey in 1989, Bosnia in 1992, and Sierra Leone in 1994.[35] There is no provision in the British immigration rules for people to be granted visas as asylum-seekers or refugees, and under the UN Convention definition, a refugee must be 'outside his country of origin' before being recognised as a refugee.

Although the British government makes it impossible for people to obtain visas to travel, this of course does not mean it is safe for people to remain in the country where they fear persecution. In 1987 the government enacted the Immigration (Carriers' Liability) Act, which imposed a fine of £1,000 per passenger on airlines that brought passengers to the UK with forged or inadequate travel documents. It effectively enlisted airline staff in immigration control, although they are unqualified in this area and unaccountable.[36] The fine was doubled in August 1991 and in April 1994 fines totalling over £60 million had been levied against carriers for breaches of this Act. Less than £8 million of this has been waived and over £20 million was reported to be still outstanding.[37]

Whether or not the imposition of carrier sanctions violates international human rights law,[38] it leads to increased dangers for refugees and asylum-seekers. They may be stopped from boarding a plane in their country of origin, and thus come to the notice of the authorities. Their details may be sent to the government when the airline is billed for the fine. Amnesty International and other groups have documented occasions where the staff of boats and airlines have placed asylum-seekers at risk of being returned to countries where they feared persecution, in order not to fall foul of this law.[39]

Adherence to international human rights standards

In its *Third Periodic Report to the UN Human Rights Committee* in 1989, the British government stated:

> The UK fully meets its obligations under the 1951 UN Convention relating to the Status of Refugees and the 1967 Protocol relating to the Status of Refugees and gives asylum to those with a well-founded fear of persecution. The number of applications has increased five-fold in the last 10 years, though the proportion who are successful has decreased from 60 per cent in 1981 to 25 per cent in 1988. This is not because criteria are now more stringent, but because increasing numbers of refugees are not fleeing political persecution, but are in reality economic migrants.[40]

In its *Fourth Periodic Report* the government states that the numbers seeking asylum continued to rise after 1988, before peaking in 1992, and that the percentage granted asylum fell dramatically.[41] In 1990, 23 per cent of all asylum-seekers had their claims recognised while in 1992 this dropped to 3 per cent.[42] The *Report* claims that:

> the trend underlines the fact that the majority of people coming into Europe as asylum-seekers in recent years have not been refugees but economic migrants.[43]

The *Report* states that the government responded to the situation by streamlining procedures and introducing new legislation, 'to ensure that unfounded applications are dealt with expeditiously and with finality, while genuine refugees continue to be protected'.[44] It outlines the main provisions of the Asylum and Immigration Appeals Act 1993 which, it claims, has reduced delays in dealing with cases, strengthened the appeal rights of asylum-seekers and made it easier for the authorities to identify claims which are 'without foundation', 'frivolous or vexatious' or 'fraudulent'.[45]

> The 1993 Act allows the Secretary of State to curtail any existing leave to enter or remain in the UK when refusing an applicant's claim for asylum. This would normally lead to the institution of deportation proceedings and the service of a notice of intention to deport would give rise to a right of appeal to an independent Special Adjudicator and thereafter to the Immigration Appeal Tribunal. Judicial review could also be sought. The 1993 Act also introduced a power to fingerprint all asylum applicants for identification purposes in order to prevent multiple applications and associated fraudulent Social Security claims.[46]

The report also describes the procedures surrounding the detention of people subject to immigration control or suspected of illegal entry. It claims that 'the power to detain is used as a last resort when there are clear and positive grounds for believing that the person will abscond if left at liberty, and after all the known circumstances of the person concerned have been taken into account'.[47] It states that 'any detained person refused asylum who has an appeal pending may apply to the Independent Appellate Authority (IAA) for bail at any stage until the appeal has been finally determined. The courts also have the power to grant a writ of habeas corpus' [that is, a writ which requires a person to justify the detention of another.]'[48]

An average of 1,500 people were detained under deportation powers each year between 1989 and 1994. Over 80 per cent of these were held for less than one month.[49] There was also a steady increase in the number of people held as alleged illegal entrants over the same period, rising from just under 2,000 in 1989 to over 3,500 in 1993.[50] The vast majority were held for less than two weeks although the number held for over three months increased dramatically, both overall and as a proportion of the total number of detainees.[51]

It is accepted that governments have a right to regulate the entry of migrants into their countries. Immigration policy is seen by most States as part of their sovereign prerogative and a necessary element of social and economic policy. International law recognises the right of States to control entry to their territories by nationals of other States, but also imposes responsibilities on them concerning the treatment of their own nationals and of foreign nationals who have been lawfully admitted into their territory.[52]

The treatment of asylum-seekers is governed by a variety of international human rights instruments. These define refugees, give them the right to seek asylum and protect them once their status has been recognised. The 1951 UN Convention Relating to the Status of Refugees states that:

> [The] term 'refugee' shall apply to any person who . . . owing to a well-founded fear of being persecuted for reasons of race, religion, nationality, membership of a particular social group or political opinion is outside the country of his nationality and is unable or, owing to such fear, unwilling to avail himself of the protection of that country.[53]

It has been noted that this definition is extremely narrow as it does not cover those fleeing from civil war, famine, drought, disasters (natural or created by humans) and poverty.[54] Even those who are fleeing from systematic and widespread human rights violations by a government may not qualify as refugees under this definition, because the Convention has been interpreted as meaning that they have to show they have a *personal* and well-founded fear of persecution.[55] The definition was drawn up principally to deal with the situation of displaced people in Europe after the Second World War, who were unable to return to the new countries and systems then created, and were already living in different countries. People continue to leave their own countries for reasons of safety, as the world situation changes, but increasing numbers do not now meet the terms of this definition.

Most refugees and asylum-seekers now come from countries of the South, and the vast majority of these remain in countries neighbouring their own. But as the numbers arriving in Western Europe have increased, many governments have begun to define 'persecution' more narrowly.[56]

The British government's record of adherence to international human rights standards has attracted controversy.[57] The government entered a blanket reservation covering immigration and nationality in its *Third Periodic Report to the UN Human Rights Committee:*

> The government of the United Kingdom reserve the right to continue to apply such immigration legislation governing entry into, stay in and departure from the United Kingdom as they may deem necessary from time to time and accordingly, their acceptance of Article 12(4) and of the other provisions of the Covenant is subject to the provisions of any such legislation as regards persons not at the time having the right under the law of the United Kingdom to enter and remain in the United Kingdom. The United Kingdom also reserves a similar right in regard to each of its dependent territories.[58]

It has also failed to ratify the Optional Protocol. These two actions have prevented any judicial testing of its immigration policy by the UN Human Rights Committee. The government has failed to ratify the Fourth Protocol of the ECHR on freedom of movement.[59] It also entered a reservation when it ratified the UN Convention on the Rights of the Child, that its provisions do not apply to immigration and nationality law.[60]

Britain's immigration restrictions have been censured by the European Commission on Human Rights on a number of occasions. In 1973 it found that the 1968 Commonwealth Immigrants Act was in breach of the European Convention on Human Rights, in that it had racial motives and breached the rights of a racial group.[61] The intention behind the Act was to exclude from the UK certain citizens of the UK and Colonies – those who were of Asian origin living in East Africa, and under pressure to leave because of the 'Africanisation' policies of the governments there. However, the case was not referred on to the Court of Human Rights and went instead to the Committee of Ministers. They did not reach the necessary two-thirds majority, so no final decision on the Act was reached. The British government failed to amend the Act despite the Commission's finding. Instead it agreed to increase slightly the number of 'special quota vouchers' issued to these British nationals, which permitted them to come to the UK. The published quota of 5000 vouchers per year since 1975 has never been granted, and the waiting time for vouchers in India was almost six years in 1981.[62]

In 1984 and 1985 the Commission and Court found that the government's immigration rules on marriage breached the Conven-

tion, in that they discriminated against women in their right to
family life. At the time, immigration rules allowed a woman to be
joined by her husband from abroad only if she was a British citizen
born in the UK or with a parent born in the UK. However, men
who were settled in the UK, whether or not they were British,
could be joined by their wives. The Commission's judgment stated
that:

> It has not been shown that the measures in question enhance
> good race relations, for, although they may respond to the
> fears of a certain section of the population, they may create
> resentment in that part of the immigrant population which views
> the policy as unfair.[63]

The government responded, not by giving women the same rights
as men but by amending the rules to remove rights from men.
Since 1988 both sexes have been subject to the same restrictions.[64]
In practice, it is still more difficult for women than men to be
joined by their partners from abroad.[65]

In 1992 the European Commission on Human Rights ruled
that the British government had breached the right to an effective
remedy before a national authority of a group of Tamils, after it
rejected their asylum claim and returned them to Sri Lanka. However, the Commission's ruling was subsequently overturned by the
European Court.[66] The British courts had initially accepted the
government's view, in a review of the immigration adjudicator's
decision, that the test of what constituted a well-founded fear of
persecution was objective and so could be assessed by the immigration adjudicator. (The British courts rejected the arguments that
the claimants' fears of persecution were reasonable.)[67] A number
of the Tamils who were sent back did subsequently suffer ill-
treatment by the Sri Lankan authorities. Another appeal, based on
the facts of the case rather than on challenging the criteria used to
make the initial decision, was upheld by the immigration
adjudicator.[68]

THE RIGHTS OF REFUGEES AND ASYLUM-SEEKERS

The British government has summarised its policy towards refugees
and asylum-seekers as being:

to meet the UK's obligations towards refugees under the UN Convention while reducing the scope for misusing asylum procedures. Where an individual does not qualify for refugee status, their individual circumstances will be taken into account and leave to remain granted in exceptional cases.[69]

In its *Fourth Periodic Report* the UK government noted that the numbers of people claiming asylum began to increase significantly towards the end of the 1980s, and it also stated that the majority of asylum-seekers coming into Europe are not refugees but economic migrants.[70] This view is shared by the governments of other countries in Western Europe and the number of inter-governmental meetings and discussions on migrant issues has increased in recent years, with the aim of dissuading people from travelling.[71] Some of the measures discussed or agreed have significant impacts on the rights of asylum-seekers: for example, the Draft Convention on the Crossing of the External Borders, the Dublin Convention and the Maastricht Treaty on European Union. There have been unofficial fora such as the Schengen Group and the Ad Hoc Group on Immigration. The latter has now been replaced by working groups set up by the K4 Committee under the Maastricht Treaty. The harmonisation of European asylum laws and procedures has taken place with little public scrutiny and has not been matched by growing democratic control.

In the UK the number of applications from asylum-seekers rose from about 4,000 per year in 1988 to 44,800 in 1991 before falling to 24,600 in 1992 and 22,370 in 1994.[72] The number of asylum-seekers who reached Western Europe in 1992 was three times the organised intake of foreign workers.[73] However, the number of asylum-seekers needs to be seen in the context of the huge global upheavals of recent years, which have resulted in vast displacements of populations. Over 90 per cent of refugees remain in the developing world and the proportion who reach Europe is extremely small. As one commentator has noted:

In global terms, 'burden-sharing' has not yet even begun. The continued failure of the North to re-settle Vietnamese refugees from Hong Kong over a period of many years is evidence of this as is the failure to deal with the refugee problem from former Yugoslavia. Looked at from this perspective, 'the refugee problem' in Europe is small and Europe's reaction hysterical.[74]

The Asylum and Immigration Appeals Act 1993

This Act came into force in July 1993. It gave all asylum-seekers refused entry the right of appeal against refusal before being sent back. A new system of asylum appeals, to be heard by special adjudicators, was set up. At the same time, new immigration rules came into force which listed factors which the Home Office must consider in asylum applications. The Home Office also made a separate policy decision to interpret the criteria more strictly, and no longer to grant people exceptional leave to remain in the UK, if they did not exactly meet the strict UN Convention criteria.[75]

Immediately before the enactment of the Asylum and Immigration Appeals Bill, the number of applications pending decisions fell dramatically, as the Home Office rushed to deal with the backlog. However, it rose again in 1993 and in 1994.[76] It appears the Act has not speeded up the appeals process.

Since its introduction, the number of asylum claims refused has also increased dramatically. In the first half of 1993, only 14 per cent of decisions were refusals. However, figures for the first quarter of 1994 show that 74 per cent of all decisions were refusals. The number of people granted exceptional leave to remain (ELR) fell from 77 per cent to 21 per cent, and the number granted asylum fell from 7 per cent to 5 per cent.

These figures are distorted slightly by the refusal of the authorities to make decisions on asylum applications in 1993 from people from the former Yugoslavia. Another potential distortion is that people have arrived in the UK (after the Home Secretary's announcement in December 1992 concerning Bosnian ex-detainees and their families) and have been given the unique status of 'temporary refugee', which applies for only six months at a time. It does not appear in the figures. If these two groups of refugees had been included, the refusal rate would have been 81 per cent.[77] The figures show a marked increase in refusals for applications from Sri Lanka, Ethiopia and Turkey, countries undergoing enormous political upheaval.

The decisions made on applications from different countries are shown in the table on page 256.[78]

The Act introduced a right of appeal for all refused asylum-seekers, but the number of successful appeals has fallen dramatically. There were 2,283 appeals to special adjudicators lodged in the first year of the Act. Of those heard, 39 were allowed and

	Refugee status		ELR		Refusal	
	1994	**(1993)**	**1994**	**(1993)**	**1994**	**(1993)**
Total %	**5**	**(7)**	**21**	**(77)**	**74**	**(16)**
Yugoslavia	2	(7)	95	(–)	4	(99)
Sri Lanka	2	(–)	16	(97)	81	(2)
Ghana	–	(1)	2	(4)	98	(94)
Turkey	14	(2)	9	(66)	77	(14)
Somalia	1	(20)	92	(95)	7	(2)
India	–	(4)	3	(29)	97	(70)
Pakistan	–	(–)	2	(31)	98	(69)
Zaire	2	(–)	2	(7)	96	(88)
Ethiopia	4	(5)	28	(98)	68	(1)
Uganda	3	(1)	8	(89)	89	(11)
Iraq	49	(1)	44	(82)	7	(1)
Former USSR	–	(17)	5	(33)	95	(50)
Iran	46	(16)	10	(77)	44	(4)
Angola	3	(19)	–	(3)	97	(85)
Sudan	29	(12)	14	(47)	57	(1)
Lebanon	4	(53)	21	(86)	75	(10)
China	11	(4)	4	(29)	85	(43)

1,030 dismissed.[79] There is less time for appellants to seek and receive legal advice because of the new 'fast-track' procedures. These apply to people whose cases the Home Office has decided are 'groundless', and are seeking entry at a port, and are handed notice of refusal in person.

Poor decision making at the Home Office often leads to unnecessary appeals. The Immigration Appeal Tribunal frequently remits cases for re-hearing by another special adjudicator, because the original decision was faulty or because the adjudicator did not explain the standard of proof used to decide the claim. By 21 July 1994, 183 people had been granted leave that year to appeal to the Tribunal; eight appeals were allowed, 33 dismissed and 80 remitted for re-hearing.[80]

'Safe third country' expulsions

Where asylum-seekers have arrived in Britain via a 'safe third country' the Home Office will deny their claim without any substantive consideration. Hundreds of asylum-seekers are expelled from Britain every year on this basis and, again, the numbers appear to be rising. In 1992 the Home Office expelled 441 asylum-seekers under the 'safe third country' rule.[81]

The Home Office expects refugees to seek asylum in the first 'safe' country they reach. It is general policy to return them to any 'safe' country through which they have travelled before reaching the UK.[82] However, the government does not consider it necessary to seek assurances from the authorities in the third country that the asylum-seeker will be readmitted and allowed to seek asylum there. In spite of repeated requests from organisations including Amnesty International, the Home Office has refused to seek such assurances even when it is highly likely that the third country will send asylum-seekers back to the country they have left.[83] For example, the Home Office has returned a number of Iranian asylum-seekers to Turkey, in spite of the Turkish authorities' practice of sending such people back to Iran without examining their asylum claims.[84]

Asylum-seekers may be expelled from the UK under this rule even if they have only spent a few hours in a 'safe third country'. Asylum-seekers have even found themselves expelled to 'safe third countries' on the basis of unscheduled transit stops, only to be sent back to the UK by the country in question or to be left in limbo between countries because no one is prepared to accept responsibility for them.[85]

Amnesty has expressed concern that the 'fast-track' appeals procedure against asylum refusals, introduced by the Asylum and Immigration Appeals Act 1993, will increase these problems. Appeals against some asylum refusals now have to be submitted within 48 hours, whereas it used to be 10 working days. The appeal – which only considers the question of return to the third country and not the merits of the asylum application itself – must be determined within seven days of the submission and is not then subject to any further appeals. The government has specified that the new procedures were primarily aimed at dealing quickly with claims which are 'without foundation'[86] and ministers have made it clear that 'the great majority of cases' in this category will be third country cases.[87] The new immigration rules also make clear that the Home Office is 'under no obligation to consult the authorities of the third country before removal.'[88]

On 8 October 1993 the High Court ruled that refugees who came to the UK via a 'safe third country' could be denied asylum provided that the special adjudicator agreed the third country was safe.[89] On 23 October 1993 two Kurdish asylum-seekers went on hunger strike to protest about their continued detention in prison. Six days later the two were expelled from Britain on the grounds that they had spent 90 minutes in the Netherlands, waiting for a ferry, and had, therefore, spent time in a 'safe third country'. The Dutch authorities responded that they did not have responsibility for the two men and placed them on a ferry back to the UK, where their applications for asylum are still being considered.

The 'safe third country' rule has no basis in international human rights law. There is no provision in either the ICCPR or the UN Convention on Refugees for limiting the right to asylum in this way. The UN High Commissioner for Refugees has made it clear that:

> none of the sources of international rules and principles relating to asylum suggest – much less prescribe – that the right to seek asylum has to be exercised in any particular country, or that a person who has been forced to escape his country to save his life or freedom would forfeit his right to seek asylum if he does not exercise it in the first country whose territory he has entered.[90]

Exceptional leave to remain

The UK's record of accepting refugees is particularly bad. In 1990 only 900 people were recognised as refugees and granted asylum. In 1991 this dropped to 505, in 1992 it was 1,115 and in 1993 it was 1,595. Given the increase in asylum claims (from 4,000 in 1988 to 22,370 in 1994),[91] this means that the proportion of applicants granted asylum has fallen sharply in the UK in recent years.

However, there was an increase in grants of exceptional leave to remain (ELR) up until the introduction of the Asylum and Immigration Appeals Act 1993. Just over 2,000 people were granted ELR in 1990 and a similar number were granted ELR in 1991, but 15,325 were granted ELR in 1992.[92] A total of 6,970 people were granted refugee status between 1988 and 1993, but 38,480 people were given ELR during the same period.[93] It has been argued that the increase in the number of grants of ELR was owing to a recognition that the definition of a refugee was too narrow – and that granting ELR status in fact acknowledged that asylum-seekers would face persecution if they were forcibly returned to their country of origin.[94] It is obviously preferable that people should remain in the UK, albeit temporarily, rather than be forcibly returned to countries where they face persecution, but the use of ELR status is nevertheless unsatisfactory. First, the decision to grant ELR is discretionary. There is no definition in the Immigration Rules or elsewhere of the criteria according to which ELR is granted. It is impossible to challenge a decision about the granting or denial of ELR in the courts. Because more and more asylum-seekers are allowed to remain in the UK only with ELR status, an increasing proportion of asylum-seekers are being treated as second-class refugees.

Second, it is administratively inefficient because it encourages additional asylum applications. People granted ELR only have temporary protection. It can subsequently be withdrawn if the Home Office believes conditions have improved in their country of origin.[95] They also have no right to family reunion under this status until four years have passed. The Home Office will consider making an exception, to consider applications from family members before this, on compassionate grounds, but this policy is discretionary, subjective and not open to any meaningful right of appeal. People granted ELR also have to wait for seven years before consideration is given to allowing them to settle. There is, therefore, a strong incentive for people who are denied asylum but granted ELR to make a fresh asylum application or to appeal against the refusal immediately. It has been argued that it would be more efficient, more cost-effective and fairer simply to grant equal protection, rights and status to all people at risk rather than to maintain the current division between asylum and ELR.[96]

Since the Asylum and Immigration Appeals Act 1993 came into force, the use of exceptional leave has been severely curtailed. In the last six months of 1993, 1,050 people were granted ELR, and 1,680 in the first six months of 1994.[97] The Home Office claimed exceptional leave was granted when it became practically hard to send people away, rather than because they needed this protection. Groups in contact with many asylum-seekers, such as the JCWI, doubt that significant numbers of people have been allowed to remain who do not have serious reasons for fearing return.

FREEDOM OF MOVEMENT

Deportations

The Home Secretary has the power in four specific circumstances to deport people who are not British citizens but who have entered the country lawfully.[98] He or she can deport:

☐ people who have entered with limited leave to remain who either overstay or break one of the conditions of entry. This can include, for example, an overseas student doing an evening job without specific permission, or a wife leaving her husband without knowing that her permission to stay has expired;

☐ if he or she deems a deportation to be 'conducive to the public good'. This power may be used to deport people who have been convicted of a criminal offence although the court has not recommended deportation, people who have deceived the immigration authorities, people considered a threat to national security and people considered a threat on political grounds;

☐ the wife [sic] or child under 18 years of someone who is being deported. This power has not been used since 1983;

☐ an adult who has been convicted of an imprisonable criminal offence when the court has recommended deportation.

An appeal may be made before deportation is carried out except in cases where the Home Secretary deems the expulsion to be conducive to the public good 'on the grounds of national security or of the relations between the UK and any other country or for reasons of a political nature'. The scope of this power is broad.[99] Article 13 of the ICCPR specifies that 'an alien lawfully in the territory' may only be expelled 'in accordance with law and shall, except where compelling reasons of national security otherwise require, be allowed to submit the reasons against his expulsion'. This provision is both narrower and more specific than the grounds allowed for deportation in British immigration law.

The power to remove people whose presence is thought to threaten national security has been given a broad interpretation. For example, during the Gulf crisis of 1990-1 (after the Iraqi invasion of Kuwait), 144 Iraqis and 11 other Middle Eastern nationals, including Palestinians, were arrested and threatened with deportation on the basis of this power: 110 were detained, and 35 of these were later designated as 'prisoners of war' by the authorities without reference to a court. Most of them were postgraduate students, but some had been settled in the UK for many years and had British spouses and families. The main evidence on which the deportations were based came from the security services and an internal government inquiry showed that mistakes had been made. In fact, those detained included a number of known opponents of the Iraqi regime.[100]

In attempting to contest deportations on grounds of national security, representations on the deportee's behalf may be heard by a panel of three lay advisers appointed by the Secretary of State. The person to be deported is not entitled to legal representation at the hearing. She or he may not hear or cross-examine witnesses from the Home Office or security services, or call his or her own witnesses. These hearings are purely advisory and the Home Secretary is under no obligation to accept the panel's rulings.[101] In the Gulf cases, 53 hearings took place. Only seven unconditionally upheld the deportation decision, 14 people were released unconditionally and 25 were held in detention pending further investigations. Those classified as 'prisoners of war' could not even go through this procedure; they had to request that the army convene a military board of enquiry into their cases. Three men did so, and were released. After the Gulf crisis ended, all the remaining detainees were released, and all the deportation decisions against them were rescinded. Although 59 people left the country after being detained, nobody was deported.[102]

These arbitrary detentions and threatened deportations were raised in submissions to the UN Human Rights Committee in 1991, in connection with the UK's *Third Periodic Report*. One Committee member made the points that:

> in the United Kingdom, the Home Secretary enjoyed sweeping powers under the Immigration Act 1971, to detain foreigners indefinitely without trial and with no right of appeal. In order to continue to enjoy those powers, the government of the United Kingdom should make an express derogation from its obligations under Articles 9 and 13 of the Covenant, and he [Mr Sadi] asked if such derogation was under consideration.[103]

The UK representative did not agree, and the powers remain. They have been used primarily against political activists such as Kani Yilmaz and Karamjit Singh Chahal.

Yilmaz, European spokesperson for the Kurdish Workers' Party the PKK, was arrested at Westminster station in central London on 26 October 1994. He was on his way to address a meeting in the Houses of Parliament. He has been held since then, under Immigration Act powers, in various high-security police stations and prisons pending his deportation on the grounds that his presence in Britain is, in the Home Secretary's opinion, 'not conducive to the public good on grounds of national security'.[104] Yilmaz fled from Turkey in 1991 after serving 10 years in prison for his membership of the PKK. He was granted political asylum in Germany and travelled around Europe carrying out political work in support of the Kurdish cause. He had visited Britain on two previous occasions with no difficulties and entered Britain perfectly openly three days before his arrest; on arrival in the UK he identified himself to immigration officers who made no attempt to detain him.[105] The Home Office claimed that Kani Yilmaz's position in the PKK meant that he was involved in terrorist activity.[106] However, he initially faced no specific charges and did not have the opportunity to defend himself against this accusation. Several weeks after his detention the German authorities requested his extradition to face charges of conspiring to commit acts of arson.[107]

Karamjit Singh Chahal, a campaigner for Sikh independence, lost a case in the High Court on 22 October 1993, challenging his deportation to India where he faces possible arrest, torture and even death.[108] He has now taken his case to the European Court of Human Rights.[109] There are no current charges against him, but he has spent over four years in a British prison under administrative detention, and could spend several more years incarcerated before the European Court of Human Rights hears his case. Chahal has lived in Britain for 22 years and has been a prominent political and religious figure in the Sikh community.[110] Two of his relatives have been shot dead by the Indian Security Forces and he was detained and tortured during a visit to India in 1984. In August 1990 Chahal was arrested and detained under the Immigration Act 1971 and served with a deportation notice. The reasons given were 'national security and other reasons of a political nature, namely the fight against international terrorism'.[111] He had previously been convicted of assault but the conviction was quashed on appeal. No charges relating to terrorism have been brought against him, so he has had no opportunity to refute the allegations of involvement in terrorism. However, he denies the allegation that he has any connection with terrorist activity.

People threatened with deportation for reasons other than national security do have a formal right of appeal under the immigration appeals system. However the Immigration Act 1988 severely limited this right for people who have been in the UK for less than seven years at the time of the deportation decision.[112] The only grounds for appeal are that there was no power in law for the Home Office to make that decision. For example, if they are being deported on grounds of overstaying leave to remain, the only grounds for appeal are that they have not overstayed and that the Home Office has granted permission to stay. Other factors, such as having a spouse and family in the UK, cannot be considered.

In its *Third Periodic Report* the British government repeated that it reserved the right to continue to apply such immigration legislation governing entry into, stay in and departure from the UK as it deemed necessary.[113] It set out the number of people removed under the government's deportation powers as follows:[114]

	1986	1987	1988
Deportation orders enforced	738	776	745
Supervised departures	80	147	743
Total	818	923	1,338

The report noted the increased use of supervised departures – those in which an individual agrees to leave the country before a deportation order is signed. This trend was confirmed in the government's *Fourth Periodic Report,* which shows that the number of supervised departures is now substantially higher than it was during the 1980s. The *Fourth Report* set out the number of removals as follows:[115]

	1989	1990	1991	1992	1993
Deportation orders enforced	652	577	733	876	850
Supervised departures	1,358	1,202	1,673	1,599	1,218

The *Third Report* noted that supervised departures meant that the intended deportee did not have to remain in detention while an order was being obtained. These departures had 'administrative benefits in that the procedure did not involve obtaining a deportation order from the Home Secretary.'[116] It implied that supervised departures were preferable unless it was essential to ensure that the person did not return to the UK. However, the report stated, the use of supervised departures was limited because the financial authority to meet their costs was restricted to cases in which a court had recommended the procedure.[117]

The 1988 immigration rules amended this restriction and permitted immigration officers to offer supervised departure to any intended deportee. This coincided with a provision of the Immigration Act 1988 coming into force which removed full rights of appeal against deportation from people who have been in the UK for less than seven years. Advisers in groups such as JCWI hear from their clients that immigration officials tell them that they have no chance of success in any appeal, and should leave as quickly as possible by agreeing to supervised departure (and thereby waiving appeal rights), rather than be detained pending a deportation order. This may be acceptable to some people, but others may wish to take the chance of appealing, in order to be able to apply for bail, and have the chance to make their own arrangements to leave.

The two reports also revealed a steady growth in the number of people being removed from the UK as alleged illegal entrants.[118] People can be treated as illegal entrants if they have:

- [] entered or sought to enter the UK without leave. This means either not seeing an immigration officer at all (for example arriving in a rowing-boat at midnight on a deserted beach), or going through the wrong immigration channel at an airport and not being stopped and examined;

- [] entered in breach of a current deportation order. It is unlikely that a person would get in using his or her own name, and there is therefore likely to be an element of deception in this;

- [] entered by deceiving an immigration officer. This includes travelling on a forged passport, lying to an immigration officer or not revealing the full facts of the situation to an immigration officer. People who are treated as illegal entrants for this reason have normal immigration stamps on their passports and may have great difficulty in understanding why they have been classified as illegal.

There is no clear distinction between people who are treated as overstayers, or who have broken a condition about work, and illegal entrants. If people in these categories are caught, they are interrogated by immigration officers. If they say anything that could indicate that their intentions on arrival were not declared to the immigration officer, they may be treated as illegal entrants. This includes people who entered as visitors but have remained longer, and people who work without getting permission. Illegal entrants can be removed from the country very quickly, with no formal appeal rights.

People treated as illegal entrants can thus be arrested, detained and removed without having any chance to contest the case. The provisions of the Immigration Act 1971 mean that there is normally no appeal against removal as an illegal entrant until after the person has been sent back. Any appeal is heard strictly on the facts of the case, meaning the basis on which the Home Office treated the person as an illegal entrant, and not on any other personal or compassionate factors.[119] Most people removed as illegal entrants have no independent review of their case. The numbers of people who have been removed are as follows:

1986	1987	1988	1989	1990	1991	1992	1993
1,142	1,566	2,196[120]	2,457	2,392	3,255	3,631	3,791[121]

Cruel, inhuman and degrading treatment during deportation

There has been concern about the way in which deportations are carried out following deaths of deportees and reports of brutality and insensitivity on the part of immigration officials, police officers and private security guards.

Joy Gardner was a Jamaican woman whose application for leave to stay in Britain had been turned down. On 28 July 1993 she died after a struggle with police officers at her home in north London, watched by her five-year-old son.[122] A letter had been sent to her and her solicitor the previous day informing her that she was being deported. The Home Office subsequently admitted that the letter was deliberately timed to arrive after she had been arrested, to reduce her chances of continuing to resist deportation.[123] She was placed in a body belt fitted with legcuffs and handcuffs and a piece of tape was placed over her mouth. She could not breathe properly and suffocated.[124] The police unit which had been involved in this and other controversial deportations was suspended, and an internal inquiry by the Metropolitan Police condemned the use of adhesive tape to restrain deportees.[125] Similar complaints of excessive brutality were made against the police in other cases. These include those of Dorothy Nwokedi, forcibly deported from Britain on 9 July 1993, Meya Mangete, deported in April 1993, Rukhsana Faqir, deported in August 1993 and an unnamed Ghanaian deported in October 1993. These cases were examined in more detail in an Amnesty International report published in July 1994.

The Amnesty report criticised the methods used by law enforcement officials to restrain people during forcible deportations from the UK. It claimed that they violated international human rights principles and constituted cruel, inhuman and degrading treatment.[126] The report highlighted a number of cases in which it believed excessive force was used by immigration officers, the police and private security guards. It called for an independent and public inquiry both into specific allegations of ill-treatment and more broadly into 'the role and accountability of all agencies involved in the deportation process, the independence of the complaints procedures and the authorisation and usage of restraint equipment and methods.'[127]

The report called on the government 'to bring to justice any law enforcement official alleged to have engaged in cruel, inhuman or degrading treatment'[128] and voiced particular concern about the accountability and standards of private security firms.[129] It also called for the establishment of an independent body to investigate specific complaints against officers.[130] Demands for an 'immigration watchdog' were first made by the Commission for Racial Equality in its 1985 report[131] and were followed up by JCWI in 1986.[132] These suggestions have not been implemented and the Home Office has maintained only its internal complaints system. In March 1993 a Complaints Audit Committee was announced, to review the effectiveness of the internal procedures.[133] It came into being in January 1994.

DETENTIONS

The regulations

About 10,000 people are detained under Immigration Act powers each year.[134] Detentions can last for minutes or months. Most people who are detained are initially stopped at a port of entry while the authorities investigate their case. Others are taken from their home or workplace because they are believed to have contravened immigration laws.

Detentions are authorised by immigration officers usually after only a cursory examination of the facts. Most people who are detained are not charged with and have not been convicted of any crime, and have not appeared in court. They are subject to administrative detention, which is entirely at the discretion of the Home Office or the immigration service. The Home Office does not have to justify these detentions in any public forum. There are no time limits on how long people can be detained and there is no watchdog body to monitor the use of detention. People can be held in administrative detention virtually anywhere.[135] Places include ships and aircraft, port immigration offices, special detention centres, police cells, remand centres and prisons.

Few detainees are informed in writing of the specific reasons for their detention. There is no time limit within which the Home Office must make a decision about someone's status, so those affected have no way of knowing how long their detention will last. An application for habeas corpus is unlikely to succeed because detainees have to prove that they are being held illegally.[136]

People detained under Immigration Act powers may apply for bail to the immigration appeals authorities, if they have an immigration appeal pending, or if they have sought entry to the UK and no decision has been made about their application for over a week. Bail applications are made to an adjudicator or the Immigration Appeal Tribunal. However, the right to apply for bail is not universally available. People detained pending deportation may only apply for bail if they have lodged an appeal against the decision to deport them.[137] Asylum-seekers have no special rights to bail but they do have rights of appeal before removal, and so they may become eligible to apply for bail after spending considerable periods of time in detention. Once a detainee has lodged an appeal against a refusal of asylum, he or she is then likely to find that the Home Office will cite the rejection of the asylum claim as a ground for opposing bail for that detainee.

Detained asylum-seekers can only obtain bail if they can find at least two people prepared to offer sureties for the application. While no minimum level is specified, a special adjudicator has stated that 'we will not normally consider granting bail unless there are two sureties offering recognizances of £2,000 each'.[138] The Joint Council for the Welfare of Immigrants has stated that sureties could be as high as £5,000 to £10,000.[139]

Detainees may make further applications for bail to the courts if they have applied to the High Court or to the Court of Appeal for a judicial review of the decision on their asylum claim. The renewed application is likely to be made towards the end of the asylum procedure by which time the detainee will probably have spent several months in detention. Technically a detainee can apply for a judicial review of the actual detention but the High Court has previously ruled that it will only overrule the Immigration Service's discretion to detain in the most extreme circumstances.[140]

Article 9 of the ICCPR specifies that anyone detained 'shall be brought promptly before a judge', that 'it shall not be a general rule that persons awaiting trial shall be detained in custody' and that people who are detained shall be entitled to challenge their detentions before a court.[141] The British government's treatment of immigration detainees, refugees and asylum-seekers is potentially in breach of all of these provisions.

The practice: fifty cases

In November 1994 there were 654 asylum-seekers held in detention.[142] Of these, 129 had been held for over six months, 233 for between two and six months, 125 for between one and two months and 167 for less than one month. There were 265 people held in prisons and 55 in police cells.[143]

The British government claims that detention is only used where necessary to prevent asylum-seekers absconding.[144] The Home Office has stated that:

> it is our policy to use detention only as a last resort. Temporary admission is granted wherever possible and detention is authorised only where there are good grounds for believing that the person will not comply with the terms of the temporary admission. In deciding whether to detain, account

is taken of all relevant circumstances including the means by which the person arrived in this country, any relevant immigration history, and any existing connections with the UK. In practice only a very small proportion of asylum-seekers is detained.

A closer analysis contradicts a number of these claims.

Between July 1993 and September 1994 Amnesty International monitored the cases of 50 detained asylum-seekers to determine whether or not their treatment accorded with international standards.[145] The cases were drawn at random from the caseloads of over 20 different legal representatives. They included detainees of 24 different nationalities, all of whom had applied for asylum after July 1993 when the procedures established by the Asylum and Immigration Appeals Act 1993 came into force and were detained when they applied for asylum. At the time of the report's publication, 33 of the cases had been fully resolved.[146]

Of the cases resolved, four of the detainees were recognised as refugees and granted asylum by the Home Office. Three were granted asylum after their appeals were allowed.[147] The proportion of successful claims (14 per cent) is significantly higher than the proportion of successful claims among all asylum-seekers (detained and not detained) during the same period which undermines the government's claim that those who are detained are those who are most likely to have their applications rejected or are submitting bogus claims. However, 10 per cent of the detainees withdrew their applications and voluntarily departed from the UK. Amnesty has expressed concern that:

> the debilitating effects of prolonged detention may cause some detainees to abandon their asylum application before it is resolved, with an attendant risk that some may return to the country from which they have fled and where they may face persecution.[148]

The seven detainees who were granted asylum spent an average of 132 days in detention.[149] For the group of 50, the average time spent in custody per detainee was 154 days. This is about three times longer than the average time a remand prisoner spends in custody before being released or convicted.[150]

These findings contradict the government's claim that the Asylum and Immigration Appeals Act 1993 would lead to shorter periods of detention. Amnesty believes that detention times have significantly *increased* since July 1993. Although the Home Office does not publish figures from which the average detention time can be calculated, its figures show that the number held for long periods has dramatically increased. For example, in April 1991 there were 120 asylum applicants who had been detained for one month or longer. In May 1992 there were 191. In April 1993 there were 230. In July 1993 there were 317. In January 1994 there were 429.[151] Of the detainees in the Amnesty study, 56 per cent spent four months or more in detention, compared with 34 per cent of asylum-seekers held in detention in April 1993, shortly before the Asylum Act came into force.[152]

The study found that none of the 50 had received at the time of their detention a written statement of the reasons for their detention, and only three received one at all.[153] This is a violation of Article 9 of the ICCPR which specifies that 'anyone who is arrested shall be informed at the time of the arrest of the reasons for his arrest and shall be promptly informed of the charges against him.'[154] None of the detainees was given a full written explanation of his or her rights while in detention or how to exercise them, nor was there any mechanism for providing detainees with such information. Amnesty expressed particular concern that detainees were not informed about how to apply for bail and that those held in prisons were not even provided with information about how to obtain specialist advice and support.[155]

Three of the detainees applied to the High Court for a judicial review of the decisions on their asylum claims. The applications were considered by the court after 97, 128 and 238 days respectively.[156] None of those detained applied to the court for bail but 19 of the 50 applied for bail to the immigration appellate authorities. In four cases this was granted, in three cases the detainees were released on temporary admission (which is not bail, but release at the discretion of the immigration officers) while in the other 12 cases bail was refused.[157] The remaining 31 did not apply for bail because they did not know two people who were able or prepared to act as sureties.[158] Among those who did not even apply for bail were two of the seven who were eventually recognised as refugees and granted asylum. The majority of detainees in the study were offered no opportunity for an independent review of the reasons for their detention *at any stage* of the detention.

Thirteen of the detainees in the Amnesty study were deemed

to be illegal entrants and one of those applying for asylum was facing deportation on other grounds.[159] This group spent an average of two months in detention before becoming eligible to apply for bail and none was subsequently granted it. However, three of these 'illegal entrants' were ultimately recognised as refugees and granted asylum.

Amnesty has expressed concern that the lack of an *automatic* hearing before a court or similar review body not only violates international human rights law but also contrasts with the rights afforded to defendants in the British criminal justice system. People charged with an imprisonable offence may be detained in custody while awaiting trial but *only* after a hearing in court, at which they may apply for bail. The court is under a duty to grant bail unless there are compelling reasons not to do so.

Inhuman and degrading treatment

There are three main immigration centres where asylum-seekers may be detained: Harmondsworth Immigration Detention Centre, Campsfield House Immigration Detention Centre and Haslar Holding Centre. Several air and sea ports have detention facilities for short-term use and asylum-seekers and other detainees are also held in the mainstream prison system. In July 1994 over 40 prisons held immigration detainees.[160] According to the government:

> immigration detention centres are run on the lines of a hostel, providing freedom of movement within a secure perimeter. Detainees are provided with three meals a day within a varied menu designed to cater for their dietary and religious requirements. They also have access to a wide range of indoor and outdoor recreational facilities, a shop, telephones and facilities for washing clothes. Provision is made for detainees to see a doctor if they require medical treatment. Arrangements are in place for legal representatives, relatives and friends to contact and visit detainees daily.[161]

Even if this were accepted at face value (and, of course, this statement cannot apply to detainees held in other places), significant concern would remain about the psychological impact of subjecting asylum-seekers to arbitrary detentions on their arrival in Britain. Three asylum-seekers have committed suicide whilst in detention since 1987: Ahmed Katangole from Uganda, Siho IyigÇven from Turkish Kurdistan and Kimpua Nsimba from Zaire.[162]

The failure of the authorities adequately to inform people of the reasons for their detention, coupled with uncertainty about how long they will be held, is likely to be particularly traumatic. As one detainee put it:

> During my stay in Haslar I found the situation like being jailed for life. Nobody informed me about the progress of my case; no court recommended me to be detained; I was only told I was not entitled to bail rights. All I could do was sit and wait. Some of us chose hunger strike as a means to draw attention to our plight; others saw suicide as a way out of their predicament . . . The ordeal of my detention has not been easy to recover from . . . Some detainees continue to fight after release to regain their normal state. One thing I know for sure: nervousness never leaves you.[163]

Three of the 50 people in Amnesty's study attempted suicide while in detention.[164]

The Medical Foundation for the Care of Victims of Torture published a study in October 1994. It focused on the experiences of 47 detained asylum-seekers, two of whom attempted suicide and eight of whom needed psychiatric care during their detentions. The Foundation concluded that detention imposes unnecessary cruelty and degradation on people already distressed by torture and loss.[165]

Amnesty criticised the lack of medical facilities in the detention centres which it described as 'rudimentary',[166] and inadequate for the care of people who may still be suffering the effects of imprisonment, torture or other traumas from which they have fled. It noted that some detainees requiring medical treatment had been transferred to prison hospital wings due to a lack of appropriate care in detention centres. It expressed concern that the government could not meet its obligations to provide asylum-seekers with medical care 'whenever necessary' when this included hospital treatment, *except* by breaching its obligation not to hold asylum-seekers with criminal remand or convicted prisoners 'whenever possible'.[167]

However, of the 606 asylum-seekers in detention on 22 June 1994, 235 (39 per cent) were held in prisons and a further 10 were in police cells.[168] The number is subject to some fluctuations – partly due to protests by some asylum-seekers about their detention, which may result in transfer to prison from a detention centre and partly due to changes in the numbers in the general prison population. On 15 April 1994 there were 276 asylum-seekers held in prisons, 111 in police cells and 265 in immigration detention centres.[169]

The main reason given for holding asylum-seekers in prisons is the lack of available space in detention centres. However, there have been cases in which it appears that asylum-seekers were deterred, by their detention, from pursuing their asylum claim in the UK.

For example, in the mid-1980s several hundred Tamils applied for political asylum in Britain in response to widespread human rights abuses perpetrated against the Tamil minority by the Sri Lankan government.[170] The government responded in May 1985 by imposing a visa requirement on all Sri Lankans – the first time that such a requirement was imposed on Commonwealth citizens – and by beginning to detain Tamil asylum-seekers on their arrival in the UK. By February 1987 there were 160 asylum-seekers in detention, and 101 of these were Tamils.

With existing facilities near to breaking point the authorities decided to convert a ship, the *Earl William*, into a holding centre.[171] The first detainees were placed aboard the *Earl William* in May 1987, two months after a similar vessel, the *Herald of Free Enterprise*, sank at Zeebrugge with the loss of 193 lives.[172] There were frequent protests that the authorities were holding them in conditions which endangered their lives. The detainees were evacuated in October 1987 when the ship burst its moorings and was holed on a sandbank during storms. The *Earl William* held around 100 asylum-seekers.[173]

Over one-half of the detainees in Amnesty's study were held in prison for at least part of the detention.[174] Amnesty expressed concern at the Immigration Service's policy of using enforced transfer to prisons as a punishment for detainees in detention centres who were perceived as 'disruptive'. Amnesty noted that these transfers took place without any formal disciplinary hearings and that there were no procedures to appeal against them.[175]

People who have lived in the UK for many years, and who may have homes or families here, may also be detained on suspicion of being illegal entrants, or because a decision has been made to deport them. According to JCWI, the first place of detention for most people arrested after having lived in the UK is usually a police cell. Regulations allow people to be detained for up to five days. In 1989 a police superintendent said:

> we had 1,500 people pass through our eight cells in the first two months of this year. The immigrants we are holding are a relatively small proportion of the total, but it is happening more often and when it does it's a great problem. Whether they are illegal or not, there should be basic human dignities and there is no dignity being kept in a small, dark grotty cell with no idea what is going to happen and when.[176]

The conditions in which asylum-seekers are held violate international human rights standards. The UN High Commissioner for Refugees has stated asylum-seekers should 'whenever possible' be held in facilities appropriate to their status and not with persons charged or convicted of criminal offences.[177]

DISCRIMINATION

On 1 January 1973 there were two separate milestones in British immigration law. Britain became a member of the European Community, now the European Union (EU). It was also the date on which the Immigration Act 1971 came into force.

The EU removes barriers to travel for citizens of the 15 EU countries, making it easier for them to travel between countries to work, do business, provide services, study or do almost anything provided they are self-supporting. Their families also have rights, even when the family members are not EU nationals themselves, to travel with them. 'Families' are broadly defined, to include a spouse, children under 21 and over 21 if dependent, dependent parents, grandparents and great-grandparents and other relatives if they have been living under the same roof. All these people have rights to join the 'worker'. Since 1 January 1994, the EU has been joined by five other white European countries, to form the European Economic Area, and nationals of all these countries have free movement rights in the whole area.[178]

By contrast, British immigration law defines restrictions rather than permissions. People who are subject to control have no right to enter, but may do so if they satisfy an immigration official that they qualify. Parts of the immigration law and rules directly discriminate on grounds of race or sex. The Immigration Act 1971 states that all people without the 'right of abode' in the UK are subject to immigration control. All British citizens have the right of abode, and so do citizens of Commonwealth countries born before 1983 who have a parent born in the UK, or Commonwealth citizen women who were married before 1983 to a man with the right of abode.[179] The majority of Commonwealth citizens with parents born in the UK are white.

The immigration rules allow Commonwealth citizens with a grandparent born in the UK to be given permission to come to live and work in the UK, and after four years to stay permanently. This entitlement, again, is likely to apply disproportionately to white people.

The immigration rules also permit young Commonwealth citizens aged between 18 and 27 to come to the UK as 'working holidaymakers' for up to two years. Historically, the vast majority of people allowed to come for this purpose have been from white Commonwealth countries. Recently more young people from other Commonwealth areas, such as west Africa and the Indian subcontinent, have become aware of the provision, often while in the UK as visitors or students, and have therefore applied to remain for this purpose. The immigration rules[180] in force from 1 October 1994 make it impossible to change status when in the UK in order to become a working holidaymaker. People therefore have to apply for entry clearance in their countries of origin, and the refusal rates for different countries vary immensely.[181]

The definition of 'family' in British immigration law and rules is narrower than in EU law. Spouses and children under 18 years old may be allowed to come provided a series of conditions are met. Parents over 65 years may be considered, again if they satisfy many conditions, including being financially dependent on the person in the UK and having no other close relatives to turn to in their country of origin. No family members have any right to come in, and they may all be refused if they fail to satisfy immigration officials of often subjective requirements.

The Asylum and Immigration Appeals Act abolished previous rights of appeal against refusal for visitors, prospective students and students enroled on courses for less than six months. It also removed rights of appeal for people who are refused because they do not meet a requirement of age, citizenship or nationality under the rules or because they are applying to remain for reasons or in circumstances not covered by the rules.[182] This leaves still more scope for immigration officials to decide applications on the basis of their own preconceived ideas, when they know that their decisions will not be reviewed by an independent body.

Attitudes and practices of immigration officials can also lead to discrimination in the operation of the rules. In 1985 the Commission for Racial Equality published a report detailing the attitudes of officers involved in making immigration decisions.[183] More recent examples are plentiful. In January 1994 it was reported that an entry clearance officer in Kingston, Jamaica, wrote a statement in connection with a woman's appeal against being refused permission to join her husband in the UK. The statement included the assertion: 'women from poor rural areas have children by different fathers as each father is required to pay maintenance'. He concluded that 'a traditional disregard of the state of matrimony has led to consistent abuse of the concept in order to secure residence abroad and it was against that background that I viewed the appellant's application'.[184] An immigration adjudicator hearing an appeal was reported to have said that he did not think the wife, who had given evidence before him, 'attractive enough for her husband to want to marry her' rather than to want to go to the UK where she lived.[185] In another case an officer felt that statements from a Bangladeshi bank were not as reliable as those from banks 'in the civilised world'.[186]

Status checking

Breach of immigration conditions is a criminal offence, and so the police are empowered to check people's immigration status if they have reason to suspect that an offence is being committed. Black people are far more likely to have their status questioned than white people[187] and this creates a circular, self-justifying argument. Because more black people are questioned, more are likely to be found to be overstayers or considered illegal entrants. This reinforces police prejudice that black people are more likely to be illegally in the country, and therefore warrant more frequent checking.

For example, figures released by the Metropolitan Police in December 1994 show that nearly half the people stopped and searched in London over the previous year were from ethnic minorities. The police stopped 132,565 white people and 95,751 black people during the year 1993–4 in London. Black people were 42 per cent of the total stopped, although they only constitute 20 per cent of the population of London and this indicates a discriminatory bias.[188]

There are many examples of individual police officers displaying racist attitudes. For example, in January 1994 the inquiry report into the death of Joy Gardner recommended banning mouth gags of the type on which she had suffocated. Mike Bennett, the Chair of the Police Federation, then said that such equipment was necessary because officers feared 'contracting HIV by being bitten'.[189] As most deportees are black, this demonstrates a racist belief that a black person is more likely than a white person to be HIV-positive.

FAMILY LIFE AND PRIVACY

Refugees and family reunion

Refugees seeking asylum in Britain face long delays before their families are allowed to join them. On average asylum-seekers have waited 14 months before a decision is made on their own applications.[190] In October 1994 the government admitted that 84 asylum-seekers have been waiting for over five years to have their asylum applications processed and one has waited over eight years.[191] If they are recognised as refugees and granted asylum they have a right to family reunion. However if they are only granted exceptional leave to remain (ELR) they have no such right. The Home Office states that it will normally consider allowing family members to come only after the first person has been in the country, with exceptional leave, for over four years. People with ELR 'must show they have the means to support and accommodate relatives without recourse to public funds and in accordance with Immigration Rules.'[192]

In practice this means that many thousands of people forced to abandon their homes and flee their country in fear of their lives, are denied the right to family reunion in Britain. They often face problems in finding employment (due to language difficulties and discrimination) and are unable to begin to settle and make new lives for themselves when close family are still in the country of danger.

Families and immigration law

It has been argued that 'the denial of family unity has been the cruellest work of our immigration law'.[193] As primary immigration has almost ended, the authorities have increasingly concentrated their efforts on reducing the numbers of dependent relatives who could come to join immigrants already settled in Britain. This has been done by changing the rules in order to make fewer people eligible and by administrative methods.

Since 1969 relatives have been required to apply for entry clearance overseas before travelling. The British government has consistently refused to post adequate numbers of staff to the British high commissions in the countries of the Indian subcontinent in order to deal with these applications in a reasonable time.[194] The waiting period between making an application and being called for interview at the British post peaked in Bangladesh at three years and two months in 1974[195] but delays of 12 to 18 months are still routine. The immigration rules on family members have also been made increasingly restrictive and have increased the scope for officials to decide on a subjective basis.[196] Turan Pekoz, a Kurdish asylum-seeker, set himself alight at the Home Office Public Enquiry Office in Croydon, in protest at the length of his separation from his family while his application was being processed.[197] He died as a result of his burns on 16 March 1993.

The one-year and primary purpose rules

The immigration rules on marriage state that a partner from abroad has to satisfy an immigration official that the partners have met each other, that they intend to stay together permanently as husband and wife, that the primary purpose of the marriage is not immigration to the UK, and that they will be able to support and accommodate themselves without recourse to public funds.

The 'primary purpose' rule specifies that a person will be refused permission to enter the country to join their spouse, fiancé or fiancée, unless an immigration official is satisfied that the marriage did not or will not take place primarily for the purpose of immigration.[198] It is insufficient for the couple to prove that they intend to live together as husband and wife. The rules have been administered so as to exclude many husbands who have been married for some years and have children by their wives.[199]

This rule is routinely used to justify intrusive and often lengthy questioning at British high commissions and embassies abroad. It has been used to prevent British citizens bringing their partners into the UK throughout the 1980s and early 1990s and now affects thousands of people every year.[200]

The rates of refusal are different for people from different countries. For example, the Home Office keeps detailed statistics showing the applications and refusals from people applying in the countries of the Indian subcontinent to come to the UK to join family members. It does not do so for any other countries. In 1992, 2,360 men from India, Pakistan and Bangladesh were allowed to come here to join their wives and families and 2,500 were refused (along with 2,160 women and children); 5,980 men and 8,250 women were allowed to come in order to marry that year. Also in 1992, 2,266 immigration appeals were heard from men from all over the world who had been refused permission to come to the UK to join their wives or fiancées; only 192 of these were from men *not* from the Indian subcontinent.[201] The vast majority of those refused were from India, Pakistan and Bangladesh.

In June 1992 the Home Office stated that it would no longer use primary purpose as a reason for refusal if a couple have been married for over five years, or if there is a child of the marriage with the right of abode in the UK.[202] This mitigates the harshness of the rule, but it is no substitute for proper rights to family life. It is also unpublicised and the written rules make no reference to it.

The 'one-year' rule causes many difficulties. Even when people have satisfied all the requirements and are able to come to the UK, they are given permission to enter for one year initially. Near the end of that year, they must apply to the Home Office for permission to settle, and the Home Office has to be satisfied about all the requirements a second time. If a marriage breaks up within the first year in the UK, the partner who came more recently from abroad may be refused permission to stay and may eventually be deported.[203] Even if the break-up is temporary, if the Home Office has been alerted to any potential problems in the marriage it is extremely difficult to satisfy the authorities that the situation has now changed, and to obtain permission to settle again. Because more women than men enter the UK through their marriage to a British national, they are disproportionately affected by this rule.[204] We believe the way in which the one-year and primary purpose rules are applied violate Articles 17 and 23 of the ICCPR.

During the first year, spouses from abroad are not entitled to welfare benefits such as income support, housing benefit and council tax benefit,[205] so if their marriage breaks up they have no means of support. Refuges for women escaping domestic violence are largely funded through housing benefit, and it may be financially more difficult for them to accommodate women who have no benefit entitlement. The immigration rules also make no provision for unmarried or same-sex partners to join their partners in the UK.

Rights of children

The British immigration rules state that the children joining their parents in the UK must satisfy officials that they are 'related as claimed' to their parents. In some countries, particularly those of the Indian subcontinent, the system of registration of births, marriages and deaths was not as highly developed as in western countries. Entry clearance officers at British high commissions, therefore, developed sophisticated systems of questioning to try and establish that families were not related.[206] They asked all members of families long lists of questions and looked for 'discrepancies' between what different members said. This meant that many children were refused permission to travel to the UK, because of 'wrong' answers given to often trivial questions. Because the appeal system worked in a similar way, and accepted statements from entry clearance officers without question, rather then subjecting them to the same scrutiny as the appellants' statements, appeals were often also unsuccessful.[207]

The of DNA genetic 'fingerprinting' made this questioning unnecessary. DNA blood tests can show that a particular couple are virtually certain to be the parents of a particular child. In 1991, the government agreed that DNA tests could be offered to first-time applicants when the relationship was the only point at issue in their application. The tests were free – but were financed by an increase in the fees for settlement entry clearance to £80 per person. Tests showed that the vast majority of children *were* related as claimed to the parents; the first 18 months of DNA testing showed that 89 per cent of children applying in Dhaka were related to at least one parent, and 78 per cent to both.[208]

Families who had previously been refused permission for their children to join them had to pay privately for DNA tests. Many did so, and with results that proved their relationship, applied again for entry clearance. But the children involved were often now over 18, and therefore no longer eligible to join their parents under the immigration rules. They were refused because of their age and because the Home Office did not accept they were 'living alone in the most exceptional compassionate circumstances', as was required under the rules for children over 18 years.[209] By mid-1992, the cases of 701 young people who had been wrongly refused entry to the UK as children had been considered. Only 126 were allowed to join their families, showing that the government has not taken responsibility for its mistakes in this area.[210]

Deportation

The Immigration Act 1971 gives the Home Secretary the power to deport the wife [sic] and children under 18 of a deportee solely on the grounds of their relationship. Factors to be considered include the existence of their own independent ties to Britain and their ability to support themselves without recourse to public funds.[211] This power remains on the statute books even though it has not been used since 1983.

The strength of family connections may be a factor militating against deportation, on compassionate or domestic grounds, but it is not decisive. The Home Office does not necessarily reverse a deportation decision because the deportee has family members in the UK. However, in 1981 the British government revoked one deportation order after the European Commission on Human Rights ruled that it might breach the applicant's right to respect for family life under Article 8 of the ECHR.[212] There are also internal Home Office instructions to officials, stating that a person who has been in a stable marriage for over two years, or who has children from a relationship, should not normally be deported.[213] These instructions refer specifically to Article 8 of the European Convention on Human Rights.

However, in June 1992 a 20-year-old Sikh woman, Dalvinder Kaur, was given notice of the Home Office's decision to deport her although she had been made the legal guardian of her sister and five brothers, aged from four to 16, a year earlier.[214] The children and their parents arrived in the UK in 1984 and applied for asylum, after their home was destroyed in rioting following the assassination of Indira Gandhi by her Sikh bodyguard. The application was refused and Dalvinder's father, a priest, was arrested and

imprisoned in January 1991. He was held in prison until his deportation to India in July 1992 where he was detained on arrival due to 'irregularities' in his travel documents. The children, three of whom had been born in Britain, were made wards of court, and placed in the care of Dalvinder after their mother went into hiding to avoid her own deportation. Their mother was deported in September 1992[215] and is now appealing to the ECHR that her right to enjoy family life has been violated.[216] The Home Office unsuccessfully attempted to strike out the wardship and then, after a lengthy gap, served notice of a deportation decision on Dalvinder Kaur. Dalvinder's appeal against the decision to deport her is still pending. The appeal was allowed by an adjudicator but the Home Office has successfully challenged this decision.

The Children Act 1989 stipulates that the welfare of the child should always be the paramount consideration. The immigration law and rules have no such stipulation and there is very little contact between family law and immigration law.

10 CENSORED: FREEDOM OF EXPRESSION AND HUMAN RIGHTS

There were six men in Birmingham, in Guildford there's four
They were picked up and tortured and framed by the law
And the filth got promotion but they're still doing time
For being Irish in the wrong place and at the wrong time
In Ireland they'll put you away in the Maze
In England they'll hold you for several long days
God help you if ever you're caught on these shores
And the coppers need someone and they walk through the
    door[1]

In November 1988 the Independent Broadcasting Authority (IBA) banned the song *Streets of Sorrow/Birmingham Six*, by the Pogues. The song questioned the convictions of the Birmingham Six[2] and the Guildford Four[3] using the above lyrics. The IBA justified its ban on the grounds that:

> the song alleges that some convicted terrorists are not guilty
> and goes on to suggest that Irish people are at a disadvantage
> in British courts of law. That allegation might solicit or invite
> support for an organisation proscribed by the Home
> Secretary's directive, in that they indicate a general
> disagreement with the way in which the British government
> responds to, and the British courts deal with, the terrorist threat
> in the UK.[4]

At that time there was already considerable public unease about the safety of the convictions of the Birmingham Six and the Guildford Four, and in October 1989 the Guildford Four's convictions were quashed. However, the IBA ban remained in force until March 1991 when the Birmingham Six were released. The IBA belatedly conceded: 'Now that the Birmingham Six are obviously not convicted terrorists, the record can be played again.'[5]

283

On 19 October 1988, the Home Secretary, Douglas Hurd, issued notices to the British Broadcasting Corporation (BBC) and the IBA, instructing them to refrain at all times from broadcasting 'any words spoken' by representatives of a number of Irish organisations, including Sinn Fein and the Ulster Defence Association.[6] The notices were issued by the Home Secretary using the discretionary powers conferred on him by the Broadcasting Act 1981[7] and the BBC Licence and Agreement,[8] which are almost identical in their wording.[9] The restrictions became known as the broadcasting ban.

Under the terms of the ban people's faces could be shown, but words had to be subtitled, read by someone else or paraphrased. Douglas Hurd said that the ban did not amount to censorship because it did not interfere with the reporting of events, but was designed to prevent 'the occasional appearance of representatives of paramilitary organisations and their political wings . . . [which] have caused widespread offence to viewers and listeners throughout the UK, particularly just after a terrorist outrage.'[10] Prime Minister, Margaret Thatcher, commented more bluntly that 'in order to beat off your enemy in war, you have to suspend your civil liberties for a time.'[11]

On 16 September 1994 the broadcasting ban was lifted, three-and-a-half weeks after the IRA announced a suspension of its military campaign of violence which had lasted for 25 years. The IRA's announcement was preceded by months of speculation about a change in republican thinking, the news that the British government had held exploratory talks with Sinn Fein, and a joint declaration on Northern Ireland by the British and Irish governments. While these developments were taking place, the British government maintained its broadcasting ban,[12] which was given a wide interpretation while it was in force. The voices of Eamonn de Valera and Sean MacBride, two of Ireland's leading statesmen, were dubbed in historical footage because they had been members of the IRA in the 1920s.[13] The words of people who were not members or supporters of any of the organisations listed were also censored – even when they were invited to participate in discussions precisely because of their independence – with the reason given that their words could be interpreted as inviting support for the same cause as a listed organisation.[14] This restriction on freedom of expression was imposed by an administrative order rather then by legislation, and lifted by a similar executive order, without reference to parliament. There were several legal challenges to the ban. In February 1991 the House of Lords rejected one challenge[15] and in 1994 the European Commission deemed inadmissible a case brought on the basis that the ban infringed Article 10 of the European Convention on Human Rights.[16]

In July 1993, the UN Human Rights Committee expressed concern that reporting restrictions in the Republic of Ireland, which had been in force since 1976 and were the model on which the British broadcasting ban was based, were an infringement of Article 19 of the International Covenant on Civil and Political Rights (ICCPR).[17] The Irish government responded, in January 1994, by not renewing the order under Section 31 of its Broadcasting Authority Act which imposed these restrictions. On 1 February 1994 the Irish parliament welcomed this decision to comply with the UN Human Rights Committee ruling.[18]

The way in which the broadcasting ban was introduced in Britain, the broad interpretation it was given, and the failure of the courts to challenge its imposition all show the inadequacy of existing constitutional protection for freedom of expression in the UK. Indeed, media censorship has increased markedly under the present government. The Prevention of Terrorism Act 1989 (PTA) and the Official Secrets Act 1989 have both made political reporting more difficult. There is no Freedom of Information Act and there is no public interest defence for disclosing sensitive information. Journalists and documentary makers who question official versions of incidents – particularly where these concern issues of political sensitivity or the security services – have found it increasingly difficult to maintain their professional integrity and remain within the law.

This is particularly disturbing because government ministers have concealed the full truth on a number of issues of political significance in the last five years. For example, in February 1994 a Foreign Office minister stated that the government's aid programme 'is not and will not be linked to arms sales'.[19] Douglas Hurd, the Foreign Secretary, subsequently told a Foreign Affairs Select Committee that the two had become temporarily entangled. The Committee's final report stated that: 'Ministerial replies to certain questions were literally true, though less open and less informative than the House has a right to expect.'[20]

In January 1991 the Prime Minister, John Major, implied that an embargo on arms sales to Iran and Iraq, laid down in 1985, was still in force – as had previously been explicitly stated by other government ministers.[21] At a subsequent trial of three businessmen accused of breaking this embargo a former government minister, Alan Clark, admitted that he had been 'economic with the actualité' in not announcing that the embargo had in fact been relaxed in 1988 and subsequently concealing this fact from parliament.[22]

Free and independent media play a crucial role in safeguarding democracy. However, the British media are subject to controls and restrictions which inhibit freedom of expression in an unjustifiable way.[23] The effects of overt State censorship and prior restraint[24] are compounded by other restrictions such as the laws of libel, obscenity and blasphemy.

The exercise of freedom of expression carries with it special responsibilities, such as respect for the rights, freedoms and reputations of others. The right to freedom of expression must be balanced against the right to privacy and the right of vulnerable groups in society to protection from those who incite hatred and violence. It is always difficult to decide the point at which to strike this balance from a civil liberties perspective. The extent to which censorship of the media is justified on grounds of 'offensiveness' is particularly difficult to determine in the areas of incitement to racial hatred, and sexually explicit or blasphemous material.[25]

The effects on freedom of expression of the concentration of media ownership and the growth of multinational media companies are also of growing concern. People's right to freedom of expression implies access to a diversity of media perspectives – as befits a pluralist society.

THE BRITISH GOVERNMENT'S RECORD

In its *Third Report to the UN Human Rights Committee*, the British government stated that it was committed to greater openness and had increased the amount of official information that it made available to the public, although it continued to oppose a Freedom of Information Act.[26] The *Fourth Periodic Report* listed a number of new laws and measures which have increased public access to official information.[27]

The *Third Report* stated that the Official Secrets Act 1989 had 'abolished the much criticised blanket protection for official information provided by Section 2 of the Official Secrets Act 1911' and had limited 'the protection of information to those areas for which criminal sanctions are absolutely necessary'.[28] The government stated that it had no plans either to repeal or extend the blasphemy laws, which criminalise attacks on Christianity but on no other religion, but the report noted that the last prosecution brought for blasphemy was in 1977.[29]

The *Third Report* stated that the government was committed to extending the scope of the Obscene Publications Act 1959, because its definition of obscenity 'does not afford adequate protection to the public against the worst type of material in circulation'.[30] It also stated that the government had established a Broadcasting Standards Council to monitor and restrict 'the portrayal of sex and violence on all forms of broadcasting'.[31]

This report outlined the statutory licensing and regulatory regimes which govern broadcasting in Britain and the proposed changes which were subsequently incorporated into the Broadcasting Act 1990.[32] It also stated that the government had opposed previous attempts to place the British press under some form of statutory control. However, it went on to state that:

in response to public and parliamentary disquiet about some activities of some sections of the press, particularly in intruding into citizens' privacy, the government has set up an independent committee to review the question of privacy and related matters.[33]

In its *Fourth Report* the government stated that the activities of some sections of the press remained a concern, that the review, chaired by Sir David Calcutt QC, had taken place and had recommended the creation of a statutory tribunal, to replace the Press Complaints Commission.[34] It also noted that a parliamentary select committee had recommended the enactment of a privacy bill and that while the government was reluctant to increase the statutory control of the press, it would be publishing a White Paper to respond to these recommendations.[35]

SECRETS AND CENSORSHIP

In a democratic society, the media must be able to probe and comment on the activities of the State. Clearly they must be subject to some restrictions in order to safeguard national security and other vital national interests, but controls on the flow of information should be kept to a minimum and should be only those that are strictly necessary.

The law provides both civil and criminal sanctions against the disclosure of unauthorised information about the activities of the State. The Official Secrets Act makes it a criminal offence to disclose or publish information that the State defines to be a secret. Civil injunctions impose prior restraint to prevent the media publishing this type of information once they have obtained it. The Contempt of Court Act, the Police and Criminal Evidence Act and the PTA require journalists to disclose the identity of sources who have only given information on condition that they remain anonymous.

Political censorship

The Official Secrets Act 1989 came into force in March 1990. It replaced Section 2 of the Official Secrets Act 1911 with a narrower but far sharper provision which allows prosecutions against which there is effectively no defence.[36]

Section 2 of the 1911 Act banned all public servants, or civilians employed under government contracts, from revealing anything about their jobs without authorisation. However, juries proved reluctant to convict when they deemed that the revelations were in the 'public interest' or were made because someone felt a 'moral duty' to disclose information.[37] Public sympathy made it difficult to prosecute successfully the civil servant Clive Ponting, for example, or former MI5-operative Cathy Massiter, who exposed official wrongdoing in the 1980s.[38] The government's ultimate failure to suppress the publication of *Spycatcher*[39] in Britain – after it had been published in a number of other countries – exposed the limitations of relying on prior restraint.[40]

The exposure of any information relating to their jobs by serving or former members of the security forces – or other 'designated persons' who have access to sensitive information – is now an absolute offence under the 1989 Act. There is no defence whatsoever, and people who expose official crime can be pros[...] under the Act. Journalists are also committing an offence if th[...] publish information which they know has been leaked in breach of the Official Secrets Act and whose publication would be 'damaging'.[41]

The enactment of the Official Secrets Act 1989 followed a series of controversies about government censorship. In 1987 Special Branch officers raided the offices of the BBC, and the *New Statesman* magazine and the houses of a number of journalists in order to suppress a film about the Zircon space-spy satellite.[42] In the same year the government banned a radio documentary, *My Country Right or Wrong,* because it featured interviews with former members of the security services.[43] A documentary concerning manipulation of the news by the government, *The Cabinet,* was also permanently suppressed.[44]

This censorship was seen to have been undertaken to avoid political embarrassment for the government. For example, Peter Wright's book *Spycatcher* alleged that senior members of the intelligence services had plotted to undermine the authority of the 1974–9 Labour government. He revealed that these activities had included illegal bugging and burgling and claimed they had driven one Labour MP to suicide.[45]

Disclosure

In April 1990 a trainee journalist, William Goodwin, was fined £5,000 by a High Court judge for refusing to comply with a court order to identify the source of an unpublished story he had written for an engineering magazine.[46] The judge told the reporter that his refusal was 'quite unacceptable' and that he was only sparing Goodwin from prison because of his youth and inexperience.[47]

The company featured in Goodwin's article feared financial loss from the publication of the story, and had won both an injunction to prevent its publication and a court order to maintain its own anonymity. However, the House of Lords ruled that Goodwin must disclose his source so that the company could sue or discipline the person.[48]

This case had considerable implications for the right of journalists to protect their sources. The British government had previously been forced to modify its contempt of court laws following a European Court ruling[49] which led to the Contempt of Court Act

f this Act provides journalists with the right to
es, except where disclosures are necessary 'in the
e, national security or for the prevention of dis-
e.' However, this has been rendered practically
e House of Lords ruling. The National Union of
UJ) backed a challenge to this ruling at the European
man Rights. The European Commission on Human
Rights d in Goodwin's favour in September 1993[50] and it is
expected that the Court will take the same view.

The Police and Criminal Evidence Act 1984 requires journalists
and photographers to hand over unpublished material to the police
if compelled to do so by a court order.[51] The police may also obtain
an order to search journalists' homes and workplaces and to seize
material which may be relevant to a criminal investigation. This
poses a serious threat to the safety of journalists and photographers
who cover demonstrations, for example, by making them vulnerable to attack by demonstrators who are seeking to conceal their
identity.[52]

The PTA 1989 makes it an offence to fail to disclose information about acts of terrorism and those thought to be involved
in perpetrating them. This has been used by the police to compel
journalists to reveal sources.[53] Some journalists have had to leave
Northern Ireland or go into hiding following death threats after
their film has been used during criminal trials. In one incident in
1988 the prosecution subpoenaed 27 journalists and photographers
to give evidence, two of whom had to be removed from Northern
Ireland for their own safety.[54]

Freedom of information

There is no general right to freedom of information in Britain and
the present British government has resisted all efforts to enact
such legislation.[55] Government records are suppressed from public
scrutiny for 30 years and this can be extended to 50 or 100
years or indefinitely where the material is considered particularly
sensitive.[56] The decision is entirely the Lord Chancellor's, there is
no legal provision for challenging it, nor any legal guidance about
what type of material is suppressed.[57] In April 1994 a new code of
practice on access to government information was published. It
gives the public rights of access to some types of non-classified
material, and allows an ombudsman to investigate complaints from

members of the public.[58] However, the rights are limited and the range of classified material remains broad.[59]

The government claims that the main categories of material which are suppressed are: distressing or embarrassing personal details about living persons or their immediate descendants, information received by the government in confidence, some papers relating to Ireland, and 'certain exceptionally sensitive papers which affect the security of the State.'[60] However, it is difficult to see how much of the material which is classified could fit even these broad topics.

For example, the records relating to field executions of British soldiers during the First World War were suppressed for 70 years, supposedly to spare their relatives from shame and embarrassment. However, when the records were finally published, they revealed that the British army had been operating a barbaric form of summary justice against young soldiers who were often suffering from post-traumatic stress disorder.[61] A campaign for posthumous pardons has been launched and a Private Member's Bill which recognises the mistakes of that policy has been brought before parliament.[62] Files on police monitoring of the National Council for Civil Liberties (NCCL) between 1935 and 1941 were opened in March 1993, though the original intention was that they were to be closed for 100 years.[63] The files reveal that members of the Council were under detailed surveillance during this period, when the NCCL was involved in monitoring clashes between anti-fascists, the police and Mosely's Blackshirts. These files have contemporary relevance, as Cathy Massiter revealed in 1985 that MI5 was still monitoring the movements of officials of the NCCL – along with trade unionists, peace activists, journalists, lawyers and politicians.[64]

There have been some advances in the area of openness.[65] In April 1994 the government introduced new rules which eased the restrictions governing which records are held for over 30 years.[66] However, the restrictions are still considerable. The Local Government (Access to Information) Act 1985 gives the public access to all full local council meetings, agendas, reports and documents. The Local Government and Housing Act 1989 also attempts to enable public scrutiny and improve the accountability of local authorities, and to prevent abuses of power by dominant political groups. It has been noted that the level of regulation over local

is in stark contrast to the absence of control over
rnment.[67]

1ave been recent legislative changes that enable indi-
discover what information State agencies hold about
ugh, again, there are significant gaps in the legislation's
scope. The Data Protection Act 1984 allows individuals to know
what information is held about them on computerised records –
but not on manual ones. The Access to Personal Files Act 1987
gives individuals the right of access to files relating to their housing
and Social Security records. The Access to Medical Reports Act
1988 gives individuals the right to see reports written about them
by a doctor for an insurance company or employer. The Access to
Health Records Act 1990 further extends individuals' rights to see
their own medical records.

Most of these legislative advances began life as Private Member's Bills. It has been argued that many of them were significantly
weakened during their passage through parliament by government
amendments which increased the exemptions for records held by
the police and other State agencies.[68]

The Data Protection Act 1984 arose from a European agreement and the European Convention on Data Protection of 1981.
However, the 1984 Act fails to comply fully with the agreed standards and has three crucial defects:

☐ it does not apply to manual records, such as card indexes,
   over which there is still no control

☐ the Data Protection Registrar, a post which was created to
   enforce the provisions of the Act, has extremely limited
   powers

☐ transfer of information is permissible for the prevention or
   detection of crime, the apprehension or prosecution of
   offenders or the collection of tax or duty.

Public Interest Immunity

The doctrine of Public Interest Immunity (PII) allows government
ministers to prevent certain documents being disclosed during litigation, on the grounds that their revelation would be contrary to
the public interest.[69] While this may be justifiable in order to protect the disclosure of sensitive documents during civil litigation,

the status of public immunity in a criminal case raises significant concerns.

In November 1992 three directors of an engineering company, Matrix Churchill, were put on trial for breaching the government's embargo on arms sales to Iraq.[70] The embargo had in fact been relaxed in 1988 – although this had been concealed from parliament – and the security services were involved in the men's activities. However, ministers had signed PII certificates suppressing details of this involvement.

In a letter to *The Times* the Attorney-General stated that ministers 'were required by law to claim public interest immunity' and that this requirement 'could not be waived.'[71] Government ministers similarly claimed that they had a duty to sign the PII certificates, on the legal advice of the Attorney-General, and that it was not a matter for their discretion, even though this could have led to the wrongful imprisonment of three people.[72]

This interpretation of the law has been widely disputed[73] and was condemned in a House of Lords judgment in 1994.[74] It has been argued that there are 'fundamental constitutional and civil libertarian objections to the view that ministers have a duty and not a discretion to claim PII.'[75] These objections are based on the reluctance of members of the judiciary to act as watchdog over the executive,[76] and their toleration of high levels of secrecy with little or no explanation.

The reluctance of the courts to intervene in PII cases can also be shown by a case taken by Liberty involving a civil servant who was sacked after losing his security clearance. Andrew Balfour had been working at the Foreign and Commonwealth Office when he was sacked. He claimed unfair dismissal and took a case to an industrial tribunal. In order to have a fair hearing he needed to explain how the security services were involved in his work. The Foreign Secretary, his employer, issued a PII certificate claiming national security as the reason for refusing to disclose the documents. The industrial tribunal accepted the argument of the government's lawyers. It decided that it could not even consider whether or not the documents should be disclosed, and that once a claim based on national security was made by the government this had to be upheld. The Court of Appeal supported the government's view and the House of Lords refused to grant leave to appeal.[77] Liberty has now lodged an appeal with the European Commission on Human Rights.

BROADCASTING AND THE NORTHERN IRELAND CONFLICT

In August 1992 Channel 4 Television and Box Productions, an independent programme maker, were fined £75,000 in the High Court for refusing to identify the source of information used in making a television documentary concerning collusion between the security forces and loyalist paramilitaries.[78] The court ruled that, in future, television companies could not give an unqualified assurance not to reveal the identity of a source where the subject related to terrorism. It was not until August 1994 that a programme-maker won a court ruling against an attempt by the police to gain access to similar material.[79]

Lord Justice Woolf stated that he fully accepted the dilemma in which this placed the television companies. He acknowledged that Channel 4 and Box Productions believed it was in the public interest to broadcast the programme. In order to obtain the information to make the programme it had been necessary to guarantee the source's anonymity, and the companies believed that revealing his name could place his life in danger. However, the court ruled that such an undertaking was impermissible because 'The 1989 Act was the law of the land and like any other law it had to be observed while it was in force.'[80] When the companies refused to comply with the court order, made under the PTA,[81] the Director of Public Prosecutions (DPP) requested that the judge use his power to sequestrate their assets. The judge rejected this option as being too drastic, but made it clear that companies could not expect to be treated with such leniency in the future.[82]

In his judgment, Lord Justice Woolf stated that 'further proceedings against individuals should not be necessary.'[83] However, in September 1992 Ben Hamilton, the programme's principal researcher, was arrested in a dawn raid and charged with perjury.[84] In November 1992 all charges against him were dropped.[85]

The use of the PTA against journalists is an erosion of freedom of expression. The powers of the PTA are extensive[86] and they are supposed to be used exclusively to prevent acts of terrorism.[87] Yet in the Channel 4 and Box Productions case, the prosecuting authorities attempted to use these powers to close a national television channel. The court's ruling has indicated that the media would have no defence against this in any future, similar cases.

Self-censorship and suppression

In April 1993 the BBC Controller of Programmes, Alan Yentob, apologised for screening a documentary that questioned the conviction of an Irishman for the killing of two soldiers. He gave the reason that it should not have been shown after news coverage of the deaths of two young boys killed in Warrington by an IRA bomb.[88] Channel 4 cancelled the screening of two dramas set in Northern Ireland at the same time.[89]

Between 1970 and June 1993, 41 programmes were suppressed by the authorities (either they were never shown or they were unfinished), the content of 33 was subject to some form of alteration (excluding the dubbing of voices after the introduction of the broadcasting ban) and 31 had their transmission delayed.[90] Both the BBC and the commercial broadcasters require programme makers to seek higher clearance in all matters relating to Northern Ireland and this so-called 'referencing-up' system has inhibited the production of many programmes through self-censorship.[91]

LIBEL AND BREACH OF CONFIDENCE

The media can be directly prevented from publishing material by injunctions, which can be obtained without giving notice to them. A judge can grant an injunction when she or he is persuaded that the material might be libellous or might amount to a breach of confidence. Article 17 of the ICCPR recognises that people's right to privacy includes protection against unjustified attacks on their honour and reputation. Clearly people need protection against false, reckless and defamatory statements. However, the British libel laws are in urgent need of reform.

London has been described as 'the libel capital of the world' because British law favours plaintiffs suing for damages more than any other country's.[92] The libel laws inhibit investigative journalists and often shield people from the legitimate scrutiny of those investigating evidence of wrongdoing. For example, it could only be revealed after the death of the media tycoon Robert Maxwell in 1991 that he had built much of his business empire by stealing from his companies' pension funds. Previous attempts to expose his business behaviour were stopped by legal restraints.[93]

Libel cases are expensive to pursue and Legal Aid is not available. However, damages can be awarded to an unlimited level. Most people are unable to afford the redress that libel litigation would offer to them, but wealthy people have the potential to bankrupt an individual or publication if they can satisfy a court that they have been libelled. The Courts and Legal Services Act 1990 gave the Court of Appeal power to reduce or increase a jury award that it considered either excessive or inadequate.[94] While this may lead to some reductions in the level of awards it also adds another expensive legal hurdle onto the libel process.

Liberty has challenged, unsuccessfully, the denial of Legal Aid to defendants in libel cases as a breach of the ECHR's provision of the right to a fair trial.[95] In 1994 Liberty launched a *pro bono* scheme with a group of City law firms. One of its first cases involved arranging free representation for two unemployed environmental activists being sued by the multinational fast-food chain McDonald's for producing a leaflet which allegedly libelled the chain.[96] Without Legal Aid many defendants are simply unable to contest libel cases and so are inhibited in a discriminatory way from exercising freedom of expression.

A libel plaintiff has to prove that the defendant published a defamatory statement about him or her. The question of what is defamatory is subjective – the definition is that it would 'lower the plaintiff in the estimation of right-thinking people.' The defence, however, must *prove*, on a balance of probabilities, that the statement was true, fair comment or was subject to some form of 'privilege',[97] and that the defendant acted honestly and without malice. It is often difficult for a publication to *prove* a statement to be true. There are numerous cases of libel being awarded where the allegations have subsequently been vindicated.[98]

The effects of the libel laws in inhibiting freedom of expression are compounded by the way in which the law relating to 'breach of confidence' has developed. A judge will not usually grant an injunction to prevent the publication of an item which is alleged to be libellous if the defendant is prepared to stand by its contents and contest the case. However, injunctions are quite often granted in cases where it is alleged that a breach of confidence has occurred.

The concept of breach of confidence was originally envisaged as being necessary to protect business secrets, but case law has extended this. It has been used to prevent a husband publishing details about his relationship with his wife,[99] to prevent employees from divulging things they may have seen or heard during the course of their employment,[100] and to prevent any revelation of information obtained under an obligation of confidence – which has been widely defined.[101] There are a number of defences to breach of confidence, including public interest. However, the law has developed unevenly and it has been argued that the courts have been too selective in their approach:

> the courts are using the doctrine to provide a form of back-door protection against certain invasions of privacy, but are producing exceptions which justify the revelation of personal sexual peccadilloes while prohibiting serious stories about dubious behaviour in public or corporate office.[102]

FREE SPEECH, HATE SPEECH AND PUBLIC MORALITY

Some commentators view freedom of expression as an absolute right.[103] They argue that State suppression of views which are controversial or unpopular, or which are regarded as inflammatory or abhorrent, sets an unacceptable boundary on free speech which does more harm to a democratic society than permitting these views to be expressed.[104] It is argued that suppression is likely to be counterproductive as it merely drives those who express these opinions underground, that suppression ignores the social climate in which these opinions are expressed and that it provides an additional cause of resentment and grievance.[105]

Rights cannot be protected by censorship and, they argue, the most effective solution to the problems caused by hate speech is more speech. Anti-censorship activists argue that restricting the expression of opinions can give a dangerous power to the government, and this restriction may be used as an alternative to improving the conditions of vulnerable groups in society.[106] They argue that those in power can promote negative attitudes by using subtle language which evades direct incitement to hatred but whose effect is more insidious.[107]

However, it is also argued that the exercise of freedom of expression carries with it special responsibilities and that some limitations are necessary and compatible with this right. There is a balance to be struck between freedom of expression and the right to privacy, the right to participate in society on equal terms, and the right to be protected from those who incite hatred.[108]

It is fairly widely accepted that restrictions on freedom of expression are necessary in order to prevent harm. However, the definition of 'harm' is not straightforward: it can be restricted to physical harm, or it can be widened – as in Article 20 of the ICCPR – to include the incitement of hostility and discrimination. The definition can mean harm to a specific individual, or it can be extended to a group or indeed to cover the whole of society. All restrictions on freedom of expression are open to objection on civil-liberties grounds. The role of the State in defining and enforcing restrictions is clearly controversial and subject to a continuing debate as societal attitudes change.

Article 19 of the ICCPR specifies that some restrictions are permissible but stresses that these must be 'necessary' and 'provided for in law'. It follows from this that any restrictions must be for a defined legitimate purpose – such as protecting the rights and freedoms of others from identifiable harm – and that they must not exceed this purpose. Restrictions must be 'provided by law' and these laws must be clear and objective. The ICCPR requires that governments take action to prevent incitement to racial hatred[109] and to provide special protection for children.[110] The ICCPR specifies that women's rights should also be safeguarded[111] and that all people should enjoy the equal protection of the law regardless of race, sex, religion, political opinion, social origin or any other status.[112] It also permits some restrictions on freedom of expression on grounds of public morality and national security.[113]

British law currently prohibits the incitement of racial hatred, but usually only in circumstances where this could lead to violence; it prohibits the production, sale, display or importation of 'obscene' material; and it protects the Christian religion from blasphemy. It is entirely consistent with the principle of freedom of expression that its exercise should be subject to the limitation that it does not interfere with the rights and freedoms of others. However, we do not believe that the British law's particular restrictions are necessary, or that they respect the principles contained in Article 19 of the ICCPR.

Incitement to racial hatred

Incitement to racial hatred is a criminal offence under Section 18 of the Public Order Act 1986 and is punishable by a maximum sentence of two years' imprisonment.

We believe that an appropriate balance must be found between freedom of expression and the protection of the rights of minorities. Liberty is opposed to the proscription of organisations and is also against restricting speech by laws of prior restraint. It would be impossible to censor all racist sentiment which can often be expressed in coded language by mainstream politicians and it is sometimes difficult to distinguish between racist comment and the expression of political opinion. However, we believe that incitement to racial hatred is an abuse of freedom of expression and that the British government is failing in its obligations to prevent organisations and individuals inciting such hatred.

Race relations and public order legislation focuses on potential threats to public order from racist organisations, publications and events. It appears insensitive to the pain and suffering they can cause to members of ethnic minorities.[114] Racist speech and literature is employed as a form of intimidation. It can be a form of racial harassment and an abuse of the right to freedom of expression, because it aims to intimidate and restrict certain groups in the enjoyment of their rights.[115]

Between 1979 and 1993 there were 70 prosecutions brought for incitement to racial hatred.[116] 'Hatred' is difficult to define, and defences have used the arguments that racist comments are more likely to arouse sympathy than incite violence,[117] that they were 'humorous', that they were not 'threatening, abusive and insulting'[118] or that they would not affect their target audience.

Prosecutions may only be brought with the consent of the Attorney-General, to whom all complaints must be submitted. The Attorney-General refers cases to the police, who refer them to the Crown Prosecution Service, which then decides whether sufficient evidence exists to justify a prosecution. It has been noted that this process is unusually tortuous and means that all prosecutions may be subject to a political veto at the first stage.[119]

The Home Office has estimated that there are between 130,000 and 140,000 incidents of racial attack and harassment every year.[120] It is difficult to establish definitively the relative importance of different causes of racial violence but clearly the climate of opinion in society plays a part and this may be shaped by groups who promote racial intolerance, discrimination and violence.

Blasphemy

Blasphemy has been a common law offence since 1967 – when the medieval blasphemy law was repealed[121] – but it has largely fallen into disuse.[122] The offence can be tried only on indictment and is punishable with a fine or imprisonment of indeterminate length.[123] The concept of blasphemy has been rendered vague and undefined as a result of this lack of judicial consideration, leading some observers to conclude that 'there is no single, comprehensive definition of the common law offence of blasphemy.'[124]

The few prosecutions for blasphemy that do occur have been brought by individuals. The last private prosecution was in 1977.[125] This conviction was upheld in the Court of Appeal and the House of Lords. A challenge to the decision was declared inadmissible by the European Commission on Human Rights[126] which ruled that it was legitimate to curb freedom of expression in order to protect the religious feelings of others.

In March 1994 the European Commission ruled that a challenge to Britain's blasphemy laws was admissible as a possible violation of freedom of expression under the ECHR.[127] The case arose after the British Board of Film Classification refused to give a licence to a film, *Visions of Ecstasy*, which they considered might be blasphemous, although it was not obscene.

Controversy about Britain's blasphemy laws arose in 1988 after an Iranian religious leader, the late Ayatollah Khomeini, placed a death sentence (*fatwah*) on the British-based writer, Salman Rushdie. The *fatwah* was issued following the publication of Rushdie's novel, *The Satanic Verses*,[128] which, it was claimed, insulted the Muslim religion. In March 1989 the Chief Metropolitan Magistrate refused to grant a summons against Rushdie and his publishers which alleged 'blasphemous libel and seditious libel at the common law'. The ruling, that the law of blasphemy in England and Wales protected only the Christian religion, was later upheld by the High Court.[129]

The privileged position that the current law of blasphemy gives to Christianity is discriminatory and offensive in a multicultural society.[130] Some have argued that the law should be extended to cover other religions, on the basis that religion is often a distin-

guishing feature of an ethnic group.[131] British law d
that the term 'race' can encompass religious grou
commentator has argued that, for some people 'it is o
easier to change one's religion than to change one's s
has observed that

> where a group identifies itself primarily by reference to its faith
> and feels that it has not only been the object of Christian
> oppression in the past but is also a vulnerable minority in
> Britain today, vilification of its fundamental beliefs may actually
> harm its interests.[134]

However, we do not believe that the right to freedom of religion
and protection from discrimination on the grounds of religious
belief should extend to restricting freedom of expression on the
grounds that certain views may offend certain religious beliefs.
This would make it necessary to define a religion – as opposed to
a sect or cult – and also to decide on the boundary between
blasphemy and theological dispute. Most religions preach revealed
truth which is in contradiction to that of other religions, and so a
high level of tolerance is essential in any pluralist society.

Pornography and sexually explicit material

The human rights debate about pornography and censorship is
necessarily vigorous. Laws must be universal in their application,
but sexual relations – and depictions of these relations – take place
within particular and variable contexts, which largely determine
their impact. It is difficult to establish what causal connection, if
any, exists between the depiction of particular sexual relations and
those relations themselves.

Some commentators argue that all pornography degrades and
exploits women.[135] Portrayals of women in sexual positions, it is
argued, degrade and oppress them because they replicate women's
subordinate position in society and in sexual relations. Pornography, therefore, is a form of discrimination.[136] Others view pornography as a form of hate speech which could be subject to the
same type of restrictions as incitement to racial hatred.[137] Images
which portray women as enjoying or deserving pain or sexual
humiliation, it is argued, legitimise violence, desensitise men to the
effects of violence and incite men to use violence against women.
Another argument is that pornography is itself a form of vio-

.1ce against women, which objectifies women as sexual objects for male consumption and institutionalises gender inequality.[138] The UN Convention on the Elimination of all forms of Discrimination Against Women has argued that 'pornography and the depiction and other commercial exploitation of women as sexual objects, rather than as individuals . . . contributes to gender-based violence.'[139]

However, there are problems with these propositions. Their definitions are wide and could cover virtually all sexually explicit material, including some lesbian and gay erotica, and feminist literature, and sexually explicit material for women's consumption. Some believe that there are benefits in increasing the availability of sexually explicit material for women, arguing that it helps to dispel ignorance, increases sexual awareness, and helps women to explore their own sexuality.[140] The objection to pornography's portrayal of gender relations could apply to a whole range of images which stereotype women in a subordinate position.

Even if pornography was defined as literature and imagery which explicitly depicted women in positions of sexual subordination and degradation, there would be problems. As one anti-censorship feminist has argued:

> women and feminists may find sensual pleasure, as well as positive affirmations of their individuality, freedom and equality, in sexually explicit imagery – including imagery that other women and feminists may find non-pleasurable, or even 'subordinating'.[141]

Some opponents of restrictions on pornography maintain that such material simply reflects women's position in society. The attack on pornography, they argue, is a dangerous limitation on freedom of expression:

> the speculative, attenuated benefits of censoring 'pornography', in terms of reducing violence and discrimination against women, are far outweighed by the substantial, demonstrable costs of such a censorship regime in terms of women's rights. Throughout history, to the present day, censorial power has been used to stifle women's sexuality, women's expression, and women's full and equal participation in our society.[142]

This argument rests on the proposition that it has not been conclusively proved that pornography causes, or contributes towards, violence and discrimination against women. And some believe that even if this *were* proved, censorship would be ineffective in suppressing pornography and could even be counter-productive by driving it underground.[143] The question of harm is deeply controversial, as studies have produced conflicting results.[144] The conclusions of numerous reports, in many different countries and using a wide variety of different research methods, are markedly varied when it comes to assessing what influence, if any, pornography has on violence against women.[145]

The obscenity laws

The Obscene Publications Act 1959[146] defines obscene publications as articles which 'tend to deprave and corrupt persons who are likely, having regard to all relevant circumstances, to read, see or hear the matter contained or embodied in it.'[147] Although its scope can include the advocacy of 'drug taking' or material which might induce violence, it is rare for the Act to be used against material of a non-sexual nature.[148] Its provisions are reinforced by a variety of other laws.

The Indecent Display (Control) Act 1981 makes the display of 'indecent' material in public a criminal offence. Sexually explicit magazines may only be lawfully displayed in shops if they are put in a separate place and marked by a warning sign. The Local Government (Miscellaneous Provisions) Act 1982 gives local authorities powers to control the siting of sex shops and cinemas.[149] The Customs Consolidation Act 1876 prohibits the importing of 'indecent or obscene' material.[150]

The Post Office Act 1953 prohibits sending, attempting to send, ordering or inviting orders for 'obscene' material.[151] The Protection of Children Act 1978 and the Children and Young Persons (Harmful Publications) Act 1955 make it an offence to take, distribute, possess or publish indecent photographs of children[152] or to produce pictorial publications which would 'tend to corrupt' a child who read them.[153] The Video Recordings Act 1984 provides for the classification of videos and makes it an offence to supply an unclassified one.[154] Part VII of the Criminal Justice and Public Order Act 1994 increases punishments with regard to some videos and computer images, principally, but not exclusively, images of minors. It also makes it an offence to possess any sexually explicit uncertified video if the police suspect that this might be used for commercial gain.

There are, in addition, a variety of common-law offenses relating to 'morality and decency' such as: conspiracy to corrupt public morals, conduct calculated or intended to corrupt public morals, conspiracy to outrage public decency, outraging public decency, obscene libel, keeping a disorderly house and public exhibition of indecent activities, pictures or things.[155]

Obscenity offenses are either tried by judge or jury or dealt with by 'forfeiture' proceedings – local magistrates can authorise the destruction of obscene articles discovered within their jurisdiction.[156] This power denies publishers who wish to defend their work the right to a jury trial. It has been argued that publishers who give notice of their wish for a jury trial should not be subject to forfeiture proceedings.[157] Given the vagueness of many of the offences, this would be a valuable safeguard against forfeiture powers turning magistrates into 'book-burners'.[158]

Customs and Excise officers have extensive powers, which are difficult to challenge.[159] Material can be confiscated and held indefinitely. A customs officer does not have to explain why material is considered obscene.[160] Prosecutions can be brought if material is deemed indecent by customs officers. There is no public interest defence, and no defence on the grounds of artistic merit in forfeiture proceedings by customs,[161] although this is available if material has been seized by the police. However, following a European Court of Justice decision in 1986, material can only be prohibited from importation from European Union States if it cannot be lawfully produced or sold in Britain.[162]

The Metropolitan Police seized 2,642 magazines and books, 13,442 photographs and 16,790 videos in the London area in 1992–3 and initiated 389 prosecutions.[163] In 1990–1 Customs and Excise seized 39,000 items which they considered indecent or obscene and initiated prosecutions against 88 people.[164] There is evidence that lesbian and gay material is more likely to be seized than equivalent heterosexual literature.[165] The obscenity laws have been criticised for being simultaneously too loose and too restrictive.[166] The tests of 'indecency' and 'obscenity' and material which 'tends to deprave and corrupt' are highly subjective and fail to acknowledge a distinction between material which is erotic and that which portrays violence. The definition of these terms is vague and we are concerned that its subjective interpretation means that the restrictions cannot be said to be 'provided by law'.

The terms allow the police, Customs and Excise and the courts considerable discretionary powers, and legal definitions of acceptability can vary in different parts of the country.[167] A former Attorney-General has commented that: 'it is often a matter of chance whether the pornographer receives large profits, a destruction order or a prison sentence.'[168] The Obscene Publications Squad prioritises policing certain types of pornography. The Independent Television Commission, the BBC[169] and the British Board of Film Classification (BBFC) have separate sets of guidelines,[170] while Customs and Excise operates a different legal regime. The result, it has been argued, is considerable legal uncertainty, with a few notable exceptions:

> officials have their lines to draw, and they draw them fairly consistently at the male groin: nudity is now acceptable and even artistic, but to erect a penis is to provoke a prosecution.[171]

For example, *Everywoman* magazine (August 1994) was banned by some distributors and bookshops because the front cover portrayed a sculpture of an erect penis. The distributors agreed to carry the magazine if a plastic bag concealed its cover.[172] And yet there is no evidence that the portrayal of male genitals is damaging.

Uncertainty surrounding the legal definitions leads to self-censorship by shops, distributors and publishers which can have particular impact on small circulation publications. Shops have refused to stock lesbian and gay erotica and some feminist literature for fear of prosecution.[173] A newsagent was threatened with prosecution for stocking the adult comic magazine, *Viz*, and copies of a 'rap' album were seized by the Obscene Publications Squad.[174] Drug workers have been threatened with prosecution if they distributed a comic that promoted safer practices of injecting.[175] In theory, any images other than single models posing for the camera could be liable to censorship. It has been argued that this seriously inhibits efforts to produce, for example, sexually explicit literature which is *not* degrading to women.[176]

The case for reform of the obscenity laws is overwhelming. However, the question of what, if anything, should replace them is deeply controversial. There have been two British government reports in recent years on obscenity and pornography, their effects and what laws should control them. In 1979 the *Williams Report* failed to establish a causal connection between pornography and physical or moral harm[177] and in 1990 the *Cumberbatch Review* also concluded that there was no proof of a definite linkage between sex crimes, violence against women and pornography.[178] Both reports questioned the reliability and methodology of other research, and have in turn had their own conclusions criticised.[179]

The Williams Committee argued for the abolition of all restraints on the written word, where it was accompanied by 'inoffensive' illustrations.[180] The central conclusion was that it was legitimate to regulate the display and sale of material which gave offence to some people, but only that which caused harm should be prohibited.[181] It called for the replacement of the existing obscenity laws with new offences to punish the production and sale of pictorial material which involved children or 'where the material gives reason to believe that actual physical harm was inflicted'.[182] It also called for the sale of all pictorial pornography to be restricted to sales from licensed sex shops.[183] The implementation of these proposals could have considerably eased the censorship of sexually explicit material for those who wished to obtain it, and protected the publishers and distributors of books from prosecution or unnecessary restrictions. However, the government responded with two pieces of legislation which gave local councils special powers to license sex shops in their areas,[184] but ignored the committee's other proposals.[185]

The *Cumberbatch Review* had a narrower brief: to review existing research on the effects of pornography, but not to make recommendations about the state of the law. It concluded that:

> Evidence of the adverse effects of pornography is far less clear-cut than some earlier reviews imply. Inconsistencies emerge between very similar studies and many interpretations of these have reached almost opposite conclusions . . . In many ways pornography seems to serve as a totem of society's ills and its convenience and tangibility as a focus make it easier to identify as a cause of some unacceptable features of life . . . But is it a matter of guilt by association?[186]

In 1992 a Canadian Supreme Court judgment distinguished between sexually explicit material which was violent, that which was non-violent but subordinating and dehumanising and that which was sexually explicit but non-violent and non-subordinating, based on mutuality and equality.[187] This followed a Royal Com-

mission report recommending that material
against women or female submissiveness shoul
effectively redefined obscenity in Canada's Crir
been argued that this might be an appropriate

Anti-censorship campaigners have vigoro'
posal as an unacceptable interference with f.
They argue that such a proposal would extend the se..
existing obscenity laws. The definition of what 'degrades' women
would be problematic and difficult to prove.[191]

It has also been suggested that women should have the right
to use civil sex-discrimination legislation to sue the pornography
industry if they can prove that they have suffered harm or injury
as a result of pornography.[192] This would not be censorship, it is
argued, because material could not be suppressed by prior restraint.
It would be up to the courts to decide whether harm was proved
or whether there was any link between pornography and anti-
social behaviour.

There are some cases in which it would be possible to prove
that harm had occurred during the production of pornography, or
in which people have had photographs of themselves used in pornography without consent.[193] Rapes and assaults are of course
crimes whether or not a camera is present, but it can be argued
that additional legislative protection is necessary because of the
nature of the pornography industry (much of which operates
underground or in legally dubious circumstances). Some feminists
argue that it is precisely because of this censorship that models are
vulnerable.[194] The Williams Committee also recommended specific
protection for photographic models against possible abuse.[195]

Taken in their entirety, the Williams Committee's proposals
could significantly liberalise Britain's obscenity laws and, at the
same time, clarify the law, focusing on people's right to protection
against abuse rather than on the concept of preserving a hazily
defined 'public morality'.

PRIVACY AND FREEDOM OF EXPRESSION

In July 1993 the government published a consultation paper proposing the creation of a new right of privacy.[196] The proposed
tort would mean that anyone who could prove they had suffered
'substantial distress' because their privacy had been infringed

have the right to claim damages in the County Court.
ymity would be considered part of privacy. In 1991 judges in
Court of Appeal had strongly expressed the view that legal
protection of privacy was necessary.[197]

The proposed tort could significantly extend the effects of the
laws of libel and breach of confidence in restricting the expression
of the media.[198] Neither truth nor fair comment would be a defence,
and although 'public interest' would be, it has been narrowly
defined in the consultation paper. Legal Aid would not be available
for people seeking to establish that their privacy had been
infringed.[199] It is argued that the tort would be used primarily by
the rich and powerful to suppress stories that the public has a
legitimate right to know:

> the mass media have published stories revealing that a former
> Chancellor of the Exchequer was overdrawn on his personal
> bank account and had repeatedly exceeded his credit-card limit,
> and used public funds to pay legal expenses in evicting a so-
> called sex therapist as his former tenant; that a minister was
> given a holiday by a friend who was the daughter of a PLO
> paymaster; that another minister had five mistresses; that an
> MP had been caught spanking teenage rent boys; that a leading
> Opposition MP had personal links with a fugitive business
> man . . . None of these stories could be said to 'relate directly'
> to a public function so as to be within the scope of the proposed
> public interest defence.[200]

Much of the support for a privacy tort has come from those
who believe that the press should be subject to greater restrictions
because journalistic standards have fallen and the system of self-
regulation through the Press Complaints Commission has failed.
There was, for example, widespread condemnation of the *Daily
Mirror* when it published a photograph of the Princess of Wales
exercising in a gym in November 1993. However, while the monarchy continues to enjoy a privileged position in the British constitution it is legitimate for members of the royal family to be subject
to press scrutiny, particularly in areas which affect their public
functions. For example, revelations about the break-up of the marriage of the heir to the throne could be said to be in the public
interest as the monarch is constitutionally prohibited from obtaining a divorce.[201]

The Campaign for Press and Broadcasting Freedom (CPBF)

believes that the problems of media intrusion and misrepresentation could best be addressed by the establishment of a statutory right of reply to inaccurate stories, and by the creation of a more effective and representative press complaints body.[202] The Campaign has promoted five separate attempts to establish a legislative right of reply, through Private Member's Bills and Ten-Minute Rule debates. Clive Soley MP's Freedom and Responsibility of the Press Bill was the most recent parliamentary attempt to establish such a system.[203] After its failure, a group of citizens, who consider themselves victims of inaccurate or sensational press reporting, established an organisation[204] to promote the right to accurate information and freedom from intrusive journalistic methods. Liberty also believes that people need to have their privacy protected – primarily from infringements by the State and public authorities. However, the individual's right of privacy must be carefully balanced against other people's rights to freedom of expression and freedom of information.[205]

OWNERSHIP AND CONTROL

Traditionally, and within civil liberties law and practice, the concerns about freedom of expression have been focused on State interference and censorship. However, there is also a growing recognition that the free market alone cannot preserve a genuine diversity of culture and communications.[206]

Several European institutions have recently recognised a wider definition of freedom of expression, which includes the positive obligations of States to ensure pluralism and diversity in the media.[207] The European Parliament has passed a resolution proposing a new directive that would limit media ownership.[208] The Committee on Civil Liberties of the European Commission, has stated:

> In the present world of nation States, social and entrepreneurial groups exercise the right to provide information according to their particular political opinions. From a democratic view, there is a legitimate demand that these social and economic groups should reflect the pluralism of the society to which they address themselves.[209]

Concentration of ownership is evident in television, radio, the press, publishing, the new media technologies of cable and satellite, and in the allied industries of distribution and retail. The British government has loosened controls on ownership, arguing that diversity and choice are best served by a competitive market.

Since 1945 there have been three Royal Commissions on the Press,[210] and all have acknowledged that the public interest is best served by freedom of expression and variety of opinion and that it is adversely affected by concentration of ownership. The Third Royal Commission concluded that links between newspapers and the broadcasting industry were undesirable:

> we regard a multiplicity of voices as essential. We do not recommend that newspaper holdings in television should be prohibited, but believe that the existing policy of ensuring that no broadcasting company is effectively controlled by a newspaper company should be maintained and strengthened to exclude effective control by newspapers in combination . . . we recommend that . . . the presumption in favour of participation by newspaper companies [in radio and television] should be abandoned.[211]

Since that report in 1977, there has been a rapid increase in the concentration of media ownership in four directions:

☐ Concentration of ownership within one medium. This applies particularly to the press, but since the Broadcasting Act 1990 it is rapidly developing in commercial broadcasting as well.

☐ Cross-media ownership. Newspaper groups have sought to develop interests in the new and potentially more lucrative electronic media, including, in particular, terrestrial and satellite television. There is also cross-media ownership across book and magazine publication, radio, cable, satellite and terrestrial television.

☐ Multinational ownership. The largest media companies are increasingly assimilating smaller companies so that they control all aspects of the production and marketing process. This means that power over the media of communication becomes increasingly concentrated in the hands of a small number of individuals. A consequence of this has been what is called transnationalisation of output; that is, the growth of products aimed at the world market in film and television

and also in other industries such as informati
publishing.

☐ Multi-sectoral integration. This occurs where
companies are controlled by, for example, pa
defence industry or property companies.[212] I
has been particular concentration within the ~~leisure~~
industries, including tourism, publishing, television rental and
the record industry.

All these factors have had an impact on editorial independence
and led to greater uniformity of views and the dominance of a
particular political and economic outlook. It has been claimed that
newspapers have become readier to argue for the interests of the
corporate world as they have come under closer proprietorial
supervision and become more closely aligned with large business
conglomerates.[213] Commentators have also noted a growth in the
number of 'advertorials', where editorial and commercial elements
become fused and where journalists are increasingly sensitive about
the needs and interests of client advertisers in writing articles.[214] It
has accompanied a drift in the press into competition for a narrow
range of stories in which public affairs news have been mar-
ginalised.[215]

Press power and democracy

Four companies control more than 85 per cent of all daily and
Sunday newspaper circulation in Britain. Rupert Murdoch's News
International Corporation owns *The Times*, *Sunday Times*, *The
Sun*, *News of the World* and *Today* and controls 34.4 per cent of
daily circulation and 37.6 per cent of Sunday circulation. The other
major players are Mirror Group Newspapers (23.3 per cent of
daily and 28.9 per cent of Sunday circulation) United Newspapers
(15.4 per cent and 10.4 per cent) and Associated Newspapers (12.3
per cent and 12.2 per cent).

The pattern of concentration in the local press is equally
marked. Over 80 per cent of the British local press is controlled
by 15 corporate owners, while over 60 per cent is owned by just
10 companies.[216] Through amalgamation, takeovers, and in some
instances exchange of titles amongst companies to achieve regional
consolidation and dominance, many parts of the country now have
a monopoly supplier of local news, even where more than one title
exists.[217]

This concentration of ownership has placed considerable power in the hands of a very few proprietors. Of the national press[218] only the *Guardian* and the *Independent* are owned by companies which do not have major interests outside the media. However, Mirror Group Newspapers has a 30 per cent stake in Newspaper Publishing, owners of the *Independent*. The Guardian Media Group owns several local newspapers and has a 15 per cent interest in GMTV and a 20 per cent interest in Trans-World Communications which owns 10 commercial radio stations.

Concentrated press power poses risks for the democratic process itself.[219] In 1987 for example, the Conservative Party had the support of 72 per cent of the national daily newspaper circulation, which considerably over-represented their electoral support and limited the range of political views available – a range which is necessary for democratic choice.

The ways in which people are influenced to vote are complex, and this is a contentious area of research and debate. However, there is evidence that the media do fashion what people think. For example, Murdoch's papers have been consistently negative about the BBC while promoting, through both editorial and advertising, News International's own satellite services on Sky. The Broadcasting Research Unit (BRU) found that 37 per cent of News International readers approved of the licence fee while 56 per cent opposed it. Among non-readers the position was markedly different, with 49 per cent approving and 44 per cent opposing it.[220]

The argument about how the press influenced voters in the 1992 General Election must take account of the impact of television coverage, which is bound by stricter limits of impartiality, and the inaccuracy of the sample polls themselves. However, there is evidence that in 1992 the pro-Conservative tabloids had a marked influence in the general election.[221] One study of the 1992 election concluded that if the parties had bought their coverage in the form of commercial advertising (looking at the size, position and prominence of articles), 'the Conservatives would have paid £1,342,000 to the *Sun*, £1,973,160 to the *Mail*, and £2,233,900 to the *Express* while Labour would have paid £1,788,000 to the *Mirror*'.[222]

On 12 April 1992 Lord McAlpine, former Treasurer of the Conservative Party, stated in the *Sunday Telegraph*:

The heroes of this campaign were Sir David English, Sir

Nicholas Lloyd, Kelvin McKenzie and the other editors of the grander Tory press. Never in the past nine years have they come out so strongly in favour of the Conservatives. Never has their attack on the Labour Party been so comprehensive. They exposed, ridiculed and humiliated that party, doing each day in their pages the job that the politicians failed to do on their bright new platforms.[223]

The *Sun* put it more succinctly in its headline 'ITS THE SUN WOT WON IT' on 11 April 1992. The media are clearly confident of their ability to wield political influence. The power and influence of major companies such as News International, however, goes beyond partisanship and poses additional threats to democracy. As commentators have noted:

> In the UK, the dominance of News International poses a
> democratic threat, and it could be argued, based on Australian
> and British experience, that Murdoch is so powerful that no
> political group dare confront his interest and seek to reduce his
> power and influence for fear that media power will be directed
> against them.[224]

The market's effects on diversity

Advocates of deregulation of media ownership have argued that regulation has traditionally been founded on the scarcity of radio frequencies or the high costs of entry into publishing. Now, they argue, the range of broadcast media and computerised newspaper production make it much easier to enter the market.

New technology has made possible the establishment of new titles. However, the *Daily Post*, *News on Sunday*, *Sunday Correspondent* and *London Daily News* all failed in a short time. *Today* and *Sunday Today* were launched with an initial outlay of £2.5 million in 1985; despite a further injection of £24 million by Lonhro, the owner of the *Observer*, *Today* was finally sold to Murdoch in 1987. The *Independent* was launched with a capital fund of £21 million in 1986, and suffered heavy losses.[225] It is now caught between Conrad Black, owner of the *Daily Telegraph* and *Sunday Telegraph*, and Rupert Murdoch, who are engaged in a price and circulation war.

Government action on concentration of ownership in the press

The Press Council had as one of its objects in 1947: 'To report publicly on developments that may tend towards greater concentration or monopoly in the press.'[226] The industry-funded Press Complaints Commission, which replaced the Press Council in 1991, has no such object. The second Royal Commission on the Press in 1962 called on the Press Council to scrutinise changes in ownership and control in the press. It also recommended new legislation to enable press amalgamations to be reviewed by an independent public body.[227]

The Monopolies and Mergers Commission, which is supposed to investigate and intervene to prevent excessive concentration of ownership in particular industries, has also failed to protect diversity of media ownership. The Commission has, so far, failed to act to prevent a single takeover in the national press.[228] Under the Fair Trading Act, the Commission is required to report on 'whether the transfer in question may be expected to operate against the public interest'. However, the burden of proof falls on the opponent of the acquisition. It has been argued that this should be reversed, in order to safeguard freedom of expression and the onus of proof should fall on the prospective acquirer to demonstrate that the merger or acquisition would not operate against the public interest.[229]

Broadcasting

The British system of controls over newspapers relies largely on self-regulation, but radio and television have developed under a system of licensing and statutory control. In Britain, television has been subject to regulations covering quality standards, impartiality, diversity, balance, breadth and range of programmes. The funding of the BBC through the licence fee, and the positive public service obligations on terrestrial broadcasters, have provided safeguards against commercial competition being the main force determining programming.

From the perspective of human rights, the public-service broadcasting system has many flaws. A service operating within the requirements to show a 'reasonable range of opinion' tends to reflect dominant views, and this marginalises the views of minorities.[230] However, in spite of its shortcomings, the regulatory system on the whole has safeguarded a mixed and comprehensive programming schedule which combines information, education and entertainment, and is free from purely commercial imperatives.

The Broadcasting Act 1990 introduced major changes in the licensing and regulation of commercial broadcasting. It replaced the strict, positive programming obligations on Channel Three companies (formerly ITV), with 'lighter touch' regulation. The Independent Broadcasting Authority (IBA), with its direct powers to mandate news, current affairs and other important elements such as children's programmes, has now been replaced by the Independent Television Commission (ITC), which has far less influence over content and schedules.

The government's 1988 White Paper, which preceded the Act, suggested:

> clear rules will be needed which impose limits on concentration of ownership and on excessive cross-media ownership in order to keep the market open for newcomers and to prevent any tendency towards editorial uniformity or domination by a few groups.[231]

The Broadcasting Act 1990 did introduce detailed rules to prevent the accumulation of licences for regional television. It also prohibited a person owning more than two regional television licences in total, more than one licence for a large region, or licences for two contiguous regions. However, the latter restriction only applied until the first licences were granted. It therefore did not prevent the merger of Tyne Tees and Yorkshire in the spring of 1992.[232] In 1994 there have been takeovers and regrouping within the largest regional television companies, and increasing share ownership of companies, independent suppliers and allied industries.[233] This growth in concentration threatens the future of the smaller companies and risks the erosion of the strong regional identity of Channel Three.

The Broadcasting Act 1990 created the Radio Authority and lifted restrictions on the ownership of radio licences. This has led to a further reduction in the number of radio stations.[234] The commercial dominance of a few companies in the radio industry has curtailed diversity and many radio stations follow similar formats.[235] The Act also introduced rules on cross-media ownership. It specified that proprietors of newspapers could hold no more than a 20 per cent interest in a body which holds a licence for a

Channel Three television service, Channel Five or national radio, and restricted Channel Three licence holders to no more than a 20 per cent stake in a national or local paper. At the time of writing, the government is conducting a review of cross-media ownership, and there is concern that it will not adequately address the high levels of concentration in the media, but will instead bow to pressure for relaxation of ownership rules. The 1990 Act applied only to channels using UK broadcast frequencies, and therefore excluded non-domestic satellite services based in Britain. At the time the Act came into force, Sky TV, a non-domestic satellite service based in Britain and owned by News International, was operating in direct competition with the smaller satellite broadcasting company, BSB.

The government argued that the Astra satellite, from which Sky TV is broadcast, was not a scarce resource, and so cross-ownership rules did not apply. However, this argument fails to take account of the dominant influence given to one company. It was also argued that an extension of the cross-media rules to include Sky TV would have led to News International relocating its operation outside the UK. This indicates that there is a need for effective control of multinationals at a transnational level.[236] Sky's unregulated competition contributed to BSB's demise. The failure to act on concentration of ownership here ran counter to the recommendation made by the 1988 Home Affairs Select Committee Report:

> We regard it as imperative that ownership of extra-terrestrial services based outside, but receivable in, the UK, should be taken into account in any future provision regarding the ownership of the UK-based channels.[237]

The former director of London Weekend Television, Greg Dyke, has highlighted what he described as a 'dependency culture' in the broadcast media which has done much to erode its independence from the government.[238] He argued that broadcasters have become increasingly reluctant to challenge a government on which they rely for their commercial success and their very existence. With the media industry lobbying the government vigorously on the question of restrictions on ownership, controversial programmes pose commercial risks which the media are becoming less willing to take.[239] The benefits to News International from the Broadcasting Act 1990, and the loss of Thames Television's franchise after its controversial investigation of the SAS killings in Gibraltar in 1988,[240] have shown that 'the lesson was there for all to see.'[241]

11 HUMAN RIGHTS IN THE WORKPLACE

FREEDOM OF ASSOCIATION IN THE WORKPLACE

The right to freedom of association is fundamental to a democracy. It is necessary to help guarantee individual human rights and, as such, is an important part of international human rights law. Participation in democratic politics requires that people are able to act in association with each other, both to secure the election of representatives and to ensure that individual opinions can be effectively expressed and individual rights protected.

In some circumstances, it is necessary that people act in association to defend their freedoms. Consequently, the right to freedom of association assumes a particular importance – it is not just an important right in itself, but one which helps guarantee the protection of other rights. Hence, understanding freedom of association is not a question of counter-posing individual and collective rights (as is often assumed), but of understanding that the right to form a freely associating collective is necessary to underpin the exercise of individual rights.

In the workplace the freely associating collective is a trade union. The right to form and join trade unions, like any other act of association, is a fundamental human right, is guaranteed by international human rights law and is a vital part of any democracy. The relationship between the employed and the employer is not equal – power rests in the hands of the employer. Despite the principle of 'equality before the law', the law does not fully take account of this imbalance. The courts assume an equality which does not exist and are extremely reluctant to interfere with 'freedom of contract' in employment law in any fundamental way. As one observer has commented:

there is in the common law of employment little notion of

justice and no acceptance at all of any idea that employees should have power to own, control, have a democratic voice in, or even be consulted about their employment. The judicial view, is uniformly that the managerial prerogative must be preserved unfettered . . . the courts insist that they cannot intervene to rectify unfair contracts, refuse to acknowledge the imbalance of contractual power between employer and employee and will not (other than exceptionally) restrain dismissals which are in breach of contract. (The Unfair Contract Terms Act 1977, which protects consumers from unfair and inequitable contracts, specifically excludes contracts of employment from its application.) The 'deregulation' of employment rights leaves the employee with theoretical equality in the employment relationship but practical subordination . . . The concept of an individual contract of employment based upon a freely negotiated bargain negotiated between individual bargainers is, of course, total legal fiction.[1]

The right of people to associate freely implies that they also have the right not to associate. To ensure freedom of association it is necessary to protect the freedom of *the* association from excessive State control and other restrictions. This does not mean that the collective, in so acting, can itself violate the rights of individuals. As long as the collective operates consistently with international human rights norms, it should be free to regulate the conduct of its own affairs.

The British government has weakened the rights of people in the workplace as part of a general undermining of trade union rights. There were 287 listed trade unions in the UK in 1993 with a total membership of about 7.68 million people, which represents about 31 per cent of the working population.[2] Successive Employment Acts have severely eroded employees' rights to freedom of association and the government has also failed to protect individuals from other attacks on their workplace rights.

THE INTERNATIONAL LABOUR ORGANISATION

In its commentary to Article 22 of the ICCPR (Freedom of Association), the UN Human Rights Committee specifies that governments must ensure that their laws conform to the guarantees set out by the International Labour Organisation's (ILO) 1948 Convention. This reflects the ILO's importance in monitoring the employment laws of individual countries and measuring them against international human rights standards. The ILO was established in 1919, becoming a specialist agency of the United Nations in 1948.[3] It holds an annual conference to which member countries are entitled to send four delegates – two government representatives, one representative of employers and one representative of employees.[4] Delegates elect its governing body, made up of members from the same three constituencies. It is staffed by an ILO office which acts as its secretariat.

One of the ILO's main functions is to set international standards for employment law. These are submitted by its governing body to the conference and adopted only with the support of at least two-thirds of the delegates present and after a lengthy consultation period.[5] These standards, or conventions, range from general principles to specific recommendations on particular industries or groups of workers. The ILO has adopted eight conventions on freedom of association, including:

□ Freedom of association and protection of the right to organise convention, 1948 (Convention No 87)

□ The right to organise and collective-bargaining convention, 1949 (Convention No 98)

□ The labour relations (public service) convention, 1978 (Convention No 151)

□ The collective-bargaining convention, 1981 (Convention No 154).

Member states must ensure that these instruments are acted on by 'the authority or authorities within whose competence the matter lies'[6] and must inform the Director General of the ILO of the measures taken. They are not obliged to change their laws or to ratify a convention but they must inform the Director General why they are not doing so.[7]

Governments must make an annual report to the ILO on what they have done to comply with the conventions.[8] These reports are examined by a Committee of Experts which reports to the annual conference and to a Committee on the Application of Standards. A Committee on Freedom of Association was set up by the govern-

319

ing body in 1951 specifically to hear complaints about breaches of this principle. Supervision and enforcement of the ILO's conventions by governments is voluntary and if they do not act the ILO can only make them the focus of *moral* judgments by the international community.

Britain and the ILO

The British government played a key role in the establishment and consolidation of the ILO and took a lead in establishing the Committee on Freedom of Association.[9] The UK has ratified 80 of the ILO's 174 conventions,[10] including Conventions 87, 98 and 151 on freedom of association.[11] However, the British government refused to ratify the most recent convention on freedom of association, No 154, dealing with collective bargaining, on the grounds that 'whilst wishing to facilitate bargaining it would not take on an obligation to promote it by direct government "intervention".'[12] This refusal reflected a new approach to industrial relations by the British government which, since 1979, has frequently been in breach of the ILO's standards.

COMPLAINTS TO THE ILO

The present British government has introduced eight successive Employment Acts: the Employment Act 1980, the Employment Act 1982, the Trade Union Act 1984, the Wages Act 1986, the Employment Act 1988, the Employment Act 1989, the Employment Act 1990 and the Trade Union Reform and Employment Rights Act 1993.[13] The measures in the first seven Acts are now contained in the Trade Union and Labour Relations (Consolidation) Act 1992. The Public Order Act 1986 and the Criminal Justice and Public Order Act 1994 also contain measures which affect trade unions and employment rights.

In its *Fourth Periodic Report to the UN Human Rights Committee*, the British government stated that:

> one of the basic principles underlying the [industrial relations] legislation which the government has introduced since 1979 is that every employee should have the right to decide whether to belong to a trade union . . . No one is any longer obliged to belong to a trade union in order to obtain employment . . .

Equally, no one is obliged to accept a requirement to leave, or not to join, a trade union.[14]

The *Report* claimed that the Trade Union Reform and Employment Rights Act 1993 had enhanced the freedom of individuals to join the trade union of their choice and provided statutory protection against discrimination in employment for those who were denied entry to or expelled from a trade union which they wished to join.[15] However, in its *Third Periodic Report*, the government defended measures introduced in 1984 which denied workers at the intelligence gathering agency, General Communications Headquarters (GCHQ), the right to join a trade union.[16]

Whatever the government's justifications, the number of complaints for alleged breaches of the ILO's conventions has grown markedly since 1979.[17] There have been complaints made to the Freedom of Association Committee about the termination of collective-bargaining rights for teachers, about the dismissal of striking seafarers, about the political vetting of building workers and about the abolition of the Civil Service Arbitration Agreement. Concerns have also been raised about the ending of collective bargaining in the newspaper industry. All were brought under Conventions 87, 98 and 151 and concerned the right to freedom of association.[18]

In some cases the ILO has ruled in the British government's favour. In May 1989 the ILO's Committee of Experts ruled that the British government's requirements that trade unions ballot their members prior to taking industrial action and that members should have a right to see their union's financial accounts were consistent with its conventions on freedom of association. The Committee also rejected complaints made against measures to improve access to the courts for union members who wished to pursue a grievance against their union. However, it has expressed serious concern about the British government's record, condemning its employment laws for breaching Convention 87 on nine counts:

☐ sacking workers at GCHQ for refusing to give up trade union membership

☐ prohibiting the disciplining of union members who refuse to participate in lawful industrial disputes

☐ prohibiting unions from paying fines incurred by their members while engaged in union action

321

☐ prohibiting secondary action in support of a lawful primary dispute

☐ prohibiting strikes which are technically secondary action only because the employer has created separate companies which nominally employ different parts of the same workforce

☐ prohibiting strikes in support of overseas workers

☐ removing the right of dismissed strikers to challenge the fairness of their dismissals.[19]

The government responded that the guarantees contained within Convention 87 were subject to respect for fundamental human rights and that it considered the 'right of every trade union member to refuse to take industrial action' to be a fundamental human right.[20] While this could be justified, by reference to freedom of conscience, if the authorities were attempting to compel people to take part in a particular form of action, it does not follow when applied to a voluntary association with its own rule book. The right of freedom of association includes the right of that freely associating collective to make its own decisions and carry out its own actions in the interests of protecting the rights of the majority of its members.

In 1992 the Freedom of Association Committee found that British law does not provide adequate protection against discrimination of trade unionists in job recruitment and fell short of the requirements of Convention 98 in not adequately protecting trade union activists.[21] The Trades Union Congress (TUC) provided evidence from individuals who had been told that they had failed to get jobs because their names were on a list compiled by an organisation called the Economic League.[22] The Economic League was financed mainly by private industry and supplied employers with the names of alleged trade unionists or 'political extremists' from files it held on up to 22,000 people.[23] The League, which went into liquidation in 1993 to be replaced by another organisation, Caprim Ltd,[24] used this list to help employers spot 'trouble-makers'. These findings were broadly endorsed by the Committee of Experts in 1994.[25] However, the British government failed to follow the recommendations.

The Freedom of Association Committee rejected complaints against the British government for its refusal to ratify the Collective-Bargaining Convention (Convention 154), despite accepting the principle that employers should recognise representative organisations.[26] However, it did make two recommendations stating that the British government should not have set aside collective-bargaining structures which already existed for public-sector employees.[27] The government has not only ignored these[28] but has since passed the Teachers' Pay and Conditions Act 1991, which enables it to impose a wage settlement on teachers even if neither the teachers nor their employers want the settlement. In the past the government was not a party to these long-standing collective-bargaining arrangements.

GCHQ

The clearest example of the British government's refusal to abide by an ILO recommendation is its ban on union membership at GCHQ. On 25 January 1984 the government banned 7,000 civil servants employed at the intelligence-gathering centre, GCHQ, from trade union membership.[29] Using powers under the Royal Prerogative, it issued a ministerial order under the Employment Protection (Consolidation) Act 1978 removing from designated staff their statutory protection against dismissal, or other disciplinary action, for being members of a trade union or participating in trade union activities.[30] Although the staff had been encouraged to join independent trade unions since 1947, they were now only permitted to join an officially approved staff association. They were either given a £1,000 bonus to leave the union or the option to transfer to another part of the Civil Service where they could preserve their union membership. If they refused to comply they would be dismissed, as 13 eventually were.

The government claimed that GCHQ had to be continually operational and that a series of industrial disputes had disrupted the flow of information which was vital to national security.[31] However, the unions had not been consulted about the ban, nor told why the government felt it necessary to impose one, despite having stated their willingness to enter into discussions about a no-disruption agreement.

Both the Appeal Court and the House of Lords accepted the government's argument that grounds of 'national security' provided a complete defence of their conduct, which would otherwise have been unlawful.[32] A complaint to the European Court of Human Rights was deemed inadmissible by the European Commission because the workers were engaged in the administration of the State.[33] However, in 1984 the ILO's Committee on Freedom of Association and its Committee of Experts upheld complaints that the ban breaches ILO Convention 87.[34] The Freedom of Association Committee stated that:

☐ the unilateral action taken by the government to deprive the category of workers of their right to belong to a trade union was not in conformity with the *Freedom of Association and Protection of the Right to Organise Convention, 1948* (Convention 87) ratified by the United Kingdom

☐ the committee considers that steps should be taken by the government to pursue negotiations with the civil servants' unions involved and a genuine effort made to reach an agreement.[35]

While the Committee of Experts accepted some of the British government's concerns, it still urged it to pursue negotiations with the unions and reach an agreement.[36] In subsequent reports the Committee stated unequivocally that 'workers at GCHQ are entitled to join the organisation of their own choosing.'[37] Furthermore, in 1989, the Committee on the Application of Standards expressed concern and regret that 13 workers had been sacked for trade union membership[38] and, when the issue was raised again in 1991 and 1992, other countries complained that the British government was ignoring the views of the ILO about a convention which it had ratified.[39]

In January 1994, the government rejected an amendment to the Intelligence Services Bill to allow GCHQ workers to 'enjoy trade union rights in accordance with ILO Convention No 87'[40] and, despite an exchange of letters with the TUC, has failed to resolve the issue.[41] The government argued that it was the Committee of Experts' interpretation of the convention which it disagreed with, rather than the principles of freedom of association or trade unionism. However, it declined the opportunity to refer the case to the UN's International Court of Justice for a definitive ruling.[42] As one observer has commented:

at every turn and in every forum, the government has been criticised, not only for its breach of convention 87 but also for its obstinate and calculated refusal to accept that it acted unlawfully and to take steps to remedy the position in accordance with the requirements of the convention.[43]

It appears that the government contemplated extending the ban's scope. In July 1992 the Ministry of Defence de-recognised unions representing 3,500 security guards on the grounds that these unions were affiliated to the Labour Party.[44] In November 1993, the government obtained an injunction to prevent the Prison Officers' Association calling industrial action, arguing that prison officers should be treated as members of the 'police service' and that their union should therefore lose its immunity.[45] The British government's continual refusal to accept the ILO's recommendations throws into question its commitment to the right to freedom of association and the principle that governments should abide by international human rights instruments to which they are a party. This is the cornerstone of international human rights standards.

TRADE UNIONS AND THE LAW

There is no right to strike in British law. Instead, trade unions are granted immunities to protect those involved in activities 'in contemplation or furtherance of a trade dispute'[46] from legal sanctions which would otherwise lead to civil law prosecutions for damages, on such grounds as:

- inducement of breach of contract
- interference with the performance of the terms of a contract
- intimidation
- conspiracy
- interference with business.[47]

Trade unions were protected from liability for damages caused by strike action from 1906 until the government removed this in 1982.[48] However, since the mid-nineteenth century judicial decisions have restricted trade union activity only for these to be subsequently removed by parliamentary legislation. In 1901 the courts made trade unions liable for unlimited damage from strike activity[49] and created the tort of civil conspiracy to be used against strike leaders.[50] In 1910 the courts outlawed political expenditure by trade unions[51] and in 1964 a judge created a new tort of intimidation which could be used against trade unions.[52] However, in each case, Parliament removed or moderated these restrictions.[53] This has had a particular effect, as one observer has commented:

> These Acts of Parliament declared that particular forms of trade union activity were not to be actionable at law if done in contemplation or furtherance of a trade dispute; that trade unions were not to be rendered unlawful because of some judicially declared unlawful characteristic (eg restraint of trade); and that trade union funds should not be wiped out by legal action for damages . . . Hence, in English trade union law there has grown up the curious pattern of 'immunities' granted by Parliament in respect of particular trade union activities which would otherwise be, because of the past activities of the judges, illegal or unlawful . . . there are no positive rights.[54]

From the 1940s until the 1970s there was a broad social and political consensus about the role of trade unions and the conduct of industrial relations.[55] The law's emphasis on the common law of contract and property rights was counterbalanced by the power of individuals organising freely associating collectives to bargain with their employers.[56] In 1968 the influential Royal Commission on Trade Unions and Employers' Associations, chaired by Lord Donovan, took the view that 'the trade union movement here is sufficiently strong to make legislation on these matters unnecessary.'[57] Indeed, there is a long-standing suspicion between trade unions and the courts in the UK which makes many trade unionists hostile to the judicial entrenchment of rights.[58]

While this belief remains strong in some quarters, support for the entrenchment of rights is growing in the UK.[59] As trade unions have had their immunities removed, the lack of any counterbalancing positive rights at the workplace has been acutely felt. There is now a curious amalgam of negative and positive rights in relation to trade unions. An individual's right not to join a trade union has been enshrined in law[60] but there is no right for trade unions to be recognised by an employer or to represent members in negotiations.

During the 1980s trade unions were increasingly restricted in their activities, their immunities removed, the law used to regulate their activities, their internal structures and organisation. The level of statutory interference has been unprecedented and marks a profound change in the evolution of trade union law in the UK. The present government has also encouraged direct legal challenges against trade unions.[61] In the 1980s employers and disaffected trade union members increasingly made use of court action against trade unions, often with tacit government support, resulting in bitter disputes – in the newspaper industry, the car industry, between seafarers and their employers and, most notably, between the National Union of Miners (NUM) and National Coal Board. Often the unions were heavily fined during these disputes, or, in the case of the NUM, had their entire assets seized.[62]

State interference in union activity was shown most clearly in the extensive preparations which the government made for the dispute with the NUM, which lasted from March 1984 until March 1985. It has been alleged that the Security Service, MI5, was deployed in a campaign to destabilise and smear the NUM and its leaders.[63] The Police Federation has subsequently condemned the secret collusion between the National Coal Board and the government which forced the police into a politically partisan role.[64]

THE FREEDOM OF ASSOCIATION

Limitations to strike action

The ILO has condemned the government for 'an excessive limitation on the exercise of the right to strike'[65] by successively narrowing the definition of a lawful trade dispute and increasing the difficulties of organising one. The principle limitations are:

☐ the removal of unions' immunity from damages caused by unofficial or unlawful industrial action, unless the union specifically repudiates the action;

☐ the outlawing of secondary action, where workers take industrial action against anyone other than their direct employer;

☐ the imposition of complex balloting requirements in advance of industrial action;

☐ restrictions on peaceful picketing;

☐ the outlawing of industrial action in support of a closed shop.

The laws are complex and their very complexity may well inhibit some trade unionists who are contemplating taking industrial action. As Lord Donaldson, one of Britain's most senior judges, commented:

> In industrial relations it is of vital importance that the worker on the shop floor, the shop steward, the local union official, the district officer and the equivalent levels in management should know what is and what is not 'offside'. And they must be able to find this out for themselves by reading plain and simple words of guidance. The judges of this court are all skilled lawyers of very considerable experience, yet it has taken us hours to ascertain what is and is not 'offside', even with the existence of highly experienced counsel. This cannot be right.[66]

The ILO was concerned that the volume and complexity of Britain's employment laws had undermined the right to freedom of association.[67] It took from 1980 to 1992 to codify all their trade union laws into a single Act of Parliament and the government did nothing to simplify the regulations.[68]

Since 1982, employers have been able to sue unions for the damage caused by industrial action if the action could be shown to be unlawful. This also enables them to apply for injunctions against trade unions contemplating such action. The courts can grant emergency injunctions against acts which might subsequently be shown to be illegal and only have to be satisfied that there is an arguable case that the act is illegal, regardless of whether this is likely to be proved at full trial. Failure to observe an injunction puts the union in contempt of court, the fines for which have no limit. The Trade Union Reform and Employment Rights Act 1993 allows any individual deprived of goods or services because of unlawful industrial action to bring proceedings to restrain such action.[69] This covers any type of disruption including overtime bans and work-to-rule. A Commissioner for Protection Against Unlawful Industrial Action has the power to take proceedings against a trade union and to compel unions to end their actions by court order.[70]

Anyone can take a union to court for an action deemed unlawful even when it had unanimous support of the union's membership and even when the employer was unwilling to use the courts. In some cases – if the dispute concerned health and safety or where there was doubt about whether the union had fulfilled all the statutory requirements – the use of the courts could inflame the situation and escalate the dispute. The increased opportunities for legal challenges to industrial action have made action more difficult to organise and therefore restricted the freedom of association.

Secondary action, the term used to describe industrial action taken by workers where the real dispute is not between themselves and their own employer, has been outlawed.[71] The typical example is a sympathy strike. All secondary action is now unlawful – a trade dispute is now defined as one which takes place only over work-related issues between workers and their employer.[72]

Trade union ballots

The conditions imposed on trade unions' ballots for industrial action restrict the possibility of such action and therefore interfere with the freedom of the association. For an industrial dispute to be lawful it must first have been authorised by a full postal ballot[73] using a standard ballot form and conducted in accordance with a code of practice.[74] The ballot form cannot carry any information about the merit of the dispute, or the union's recommendation, although this can also be circulated, but must contain a statutory worded warning each member that 'if you take part in a strike or other industrial action, you may be in breach of your contract of employment.'[75] This wording must be used even when the action being contemplated is not in breach of contract, such as a work to rule or a ban on voluntary overtime.

A ballot's validity expires if the industrial action is not taken within four weeks of the ballot being conducted.[76] A ballot can be held only if the union genuinely intends to take industrial action, rather than just to test its members' strength of feeling on a particular issue. A ballot should not be held unless the members have shown a desire for one, although it is not specified how they should do this before having a ballot. The ballots must be supervised by independent scrutineers who are required to produce a report within four weeks.

The Trade Union Reform and Employment Rights Act 1993 requires unions to give employers seven days' written notice of any ballot for industrial action, specifying those who are to be balloted and sending a sample copy of the voting paper. A separate notice must be sent seven days before any industrial action specifying those being 'induced to take part . . . in the industrial action' and the specific date of the strike or strikes.[77]

In February 1994, the Court of Appeal extended the scope of this Act by ruling that all trade unions must now identify all members being balloted and subsequently induced to take part in industrial actions to their employers.[78] The court upheld an injunction against strike action at a college because the lecturers' union had not given the names of the members who had been balloted about the dispute.[79] Previously the government had provided assurances that names would rarely, if ever, be required.[80] The court's interpretation means that trade unions are now routinely required to supply lists of members to their employers.[81] Liberty believes this is a fundamental breach of the right to privacy and freedom of association as the members concerned may wish to conceal their union membership from their employers and it has lodged an appeal to the European Court of Human Rights on behalf of the National Association of Teachers in Further and Higher Education (NATFHE) and five of its members.

The increasingly casual nature of employment practices and the growth of self-employment and sub-contracting also make ballots extremely difficult to organise. Postal ballots, which can take up to a month to organise, can be even more difficult amongst a transient workforce or with high union membership turnover.

Picketing

The Employment Act 1980 outlawed secondary picketing by restricting lawful picketing to that taking place at or near the place of work.[82] A code of practice issued under the Act set out new rules for lawful picketing[83] which, if not observed, made pickets liable for inducing workers to breach contracts. They could also be liable for the civil offences of trespass, nuisance and unreasonable harassment, and a variety of criminal offences such as obstruction of the public highway, obstruction of a police officer, disorderly conduct and breach of the peace.

The number of pickets allowed to stand outside a workplace has long been subject to restrictions under the common law.[84] During the miners' strike of 1984–5 the High Court limited the number to six[85] which was also recommended in the Code of Practice on Picketing. The Public Order Act 1986 allows the police to limit the actions of pickets still further.[86] The Criminal Justice and Public Order Act 1994 creates the new criminal offence of disruptive trespass, which is defined as trespass that occurs with the intention of obstructing, intimidating or influencing the lawful activities of others.[87] It also makes it a criminal offence to disobey a police officer, of any rank, if told to leave private land.[88] Although not primarily aimed at trade unionists, these powers could be used against pickets at a workplace if the land belongs to the employer, or against trade union activists organising consumer boycotts in support of an industrial dispute.

Trade union internal affairs

It is a basic democratic right for trade union members to decide how to conduct their union's internal affairs and to be able to draw up their own constitution and rule book, although the ILO permits governments to promote democratic practices within trade unions. This is set out in Article 3 of the ILO's Convention 87:

☐ Workers' and employers' organisations shall have the right to draw up their constitutions and rules, to elect their representatives in full freedom, to organise their administration and activities and to formulate their programmes.

☐ The public authorities shall refrain from any interference which would restrict this right or impede the lawful exercise thereof.[89]

Over the past 15 years a succession of laws and regulations have undermined the autonomy of trade unions, greatly increasing State interference in their internal affairs. Many reforms are not objectionable in themselves but interference in union activity has increased, such as the imposition of postal ballots and other regulations of trade union votes and elections;[90] the requirement to submit annual financial returns to a certification officer[91] and publish full financial details, including salaries of executives; new requirements on expenditure, the collection of subscriptions and the control of union membership. A new Commissioner has been established specifically to litigate against trade unions.[92]

Attempts have been made to prevent trade unions engaging in political activities. The Employment Act 1984 required trade unions with political funds to ballot their members once every 10 years.[93] Subsequent laws have specified that ballots must be fully postal[94] and observed by an independent scrutineer.[95] The definition of what constitutes political expenditure now includes the production of any material which might influence people's voting intentions.[96] This means, for example, that campaigns against privatisation of public utilities will probably have to be paid for out of political rather than general funds.[97]

Trade union membership

The European Court of Human Rights has ruled that people should have a right not to be discriminated against because they have refused to join a trade union.[98] The government has also made it automatically unfair to dismiss or refuse to employ someone because he or she refuses to join a trade union.[99] However, freedom of association also involves the right of trade unions to determine whom they accept or retain as members.[100] This allows unions to enter into inter-union agreements to prevent poaching of members and to ensure that those within the union abide by the rules and do not undermine collective decisions. Nevertheless, the Trade Union Reform and Employment Rights Act 1993 specifies that an individual may not be lawfully excluded from one union in a workplace where the majority belongs to another, or where an inter-union agreement exists to prevent poaching.[101]

The common law already provides the individual with a right to challenge his or her expulsion from, or discipline by, a union on the grounds of its own rules[102] or on the grounds of natural justice.[103] The government has added the right of individuals not to be 'unreasonably' excluded or expelled from union membership or to be 'unjustifiably' disciplined for a breach of union rules.[104] Industrial tribunals usually decide what constitutes unreasonable or unjustifiable actions[105] but the government has specified that disciplining a member for failing to take part in industrial action constitutes an 'unjustifiable charge'.[106]

EMPLOYEES' RIGHTS AND DISCRIMINATION

Industrial tribunals

Industrial tribunals usually consist of a chairperson who is a lawyer, and two others, one representing employers and one representing employees.[107] Industrial tribunals deal with claims connected with unfair dismissal, trade union rights, redundancy, equal pay and race and sex discrimination. They can award compensation, reinstatement, re-engagement or equal pay. Either side can appeal against decisions at an Employment Appeal Tribunal (EAT). The decisions of EATs create precedents which subsequent tribunals must follow.

Workers have a right to a statement of the principal terms and conditions of their contract of employment and a right to a statement of the reasons for any dismissal,[108] to compensation if they have been wrongfully dismissed, to compensation for racial and sexual harassment and to equal pay and treatment between the sexes.[109] Women have a right to maternity pay and to be able to return to work after maternity leave.[110] Employees have a right to redundancy payment and sick payment, to the disclosure of certain information by their employer and to the terms and conditions established by collective agreements in the same industry and locality.[111] However, the government removed or diluted many of these rights and restricted their effectiveness by denying people access to industrial tribunals. In 1979 it extended the qualifying period during which workers could bring complaints to an industrial tribunal about wrongful dismissal from six months to one year[112] and in 1985 this was extended to two years.[113] In 1980 it reversed the burden of proof in unfair dismissal cases, placing it on the employee, and stated that tribunals should take into account the size and administrative resources of a firm when deciding cases.[114] In 1989 it gave industrial tribunals the power to demand deposits of up to £150 from applicants before they hear the case.[115]

The number of claims of unfair dismissal has steadily increased, reaching record levels in 1993. However, the proportion of cases where an industrial tribunal hearing has resulted in reinstatement is small and has been falling. Over 40,000 individuals submitted applications to industrial tribunals alleging unfair dismissals in 1993, 50 per cent higher than in 1983.[116] The proportion of cases where tribunals have awarded workers the right to be reinstated or re-engaged has fallen from 0.33 per cent in 1989-90 to 0.17 per cent in 1993-4.[117]

In 1994, the government initiated a consultation process about the reform of the industrial tribunal system 'with a view to identifying any changes which would help them to cope with an increasing volume and complexity of cases with reduced delays, while containing demands on public expenditure.'[118] In December 1994 the

Department of Employment published a consultation paper which focused on ways of increasing the proportion of disputes which could be resolved without reference to industrial tribunals.[119] In effect, this will reduce the right of people to challenge unfair dismissals in front of tribunals, particularly given the increased powers to strike out certain cases granted to the chairs of industrial tribunals in the Trade Union Reform and Employment Rights Act 1993.[120]

Fair wages policy

There have been other changes to the law on individual employment rights. Some of these have principally been to bring the UK into line with European Union directives, which take precedent over British law, and have generally improved the rights of employees at work. Others have been aimed at reducing the burdens on business by weakening or abolishing existing rights.[121]

In 1982, the government rescinded the Fair Wages Resolution, which had instructed government departments to insist that contractors should pay rates and observe hours and conditions no less favourable than those established by the trade union for that industry.[122] In 1986 it restricted the powers of Wage Councils, which set minimum wages in certain industries, and removed from their scope all workers under the age of 21.[123] In 1993 the government abolished the Wage Councils,[124] making the UK almost alone in the European Union in not providing employees with a minimum wage enforced by a labour inspectorate or by legally binding collective agreements.[125] In 1989, the government repealed protective legislation regulating the hours of work of young people and exempted employers with fewer than 20 employees from the obligation to provide their workers with the particulars of disciplinary procedures.[126]

The Trade Union Reform and Employment Rights Act 1993 strengthened the right of pregnant women to protection from unfair dismissal[127] and the right of health and safety representatives to protection against victimisation.[128] It also ensured the rights of workers in firms which have changed ownership to retain their original terms and conditions, and gave part-time workers the right to written confirmation of these.[129] But the same Act removed the statutory role of the Arbitration Conciliation and Advisory Service (ACAS) to encourage the development of collective bargaining and

downgraded its Chair.[130] It also enabled the chairs of industrial
tribunals to hear complaints on their own in some circumstances,
including ones where 'grounds of national security' apply.[131] The
Act prohibits local authorities from inserting clauses in contracts
which require contractors to use union labour or to recognise trade
unions.[132] It forbids local authorities from taking into account
employers' records on employment rights and industrial relations
when awarding contracts.[133] In May 1993, the government dropped the requirement that private contractors meet equal opportunities employment obligations when bidding for government
contracts.[134]

Discrimination against trade unionists

Article 26 of the ICCPR specifies that no one shall be discriminated
against on the grounds of race, religion, gender, political or other
opinion. In its *Fourth Periodic Report to the UN Human Rights
Committee*, the British government stated that it was committed
to provide 'comprehensive protection against discrimination in
employment on the grounds of an individual's membership or non-
membership of a trade union.'[135] This decision was overturned by
the House of Lords in March 1995. However, Section 13 of the
Trade Union Reform and Employment Rights Act 1993 authorises
employers to discriminate against trade union members in matters
such as pay and conditions of employment. This section was
inserted into the Bill at a late stage in order to reverse the effects
of a judgment of the Court of Appeal which said that it was
unlawful for a newspaper to pay a journalist less than his colleagues
because he refused to give up his trade union membership.[136]

Although the Employment Protection (Consolidation) Act
1978 provides workers with protection from *dismissal* or *victimisation* on the grounds of trade union membership or activity[137] and
the Employment Act 1990 makes it unlawful for an employer to
refuse to *employ* someone on membership grounds,[138] there is no
law to protect people who are refused *employment* for trade union
activity.[139] While the Employment Act 1990 made it unlawful to
refuse to employ someone either because they are, or are not, a
member of a trade union,[140] there is no protection against applicants being refused employment because they are identified as
trade union activists. There is also no protection against the mass
dismissal of workers for breach of contract, if they have taken part

in a lawful industrial dispute, although there is some protection against selective dismissals.[141] The same Act also removed the rights of workers, who had been dismissed selectively after taking part in unofficial action, from taking their case to an industrial tribunal and outlawed industrial action in support of such dismissed unofficial strikers.[142]

Other discrimination

The reduction of employment rights had a disproportionate impact on women and ethnic minorities because these people often have part-time, low-paid jobs often with casual contracts and poor conditions of employment.[143] Many measures improved the position of women and part-time workers, although it is significant that most of the improvements have been as a result of pressure from the European Union.[144]

The Trade Union Reform and Employment Rights Act 1993 gives all pregnant women the right to 14 weeks' paid maternity leave, to protection against dismissal on grounds of pregnancy or child birth, to demand written reasons for dismissal during the pregnancy or maternity leave, to protection of employment status and other contractual rights, to specific health and safety protection and to suitable alternative employment if made redundant whilst on maternity leave.[145] This extends rights of maternity leave to part-time workers and those who have not worked continuously for the same employer for a certain period. Prior to this the government had effectively reduced the numbers of women entitled to maternity leave by extending the necessary qualifying period for which workers had to be employed before they were protected from unfair dismissals.[146] It had also exempted employees of small firms from this protection.[147]

An estimated 501,000 women are employed in paid work carried out from home.[148] Women taking on waged work at home have virtually no statutory employment protection, are not covered by health and safety legislation.[149] The limited financial protection that was offered to some homeworkers by Wage Councils has now disappeared and poor trade union organisation means that women who work from home often experience considerable isolation and vulnerability. Many people, usually women, are brought into this country on their employers' passports and virtually treated as slaves because they are denied effective protection from exploitation.[150]

The abolition of Wage Councils also affects women and ethnic minorities disproportionately. Women constitute about 80 per cent of workers in industries which were previously regulated by Wage Councils.[151] Black workers – male and female – are also concentrated in these industries. Studies have concluded that black women were paid between 10 and 25 per cent less than white women.[152]

There is no legislation prohibiting discrimination on the grounds of sexual orientation, age or disability. The laws on race and sex discrimination make provision for immediate and relatively comprehensive protection, but employees who believe they are subject to discrimination on other grounds have no option but to resign from their job and claim 'constructive dismissal'. Such claims are extremely difficult to win.[153] Cases against discrimination have to be taken on an individual basis and even where they are won there is no guarantee that it will lead to a change in the employment practices which led to the original complaint.[154] Although it can be argued that tackling inequality requires collective remedies, British law does not allow for 'class actions' to be brought on behalf of groups of workers.[155]

VETTING AND GAGGING

Civil servants

Liberty has repeatedly expressed concern about the rules and regulations which restrict the rights of civil servants.[156] It is estimated that there are over 100 statutes which make disclosure of information by civil servants a criminal offence.[157] The Official Secrets Act 1989 makes it an offence for former or serving members of the security services to expose any information relating to their jobs – or for other 'designated persons' who have access to sensitive information to do so.[158] There is no defence on grounds of 'public good' to this offence.

In its *Third Periodic Report*, the British government acknowledged that many civil servants and local government officers are barred from participating in national politics and must sometimes seek permission to participate in local politics.[159] It also stated that certain civil servants are positively vetted for their political views. The trustworthiness of civil servants is measured by 'the degree to which they have assimilated themselves' into society and their 'length of residence in the United Kingdom'.[160]

The Housing and Local Government Act 1989 also prohibits local government workers in 'politically restricted posts' from holding office in a political party at any level,[161] while the Local Government Officers (Political Restrictions) Regulations 1990 prohibit such workers from engaging in most forms of political activity. The term 'politically restricted posts' covers all officers earning over £19,500. This is a clear infringement of the right to freedom of expression and the right to political participation, as guaranteed by Articles 19 and 25 of the ICCPR.

The government argues that it positively vets civil servants and restricts some of them from engaging in political activity in order to remove 'potential subversives' and, it claims, to promote the objective of a politically neutral public service.[162] However, the increasing use of short-term contracts and the appointment of government 'advisors' to key positions of influence has led some observers to warn of a worrying politicisation of the Civil Service.[163] In 1985 the government announced that members of any 'subversive group acknowledged as such by the Minister, whose aims are to undermine or overthrow parliamentary democracy in the UK and Northern Ireland by political, industrial or violent means'[164] would be barred. In 1990 it announced that it would positively vet potential employees 'in connection with work the nature of which is vital to the security of the State.'[165] Such actions are in breach of Articles 19 and 25.

A blanket ban against employing homosexuals in the Diplomatic Service was removed in 1990, although homosexuality is still a factor considered by the Diplomatic Service's vetting process. Between 1982 and 1992 half the people who lost their security clearance did so because they were gay.[166]

Whistleblowing

Employees are often amongst the first to know if there is something wrong where they work.[167] 'Whistleblowers' are employees who highlight concerns about health and safety, financial and other irregularities, or who generally protest at their employer's policies and practices. Their protection from victimisation is inadequate. In 1994 a new charity was established, Public Concern at Work, to protect and advise people who speak out about safety and malpractice.[168] In its first annual report it stated that it had received 1,500 enquiries, including 620 requests for legal advice. Over half of these involved allegations of serious malpractice which threatened the public or amounted to a serious breach of law.[169]

The importance of whistleblowers was highlighted by inquiries into the Piper Alpha oil rig disaster, in which 167 workers died, and the capsizing of the ship, *Herald of Free Enterprise*, in which 193 people were killed. These heard that employees had doubts about the companies' safety precautions but had not spoken out.[170] Similarly, during an investigation into the multi-million pound fraud at the Bank of Credit and Commerce International, it emerged that an internal auditor, who had expressed doubts about financial irregularities, had been made redundant.[171]

There have also been concerns expressed about employees in the National Health Service (NHS) who have been dismissed after highlighting health care deficiencies.[172] According to a survey conducted in 1993, 93 per cent of nurses were less likely to speak 'on the record' to journalists than they were two years before and fear of management was cited as a major reason.[173] Research shows that NHS employees believe that going to the media is the best way to get results, although many also believe that they may be unfairly disciplined for doing so.[174]

More employers are inserting 'confidentiality clauses' into employment contracts, barring employees from disclosing information about them in any circumstances and threatening those who do with dismissal.[175] This practice is particularly marked in the NHS and has accompanied a large scale restructuring of the service and the creation of an internal market for health care.[176] In December 1994 the *British Medical Journal* cited 30 cases from the previous two years in which doctors had been prevented from criticising the new structure.[177]

SOCIAL AND ECONOMIC CONSEQUENCES

Over the last 15 years the British government has been attempting to hold down labour costs and restrict workers' rights in order to encourage inward investment in the UK. The price of such a policy has been the erosion of employees' rights and a simultaneous increase in inequality. Although government representatives have told the ILO that it is not opposed to the principles of freedom of association at the workplace and trade unionism, its official publications can imply this. In 1991 a Department of Trade and Industry booklet, *Britain the Preferred Location*, stated that:

> The overall cost of labour in Britain is significantly below that of other major European industrial countries . . . There is no legal requirement for a company in Britain to recognise a union. Many companies – especially foreign-owned ones do not do so. Throughout Britain as a whole the number and percentage of employees who are members of trade unions has been falling since 1979 . . . The balance of power in industrial relations has shifted significantly since 1979 . . . effective legal action can be taken against any union which seeks to organise unlawful industrial action; organisation of industrial action will always be unlawful if, for example, the industrial action is 'secondary' (or 'sympathy') action taken by workers whose employer is not party to the dispute to which the 'primary' action relates; or if it is not wholly or mainly about employment matters; or if it consists of picketing away from the pickets' own place of work; legal proceedings can be brought to restrain a union from organising industrial action if it does so without first obtaining majority support from a properly conducted secret ballot of its members.[178]

The number of industrial disputes has dropped markedly – in the 12 months to October 1994 there were 403,000 days lost through strike action compared to 29.5 million in 1979,[179] whilst in 1993 there was a total of 211 strikes, the lowest number since records began in 1891.[180] This may be indicative of the weakening power of employees to organise collectively and to bargain with their employers.

At the same time inequality has increased in the UK over the last 15 years. While company directors have awarded themselves huge pay rises, public sector pay has been held down. A survey by the Labour Research Department found that between 1993 and 1994 average boardroom pay for directors rose by 19.2 per cent compared to an underlying average increase for all employees of 2.8 per cent.[181] According to the Low-Pay Unit, employers are increasingly offering very low paid, part-time employment, for which the weekly wage falls below £57 in order to avoid paying National Insurance contributions.[182] In 1979, 9 per cent of the population lived on an income less than half the average. By 1989 this had increased to 22 per cent of the population.[183] The income of the poorest fifth of households fell 20 per cent during the 1980s while the income of the top fifth rose by over 30 per cent.[184]

Short-term, part-time and self-employed workers

The number of workers on short-term and individual contracts has grown significantly as have the number of part-time and self-employed workers, who have fewer statutory rights and protections.[185] Records on the number of part-time workers are only available from 1984 but the number since that date has steadily increased, by a greater proportion than the overall increase in the size of the workforce.[186] Between 1979 and 1993 the number of men in full-time employment dropped by almost three million.[187] In the spring of 1994 there were 732,000 employees on fixed-term contracts, 3 per cent of the workforce, 3,208,000 self-employed workers, 13 per cent of the workforce, and 6,006,000 workers who were working part-time. In total 9,076,000 belonged to one or more of these categories, now comprising 36 per cent of the total workforce.[188]

Between 1981 and 1991 the numbers of self-employed workers grew from around 2.2 million to nearly 3.3 million, of whom one million work alone.[189] Some observers have claimed that much of this growth rests on a legal fiction which has been deliberately encouraged by changes to tax legislation[190] and that many workers are now engaged on a contractual basis who should be classified as directly employed.[191] This is particularly noticeable in the building industry where a massive growth in the numbers of self-employed workers, is believed to have contributed to the industry's worsening safety record.[192]

Privatisation of major industries has significantly weakened the collective-bargaining structures for those workers affected. Long-standing employment agreements have been swept away and inferior conditions imposed on workers.[193] In the remaining nationalised industries, such as coal mining and the railways, State employers have been imposing new terms and conditions to create a more 'flexible workforce' in the run-up to privatisation.[194]

Health and safety

One of the most notable consequences of the erosion of workplace rights and the right to freedom of association in the workplace, has been a deterioration in health and safety standards.[195] Maintaining good standards of health and safety in the workplace requires co-operation between employers and staff using recognised structures.

While the Health and Safety at Work Act 1974 provides statutory regulations, the enforcement of these provisions has never been adequate and has deteriorated markedly during the 1980s.[196] The Health and Safety Executive (HSE), which was established to enforce the Act's provisions, has never been given adequate resources to carry out its task and the government has preferred to encourage 'self-regulation' rather than official enforcement.[197] The number of HSE inspectors in England and Wales was cut from 579 in 1979 to 468 in 1988 and was still below the 1979 level in 1994.[198] According to the HSE around 90 per cent of fatal accidents at work are avoidable and about 70 per cent are directly attributable to management negligence.[199] Most do not even result in a prosecution. Between April 1992 and March 1993 there were 346 reported deaths at the workplace, only 55 of which resulted in prosecutions.[200] No company director has ever been gaoled for causing the death of a worker, even when it has been proved that they knew they were making them work in an unsafe environment.[201]

The weakening of trade union organisation and changes in employment patterns have left particular groups such as temporary, part-time or 'self-employed' workers especially vulnerable. The construction industry, North Sea oil operations and agricultural work provide stark illustrations of this.[202] All three are characterised by organisational fragmentation, transient workforces with little job security, and have employers who are traditionally hostile to trade unionism.[203] All three also have appalling safety records. The construction industry, one of the largest sectors of the economy, is deregulated. Often dozens of sub-contractors operate on a single site managed by a large contractor, while over half the industry's workforce is now technically self-employed and engaged by firms on a contractual basis. This has led to casual employment practices with a high turnover of labour in which there has been widespread vetting and victimisation of trade union activists.[204]

Without effective protections of freedom of association or security of employment, workers in the building industry are often forced to perform unsafe tasks or risk the sack:[205] they are electrocuted because they have not been told about the location of cables; suffocate in trenches which have not been properly shored up, or have been dug next to walls; fall from roofs or scaffolding because guard rails have been taken away or have not been properly secured; are mangled by machinery where the safety guards have been removed; are hit by masonry; are run over by dumper trucks or trains; and are drowned, gassed, burnt or poisoned because safety precautions are regularly side-stepped and ignored.[206] The HSE recorded that there were 1,172 fatal injuries in the building industry between 1981 and 1992–3, and this is possibly an under-estimate owing to lack of reporting.[207] Work-related illnesses, such as bronchitis, cancer and asbestosis, have claimed the lives of thousands more.[208]

The practices which lead to these figures are illegal but the HSE has inadequate resources to police the industry. There are only 100 HSE inspectors covering the whole construction industry which means that an employer can expect to be visited, on average, only once every 12 years.[209] Where prosecutions do occur they are usually brought by HSE inspectors for breaches of the Health and Safety at Work Act 1974 and are held in magistrates courts where the punishment is usually a small fine.

The effects of the lack of union protection are shown in the oil industry where, in 1990, employers refused to recognise a rank and file trade union body, the Offshore Industry Liaison Commit-tee, which had grown out of a series of industrial disputes about safety conditions.[210] The employers have since victimised many of its members, effectively denying workers representation by the trade union of their choice.[211]

Many workers in the oil industry believe that the lack of a recognised independent trade union organisation has contributed to its poor safety record,[212] the worst case of which was the Piper Alpha oil disaster in 1988, when 167 workers burned to death. A public inquiry into the disaster recommended that safety commit-tees be established on the oil rigs and safety representatives be given protection against victimisation.[213] However, in August 1990, 726 oil workers were sacked for threatening a 24 hour strike in protest at the poor safety conditions still prevailing.[214]

The criminal law could be used more often to prosecute employers and, in particular, to charge individual company direc-tors with reckless manslaughter.[215] However, it appears that HSE inspectors have insufficient grounding in criminal law, and that the police and Crown Prosecution Service are reluctant to involve themselves in prosecutions even where it can be shown that the actions, or inactions, of individual employers directly caused a death. As one observer has commented:

> It hasn't . . . been the lack of laws that has stopped prosecutions but the lack of will to enforce them. The CPS and police do not treat workplace deaths as worthy of even the slightest suspicion or the most cursory investigation. In effect such deaths have become decriminalised.[216]

In the absence of individual legal protection, the collective protection that trade unions can provide becomes even more vital. 'Absolute employer power', it has been argued, 'gives rise to minimal responsibility for worker safety, and thereby maximises risks.'[217] Independent safety representatives and protection against their victimisation are necessary to help create a safety culture at work.

CONCLUSIONS

The impact of changing economic circumstances, eight successive employment laws and the Conservative government's hostility to the notion of collective bargaining have profoundly altered the rights of individuals in the workplace. Where previously the employee could rely on freedom of association and the collective power which this brought, through trade unions, to counter-balance the law's emphasis on the employer's contract and property rights, the erosion of this power has left employees vulnerable and defenceless.

This weakness was acknowledged by the European Court of Justice in June 1994 when it decided that the UK had failed to ensure the provision of mechanisms to enable workers to be consulted over redundancies and transfers of employment.[218] It is clear that the UK will be obliged to introduce legislation to correct this but the TUC is keen to ensure that, when such enabling legislation *is* introduced, it provides as wide a scope as possible for consultation within the workplace. While the TUC's proposals would give trade unions some protection, as collective organisations, they emphasise the need for unions to recruit members in order to win recognition, rather than arguing for an automatic incorporated role for unions in the workplace.[219]

To protect freedom of association at the workplace, employees' rights need to be a part of an integrated and comprehensive system of labour standards in which substantive rights are supported by a procedural framework for collective participation. The enactment of a comprehensive labour code, with statutory rights to workplace representation, should be an essential part of wider constitutional reforms in which employees are granted legally enforceable rights.

APPENDIX 1
LIBERTY'S BILL OF RIGHTS

PART ONE

Article 1
The Right to Protection under a Bill of Rights

The rights and freedoms set out below shall be known as the UK Bill of Rights. The Bill shall have the force of law and shall apply to all individuals within the jurisdiction of the UK without distinction of any kind. It shall be incumbent on the State to adopt such legislative or other measures as may be necessary to give effect to the rights and freedoms in this Bill.

Article 2
The Right to Life

1. Everyone's right to life, from the moment of birth, shall be protected by law. No one shall be deprived of life.

2. Deprivation of life shall not contravene this Article when it results from the use of force which is no more than absolutely necessary in defence of any person from unlawful violence, which could reasonably be expected to result in loss of life.

3. No one shall be condemned to death or executed.

Article 3
The Right to Freedom from Torture and Ill-Treatment

1. No one shall be subjected to torture or to cruel, inhuman or degrading treatment or punishment.

2. No one shall be subjected without their express and informed consent to medical or scientific experimentation, testing or research.

Article 4
The Right to Freedom from Slavery and Forced Labour

1. No one shall be held in slavery or servitude.

2. No one shall be required to perform forced or compulsory labour other than in the ordinary course of detention imposed according to the provisions of Article 5 or during conditional release from such detention.

Appendix 1

Article 5
The Right to Liberty and Security from Arbitrary Arrest and Detention

1. Everyone has the right to liberty and security of person. No one shall be deprived of their liberty save on reasonable grounds in the following cases and in accordance with a fair and just procedure prescribed by law:

(a) the lawful detention of a person after conviction of a crime by a competent court;

(b) the lawful arrest or detention of a person for non-compliance with the lawful order of the court;

(c) the lawful arrest or detention of a person for the purpose of bringing them before a competent legal authority on reasonable suspicion of having committed a specific offence or when there are reasonable grounds for suspecting either that a specific offence is being attempted or that a person is fleeing after having committed a specific offence;

(d) nothing in this Article shall prevent the involuntary admission into designated health facilities under strict medical supervision and on the basis of sound medical advice of:

(i) persons where the circumstances are such that proper precautions to prevent the spread of a notifiable and serious infectious disease cannot be taken and where there is a serious risk of infection to other people if the person suffering from the said disease is not detained in hospital;

(ii) persons suffering from mental illness of a nature or degree which makes detention strictly necessary to prevent imminent and serious physical harm to themselves or others provided that the involuntary admission is initially for a short period and is subject to regular review by an independent body governed by the principles of natural justice laid down in Article 6.

2. Everyone who is deprived of their liberty on any of the grounds in this Article shall have the following rights:

(a) they shall be informed, at the time of their detention or involuntary admission, and in a language which they understand, of the reasons for their detention and shall be informed promptly of any charges against them;

(b) they shall be entitled to consult a lawyer free of charge at any time;

(c) if they are charged with a crime they shall be advised that they are not required to say anything unless they wish to do so but what they say may be given in evidence against them;

(d) they shall be entitled to have their whereabouts notified to a person of their choice without delay.

3. Anyone arrested or detained on a criminal charge shall be brought promptly and without delay before a judge or other officer authorised by law to exercise judicial power and shall be entitled to trial within a reasonable time or to release. It shall be the general rule that persons awaiting trial shall not be detained in custody but may be subject to guarantees to appear for trial.

4. Anyone who is deprived of their liberty under any of the grounds in this Article shall be entitled to take proceedings before a court without delay, in order that the court may decide speedily on the lawfulness of the detention and order their release if the detention is not lawful.

5. No one shall be deprived of their liberty solely on the grounds of inability to fulfil a contractual obligation, pay a debt or pay a fine.

6. All persons deprived of their liberty shall be treated with humanity and with respect for the inherent dignity of the human person.

7. (a) Accused persons in detention shall, save in exceptional circumstances, be segregated from convicted persons and shall be subject to separate treatment in accordance with their status as unconvicted persons.

(b) Accused juveniles in detention shall be separated from adults and brought as speedily as possible for adjudication.

8. Convicted juveniles shall be segregated from adults and accorded treatment appropriate to their age and legal status.

9. The regime of custodial institutions should seek to minimise any differences between prison life and life at liberty which tend to lessen the responsibility of the prisoners or the respect due to their dignity as human beings.

Article 6
The Right to a Fair and Public Trial or Hearing

1. All persons are equal before the law and are entitled without discrimination to the equal protection of the law.

2. In the determination of any civil rights and obligations or of any criminal charge everyone is entitled to:

(a) a fair and public hearing within a reasonable time by an independent and impartial court or tribunal established by law. Judgment shall be pronounced publicly *in all circumstances* but the press and public may be excluded from, or reporting restrictions applied to, all or part of the trial in the following circumstances:

(i) where the interests of children and juveniles require;

(ii) where it is strictly necessary and to the extent that it is strictly necessary in a democratic society to protect the private lives of the parties or witnesses. In criminal proceedings the private life of the defendant shall be protected by restrictions only to the extent that any such publicity would result in the identification of a vulnerable witness or victim;

(iii) where, in the opinion of the court, it is strictly necessary, and to the extent that it is strictly necessary in a democratic society, in exceptional circumstances, to protect public safety;

(iv) where, in the opinion of the court, it is strictly necessary, and to the extent that it is strictly necessary in a democratic society, in exceptional circumstances, to enable the hearing to continue. During the course of any hearing the public, or sections thereof, may be excluded from specific sessions in such circumstances but reporting restrictions may not apply;

(v) where it is strictly necessary, and to the extent that it is strictly necessary in a democratic society, when there is a substantial risk, in the opinion of the court, that publicity would seriously prejudice the interests of justice. Reporting restrictions only, on all or part of the trial, may be applied in these specific circumstances. The risk of impediment or prejudice must in these circumstances be more than is merely incidental to publicity which is in the public interest;

(b) be present at any hearing and to represent themselves in person or be represented through legal assistance of their own choosing; to be informed of this right and if without sufficient means to pay for legal assistance to be given it free when the interests of justice so require;

(c) a right of appeal to a higher court from an unfavourable decision of any court or tribunal and this shall include the right of everyone convicted of a crime to appeal against conviction and sentence. Subject to any conditions prescribed by law there shall be a final right of appeal to the Supreme Court.

3. Everyone charged with a criminal offence shall be presumed innocent until proved guilty according to law.

4. Everyone charged with a criminal offence shall have the following minimum rights:

(a) to be informed promptly and in detail in a language which they understand of the nature and cause of the charge against them;

(b) to have adequate time and facilities for the preparation of their defence, to communicate privately with counsel of their own choosing and to be given access to all relevant documents and witness statements that will assist them in their defence;

(c) to be tried without undue delay;

(d) to examine or have examined the witnesses against them, including expert witnesses, and to obtain the attendance and examination of witnesses on their behalf under the same conditions as witnesses against them;

(e) to have the free assistance of an interpreter if they cannot understand or speak the language used in court;

(f) not to be compelled or coerced to give evidence in their defence or to testify against themselves or to confess guilt;

(g) to be tried by a jury of their peers in all cases involving potential loss of liberty.

5. In the case of juveniles the procedure shall be such as will take account of their age.

6. When a person has by a final decision been convicted of a criminal offence and has suffered punishment as a result of such a conviction, that person shall have the right to have their case reviewed and investigated by an independent body if substantial doubt arises about the conviction, whether as a result of new evidence or in any other way.

7. (a) A confession of guilt by the accused shall be accepted as valid evidence in any criminal proceedings only if it is made without coercion or inducement of any kind in the presence of a solicitor and if it can be corroborated by independent evidence which implicates the defendant in the crime.

(b) Other evidence which was obtained in breach of the law, including this Bill of Rights, shall not be admitted in evidence in any criminal or other proceedings.

8. No one shall be liable to be tried or punished again for an offence for which they have already been finally convicted or acquitted in accordance with the law and penal procedure.

Article 7
The Right to Justice Concerning Retrospective Offences

1. No one shall be held guilty of any criminal offence on account of any act or omission which did not constitute a criminal offence under national or international law at the time it was committed. Nor shall a heavier penalty be imposed than the one that was applicable at the time the criminal offence was committed. If, subsequent to the commission of

the offence, provision is made by law for the imp
penalty, the offender shall benefit thereby.

2. Nothing in this Article shall prejudice the trial and
person for an act or omission which constitutes the cr
a crime against humanity.

Article 8
The Right to Personal Privacy

1. Everyone has the right to respect for their private and family life, their home and their correspondence.

2. Everyone has the right to the protection of the law against interference with their privacy, family, home or correspondence and against attacks on their reputation.

3. Everyone has the right to know what public and private authorities hold information on them and for what purposes the information has been collected and will be used.

4. Everyone has the right of access to information held on them by any public or private authority, and to withhold consent to personal information being disclosed to a third party.

5. Everyone has the right to be secure against unreasonable search and seizure and all searches and seizures must be prescribed by law in accordance with the following safeguards:

(a) unless it is strictly impractical to do so all searches must be authorised in advance by a court;

(b) the reasons for the search and any documents or other authorisation for the search shall be given to the person searched or the occupier of the premises before the search takes place;

(c) a written list of seized items shall be provided at the end of the search.

6. No one shall be required to obtain or carry on their person a document for the sole purpose of establishing their identity.

7. Anyone affected by inaccurate statements disseminated to the public in general by any medium of communication has the right to reply or make a correction using the same communication outlet, under such conditions as the law may establish.

8. The rights set out in Clauses 2 and 4 are subject only to such limits as are prescribed by law, strictly necessary and demonstrably justified in a democratic society for:

protection of the rights and freedoms of others as laid down in
Bill and;

(b) the protection of public safety to the extent that is strictly necessary
in exceptional circumstances.

Article 9
The Right to Freedom of Conscience

1. Everyone has the right to freedom of thought, conscience and religion
(including the right to no religion) and to hold their own opinions. These
rights include freedom to change one's religion or beliefs and freedom
either alone or in community with others and in public or in private,
to manifest one's religion or beliefs in worship, teaching, practice and
observance.

2. Freedom to manifest one's religion or beliefs shall be subject to such
limits as are prescribed by law, strictly necessary and demonstrably justified
in a democratic society for the protection of other individuals from imminent physical harm and for the protection of the rights and freedoms of
others as laid down in this Bill.

Article 10
The Right to Freedom of Information and Expression

1. Everyone shall have the right to freedom of expression. This right shall
include freedom to seek, receive and impart information and ideas of all
kinds regardless of frontiers either orally, in writing or in print, in the
form of art, or through any media of their choice subject only to such
limits as are prescribed by law, strictly necessary and demonstrably justified
in a democratic society for the protection of individuals from imminent
physical harm or to prevent incitement to racial hatred and for the protection of the rights and freedoms of others as laid down in this Bill.

2. Everyone shall have the right of access to official information held by
public authorities subject only to such limits as are prescribed by law,
strictly necessary and demonstrably justified in a democratic society, for:

(a) the protection of the rights and freedoms of others as laid down in
this Bill;

(b) the protection of public safety to the extent that is strictly necessary
in exceptional circumstances. Nothing in this clause shall prohibit access
to public information which it is in the public interest to acquire.

3. This Article shall not prevent the State from requiring the licensing of
broadcasting, television or cinema enterprises.

Article 11
The Right to Organise and Demonstrate

1. Everyone has the right to freedom of peaceful assembly and to freedom of association with others, including the right to form and join trade unions for the protection of their interests. No restrictions shall be placed on the exercise of these rights other than the right to freedom of assembly and only provided that such restrictions are prescribed by law and are strictly necessary and demonstrably justified in a democratic society for the protection of individuals from imminent physical harm.

2. All workers and employees shall enjoy adequate protection against acts of anti-union discrimination in respect of their employment. Such protection shall apply more particularly in respect of acts calculated to:

(a) make the employment of workers subject to the condition that they shall not join a trade union or shall relinquish trade union membership;

(b) cause the dismissal of or otherwise prejudice a worker by reason of union membership.

Article 12
The Right of All to Marry and Divorce

1. Everyone of marriageable age shall have the right to marry the spouse of their choice without discrimination on any grounds. No marriage shall be entered into without the full consent of the intending spouses. Everyone who is married shall also have the right to divorce, subject only to such proceedings as are necessary to guarantee the protection of any children of the marriage, and to ensure an equitable disposition of any property jointly held by the parties to the marriage.

2. Everyone of marriageable age shall have the right to found a family.

Article 13
The Rights of Children

1. Every child shall have the right without discrimination on any ground to such measures of protection on the part of the family, society and the state as are required by children's status as a minor. Children's rights as well as needs must be taken into account and their rights under this Bill shall apply in full subject only to such limits which are prescribed by law, strictly necessary and demonstrably justified in a democratic society for their right to protection under this Article.

2. The child shall be protected from all forms of neglect, cruelty and exploitation whilst paying due regard to the rights of the child as laid down in this Bill.

shall recognise equal rights for children born out of wedlock
born in wedlock.

hild born in the UK is entitled to UK citizenship and nationality.

Article 14
The Right to Freedom from Discrimination

1. The equal protection of the law and the enjoyment of rights, whether
referred to in this Bill of Rights or not, shall be secured without discrimination on any ground such as gender, race, colour, language, religion,
political or other opinion, ethnic, national or social origin, nationality or
citizenship, mental or physical disability or illness, sexual orientation,
gender identity, age, marital, economic or other status.

2. All persons belonging to ethnic, religious, linguistic, cultural or national
minorities shall not be denied the right, in community with other members
of their group, to use their own language and manifest their own culture
or religion subject to the limitations in Article 9(2).

3. This article shall not preclude any law, programme or activity that has
as its objective the amelioration of conditions of individuals or groups
disadvantaged on any of the grounds listed in this Article. Neither shall it
preclude any differential services or entitlements based on special needs
or genuine occupational qualifications.

4. Any conduct which is threatening, abusive and insulting and which is
intended or which is likely, having regard to all the circumstances, to stir
up racial hatred or hatred is in breach of this Bill.

Article 15
The Right to a Human Rights Education

Everyone has the right to an education which prepares them to participate
fully in society and the democratic process, to understand and respect
human rights, including the rights in this Bill, and to respect diversity and
minority rights.

Article 16
The Right to Democratic Participation

1. The will of the people shall be the basis of the authority of government.
This shall be expressed in the following ways:
    every adult British citizen and every adult settled or ordinarily resident
in the UK shall have the right and opportunity to:

(a) take part in the conduct of public affairs both directly and through
freely chosen representatives;

(b) vote and stand for election at periodic elections which shall be by universal and equal suffrage and shall be held by secret ballot guaranteeing the free expression of the will of the electorate;

(c) have access, on general terms of equality, to public service.

Nothing in this clause can be construed as limiting any rights to democratic participation to which any group not specifically mentioned in this Article is currently entitled.

2. The right to vote in any election shall not be denied or abridged for any reason.

Article 17
The Right to Freedom of Movement

1. Everyone within the UK shall have the right to liberty of movement and freedom to choose their residence within that territory.

2. Everyone shall be free to leave the UK and no one who is settled in the UK shall thereby forfeit the right to return, regardless of length of absence.

3. Every British national shall be entitled to enter the territory of the UK and to a valid passport.

4. No restrictions shall be placed on the exercise of the rights in this Article other than the limitations to liberty and those concerning security of person in Article 5(1). The rights set out in Article 17(1) may also be subject to such limits as are prescribed by law, strictly necessary and demonstrably justified in a democratic society for the protection of individuals from imminent physical harm.

Article 18
The Right to Natural Justice concerning Deportation Laws and Procedures

1. No British national or any individual settled in the UK shall be deported from the UK.

2. No one in the UK may be deported or removed until a decision is reached in accordance with the law and the principles of due process set out in Articles 5 and 6. Anyone subject to a deportation order or threatened with removal as an illegal entrant must, before the deportation or removal, be allowed to appeal. They must be allowed to submit reasons against their deportation or removal and to have their case reviewed by, and be represented for the purpose before, an independent and impartial court or tribunal established by law.

3. It shall be the general rule that persons subject to a deportation order

or threatened with removal shall not be detained in custody but may be subject to guarantees to appear before a court or tribunal.

4. Collective expulsion of aliens is prohibited.

Article 19
The Right to Asylum

1. Every person has the right to seek and be granted asylum in the UK in accordance with the law of the UK and international conventions if they are being pursued for political offences or have a well-founded fear of persecution for reasons of gender, race, colour, language, religion, political or other opinion, ethnic, national or social origin, age, nationality or citizenship, mental or physical disability or illness, sexual orientation or gender identity.

2. No penalties shall be imposed on any individual or body on account of the illegal entry or presence of refugees or asylum seekers who, coming from a territory where their life or freedom was threatened under the terms of Clause 1, seek to enter or are present in the territory without authorisation provided they present themselves without undue delay to the authorities and show good cause for their illegal entry or presence.

3. No refugee or asylum seeker shall be deported or removed to the frontiers of any territories where their life or freedom would be threatened on account of any of the grounds in Clause 1. No deportations or removals shall take place other than according to the procedures set out in Article 18(2) which in all cases includes a right to appeal.

Article 20
The Right not to be Extradited without Adequate Safeguards

1. No one shall be extradited from the UK to face criminal charges elsewhere unless the country requesting extradition has proved to a court that there is an arguable case that a serious criminal offence was committed by that person. Such persons shall be protected by the rights of due process provided for by Articles 5 and 6.

2. No one shall be extradited from the UK unless the alleged offence would be an offence under UK law.

3. No one shall be extradited from the UK if it appears to the court that:

(a) the alleged offence is an offence under military law which is not also an offence under the general criminal law;

(b) the request for the individual's return is in fact made for the purpose of prosecuting or punishing that person on account of gender, race, colour, language, religion, political or other opinion, ethnic, national or social origin, age, nationality or citizenship, mental or physical disability or illness, sexual orientation or gender identity;

(c) the individual might, if returned, be prejudiced during the course of the trial or punished, detained or face restrictions in personal liberty for any of the reasons in Article 20(3)(b);

PART TWO: APPLICABILITY AND DEFINITIONS

Article 21

The rights in this Bill apply only to natural persons from the moment of their birth and the terms 'individual', 'everyone', or 'no one' shall be construed as having this meaning alone.

Article 22

Unless otherwise specified, every individual within the jurisdiction of the United Kingdom shall enjoy the fundamental rights and freedom secured in this Bill against:

(a) any act or omission by the legislative, executive, judiciary or crown;

(b) any act or omission by any individual or body in the performance of any public function.

Article 23

In addition to the provisions in Articles 21 and 22, the following provisions shall have effect for the interpretation of this Bill.

The term 'slavery' under Article 4 refers to the condition of being wholly in the legal possession of another person, whilst the term 'servitude' covers debt-serfdom, being sold into marriage and sham adoptions. Whilst both these terms refer to the status of an individual, forced or compulsory labour characterises the type of work which is performed.

The term 'security of person' in Article 5 means protection against arbitrary arrest and detention.

The term 'civil rights and obligations' in Article 6 covers any question which a court or tribunal is empowered to determine, including any matter involving a dispute with government departments, local authorities and any other public body.

The term 'criminal charge' in Article 6 includes contempt of court and any matter which falls within the jurisdiction of a disciplinary body as a result of which a person found guilty may be deprived of liberty, or lose remission on a prison sentence.

The term 'public interest' in Articles 6 and 10 refers to official information which reveals the existence of crime, corruption, danger to the public, serious misconduct, abuse of authority or neglect in the performance of official duty.

The term 'public safety' in Articles 6, 8 and 10 means the ability of people to engage in ordinary social activity without demonstrable danger of physical harm.

The term 'crime against humanity' in Article 7 derives from the 1945 Nuremburg trial at the end of the Second World War and the term 'genocide' is defined in the 1948 Convention on the Prevention and Punishment of the Crime of Genocide which has been ratified by the UK.

The term 'adult' in Articles 8 and 16 refers to any natural person of 18 years or more.

The 'right to assembly' in Article 11 refers to the right to demonstrate, march and hold public and private meetings, and the 'right of association' refers to the right to join any organisation without interference from the state.

The term 'marriageable age' in Article 12 refers to any natural person of 16 years or more.

The term 'child' in Article 13 refers to every natural person from the moment of their birth to the age of 18.

The term 'settled' in Articles 16, 17 and 18 refers to being resident in the UK without any restrictions on the period of stay (although still subject to immigration control).

The term 'ordinarily resident' in Article 16 refers to being in a particular country, voluntarily and for settled purposes, as part of the regular order of life for the time being, whether of short or long-term duration.

The term 'serious criminal offence' in Article 20 refers to any offence for which the penalty involved is 12 months' imprisonment or more.

REMEDIES AND ENFORCEMENT – ARTICLES 24-35

Article 24

1. Everyone whose rights and freedoms as set forth in this Bill are being, have been or are about to be directly violated shall have an effective remedy before an independent and impartial tribunal or court. They shall

be entitled to a declaration of their rights and to the appropriate remedy as follows:

(a) in all cases reasonable financial compensation for breaches of the Bill;

(b) an injunction restraining breaches of the rights and freedoms contained in this Bill;

(c) an order to enforce the rights provided in this Bill;

(d) an order quashing the decision of a public body, court or tribunal which has breached the provisions of this Bill.

2. Anyone who has been convicted of a crime where it has subsequently been shown there has been a miscarriage of justice shall have an enforceable right to financial compensation.

3. All such remedies will be available against the State, the Crown and any individual or body in the performance of any public function. Any group of persons whose individual rights under this Bill have been, are being, or are about to be directly violated shall be entitled to take action as a group or in cases where the court declares it to be in the interests of justice, be represented by a non-governmental or quasi-governmental non-profitmaking organisation.

Article 25

If the validity of any Act of Parliament in relation to this Bill of Rights is challenged in the course of proceedings in a minor court or tribunal and there is an arguable case for proceeding on that issue, the court or tribunal shall refer the question to the High Court.

Article 26

1. Any acts, decisions or omissions by any of the individuals or bodies listed in Article 22, including the Crown, whether or not their powers are conferred by Act of Parliament, subordinate legislation passed or common law judgment made before or after this Bill of Rights has come into force, shall be subject to this Bill of Rights.

2. This Article shall not affect the legality of any acts, decisions or omissions prior to the coming into force of this Bill of Rights.

Article 27

Any Act of Parliament passed before this Bill of Rights has come into force and any subordinate legislation passed or common law judgment made before or after this Bill of Rights has come into force shall be so construed and applied as not to abrogate, abridge or infringe, whether directly or indirectly, any of the rights and freedoms in this Bill of Rights;

and insofar as any such law or provision thereof is incapable of such construction or application, it shall cease to have effect.

Article 28

Any Act of Parliament passed after this Bill of Rights has come into force shall be so construed and applied as not to abrogate, abridge or infringe, whether directly or indirectly, any of the rights or freedoms in this Bill of Rights and any such Act shall be so construed and applied as not to repeal or amend any provision of this Bill of Rights. Insofar as any Act passed after this Bill of Rights has come into force is incapable of such a construction or application it shall not have effect except under the following circumstances:

(a) where such an Act or provision thereof, or re-enactment of previous legislation, expressly declares within the legislation itself that it shall take effect in breach of the Bill of Rights;

(b) where the Human Rights Scrutiny Committee, acting in accordance with its powers under Article 31, makes a declaration of rights on a two-thirds majority that an Act of Parliament or provision thereof is in accordance with the meaning, intention and spirit of this Bill of Rights and this has been confirmed by a resolution of a simple majority of both Houses of Parliament and this is expressly declared within the legislation itself. In such circumstances no court shall decline to apply an Act or provision thereof by reason only that it judges it to be inconsistent with any provision of this Bill of Rights. Nothing in this clause shall prejudice the right of the courts to express a view as to whether the said legislation or provision thereof is in breach of this Bill.

Article 29

An Act or a provision of an Act in respect of which an express declaration has been made under Article 28 shall operate as it would have but for this Bill of Rights except that in the case of declarations made under Article 28(a) the Act or provision shall cease to have effect five years after it comes into force (or any such earlier date as may be specified in the declaration) after which time the Act or provision will be deemed to have been repealed. The period in which any Act, or provision thereof, passed in accordance with the Powers under Article 28(a) comes into force can be delayed by a simple majority of the second chamber of the legislature for up to five years.

Article 30

The powers of declaration under Article 28(a) and (b) do not apply to the following Articles: 1, 2, 3, 4(1), 7, 9(1), 14(1), 16 and any Act of Parliament, subordinate legislation or common law judgment or provision thereof passed before or after this Bill of Rights comes into force which is judged by the High Court to be incapable of a construction or application which upholds the rights in these Articles shall cease to have effect.

Article 31

A Human Rights Scrutiny Committee shall be elected by Members of the House of Commons as a Committee of the House of Commons on which no member of the executive shall sit. It shall have 15 members and a Chair. The Chair of the Committee shall be elected by the Committee members and shall have no voting rights. The Committee shall have the following functions:

(a) to scrutinise Acts of Parliament and provisions thereof for compliance with this Bill of Rights when requested to do so by a minister or after a resolution of one third of either House of Parliament or by the Human Rights Commission in such circumstances where a ruling of the Supreme Court has declared an Act of Parliament or provision thereof, passed subsequent to this Bill of Rights coming into force, to be in breach or otherwise of this Bill.

(i) Should the Human Rights Scrutiny Committee, on giving due consideration to the advice of the Human Rights Commission, make a declaration of rights by a two-thirds majority to the effect that the said Act or provision thereof is in accordance with the meaning, intention and spirit of this Bill of Rights and this is confirmed by a resolution of a simple majority of both Houses of Parliament at the final reading of the Bill in question and is expressly declared within the legislation itself, no court shall decline to apply the Act or provision thereof by reason only that it judges it to be in breach of this Bill of Rights other than in relation to the Articles listed under Article 30.

(ii) Should the Human Rights Scrutiny Committee, on giving due consideration to the advice of the Human Rights Commission, declare by a two-thirds majority that the said legislation or provision thereof is in breach of the meaning, intention or spirit of this Bill of Rights an express declaration within the legislation itself under the powers conferred by Article 28(a) will be required to enable the legislation to proceed.

(iii) Should less than two-thirds of the Committee agree on a resolution in either of the circumstances in Article 31(a) subsections (i) and (ii), the legislation in question will proceed in the normal way and be subject to the ruling of the Courts under Article 28.

(b) to scrutinise any proposed amendments to the Bill of Rights and to express a view on whether such an amendment should be supported or otherwise, having given due consideration to the advice of the Human Rights Commission in this regard;

(c) to appoint the Commissioners and Chair of the Human Rights Commission;

(d) to receive the annual report of the Human Rights Commission, lay a copy of the report before both Houses of Parliament and cause the report to be published;

(e) to receive and advise Parliament on any other reports of the Human Rights Commission under Article 32(b) to (e).

Article 32

There shall be a body of Commissioners named the Human Rights Commission with the following functions:

(a) at its own discretion to request the Human Rights Scrutiny Committee to review Acts of Parliament or provisions thereof overturned by the courts and to express a view, which shall be announced in public, on all legislation or provisions thereof to be reviewed by the Human Rights Scrutiny Committee prior to the Committee exercising its powers of review under Article 31(a)(i) or (ii);

(b) at its own initiative or at the request of the executive, legislature, Supreme Court or Human Rights Scrutiny Committee to advise whether any current legislation or provisions thereof is consistent with or contrary to the Bill of Rights;

(c) at its own initiative or at the request of the executive, legislature, or Human Rights Scrutiny Committee to advise whether any proposed legislation or provisions thereof is consistent with or contrary to the Bill of Rights, including any proposed amendments to the Bill of Rights itself;

(d) at its own initiative or at the request of the executive, legislature or Human Rights Scrutiny Committee to advise on any new legislation required to comply with this Bill of Rights and relevant regional or international human rights instruments ratified by the UK;

(e) to keep under review the Bill of Rights 1994 and advise the executive, legislature or Human Rights Scrutiny Committee where revisions are required to enhance human rights;

(f) to provide the Human Rights Scrutiny Committee with an annual report which shall include a general survey of human rights developments in the relevant period in so far as these relate to the rights and freedoms in this Bill of Rights;

(g) to directly assist individuals who are actual or prospective complainants under the Bill of Rights who apply to the Commission for assistance provided that the Commission considers one or more of the following apply:

(i) the case raises a question of general principle;

(ii) it is unreasonable, having regard to the complexity or cost of the case, to expect the applicant to deal with it unaided;

(iii) the case has implications for a group or category of individuals.

(h) There shall be no less than 15 and no more than 25 commissioners appointed on a part or full time basis for a five-year term by an ad hoc Appointments Committee of three members of the Human Rights Scrutiny Committee. One of their number shall be appointed Chair by the Appointments Committee. The commissioners shall be drawn in equal proportion from the following three categories:

(i) the legal profession, including legal academics, practising lawyers and judges;

(ii) human rights non-government organisations;

(iii) lay members of the community, reflecting in so far as is possible the categories laid down in Article 14, who have knowledge or experience of abuses of the rights and freedoms in this Bill of Rights. The Commissioners may appoint such officers as they think fit in furtherance of the aims of the Commission subject to the approval of the Civil Service as to numbers and remuneration.

Article 33

1. An amendment to this Bill of Rights shall only be made through an Act of Parliament following a resolution of a two-thirds majority of both Houses of Parliament on the final reading of the Bill in question having given due consideration to the advice of the Human Rights Scrutiny Committee. The coming into force of any such amendment may be delayed by a simple majority of the second chamber of the legislature for five years.

2. Repeal of this Bill of Rights can be made only by a resolution of a two-thirds majority of both Houses of Parliament on the final reading of the Bill in question having given due consideration to the advice of the Human Rights Scrutiny Committee, and the coming into force of such an Act will be delayed for five years.

Article 34

The fundamental rights and freedoms in this Bill of Rights are in addition to, and not in derogation from, any other fundamental rights and freedoms given to the individual by any statutory body or international or regional instrument ratified by the UK.

Article 35

1. Any court or tribunal which is called on to interpret or apply the Bill of Rights, and any body, including the Human Rights Scrutiny Committee and Commission, which is called on to assess the effect of the Bill on any other enactment shall pay due regard to the following:

(a) the European Convention on Human Rights and Fundamental Freedoms, the International Covenant on Civil and Political Rights and any other international or regional treaty ratified by the UK concerning the rights and freedoms in this Bill;

(b) reports and expressions of views on human rights by the European Commission of Human Rights, the Council of Europe and the United Nations Human Rights Committee;

(c) judgments and advisory opinions of the European Court of Human Rights.

2. This Article shall not be construed as limiting or derogating from any rights or freedoms in this Bill which are not contained or not contained to the same degree in any of the aforementioned Instruments.

APPENDIX 2
INTERNATIONAL COVENANT ON CIVIL AND POLITICAL RIGHTS

PREAMBLE

The States Parties to the present Covenant,

CONSIDERING that, in accordance with the principles proclaimed in the Charter of the United Nations, recognition of the inherent dignity and of the equal and inalienable rights of all members of the human family is the foundation of freedom, justice and peace in the world,

RECOGNISING that these rights derive from the inherent dignity of the human person,

RECOGNISNG that, in accordance with the Universal Declaration of Human Rights, the ideal of free human beings enjoying civil and political freedom from fear and want can only be achieved if conditions are created whereby everyone may enjoy his civil and political rights, as well as his economic, social and cultural rights,

CONSIDERING the obligation of the States under the Charter of the United Nations to promote universal respect for, and observance of, human rights and freedoms,

REALISING that the individual, having duties to other individuals and to the community to which he belongs, is under a responsibility to strive for the promotion and observance of the rights recognised in the present Covenant,

AGREE upon the following articles:

PART I
Article 1

1. All peoples have the right of self-determination. By virtue of that right they freely determine their political status and freely pursue their economic, social and cultural development.

2. All peoples may, for their own ends, freely dispose of their natural wealth and resources without prejudice to any obligations arising out of international economic co-operation, based upon the principle of mutual benefit and international law. In no case may a people be deprived of its own means of subsistence.

3. The States Parties to the present Covenant, including those having

responsibility for the administration of Non-Self-Governing and Trust Territories, shall promote the realisation of the right of self-determination, shall respect that right, in conformity with the provisions of the Charter of the United Nations.

PART II

Article 2

1. Each State Party to the present Covenant undertakes to respect and to ensure to all individuals within its territory and subject to its jurisdiction the rights recognised in the present Covenant, without distinction of any kind, such as race, colour, sex, language, religion, political or other opinion, national or social origin, property, birth or other status.

2. Where not already provided for by existing legislative or other measures, each State Party to the present Covenant undertakes to take the necessary steps, in accordance with its constitutional processes and with the provisions of the present Covenant, to adopt such legislative or other measures as may be necessary to give effect to the rights recognised in the present Covenant.

3. Each State Party to the present Covenant undertakes:

(a) To ensure that any person whose rights or freedoms as herein recognised are violated shall have an effective remedy, notwithstanding that the violation has been committed by persons acting in an official capacity;

(b) To ensure that any person claiming such a remedy shall have his right thereto determined by competent judicial, administrative or legislative authorities, or by any other competent authority provided for by the legal system of the State, and to develop the possibilities of judicial remedy;

(c) To ensure that the competent authorities shall enforce such remedies when granted.

Article 3

The States Parties to the present Covenant undertake to ensure the equal right of men and women to the enjoyment of all civil and political rights set forth in the present Covenant.

Article 4

1. In time of public emergency which threatens the life of the nation and the existence of which is officially proclaimed, the States Parties to the present Covenant may take measures derogating from their obligations under the present Covenant to the extent strictly required by the exigencies of the situation, provided that such measures are not inconsistent with

their other obligations under international law and do not involve discrimination solely on the ground of race, colour, sex, language, religion or social origin.

2. No derogation from articles 6, 7, 8 (paragraphs 1 and 2), 11, 15, 16 and 18 may be made under this provision.

3. Any State Party to the present Covenant availing itself of the right of derogation shall immediately inform the other States Parties to the present Covenant, through the intermediary of the Secretary-General of the United Nations, of the provisions from which it has derogated and of the reasons by which it was actuated. A further communication shall be made, through the same intermediary, on the date on which it terminates such derogation.

Article 5

1. Nothing in the present Covenant may be interpreted as implying for any State, group or person any right to engage in any activity or perform any act aimed at the destruction of any of the rights and freedoms recognised herein or at their limitation to a greater extent than is provided for in the present Covenant.

2. There shall be no restriction upon or derogation from any of the fundamental human rights recognised or existing in any State Party to the present Covenant pursuant to law, conventions, regulations or custom on the pretext that the present Covenant does not recognise such rights or that it recognises them to a lesser extent.

PART III

Article 6

1. Every human being has the inherent right to life. This right shall be protected by law. No one shall be arbitrarily deprived of his life.

2. In countries which have not abolished the death penalty, sentence of death may be imposed only for the most serious crimes in accordance with the law in force at the time of the commission of the crime and not contrary to the provisions of the present Covenant and to the Convention on the Prevention and Punishment of the Crime of Genocide. This penalty can only be carried out pursuant to a final judgment rendered by a competent court.

3. When deprivation of life constitutes the crime of genocide, it is understood that nothing in this article shall authorise any State Party to the present Covenant to derogate in any way from any obligation assumed under the provisions of the Convention on the Prevention and Punishment of the Crime of Genocide.

4. Anyone sentenced to death shall have the right to seek pardon or commutation of the sentence. Amnesty, pardon or commutation of the sentence of death may be granted in all cases.

5. Sentence of death shall not be imposed for crimes committed by persons below eighteen years of age and shall not be carried out on pregnant women.

6. Nothing in this article shall be invoked to delay or to prevent the abolition of capital punishment by any State Party to the present Covenant.

Article 7

No one shall be subjected to torture or to cruel, inhuman or degrading treatment or punishment. In particular, no one shall be subject without his free consent to medical or scientific experimentation.

Article 8

1. No one shall be held in slavery; slavery and the slave-trade in all their forms shall be prohibited.

2. No one shall be held in servitude.

3. (a) No one shall be required to perform forced or compulsory labour;

(b) Paragraph 3(a) shall not be held to preclude, in countries where imprisonment with hard labour may be imposed as a punishment for a crime, the performance of hard labour in pursuance of a sentence to such punishment by a competent court;

(c) For the purpose of this paragraph the term 'forced or compulsory labour' shall not include:

(i) Any work or service, not referred to in subparagraph (b), normally required of a person who is under detention in consequence of a lawful order of a court, or of a person during conditional release from such detention;

(ii) Any service of a military character and, in countries where conscientious objection is recognised, any national service required by law of conscientious objectors;

(iii) Any service exacted in cases of emergency or calamity threatening the life or well-being of the community;

(iv) Any work or service which forms part of normal civil obligations.

Article 9

1. Everyone has the right to liberty and security of person. No one shall be subjected to arbitrary arrest or detention. No one shall be deprived of

his liberty except on such grounds and in accordance with such procedure as are established by law.

2. Anyone who is arrested shall be informed, at the time of arrest, of the reasons for his arrest and shall be promptly informed of any charges against him.

3. Anyone arrested or detained on a criminal charge shall be brought promptly before a judge or other officer authorised by law to exercise judicial power and shall be entitled to trial within a reasonable time or to release. It shall not be the general rule that persons awaiting trial shall be detained in custody, but release may be subject to guarantees to appear for trial, at any other stage of the judicial proceedings, and, should occasion arise, for execution of the judgment.

4. Anyone who is deprived of his liberty by arrest or detention shall be entitled to take proceedings before a court, in order that that court may decide without delay on the lawfulness of his detention and order his release if the detention is not lawful.

5. Anyone who has been the victim of unlawful arrest or detention shall have an enforceable right to compensation.

Article 10

1. All persons deprived of their liberty shall be treated with humanity and with respect for the inherent dignity of the human person.

2. (a) Accused persons shall, save in exceptional circumstances, be segregated from convicted persons and shall be subject to separate treatment appropriate to their status as unconvicted persons;

(b) Accused juvenile persons shall be separated from adults and brought as speedily as possible for adjudication.

3. The penitentiary system shall comprise treatment of prisoners the essential aim of which shall be their reformation and social rehabilitation. Juvenile offenders shall be segregated from adults and be accorded treatment appropriate to their age and legal status.

Article 11

No one shall be imprisoned merely on the ground of inability to fulfil a contractual obligation.

Article 12

1. Everyone lawfully within the territory of a State shall, within that territory, have the right to liberty of movement and freedom to choose his residence.

2. Everyone shall be free to leave any country, including his own.

3. The above-mentioned rights shall not be subject to any restrictions except those which are provided by law, are necessary to protect national security, public order (ordre public), public health or morals or the rights and freedoms of others, and are consistent with the other rights recognised in the present Covenant.

4. No one shall be arbitrarily deprived of the right to enter his own country.

Article 13

An alien lawfully in the territory of a State Party to the present Covenant may be expelled therefrom only in pursuance of a decision reached in accordance with law and shall, except where compelling reasons of national security otherwise require, be allowed to submit the reasons against his expulsion and to have his case reviewed by, and be presented for the purpose before, the competent authority or a person or persons especially designated by the competent authority.

Article 14

1. All persons shall be equal before the courts and tribunals. In the determination of any criminal charge against him, or his rights and obligations in a suit at law, everyone shall be entitled to a fair and public hearing by a competent, independent and impartial tribunal established by law. The Press and the public may be excluded from all or part of a trail for reasons of morals, public order (ordre public) or national security in a democratic society, or when the interest of the private lives of the parties so requires, or to the extent strictly necessary in the opinion of the court in special circumstances where publicity would prejudice the interests of justice; but any judgment rendered in a criminal case or in a suit at law shall be made public except where the interests of juvenile persons otherwise requires or the proceedings concern matrimonial disputes or the guardianship of children.

2. Everyone charged with a criminal offence shall have the right to be presumed innocent until proved guilty according to law.

3. In the determination of any criminal charge against him, everyone shall be entitled to the following minimum guarantees, in full equality:

(a) To be informed promptly and in detail in a language which he understands of the nature and cause of the charge against him;

(b) To have adequate time and facilities for the preparation of his defence and to communicate with counsel of his own choosing;

(c) To be tried without undue delay;

(d) To be tried in his presence, and to defend himself in person or through legal assistance of his own choosing; to be informed, if he does not have legal assistance, of this right and to have legal assistance assigned to him, in any case where the interests of justice so require; and without payment by him in any such case if he does not have sufficient means to pay for it;

(e) To examine, or have examined, the witnesses against him and to obtain the attendance and examination of witnesses on his behalf under the same conditions as witnesses against him;

(f) To have the free assistance of an interpreter if he cannot understand or speak the language used in court;

(g) Not to be compelled to testify against himself or to confess guilt.

4. In the case of juvenile persons, the procedure shall be such as will take account of their age and the desirability of promoting their rehabilitation.

5. Everyone convicted of a crime shall have the right to his conviction and sentence being reviewed by a higher tribunal according to law.

6. When a person has by a final decision been convicted of a criminal offence and when subsequently his conviction has been reversed or he has been pardoned on the ground that a new or newly discovered fact shows conclusively that there has been a miscarriage of justice, the person who has suffered punishment as a result of such conviction shall be compensated according to law, unless it is proved that the non-disclosure of the unknown fact in time is wholly or partly attributable to him.

7. No one shall be liable to be tried or punished again for an offence for which he has already been finally convicted or acquitted in accordance with the law and penal procedure of each country.

Article 15

1. No one shall be held guilty of any criminal offence on account of any act or omission which did not constitute a criminal offence, under national or international law, at the time when it was committed. Nor shall a heavier penalty be imposed than the one that was applicable at the time when the criminal offence was committed. If, subsequent to the commission of the offence, provision is made by law for the imposition of a lighter penalty, the offender shall benefit thereby.

2. Nothing in this article shall prejudice the trial and punishment of any person for any act or omission which, at the time when it was committed, was criminal according to the general principles of law recognised by the community of nations.

Article 16

Everyone shall have the right to recognition everywhere as a person before the law.

Article 17

1. No one shall be subjected to arbitrary or unlawful interference with his privacy, family, home or correspondence, nor to unlawful attacks on his honour and reputation.

2. Everyone has the right to the protection of the law against such interference or attacks.

Article 18

1. Everyone shall have the right to freedom of thought, conscience and religion. This right shall include freedom to have or to adopt a religion or belief of his choice, and freedom, either individually or in community with others and in public or private, to manifest his religion or belief in worship, observance, practice and teaching.

2. No one shall be subject to coercion which would impair his freedom to have or to adopt a religion or belief of his choice.

3. Freedom to manifest one's religion or beliefs may be subject only to such limitations as are prescribed by law and are necessary to protect public safety, order, health or morals or the fundamental rights and freedoms of others.

4. The States Parties to the present Covenant undertake to have respect for the liberty of parents and, when applicable, legal guardians to ensure the religious and moral education of their children in conformity with their own convictions.

Article 19

1. Everyone shall have the right to hold opinions without interference.

2. Everyone shall have the right to freedom of expression; this right shall include freedom to seek, receive and impart information and ideas of all kinds, regardless of frontiers, either orally, in writing or in print, in the form of art, or through any other media of his choice.

3. The exercise of the rights provided for in paragraph 2 of this article carries with it special duties and responsibilities. It may therefore be subject to certain restrictions, but these shall only be such as are provided by law and are necessary:

(a) For respect of the rights or reputations of others;

Appendix 2

(b) For the protection of national security or of public order (ordre public), or of public health or morals.

Article 20

1. Any propaganda for war shall be prohibited by law.

2. Any advocacy of national, racial or religious hatred that constitutes incitement to discrimination, hostility or violence shall be prohibited by law.

Article 21

The right of peaceful assembly shall be recognised. No restrictions may be placed on the exercise of this right other than those imposed in conformity with the law and which are necessary in a democratic society in the interests of national security or public safety, public order (ordre public), the protection of public health or morals or the protection of the rights and freedoms of others.

Article 22

1. Everyone shall have the right to freedom of association with others, including the right to form and join trade unions for the protection of his interests.

2. No restrictions may be placed on the exercise of this right other than those which are prescribed by law and which are necessary in a democratic society in the interests of national security or public safety, public order (ordre public), the protection of public health or morals or the protection of the rights and freedoms of others. This article shall not prevent the imposition of lawful restrictions on members of the armed forces and of the police in their exercise of this right.

3. Nothing in this article shall authorise States Parties to the International Labour Organisation Convention of 1948 concerning Freedom of Association and Protection of the Right to Organise to take legislative measures which would prejudice, or to apply the law in such a manner as to prejudice, the guarantees provided for in that Convention.

Article 23

1. The family is the natural and fundamental group unit of society and is entitled to protection by society and the State.

2. The right of men and women of marriageable age to marry and to found a family shall be recognised.

3. No marriage shall be entered into without the free and full consent of the intending spouses.

373

4. States Parties to the present Covenant shall take appropriate steps to ensure equality of rights and responsibilities of spouses as to marriage, during marriage and at its dissolution. In the case of dissolution, provision shall be made for the necessary protection of any children.

Article 24

1. Every child shall have, without any discrimination as to race, colour, sex, language, religion, national or social origin, property or birth, the right to such measures of protection as are required by his status as a minor, on the part of h is family, society and the State.

2. Every child shall be registered immediately after birth and shall have a name.

3. Every child has the right to acquire a nationality.

Article 25

Every citizen shall have the right and the opportunity, without any of the distinctions mentioned in article 2 and without unreasonable restrictions:

(a) To take part in the conduct of public affairs, directly or through freely chosen representatives;

(b) To vote and be elected at genuine periodic elections which shall be by universal and equal suffrage and shall be held by secret ballot, guaranteeing the free expression of the will of the electors;

(c) To have access, on general terms of equality, to public service in his country.

Article 26

All persons are equal before the law and are entitled without any discrimination to the equal protection of the law. In this respect, the law shall prohibit any discrimination and guarantee to all persons equal and effective protection against discrimination or any ground such as race, colour, sex, language, religion, political or other opinion, national or social origin, property, birth or other status.

Article 27

In those States in which ethnic, religious or linguistic minorities exist, persons belonging to such minorities shall not be denied the right, in community with the other members of their group, to enjoy their own culture, to profess and practise their own religion, or to use their own language.

ACKNOWLEDGEMENTS

Partner organisations in Liberty's Human Rights Convention project: Anti-Racist Alliance, Article 19, British Council of Organisations of Disabled People, Campaign for Press and Broadcasting Freedom, Change, Charter 88, the Fawcett Society, Institute of Employment Rights, Joint Council for the Welfare of Immigrants, Law Centres Federation, MIND, Prison Reform Trust, Refugee Council, Scottish Council for Civil Liberties, Society of Black Lawyers, Southall Black Sisters, Stonewall, UK Forum on HIV and Human Rights. Other organisations to which thanks are due are Asylum Aid, OutRage! and the Women's National Commission.

In addition, Liberty gratefully acknowledges the assistance of Georgina Ashworth, Ian Bynoe, Nicholas Blake, Bill Bowring, Stephen Bradshaw, Cathy Bryan, Avedon Carol, Christine Chinkin, Martin Collins, Jane Connors, Louise Christian, Harry Cocks, Simon Creighton, Richard Dunstan, Sue Easton, Michael Ellman, Kate Foley, Roz Foley, Conor Gearty, Pam Giddy, Caroline Gooding, Pauline Graham, Alex Hamilton, Jonathan Hardy, Kate Harrison, Siwan Hayward, Marylin Howard, Rachel Hurst, Kelly Johnson, Carolyn Jones, Stephanie Kaminsky, Roz Kaveney, Francesca Klug, Philip Leach, Fiona Mactaggart, Sheena McMurtrie, Elizabeth Meehan, Qudsia Mirza, Sharron Nelles, Louise Pirouet, Nettie Pollard, Sue Pratt, Kevin Pringle, Vicky Randall, Margherita Rendel, Mary Sainsbury, Sue Shutter, Mary-Ann Stephenson, Hannana Siddiqui, Stefan Simanowitz, Kathy Sutton, Peter Tatchell, Alan Thomas, Shaun Trevisick, Alison Vickers, John Wadham, Jenny Watson, Jenny Willmott, Elizabeth Wilson, Jane Winter, Charlotte Wright and Richard Wood.

Chapter 8 is based on the MIND/Liberty report *People with Mental Health Problems and Learning Disability*. Liberty would like to thank Camilla Parker, solicitor, who substantially updated and revised the report for this chapter and Jenny Willmot for her contribution to the section on gay and lesbian issues.

Particular thanks should go to Matthew Brown, Renée Harris and Kate Wilkinson, who edited the reports in their initial format.

NOTES

1 Democracy and Human Rights in the UK

1. *BBC and Vacher's General Election*, BBC News and Current Affairs and Vacher's Publications, 1992, at 14.
2. F.S.W. Craig (ed.), *British Electoral Facts 1832–1987*, Parliamentary Research Services, 1989, at 53, lists the following results for this century:

Date	Winning Party	% of Vote	Date	Winning Party	% of Vote
1900	Con	50.3	1950	Lab	46.1
1906	Lib	49.4	1951	Con	48.0 (Lab won 48.8)
1910	Lib	43.5	1955	Con	49.7
1910	Lib	44.4	1959	Con	49.4
1918	Con (Nat)	38.7	1964	Lab	44.1
1922	Con	38.5	1966	Lab	48.0
1923	Lab (Min)	30.7	1970	Con	46.4
1924	Con	46.8	1974	Lab	37.2
1929	Lab (Min)	37.1	1974	Lab	39.2
1931	Con (Nat)	67.2	1979	Con	43.9
1935	Con (Nat)	53.3	1983	Con	42.4
1945	Lab	48.0	1987	Con	42.3
1950	Lab	46.1	1992	Con	41.9

The vagaries of the present voting system are starkly illustrated by the 1951 poll, where the Labour Party won a higher percentage of the vote than the Conservatives but lost the election.
3. 'British government' in this book refers to the United Kingdom Government of Great Britain and Northern Ireland.
4. See Wade and Bradley, *Constitutional and Administrative Law* (11th Edn by Bradley and Ewing), Longman, 1993, at 65–96. The doctrine of parliamentary sovereignty has been partially modified by British membership of the European Union.
5. *Vacher's Parliamentary Companion*, Vacher's Publications, August 1993, lists 382 life peers from a total of 1,223.
6. Ibid., 113 peers take the Labour Whip; of the 775 hereditary peers, 13 take the Labour Whip.
7. Wade and Bradley, 1993, at 51.

8. s75 of the Government of Ireland Act 1920, re-enacted by the 1949 Ireland Act and the 1973 Northern Ireland Constitution Act.
9. See Michael Spencer, *1992 And All That, Civil Liberties in the Balance*, the Civil Liberties Trust, 1990.
10. *Irish Times*, 'Delors Says Sovereignty Now Passing to the EC', 7 August 1988.
11. The Maastricht Treaty proposes that the parliament should have the right to veto the appointment of the President and of the Commission.
12. Wade and Bradley, 1993, at 127–54. Parliament does have the power to reject the budget in its entirety but not to scrutinise or amend it.
13. *Third Periodic Report by the Government of the United Kingdom of Great Britain and Northern Ireland to the United Nations Human Rights Committee Under Article 40, International Covenant on Civil and Political Rights*, October 1989, at 8.
14. *Fourth Periodic Report by the Government of the United Kingdom of Great Britain and Northern Ireland to the United Nations Human Rights Committee Under Article 40, International Covenant on Civil and Political Rights*, 1994, para 17.
15. Ibid., at 2–3.
16. Ibid., para 5.
17. Ibid., para 6.
18. For example, Liberty, *A People's Charter*, NCCL, 1991, and Robert Blackburn (ed.), *A Written Constitution for the United Kingdom*, IPPR, 1993.
19. Wade and Bradley, 1993, at 252–3.
20. Ibid., at 253–4. Between 1957 and 1963, before the Conservative Party chose its leaders by democratic election, the way this discretionary power was exercised caused considerable unease.
21. Wade and Bradley, 1993, at 245–69.
22. *China Navigation Co Ltd v. A-G (1932) 2 KB 197*; *Chandler v. DPP (1964) AC 763*; Crown Proceedings Act 1947.
23. Wade and Bradley, 1993, at 267.
24. Erskine May, *Parliamentary Practice, The Law, Privileges, Proceedings and Usage of Parliament* (Sir C. Gordon [ed.], 20th edn), Butterworth, 1983, at 338.
25. *Daily Telegraph*, 'A Relaxed View of the Rules', 14 December 1993.
26. Wade and Bradley, 1993, at 264–9.
27. Ibid., at 74.
28. Ibid., at 26–9.
29. For example, the prorogation (discontinuation) of Northern Ireland's Stormont parliament followed decades of convention and practice that all matters relating to Northern Ireland could only be discussed there rather than at Westminster.
30. *Hansard*, The Gulf, 21 January 1991, Cols 23–112.
31. Ibid., at 219–20. Adjournment debates take place at the end of the day's public business and provide limited opportunities for discussion.
32. Wade and Bradley, 1993, at 325. Neither the Gulf nor the Falklands conflicts were formally declared as wars. After a declaration of war the government's power to exercise its prerogative powers is greatly extended.
33. *Hansard*, 15 February 1993, Cols 27–38.
34. Ibid.

35. *Hansard,* Treaty of Maastricht (Social Policy), 22 and 23 July 1993, Cols 521–613 and 627–725. The government was defeated on the first substantive vote by 324 votes to 316. It won the confidence motion by 339 votes to 299.
36. See *Public Law,* Sweet and Maxwell, Autumn 1993, at 402–7 for a more detailed discussion.
37. Ibid., at 114–15.
38. See Paddy Hillyard and Janie Piercy-Smith, *The Coercive State*, Fontana, 1988, at 111–42. News reporters had to have their copy approved by as many as five different censors who in some cases changed the direct sense of articles. It took an average of 23 days for documentary footage of the conflict to arrive back in Britain because of obstructions by the authorities.
39. Lord Hailsham, *On the Constitution*, HarperCollins, 1992, at 21–2.
40. Ferdinand Mount, *The British Constitution Now*, Heinemann, 1992, at 107–9.
41. Ibid., at 108.
42. For example, *Guardian,* 'Anger at Tebbit Attack', 11 April 1988 – Prince Charles publicly clashed with Norman Tebbit, a government minister, over unemployment. *The Sunday Times,* 'Queen Dismayed by "Uncaring" Thatcher', 20 July 1986 – The Queen is reported to have been opposed to the government's reluctance to apply sanctions against South Africa. *Daily Mail,* 'Does Britain Need a Terracotta Duke?', 17 October 1986 – A political storm followed the reporting of private remarks by Prince Philip, the Queen's husband, which were alleged to have been racist.
43. *The Times,* 'Archdeacon Raises Wider Unease over Monarchy', 10 December 1993.
44. Peter Wright, *Spycatcher,* Viking, 1987, at 368–72.
45. Georgina Ashworth, *When Will Democracy Include Women?*, Change Thinkbook VII Calverts Press, 1992, at 4.
46. Wade and Bradley, 1993, at 160.
47. *Third Periodic Report,* 1989, at 16.
48. Ibid.
49. *Chief Metropolitan Stipendiary Magistrate* ex parte *P Chaudrey* (1991) 1 QB 427.
50. See Vacher's Publications, 1993.
51. Ibid.
52. The Labour Party, *Statements to Conference,* October 1993, at 35.
53. Vacher's Publications, 1993.
54. Lord Hailsham, *Halsbury's Laws of England* (4th Edn), 1974, Butterworth, vol 8, at 722–35.
55. Wade and Bradley, 1953, at 205.
56. Ibid., at 204–10.
57. The Labour Party, 1993, at 35, proposes replacing the House of Lords with an elected second chamber. *We The People...Towards a Written Constitution,* Liberal Democrats, 1990, included a pledge to replace the House of Lords with an elected second chamber.
58. *Independent,* 'Arafat Treated to a Commons Sandstorm', 15 December 1993.
59. *Public Law,* 'Recent Developments in the Use of Guillotine Motions', Winter 1990, at 496. The minority Labour government of 1979 set the previous record by using the guillotine 11 times in one year.

60. Ibid.
61. Wade and Bradley, 1993, at 623.
62. Ibid., at 625.
63. The Fawcett Society, Uncovering Discrimination, A Response to the UK Government Second Report on the United Nations Convention on all forms of Discrimination Against Women, 1993 (unnumbered).
64. Ibid.
65. Fact Sheet No 5, Appendix C, House of Commons Public Information Office.
66. Wade and Bradley, 1993, at 160.
67. Observer, 'Women Ordained in Church Revolution', 13 March 1994.
68. The Fawcett Society, 1993.
69. Independent, 'Whitehall Set to Remain Male Bastion', 10 May 1993.
70. Kevin Morgan and Ellis Roberts, The Democratic Deficit: A Guide to Quangoland, Cardiff University Papers in Planning Research no 144, 1993, at 19.
71. Ashworth, 1992, at 3.
72. Sunday Telegraph, 'The Diary', 12 April 1992.
73. Population Trends, Office of Population Censuses and Surveys, HMSO, Summer 1991, at 1.
74. Ibid., at 2.
75. Ibid., at 7–11.
76. S2, Para 6, Local Government Finance Act 1988.
77. 'London Loses Over 70,000 Voters', Association of London Authorities, 7 December 1992.
78. Ibid.
79. See Jeremy Smith and Iain McLean, The UK Poll Tax and the Declining Electoral Roll: Consequences for London, University of Warwick, 1992.
80. Ibid., at 3–9.
81. Ibid.
82. Polls Apart: Disabled People and the 1992 General Election, Spastics Society, July 1992.
83. The Electoral Process, RNIB, undated.
84. Campaign for Voting Rights for Homeless People, CHAR, November 1993.
85. Hansard, Written Answer from the Home Secretary, 2 March 1992, Col 43.
86. Sue Shutter, Immigration and Nationality Law Handbook, Joint Council for the Welfare of Immigrants, 1992, at 212.
87. Liberty and Anti-Racist Alliance, Racism: The Destruction of Civil and Political Liberties, NCCL, October 1993.
88. s1 Representation of the People Act 1983.
89. See Howard Davis and John Stewart, The Growth of Government By Appointment. Implications for Local Democracy, Institute for Local Government Studies, University of Birmingham, 1993. See also, Jack Straw MP, The Growth of the Unelected State, A Report on the Transfer of Powers from Elected Local Authorities to Unelected Quangos, and Labour's Response, September 1993.
90. See Norman Lewis and Diane Longley, Accountability in Education, Social Services and Health, European Policy Forum, December 1992.
91. Hansard, Written Answer, 27 July 1993, Col 909.
92. The Financial Times, 'Resurgence of Quangos Defies Thatcherite Initiative', 14 January 1993.

93. *Audit Commission Report and Accounts*, HMSO, 1993.
94. Morgan and Roberts, 1993, at 25–30.
95. *Observer*, John McGhie, 'Tories Put Friends in High Places', 4 July 1993.
96. *Independent on Sunday*, 'Whatever Happened to Democracy', 28 March 1993.
97. See David Marquand et al., *The New Centralism: Britain Out of Step in Europe*, Basil Blackwell, 1989.
98. *Hansard*, Written Answer, 28 October 1993, Cols 735–8, lists the nominees.
99. Paul Bongers, *Local Government in the Single European Market*, Longman, 1992, at 102–5 and 132. See also, *Conference on the European Charter of Local Self-Government, Barcelona 23–25 January 1992*, Council of Europe Press, 1993, Studies and Text no 27.
100. Tony Byrne, *Local Government in Britain*, Penguin, 1992, at 221.
101. Ibid., at 360.
102. See *Passing the Bucks: The Impact of Standard Spending Assessments on Economy, Efficiency and Effectiveness*, HMSO, 1993.
103. See Straw, 1993, at 5.
104. Professor John Stewart, *Accountability to the Public*, European Policy Forum, December 1992, at 5.
105. s4 of The Welsh Language Act 1967 repealed the provision in the Wales and Berwick Act 1746 that the term 'England', when used in an Act of Parliament, should be taken to include the dominion of Wales and the town of Berwick-on-Tweed.
106. Wade and Bradley, 1993, at 39. Wales was militarily defeated by England in the thirteenth century. In 1536 an act of the English parliament united Wales with England and granted Welsh representation in the English parliament.
107. Ibid.
108. Wade and Bradley, 1993, at 38–9. In 1906 a Welsh Department of Board Education was established. The Church of England, to which few Welsh people belonged, was disestablished in 1914. In 1964 the Welsh Office was created which grew rapidly, accompanied by a growing number of other all-Wales bodies.
109. See John Osmond, *The Democratic Challenge*, Gower Press, 1992, at 12–14.
110. Ibid., 26–32.
111. Wade and Bradley, *Constitutional and Administrative Law*, Longman (10th edition) at 404. 79% voted against and 21% in favour, on a turnout of 58%.
112. See Osmond, 1992.
113. Support for the creation of a Welsh Assembly was in all three parties' 1992 general election manifestos.
114. See BBC News and Current Affairs and Vacher's Publications, 1992.
115. Vacher's Publications, 1993.
116. Ibid.
117. Morgan and Roberts, 1993, at 24.
118. Ibid., at 22.
119. Ibid., at 5.
120. Ibid., at 7.
121. Osmond, 1992, at 16–21.
122. Ibid., at 19.
123. Ibid., at 16.

124. *Western Mail*, 'Quangos out of Control', 15 September 1993.
125. Morgan and Roberts, 1993, at 28.
126. Ibid.
127. J.A.G. Griffiths and Michael Ryle, *Parliament: Functions, Practice and Procedures*, Sweet and Maxwell, 1989, at 361.
128. *House of Commons Journal*, 1974–5, at 92.
129. Osmond, 1992, at 33.
130. Craig (ed.), 1989, at 150. The vote was 51.6% in favour and 48.4% against on a 63.6% turnout.
131. See Andrew Marr, *The Battle for Scotland*, Penguin, 1992.
132. The Act of Adjournment passed on 25 March 1707 stated that the parliament was to meet again in April the following year.
133. Government of Scotland Bills: 1906, 1908, 1911, 1912, 1913, 1914, 1919, 1920, 1922 (and a Government of Wales and Scotland Bill) 1924, 1926, 1927, 1928, 1967, 1974 (Scotland and Wales), 1976 (Scotland and Wales), 1986, 1987, 1989.
134. See Marr, 1992 for more details.
135. Wade and Bradley, 1993, at 50–1.
136. s85 Scotland Act 1978.
137. Craig (ed.), 1989, at 147. The vote was 58.4% for and 41.6% against. The turnout was 61.7%. This means that only 36% of the population on the electoral register voted in favour of the proposal.
138. *Towards Scotland's Parliament: Report to the Scottish People by the Scottish Constitutional Convention*, Edinburgh, 1990.
139. *Independence in Europe – Make it Happen Now!*, Scottish National Party general election manifesto 1992.
140. The Labour Party, Liberal Democrats, Scottish National Party and Conservative Party all favour Scotland's membership of the European Community and the process of European integration. Only the Green Party and the British National Party, neither of which have parliamentary representation, oppose this. The main parties all support the Maastricht Treaty and only the Conservatives oppose inclusion of the Social Chapter.
141. See for example, *The Modern Law Review*, Professor Neil MacCormick, 'Beyond the Sovereign State', January 1993.
142. BBC News and Current Affairs and Vacher's Publications, 1992. The Labour Party won 39% and 49 seats, compared to 42.4% in the 1987 general election. The Liberal Democrats won 13.1% and 9 seats compared to 19.2% in 1987. The Scottish National Party won 21.5% and 3 seats compared with 14% in 1987.
143. Craig (ed.), 1989, at 2, 47 and 49. The Conservatives won 25.7% of the vote in 1992 compared with 24% in the 1987 election and 28.4% in 1983.
144. See Marr, 1992.
145. Article 18, Act of Union 1707.
146. Article 19, Act of Union 1707.
147. Wade and Bradley, 1993, at 397–407.
148. *MacCormick v. Lord Advocate* (1953) SLT 255.
149. Wade and Bradley, 1993, at 397–407.
150. Marr, 1992, at 176–80. A pledge to include the Community Charge Act 1987 was included in the Conservatives' manifesto of the same year. The impli-

cations of the tax were highlighted by the other main parties and are believed to have contributed to the large swing against the Conservatives.

151. *Make a Date With Democracy, Proceedings of Charter 88's First Constitutional Convention*, Charter 88, 1990, at 34–41.
152. Figures released by the Department of Employment in November 1993 showed the unemployment rate in Scotland had dropped below the UK average for the first time in over two decades.
153. *Regions*, Regional Studies Association, August 1993.
154. See Hamish Paton, *Scotland's Second Chance, Energy and Opportunity – Post 1993*, Scottish Centre for Economic and Social Research, August 1992.
155. *Recovery in Scotland Make It Happen Now!*, Scottish National Party, 1992.
156. See *The Great Gas Robbery*, SNP research department, February 1990, October 1993.
157. *Steel Industrial Statistics*, UK Steel Information Service, 12 November 1993. Factors other than discrimination undoubtedly account for the collapse of the Scottish steel industry but the contrast between Scotland and England is noteworthy.
158. *Scotsman*, 'Laing Urged to put Job on Line over Rosyth', 10 June 1993.
159. See Spencer, 1990, and Liberty, *Memorandum on the European Community Accession to the European Convention on Human Rights*, February 1992. See *Official Journal of the European Communities*, 18 July 1988, C77, at 229, in which the European Parliament passed a resolution drawing attention to the 'democratic deficit'. In 1992 it adopted the *Final Report on the Intergovernmental Conference in the Context of Parliament's Strategy for European Union*, A3–0123/92, European Parliament 1990, David Martin (rapporteur).
160. For more details see *Maastricht: The Treaty on European Union – The Position of the European Parliament*, Office for Official Publications of the European Communities, 1992.
161. *Costa v. ENEL*, Case 6/64 (1964) CMLR 425.
162. Wade and Bradley, 1993, at 334–5.
163. Ibid.
164. Article 21 of the UN's *Universal Declaration on Human Rights* states that: 'Everyone shall have the right to take part in the government of his country, directly or through freely chosen representatives . . . The will of the people shall be the basis of the authority of government.' Article 3 of the first protocol of the *European Convention on Human Rights* states that free elections should be held 'which will ensure the free expression of the people in the choice of the legislature.'
165. *The European Community and Human Rights*, European File 5/89, Office for Official Publications of the European Communities, Luxembourg, 1989, cited in Spencer, 1990, at 131.
166. See Spencer, 1990, at 132. The Single European Act 1987 (SEA) inserted two new Articles, 118a and 118b, into the 1957 Treaty of Rome. The first concerns health and safety and allows the Commission to issue binding Directives on member states by a qualified majority voting system. The second urges the Commission to develop dialogue between workers and employers at a European level to promote 'relations based on agreement'. The SEA did also refer to the ECHR without giving it legal force.

Notes

167. Spencer, 1990, at 133.
168. *Report from the Select Committee on the Committee Work of the House*, 1991–2, House of Lords Paper 35, vol II, at 226.
169. Spencer, 1990, at 133.
170. *International Handelsgesellschaft*, case 11/70 (1970) ECR 1125, at 1134.
171. Wade and Bradley, 1993, at 424. France ratified the Convention in 1974. It was the last member to do so.
172. For a discussion of the consequences of ratification see House of Lords Report, *Human Rights Re-Examined, Session 1992–3, Third Report*, HL Paper 10.
173. Spencer, 1990, at 135–6.
174. *House of Commons Foreign Affairs Committee*, Second Report 1992–3, para 111.
175. Ibid.
176. Article 25 of the ECHR provides a right of individual petition.
177. *State of the Question of Accession by the European Community to the European Convention on Human Rights*, Féderation Internationale des Droits de l'Homme, 1993.
178. Different members of the Council send different-sized delegations. Decisions can be reached if they are in line with proposals from the Commission by a vote of 54 of the 76 members. If the Council wishes to deviate from the Commission's proposals, unanimity is required.
179. See *Memorandum to an Enquiry by the House of Lords Select Committee on the European Communities into Parliamentary Scrutiny of Inter-Governmental Co-operation*, NCCL, May 1993.
180. See *House of Lords Scrutiny of the Intergovernmental Pillars of the European Union, Session 1992–3, Twenty-eighth Report*, HL Paper 124.

2 Criminal Justice and Human Rights

1. *R v. Callaghan and Others* (1992) 2 All ER 417.
2. Chris Mullin, *Error of Judgment: The Truth About the Birmingham Bombings*, Poolbeg, 1987 at 237–43.
3. *R v. Richardson and Others, The Times*, 'Law report', 20 October 1989.
4. *Brathwaite v. UK*, 18 April 1991 No 15/23/89 (Appeal Court Judgment Lord Justice Farquharson 25 Nov–5 Dec 1991).
5. See David Rose, *A Climate of Fear: The Murder of PC Blakelock and the Case of the Tottenham Three*, Bloomsbury, 1992.
6. *Daily Telegraph* 'Infertility Cited as Proof of Convicted Killer's Innocence', 18 February 1992.
7. *Hansard*, Written Answer, 28 February 1992, col 653.
8. *R v. Miller, Paris and Abdullahi, The Times*, 'Law report', 24 December 1992, CA.
9. *R v. Ward, The Times*, 'Law report', 8 June 1992.
10. See Liberty, *A Case to Answer: A Dossier of 111 Cases Where the Conviction May be Unsafe*, 1992; and Liberty, *Further Cases to Answer: A Revised Dossier of 163 Cases Where the Convictions May be Unsafe*, 1992. This dossier is continually being updated and now contains over 200 cases.
11. *The Royal Commission on Criminal Justice Report*, Chairman Viscount Runciman, HMSO, Cm 2263, 1993.

12. Mike McConville and Lee Bridges (ed.), *Criminal Justice in Crisis*, Legal Research Institute, 1994, at xv.
13. Royal Commission, 1993, recommendation 22.
14. Ibid., recommendations 13–21.
15. Ibid., recommendation 114.
16. Ibid., recommendations 156–63.
17. Ibid., recommendations 132–8.
18. *Fourth Periodic Report by the Government of the United Kingdom of Great Britain and Northern Ireland to the United Nations Human Rights Committee Under Article 40, International Covenant on Civil and Political Rights*, 1994, para 315.
19. See Liberty, *Let Justice Be Done: Report to the Commission on Criminal Justice*, 1991; see also, Peter Thornton QC, Ann Mallalieu QC and Anthony Scrivener QC, *Justice on Trial: Report on the Independent Civil Liberty Panel on Criminal Justice*, Civil Liberties Trust, 1992.
20. Royal Commission, 1993, recommendations 331–52.
21. Ibid., recommendations 82–90.
22. *Independent* 'Howard Seeks to Placate "Angry Majority" ', 7 October 1993.
23. *Hansard*, Bills Presented, 16 December 1993 col 1297.
24. *Hansard*, Royal Assent, 3 November 1994, col 1631.
25. *HMSO Daily List*, Statutory Instruments issued on 30 January 1995, *The Criminal Justice and Public Order Act 1994 (Commencement No 5 and Transitional Provisions) Order 1995*, 31 January 1995.
26. ss44 and 46 Criminal Justice and Public Order Act 1994.
27. s32 Criminal Justice and Public Order Act 1994.
28. s82 Criminal Justice and Public Order Act 1994.
29. ss60 and 81 Criminal Justice and Public Order Act 1994.
30. ss61–80 Criminal Justice and Public Order Act 1994.
31. ss1–15 Criminal Justice and Public Order Act 1994.
32. ss54–59 Criminal Justice and Public Order Act 1994.
33. *Independent*, 24 March 1994.
34. See Beverly Steventon, *The Ability to Challenge DNA Evidence*, Royal Commission on Criminal Justice, Research Study 9, HMSO, 1993.
35. See Paul Roberts and Chris Willmore *The Role of Forensic Science Evidence in Criminal Proceedings*, Royal Commission on Criminal Justice, Research Study 11, HMSO, 1993.
36. For example *R* v. *Callaghan and Others* (1992) 2 All ER 417 and *R* v. *Ward*, *The Times*, 'Law report', 8 June 1992.
37. Ibid.
38. Chris Mullin, *Error of Judgment: The Truth About the Birmingham Bombings*, Poolbeg, 1987.
39. See James Wood and Adam Crawford, *The Right of Silence, the Case for Retention*, the Civil Liberties Trust, 1989.
40. See also, Mike McConville and Dr Jacqueline Hodgson, *Custodial Legal Advice and the Right to Silence* and Joyce Plotnikoff, *Information and Advice for Prisoners About Grounds for Appeal*, Research for the Royal Commission on Criminal Justice, 1993.
41. See *The Right of Silence, Liberty Parliamentary Briefing*, NCCL, 1993.
42. Ibid.

43. See Michael Mansfield *Presumed Guilty, the British Criminal Justice System Exposed*, Heinemann, 1993.
44. See Clive Walker and Keir Starmer (eds), *Justice in Error*, Blackstone Press, 1993.
45. See Andrew Sanders and Richard Young, *Criminal Justice*, Butterworth, 1994.
46. Andrew Sanders et al., *Advice and Assistance at Police Stations and the 24-hour Duty Solicitors Scheme*, Lord Chancellor's Department, 1989, at 59.
47. McConville and Hodgson, 1993, at 176.
48. *Murray* v. *UK* (27 June 1994) App 1 No 18731/91.
49. Ibid.
50. *CRE Connections*, January 1995.
51. s66 Police and Criminal Evidence Act 1984 (Codes of Practice). Under the Act the Home Secretary can issue codes of practice delineating minimum standards of conduct.
52. s24 Police and Criminal Evidence Act 1984.
53. s116 Police and Criminal Evidence Act 1984.
54. ss41–44 Police and Criminal Evidence Act 1984.
55. Police powers are contained in the Act itself, not the codes. Thus, power to deny access to solicitors is in the Act, while responsibility to inform suspects of the right to contact a solicitor is in a code.
56. ss81–100 Police and Criminal Evidence Act 1984.
57. See Harrison and Cragg, *Police Misconduct*, Legal Action Group, 1991.
58. *Independent*, 'Police Took Action in 20% of Discipline Cases', 15 April 1993.
59. *Hansard*, Written Answer, 9 February 1995, cols 378–9.
60. ss56–8 Police and Criminal Evidence Act 1984. Access can be delayed if, as a result of contact with a solicitor, police believe that evidence or property will be tampered with or other suspects notified. See also, Geoffrey Robertson, *Freedom, The Individual and the Law*, Penguin, 1989, at 39.
61. Sanders and Bridges, *Criminal Law Review 495*, 'Access to Advice and Police Malpractice' (1990), at 499.
62. See Gisli Gudjonsson, Isabel Clare, Susan Rutter and John Pearce, *Persons at Risk During Interviews in Police Custody: The Identification of Vulnerabilities*, Royal Commission on Criminal Justice, Research Study 12, HMSO, 1993 at 18.
63. See Andrew Sanders, et al., 1989.
64. McConville and Hodgson, 1993. at 191–2.
65. *Guardian*, 'Mackay Calls for Legal Aid Bar on Rich', 21 December 1994.
66. See Richard Young, Timothy Maloney and Andrew Sanders, *In the Interests of Justice?: The Declaration of Criminal Legal Aid Applications by Magistrates' Courts in England and Wales*, Report to the Legal Aid Board, 1992.
67. *R* v. *Lord Chancellor* ex parte the Law Society, *Independent*, 4 May 1993.
68. *R* v. *Richardson and Others*, *The Times*, 'Law report', 20 October 1989 and *R* v. *Ward*, *The Times*, 'Law report', 8 June 1992.
69. *R* v. *Ward*, *The Times*, 'Law report', 8 June 1992.
70. *R* v. *Johnson, Davis and Row*, *Independent*, 22 January 1993.
71. *R* v. *Bromley Justices* ex parte *Smith*, 4 November 1994.
72. Liberty, *Unequal Before the Law*, 1992 (citing statistics for 1990) at 2.
73. Ibid.

74. Roger Hood, *Race and Sentencing: Report for the Commission for Racial Equality*, Clarendon Press, 1992, at 40.
75. Thornton, Mallalieu and Scrivener, 1992, at 24–35.
76. Ibid., at 24.
77. Ibid.
78. Ibid.
79. See Kate Malleson, *A Review of the Appeals Process*, Royal Commission on Criminal Justice, Research Studies 17 and 18, HMSO, 1993.
80. Mullin, 1987, at 216.
81. s17 of the Criminal Appeals Act 1968.
82. Paul Hill, *Stolen Years*, Corgi, 1991, at 262–70.
83. Criminal Appeal Bill, 23 February 1995.
84. Clause 17 Criminal Appeal Bill.
85. Clauses 1 and 2 Criminal Appeal Bill. Cases will no longer be referred automatically on points in law.
86. See Stephen Livingstone and Tim Owen, *Prison Law*, Clarendon Press, 1993.
87. *Prison Disturbances April 1990, Report of an Inquiry* (Woolf Report), HMSO, Cm 1456, 1991, paras. 11.81–11.112.
88. CPT, para 57, 26 November 1991.
89. *Guardian*, 'Tumim Blames Overcrowding for "Well Below Standard" Jail', 15 February 1995.
90. Martin Wasik and Richard Taylor, *Blackstone's Guide to the Criminal Justice Act 1991*, Blackstone Press, 2nd edn, 1994, at 2. Council of Europe figures show UK custodial population 97.4 per 100,000: France (81.1), Sweden (50.6), Greece (44) and Holland (40).
91. *Fourth Periodic Report*, 1994, para 196.
92. *Hansard*, Written Answer, 20 December 1994, col 1203. On 1 September 1993 there were 53,400 people in British prisons over 4000 fewer prisoners than in February 1995.
93. Prison population of England and Wales, 24 February 1995–50,699 (letter from Home Office, S2 Division, 28 February 1995). Total prison population of Northern Ireland, 27 February 1995–1,845 (letter from Northern Ireland Office, statistics and research branch 28 February 1995). Scottish Office unable to give precise figures but estimate the Scottish prison population at 5,650 (letter from Scottish Office, home and health department, 28 February 1995).
94. *Fourth Periodic Report*, 1994, para 197.
95. s1 of the Criminal Justice Act 1991 states that offenders should be imprisoned for 'serious offences' only and created a set of criteria to assist the courts in determining when the imposition of a custodial sentence is appropriate. This was amended in s66 of the Criminal Justice Act 1993. s29 of the Criminal Justice Act 1991 required courts to disregard an offender's previous convictions when passing sentence. This provision was repealed by the Criminal Justice Act 1993.
96. *NACRO Briefing*, 'Prison Overcrowding', National Association for the Care and Rehabilitation of Offenders, July 1994.
97. Ibid.
98. *Fourth Periodic Report*, 1994, para 201.
99. Ibid., para 203.

100. *Hansard*, Written Answer, 5 May 1994, col 626.
101. Prison Reform Trust, *Prison Report*, 20 (1992), 17.
102. *Guardian*, 'Jail Security Crackdown Will Halt Reform Schemes', 31 January 1995.
103. Michael Howard, 'Conference Speech', Conservative Central Office, 13 October 1994.
104. *Guardian*, 31 January 1995.
105. *NACRO Briefing*, July 1994.
106. Woolf, 1991, para 14.225.
107. *Fourth Periodic Report*, 1994, para 248.
108. Letter to Liberty's legal department from Mairead UiAdhmaill, 23 January 1995.
109. *Campbell v. UK* (1992), 15 EHRR 137, series A, No 233.
110. Prisoners Advice Service, unpublished report 1995.
111. *Knight v. Home Office* (1990) 3 All ER 237.
112. *The Howard League, Fact Sheet 11 on Remand in Custody*, Howard League for Penal Reform, 1994.
113. *Hansard*, Written Answer, 14 December 1994, col 644.
114. Livingstone and Owen, 1993, at 121.
115. *Hansard*, Written Answer, 5 May 1994, col 626: 41 deaths in prisons, 1992, 20 remand prisoners; 47 deaths, 1993, 24 remand prisoners.
116. Howard League, 1994, in 1991 74,603 people spent time in prison on remand. Of these, 31,489 subsequently received a prison sentence, 14,216 were given a non-custodial sentence by the courts, 2,418 were found not guilty or charges were not proceeded with and 26,480 people's disposal was not recorded but they were not sent to a prison in England and Wales.
117. NACRO Briefing, July 1994.
118. Woolf, 1991, para 14.293.
119. Livingstone and Owen, 1993, at 76.
120. David Feldman, *Civil Liberties and Human Rights in England and Wales*, Clarendon Press, 1993, at 280.
121. *Becker v. Home Office* (1972), *Submission to Phase 2 of the Woolf Inquiry into Prison Disturbances*, September 1990, Prison Reform Trust, at 12.
122. Livingstone and Owen, 1993, at 19.
123. *Guardian*, 'Prison Governors Plead for Legal Curb on Overcrowding', 10 May 1994.
124. *R v. Governor of Parkhurst Prison* ex parte *Hague; Weldon v. Home Office* (1990), 3 WLR 1253; (1991) 3 All ER 733.
125. Circular Instructions (CI) were internal administrative directives to which prisoners had no access. They were replaced with Advice to the Governors (AI) in 1992. CI 37/90 was replaced by A I 28/93.
126. Livingstone and Owen, 1993, at 45.
127. Woolf, 1991, para. 14.345
128. Livingstone and Owen, 1993, at 29.
129. Circular Instruction 26/1990.
130. Livingstone and Owen, 1993, at 37.
131. *Campbell and Fell v. UK*, 7 EHRR 165, Series A, No 80.
132. Backed-up by Standing Order 1992/514.
133. Loss of remission can no longer be imposed.

134. *Daily Mail* (29 September 1994, 'Instant Jail Justice') reports that the Home Secretary has plans to give prison governors the power to increase the sentences they can impose beyond the current maximum of 28 days.
135. Prisoners Advice Service, unofficial figure from Home Office employees who review adjudications.
136. *Hansard*, Written Answer, 8 December 1994, col 332. Concerns have been raised as to the standard of care afforded prisoners in privately run or contracted-out prisons and remand centres. In Doncaster prison for example only 60 (14%) of the 450 staff have had any experience in the prison service.
137. Letter to Liberty's legal department from Derek Lewis, Director General, HM Prison Service, 29 November 1994.
138. Prison Reform Trust, unpublished report 1995.
137. Ibid.
140. Ibid.
141. Prisoners Advice Service, unpublished report, February 1995. Prisoners who are being reviewed under the new system are facing delays of between 3 and 6 months from their parole date before receiving an answer.
142. *Weeks v. UK* 1988, 10 EHRR 293; *Wilson and Gunnell v. UK*, 1990, EHRR, 666.
143. Article 6.1, the right to fair trial.
144. *Fourth Periodic Report*, 1994, para 222.
145. Section 34, *Criminal Justice Act 1991*.
146. *Taylor v. UK* – Preliminary hearing 2 December 1994.
147. These changes followed the decision in the House of Lords in *R v. Secretary of State for the Home Department* ex parte *Doody* 1993 3 WLR 154).
148. *R v. Secretary of State* ex parte *Raja and Riaz*, 16 December 1994 DC.
149. Feldman, 1993, at 298. In the case of *R v. Secretary of State* ex parte *Cox*, Popperwell described as perverse the Home Secretary's decision to cancel the provisional release date of a life sentence prisoner who, whilst at a pre-release hostel, was found in possession of a fraudulent tax disc and a small amount of cannabis. Without Popperwell's intervention he would have remained in a closed prison for several years.
150. s39, *Criminal Justice Act 1991*.
151. *Weeks v. UK* (1988) 10 EHRR 293.
152. *Hussain and Singh v. UK*, App no 21928/93. Ruling – 19 December 1994.
153. See Una Padel, Rose Twidale, John Porter, *HIV Education in Prisons*, Health Education Authority, in association with SCODA, 1992.
154. Ibid.
155. Ibid.
156. Ibid.
157. Ibid.
158. *Third Periodic Report by the Government of the United Kingdom of Great Britain and Northern Ireland to the United Nations Human Rights Committee Under Article 40, International Covenant on Civil and Political Rights*, 1989, at 11.
159. Hood, 1992, at 3.
160. Ibid.
161. Ibid., at 178.
162. *Third Periodic Report*, 1989, at 11.

Notes

163. *Fourth Periodic Report*, 1994, paras 26 and 27.
164. See Hood, 1992, at 127–31.
165. *Third Periodic Report*, 1989, at 11–12.
166. See Liberty, *Further Cases To Answer*, 1992.
167. Correspondence received by Liberty (legal department).
168. Ibid.
169. *Home Office Statistical Bulletin*, June 1989.
170. *Race and the Law*, Labour Research, August 1992, at 10 (citing studies of Bristol, Bath and London by the Commission for Racial Equality).
171. *Deadly Silence: Black Deaths in Custody*, Institute of Race Relations, 1991, at 68 (citing NACRO, *Race and Criminal Justice*, 1989).
172. Andy Shallice and Paul Gordon *Black People, White Justice? Race and the Criminal Justice System*, 1990 and *Deadly Silence*, at 68.
173. *Hansard*, Written Answer, 11 November 1991, Cols 339. Roger Hood concludes that the over-representation of black women prisoners in the areas he studied, 'was due entirely to the number and the legally relevant characteristics of those appearing in Crown Court and not to any overall discrimination in the way in which they are treated by the courts'. Hood, 1992, at 207.
174. Ibid.
175. *Labour Research*, August 1992.
176. *Newham Monitor Quarterly Bulletin*, Spring 1993.
177. *R v. McKenzie* (1992) NLJ 1162.
178. *R v. Ward* (1992) 96 Cr App R 1, *The Times*, 8 June 1992.
179. *R v. Kiszko* (1978) 68 Cr App R 62 (1992) *The Times*, 18 February 1992.
180. *Guardian*, 'Denied a Fair Hearing', 6 October 1993.
181. Council for the Advancement of Communication with Deaf People, *1993 Directory*, Durham University, 1993.
182. *Daily Telegraph*, 'Deaf Boy's Confession "Concocted by Police",' 8 February 1994.
183. *British Deaf News*, 'Deaf People Want Equality in Jury Service', November 1993.
184. *Daily Telegraph*, 'Judge Rejects the First Deaf Juror', 21 January 1994.
185. See for example, Seear and Player, *Women in the Penal System*, Howard League for Penal Reform, 1986, at 4.
186. Women's National Commission, *Women and Prison, Report of an ad-hoc Working Group*, Cabinet Office, February 1991, at 2.
187. *Hansard*, Written Answer, 22 March 1993, col 447.
188. Hood, 1992, at 176–7.
189. Helena Kennedy, *Eve Was Framed*, Chatto and Windus, 1992, at 65–81.
190. Seear and Player, 1986, at 3.
191. Women's National Commission, *Women and Prison, Report of an ad-hoc Working Group*, Cabinet Office, February 1991, at 12.
192. *Submission to the Royal Commission on Criminal Justice*, Hackney Council Women's Unit, 1991, at 17.
193. Women's National Commission, 1991, at 12–13.
194. Ibid.
195. Ibid., at 16. In 1989 2,500 women were sentenced to immediate custody. In the same year 180,700 women were fined and 685 women were imprisoned for non-payment of fines.

389

196. *Hansard*, Written Answer, 22 March 1993, col 446.
197. Women's National Commission, 1991, at 7. The figures it cites are for 1989. These show that 30% of untried and 47% of convicted unsentenced women prisoners remanded in custody were subsequently freed or given a non-custodial sentence, compared to 23% and 32% respectively of men.
198. Silvia Casale, *Women Inside: The Experience of Women Remand Prisoners in Holloway*, Civil Liberties Trust, 1989, at 13.
199. *Report of an Unannounced Short Inspection by HM Inspectorate of Prisons to HM Prison Durham*, 28 April 1993, at 28.
200. Committee on the Administration of Justice, *Annual Report 1992–3*. In November 1992, the government's Inter-Departmental Working Group on the Transfer of Prisoners recommended that prisoners from Northern Ireland be transferred to Northern Ireland to serve their sentences nearer their families.
201. *Observer* 'Six IRA Men to be Sent Home', 4 September 1994.
202. Sinn Fein Prisoner of War Department, February 1995.
203. See *Prison Disturbances April 1990, Report of an Inquiry by the Rt Hon Lord Justice Woolf and his Honour Judge Stephen Tumin*, HMSO, 1991, Section 15, Recommendations and Proposals, at 433–4.
204. Women's National Commission, 1991, at 3.
205. Mary Eaton, *Women After Prison*, Oxford University Press, 1993, at 36.
206. Women's National Commission, 1991, at 33.
207. Ibid., at 25.
208. Eaton, 1993, at 30.
209. *Hansard*, Written Answer, 31 January 1994, cols 563–8.
210. Kennedy, 1992, at 184.
211. Ibid.
212. See Paddy Hillyard, *Suspect Community, People's Experiences of the Prevention of Terrorism Acts in Britain*, Pluto Press, 1993.
213. Ibid.
214. *Guardian*, 'Muslim Fights Jail Strip Searches', 15 February 1994.
215. *Hansard*, Written Answers, 14 April 1993, col 626. Most metal detectors will not detect syringes but the police scientific branch has been commissioned to design one that will. X-ray machines are another alternative. Various forensic tests can establish if people have been in contact with drugs or explosives.
216. See *Strip-searching, Personal Testimonies, Report of an Inquiry into the Psychological Effects of Strip-searching*, the United Campaign Against Strip-searching, 1989.
217. *Hansard*, Written Answer, 16 June 1993, col 576.
218. *Hansard*, Written Answer, 10 February 1989, cols 836–7.
219. Ibid.
220. Ibid.
221. Men can also be prosecuted for offences relating to prostitution but this report focuses on their effects on women.
222. s1 The Street Offenses Act 1959. This makes it an offence 'for a common prostitute to loiter and solicit for the purposes of prostitution.'
223. See Frederique Delacoste and Priscilla Alexander, *Sex Work, Writings by Women in the Sex Industry*, Virago, 1988.
224. *English Collective of Prostitutes statement*, 13 September 1993.
225. Ibid.

226. s33 Sexual Offenses Act 1956.
227. s34 Sexual Offenses Act 1956.
228. *Independent on Sunday*, 'CPS Accused of Ignoring Rape Against Prostitutes', 25 July 1993.
229. See Delacoste and Alexander, 1989.
230. Caroline Gooding, *Trouble with the Law?*, GMP, 1992, at 217.
231. s12 Sexual Offenses Act 1956.
232. s13 Sexual Offenses Act 1956.
233. s1 Sexual Offenses Act 1967.
234. s145 Criminal Justice and Public Order Act 1994.
235. Gooding, 1992, at 219.
236. For example, *Pink Paper*, 'Thirty-eight Men Arrested in Police Swoop on Gay Party', 16 May 1993.
237. s36 Disorderly House Act 1751.
238. *Pink Paper*, 'Police Arrest 13 in Club Swoop', 29 April 1994.
239. *Capital Gay*, 'Crowd Mobs Raid Officers in Mineshaft Protest', 13 May 1994.
240. *R v. Brown and Others*, NLJ Law Reports, 19 March 1993.
241. *The Times*, '15 Men Convicted of Degrading and Vicious Practices', 20 December 1990.
242. See for example, *Pink Paper*, 16 May 1993.
243. *Laskey v. UK*, 18 January 1995 App l No 21627/93.
244. Paul Crane, *Gays and the Law*, Pluto Press, 1982, at 36.
245. Ibid., at 16.
246. *New Law Journal*, 'Homosexuality and the Police', 6 March 1992.
247. s5 Public Order Act 1936 or s54(13) Metropolitan Police Act 1939.
248. *Independent*, 'Smoke Stirs Passengers Unmoved by Public Sex', 7 August 1992. Other passengers eventually objected when the couple had a post-coital cigarette in a no smoking carriage.
249. *Independent on Sunday*, 'Police "Stirred up Anti-gay Protest",' 27 October 1991.
250. Peter Tatchell, *Europe in the Pink*, GMP, 1992, at 87.
251. *Masterson v. Holden* (1986) 3 All ER 39. Two men were convicted of insulting behaviour after they had been seen kissing at a bus stop at 1.55 am.
252. *Gay Times*, 'Police Threaten Men for Holding Hands', July 1988.
253. *Pink Paper*, 'Gay Scotsman in Frock Fight', 14 October 1989.
254. *R v. Kirkupp* (1992) 96 Cr App R 352. See also, Helen Power, *New Law Journal*, 'Entrapment and Gay Rights', 15 January 1993.
255. *R v. Gray* (1981) 74 Cr App 324 CA.
256. s4(1) Sexual Offenses Act 1967.
257. *Gay London Policing*, GALOP, 10th Annual Report, 1992
258. See Walmsely and White for the Home Office, *Sexual Offenses, Consent and Sentencing*, HMSO, 1979.
259. Home Office, *Crime Statistics 1990*, HMSO, 1992, Table 2.11, at 49.
260. *Pink Paper*, 'Criminal Injustice', 26 October 1991.
261. *Pink Paper*, 'Labour MP wants Inquiry', 6 July 1991.
262. Helena Jeffs, *Age of consent for male homosexual acts*, Research Paper 94/12, Home Affairs Section, House of Commons Library, 20 January 1994, at 56.

263. Ibid.
264. Ibid., at 58.
265. Ibid., at 56.
266. Ibid., at 57.
267. Ibid., at 58.
268. Ibid.
269. Gooding, 1992, at 221.
270. s1 Sexual Offenses Act 1967.
271. s1(b) Sexual Offenses Act 1967.
272. *Pink Paper,* 'Criminal Injustice', 26 October 1991.
273. Gooding, 1992, at 230.
274. Tatchell, 1992, at 89.
275. Ibid.
276. *Pink Paper,* 'Criminal Injustice', 26 October 1991.
277. s37 Sexual Offenses Act 1956, and Schedule II (32).
278. s1(b) Sexual Offices Act 1967.
279. Gooding, 1992, at 215.
280. Crane, 1982, at 41.
281. *Pink Paper,* 'Police to Blame for 21% of Anti-gay Abuse', 22 November 1992.
282. Ben Summerskill, 'Lesbian and Gay Police Officers in the Met', in *Policing Without Prejudice,* the Association of London Authorities, March 1991.
283. *Pink Paper,* 'Brighton Rape Sparks Police Row', 1 April 1994.
284. Ibid.
285. *Capital Gay,* 'Police Chief in "Lezzie" Jibe Reinstated', 6 May 1994.
286. Gooding, 1992, at 281–2.
287. Adam Sampson, *Acts of Abuse,* Routledge, 1992, at 83–5.
288. Gooding, 1992, at 282.
289. Crane, 1982, at 59.
290. Gooding, 1992, at 281–2.

3 Racism in England and Wales

1. The Natt case was reported extensively in the British media including all the national newspapers and main television news bulletins. We are grateful to the Newham Monitoring Project who helped highlight the case. The details are taken from their *1992/3 Annual Report.*
2. *Police Review,* 7 August 1992.
3. The terms black and ethnic minority are both used in an inclusive sense in this report, to mean non-white minority groups. The experiences of Irish people, Jewish people and Travellers are addressed separately.
4. *Guardian,* 17 September 1993, 'Far Right British National Party wins Council seat in East End'. The results were: British National Party, 1,480; Labour, 1,473; Liberal Democrats, 1,284; Conservatives, 134.
5. Martin Walker, *The National Front,* Fontana, 1977, at 198. In May 1976 two candidates of the National Party, a splinter from the National Front, were elected to council seats in Blackburn, Lancashire.
6. *Searchlight,* June 1994.
7. *Second Review of the Race Relations Act 1976:* Commission for Racial Equal-

ity, 1992, at 12. See also, *Second Review of the Race Relations Act 1976: A Consultative Paper*, CRE, 1991, at 12.

8. *Fourth Periodic Report by the Government of the United Kingdom of Great Britain and Northern Ireland to the United Nations Human Rights Committee Under Article 40, International Covenant on Civil and Political Rights*, 1994, para 22.

9. *National Monitor 1991 Census of Great Britain*, Table J, Ethnic Groups, Cen 91 CM56, OPCS, December 1992. According to the Census, 94.5% of the population of Great Britain is white while 5.5% is non-white.

Black Caribbean	0.9%	Pakistani	0.9%
African	0.4%	Bangladeshi	0.3%
Other	0.3%	Chinese	0.3%
Indian	1.5%	Other Asian	0.4%
		Other	0.5%

10. *Third Periodic Report by the Government of the United Kingdom of Great Britain and Northern Ireland to the United Nations Human Rights Committee Under Article 40, International Covenant on Civil and Political Rights*, October 1989, para 21.

11. *Third Periodic Report*, 1989, para 23.

12. *Fourth Periodic Report*, 1994, para 19.

13. Ibid., para 38.

14. Ibid., para 28.

15. s154 Criminal Justice and Public Order Act 1994.

16. ss4–15 Race Relations Act 1976.

17. Ibid., ss17–19.

18. Ibid., ss21–4.

19. Ibid., s20.

20. Ibid., s1.

21. s17–23 Public Order Act 1986.

22. s43 Race Relations Act 1976.

23. Ibid.

24. *Fourth Periodic Report*, 1994, para 33.

25. *Third Periodic Report*, 1989, at 15.

26. Ibid., at 114–15.

27. *Third Periodic Report*, 1989, at 15.

28. Consultation Review, CRE, 1991, at 5.

29. s1 Race Relations Act 1976.

30. Ibid.

31. *Kuldip Singh v. British Rail Engineering Ltd* (1986) ICR 22.

32. *Perera v. Civil Service Commission* (1983) IRLR 166.

33. *Wong v. GLC* EAT 524/79.

34. s2 Race Relations Act 1976.

35. CRE Review, 1992, at 28.

36. Ibid., at 28–9.

37. Ibid., at 19.

38. *Amin v. Entry Clearance Officer, Bombay* (1983) All ER 864.

39. s41 Race Relations Act 1976.

40. *Review of the Race Relations Act 1976: Proposals for Change*, CRE, 1985, at 9.
41. s75 Race Relations Act 1976.
42. See *Irish Post*, 6 February 1993. This details the case of a British born man refused a job at the government's intelligence gathering centre, GCHQ, because his parents were born in Ireland.
43. *CRE Review*, 1985, at 8.
44. *CRE Review*, 1992, at 12.
45. Ibid.
46. Ibid.
47. *Large Companies and Racial Equality*, Commission for Racial Equality, 1995, at 28.
48. Ibid., at 9–10.
49. Ibid., at 28.
50. Ibid., at 29.
51. *CRE Review*, 1985, at 17–18 and *CRE Review*, 1992, at 51–3.
52. Ibid.
53. Trevor Jones, *Britain's Ethnic Minorities*, Policy Studies Institute, 1993, table 5.1., at 112–31.
54. Ibid., table 4.18, at 106.
55. See Colin Brown, *Black and White Britain: The Third PSI Survey*, Policy Studies Institute, 1982.
56. See *Black Workers in the Labour Market, a report on black workers in the labour market in 1993 and their access to education and training opportunities*, Trades Union Congress, 1994.
57. Jones, 1993, at 35–6.
58. *Black and Ethnic Minority Women and Men in Britain 1994*, Equal Opportunities Commission and Commission for Racial Equality, 1994, at 21.
59. See Commission for Racial Equality, *Sorry It's Gone: Testing for Racial Discrimination in the Private Rented Sector*, CRE, 1990.
60. See Commission for Racial Equality, *Out of Order: The Report of a Formal Investigation into the London Borough of Southwark*, CRE, 1990.
61. CARF, '1981–1991 How Racist is Britain?', Campaign Against Racism and Fascism, June/Aug 1991, at 8–11.
62. Ibid.
63. See Commission for Racial Equality, *Homelessness and Discrimination: Report of a Formal Investigation into the London Borough of Tower Hamlets*, CRE, 1988.
64. *Observer*, 'Asian Families Forced to Live on Race-Hate Estate', 21 March 1993.
65. The leaflets produced in the September 1993 by-election were published by the Island Liberal Focus Team. The bogus Labour Party leaflet was produced anonymously although Liberal Party members admitted in court that they had published it.
66. *R* v. *Secretary of State for the Environment* ex parte *Tower Hamlets London Borough Council*, *The Times*, 'Law report', 9 April 1993.
67. s4 Asylum and Immigration Appeals Act 1993.
68. Richard Skellington and Paulette Morris, *'Race' in Britain Today*, Sage Publications/Open University, 1992, at 99.

69. Cary Oppenheim, *Poverty: The Facts*, Child Poverty Action Group, 1990, at 53.
70. See National Association of Citizens Advice Bureau (NACAB), *Homelessness: A National Survey of CAB Clients*, 1988.
71. *CRE Review*, 1992, at 13.
72. *Independent*, 'Race Bias Case Blighted Career', 2 July 1993.
73. See Chetan Bhatt, *AIDS and the Black Community*, Black HIV/AIDS Network (BHAN), 1991.
74. Ibid. See also, *Sun*, 'Mum, Baby and AIDS Midwife', 23 February 1993.
75. The UK Forum is an umbrella grouping of organisations providing frontline advice and counselling as well as research and information on issues around HIV and AIDS.
76. Ibid.
77. Sue Shutter, *Immigration and Nationality Law Handbook*, Joint Council for the Welfare of Immigrants, 1992, at 124–42.
78. Ibid.
79. Ibid.
80. s3 Asylum and Immigration Appeals Act 1993.
81. Ibid.
82. See Oppenheim, 1990, at 89.
83. *Fourth Periodic Report*, 1994, para 449.
84. Ibid., para 447.
85. Ibid., para 450.
86. Skellington, 1992, at 104.
87. *Fourth Periodic Report*, 1994, para 37.
88. Ibid.
89. *Independent*, 'Women and Blacks: More Chances but less Promotion', 28 April 1989.
90. Skellington, *supra* note 73, at 106.
91. Ibid.
92. Ibid.
93. *Law Society Gazette*, 4 November 1992, at 7 and 13 January 1993, at 3.
94. Dame Jocelyn Barrow, *The Committee of Inquiry into Equal Opportunities on the Bar Vocational Report, Interim Report*, The General Council of the Bar, Executive Summary, September 1993, at 3.
95. *Guardian*, 'More Black Students pass Bar Exam but Race Gap Remains', 14 August 1993.
96. *Fourth Periodic Report*, 1994, para 452.
97. Ibid., para 453.
98. Ibid., para 451.
99. Ibid.
100. *Equal Opportunities Review* 35, Jan/Feb 1991, at 6–7.
101. *Daily Telegraph*, '25,000 for Race Taunt Asian PC', 5 May 1993.
102. *Daily Telegraph*, 'Immigrant Total Reaches Record' 7 February 1992, citing *International Migration 1990*, Office of Population Census and Surveys, HMSO.
103. Paul Gordon, *Racial Violence and Harassment*, Runnymede Research Report, Runnymede Trust, 2nd edn, 1990, at 22.
104. Gordon, 1990, at 38.

105. See Francesca Klug, *Racist Attacks*, Runnymede Trust, 1982.
106. Transcript from World in Action Television Documentary, 1 January 1978.
107. Gordon, 1990.
108. *Searchlight*, February 1985.
109. See *Runnymede Trust Bulletin*, 'The Press and Refugees', November 1992; also *CARF*, 'Media File', Jan/Feb 1992.
110. Ibid., 'Tebbit Cricket Loyalty Test', June 1990.
111. Transcript of speech in Bolton, 28 May 1993.
112. *Guardian*, letters page, 'Racism and a Fantasy World', 8 July 1993.
113. Robert Moore, *Racism and Resistance*, in Gordon, 1990, at 11.
114. *Fourth Periodic Report*, 1994, para 28.
115. Ibid.
116. *Guardian*, 'MPs told Race Attacks May Top 130,000 a Year', 15 July 1993.
117. Home Affairs Committee, *Racial Attacks and Harassment, Third Report*, vol I, Session 1993–94, para 21.
118. Ibid., para 22.
119. Ibid., paras 24–5.
120. Ibid., paras 26–48.
121. Ibid., para 82.
122. CARF, *Evidence of the Campaign Against Racism and Fascism to the Home Affairs Committee Inquiry into Racially Motivated Attacks and Harassment*, CARF, 1993, at 2.
123. *Racial Abuse, An Everyday Experience for Some Londoners, A Submission by the Association of London Authorities to the House of Commons Home Affairs Committee Inquiry into Racially-Motivated Attacks and Harassment*, June 1993, at 4.
124. See Ruth Hall, *Ask Any Woman: A London Inquiry Into Rape and Sexual Assault*, Falling Wall Press, 1985.
125. CARF, 1993, at 1. In the case of 15–year-old Navid Sadiq, killed in January 1992, the motive may have been robbery although the perpetrator was clearly a racist. Other cases accepted as purely racially motivated were: Panchadcharam Sahitharan, Mohammed Sarwar, Siddik Dada, Rohit Duggal, Ruhullah Aramesh, Ashiq Hussain, Aziz Miah, Donald Palmer and Sher Sagoo.
126. Runnymede Trust, 'Racist Violence and White Exclusionism', *Runnymede Trust Bulletin*, September 1992.
127. Ibid.
128. Newham Monitoring Project *Annual Report 1992/3* provides illustrations of the way the practice works, at 6–15.
129. *Daily Telegraph*, 'Whites-only Club Illegal Rules Judge', 29 January 1992.
130. See *Southall, the birth of a black community*, Institute for Race Relations and Southall Rights, 1981.
131. *Independent Magazine*, 'The Colour of Blood', 12 June 1993.
132. Gordon, 1990, at 20.
133. Ibid.
134. *The Voice*, 'You Just Don't Give a Damn', 11 May 1993.
135. See *Anti-Racist Alliance Submission to the Home Affairs Select Committee*, 9 July 1993.
136. Ibid.
137. *The Response to Racial Attacks and Harassment: Guidance for the Statutory*

Agencies, Report of the Inter-Departmental Racial Attacks Group, Home
Office, 1989, paras 110–15.

138. For example, in February 1993, Metropolitan Police Chief Commissioner,
Paul Condon, stated in his first major speech to a conference on racial and
sexual harassment: 'the police must be intolerant of those who indulge in
racial abuse, and intolerant of those who use hatred and violence as the tools
of their own expression. But if we are to be intolerant of those outside the
police service who fail to treat their fellow human beings with dignity and
respect, we must be equally intolerant of our own colleagues who fail to reach
the required standards.' *Police Review*, 'Condon Says no Quarter Will be
Given on Sex Harassment', 5 March 1993.
139. CARF, 1993, at 5–6.
140. Ibid.
141. Ibid.
142. s154 Criminal Justice and Public Order Act 1994.
143. See *UN, Report of the Committee on the Elimination of Racial Discrimination*, UN General Assembly, Official Records, Forty-eighth Session, Sup-
plement no 18 (A/48/18), at 80–1.
144. *Third Periodic Report*, 1989, para 274.
145. Ibid., para 275.
146. *Fourth Periodic Report*, 1994, para 381.
147. *Hansard*, Written Answers, 18 January, 1993 Col 4.
148. Sandra Coliver (ed.), *Striking the Balance: Hate Speech, Freedom of
Expression and Non discrimination*, Article 19, 1992, see Joanna Oyediran,
'The UK's Compliance with Article 4 of the International Convention on the
Elimination of all forms of Racial Discrimination', at 246
149. *R v. Jordan and Tyndall* (1963) Crim LR 124, CCA. Colin Jordan and John
Tyndall were leading members of Spearhead, a paramilitary group associated
with the British National Party and the National Socialist Movement. They
were seen at various times drilling in uniform, exchanging Nazi salutes and
taking part in survivalist training exercises. A search of their headquarters
revealed a cache of arms and neo-Nazi paraphernalia.
150. *Third Periodic Report*, 1989, para 263.
151. Oyediran, 1992, at 251.
152. See CARF, 1993, at appendix 2.
153. See 'The Murderers Are Amongst Us: The Criminal Records of Britain's
Racists', *Searchlight*, 1985.
154. Ibid.
155. Greenwich Action Committee Against Racist Attacks monitors reported racist
incidents on the basis of returns from the police, hospitals and local authority
housing and social services. During the period May 1991/2 there were 800
incidents. From May 1992/3 this had increased to 1,500.
156. *Hansard*, Racial Violence, 21 May 1993, Col 541. They were: Roland Adams
(aged 15, February 1991); Orville Blair (25, May 1991); Rohit Duggal (16,
July 1992); and Stephen Lawrence (18, April 1993); all stabbed to death.
157. s20 Prevention of Terrorism (Temporary Provisions) Act 1989.
158. Two groups appear in Schedule 1 of the Prevention of Terrorism Act 1989:
The Irish Republican Army and the Irish National Liberation Army. Section

1 (2)(a) allows the Secretary of State to add any organisation 'which appears to him to be concerned in, or in promoting or encouraging, terrorism'.

159. ss2–3 Prevention of Terrorism (Temporary) Provisions Act 1989.

160. Both the BBC and the IBA are subject to reserved government powers which incorporate the power, vested in the Home Secretary, to include or exclude specific items. In a letter to both organisations in October 1988, the Home Secretary instructed them to 'refrain at all times from sending any broadcast matter which consists of or includes any words . . . (a) where the person speaking the words represents or purports to represent an organisation specified below, or (b) the words support or solicit or invite support for such an organisation.' The organisations listed included: the IRA, the INLA and the UVF. These are all proscribed as well as Sinn Fein, Republican Sinn Fein and the UDA, which were all at the time legal bodies.

161. *Observer*, 'Twenty-five Years of the Troubles', 11 July 1993.

162. Gordon, 1990, lists 43 murders between 1981 and 1989 where the victim was black and the motivation appears to have been racial. This figure includes 13 young people killed in the Deptford fire in 1981 which is discussed earlier in the book. CARF, 1993, documented 10 murders in 1992 and two in 1991. Because of difficulties determining what constitutes a racial attack both CARF and Runnymede believe these figures may be an underestimate.

163. *R v. McLaughlin and O'Loughlin* (1987) 85 Cr App R 157.

164. *Magill Magazine*, 'A Tale of Two Bombers', February 1989.

165. *Evening Standard*, 'London on Bombs Alert', 12 November 1985.

166. See Paddy Hillyard, *Suspect Community: People's Experiences of the Prevention of Terrorism Act*, Pluto Press, 1993.

167. Ibid.

168. Patrick Lawlor, *Just News*, May 1990, at 6–7.

169. *Searchlight*, January 1987.

170. Ibid.

171. *Guardian*, 2 November 1985.

172. *Searchlight*, January 1987.

173. Ibid.

174. *The Sunday Times*, 'Exposed: Labour Trickery that Hyped BNP to Election Victory', 19 September 1993.

175. Institute of Jewish Affairs, *Antisemitism World Report 1993*, 1993, at 61.

176. Ibid.

177. Ibid.

178. Ibid.

179. In July 1993 the CRE announced it was launching its first ever study into anti-Irish discrimination.

180. See Liam Greenslade, *The Irish in Britain in the 1990s: a Preliminary Analysis of the 1991 Census*, University of Liverpool, 1993.

181. *Runnymede Trust*, 'The Irish in Britain – Profile of a Hidden Experience', Runnymede Trust Bulletin, April 1993.

182. Liam Greenslade, *White Skins, White Masks: Mental Illness and the Irish in Britain*, Paper presented at the British Sociological Association Annual Conference, University of Manchester, 1991, at 5.

183. See Tom Connor, *The London Irish*, London Strategic Policy Unit, 1988.

184. Ibid. See also, Haringey Council, *Equal Opportunities: The Irish Dimension: An Agenda for Change* (no date).
185. Industrial Tribunal Case no 62824/93. CRE news release, 7 June 1994.
186. The 1991 National Prison Survey interviewed 10% of the male prison population and 20% of the female prison population. The survey asked prisoners which country they were born in. 1% of the 3,831 of the prisoners who answered the question said they were born in Northern Ireland and 1.8% said they were born in the Republic of Ireland.
187. Correspondence between Liberty and the Home Office.
188. Speech by Harry Fletcher, Deputy General Secretary of the National Association of Probation Officers to a conference organised by the Action Group for Irish Youth. The study was conducted by Middlesex Probation Service in 1991. Quoted in the February edition of NAPO's magazine, *NAPO News*.
189. See Murphy, Flynn and Tucker, *Racial Attacks and Harassment of Irish People*, Action Group for Irish Youth, 1993 and Liz Curtis, *Nothing But The Same Old Story: The Roots of Anti-Irish Racism*, Information on Ireland, 1984.
190. *Hansard*, Oral Questions, 20 July 1993, Col 194.
191. *First Tuesday*, Yorkshire Television, 6 July 1993.
192. *Commission for Racial Equality v. Dutton* (1989) 1 All ER 306, Court of Appeal.
193. Complaints to Liberty's Legal Department by Travellers have increased considerably over the last two years.
194. See Liberty, *The Road to Nowhere? A Report on the Government's Proposals to Reform the 1968 Caravan Sites Act*, March 1993.
195. Ibid.
196. See Safe Childbirth for Travellers Campaign, Save the Children Fund, *Response to the Government Proposal to Repeal the Caravan Sites Act 1968*, November 1992.
197. *Hansard*, Caravan Sites (Amendment) Bill 5 February 1993, Col 613–14.

4 Northern Ireland

1. *An Phoblacht/Republican News*, 1 September 1994, statement issued in the name of P. O'Neill, Irish Republican Publicity Bureau, Dublin.
2. *Guardian*, 'Loyalists order a Ceasefire', 13 October 1994.
3. *Daily Telegraph*, 'Major Agrees to Talks with Sinn Fein', 22 October 1994.
4. Letter from 10 Downing Street, 4 November 1994.
5. NCCL, *A People's Charter, Liberty's Bill of Rights, A Consultation Document*, 1991, at 113. Between 1959 and 1990, the European Court gave 37 judgments against the British government and found that it had violated at least one article of the Convention on 27 occasions. The next most frequent offender, Austria, has been in breach on 15 occasions. In 1991 Italy overtook Britain as the most frequent violator and Britain now ranks second.
6. *Ireland v. UK* (1978) Case No 5310/71.
7. Fox, Campbell and Hartley v. UK (1990) Case Nos 1224/86 and 12383/86.
8. *Brogan and Others v. UK* (1988) Case Nos 11209/84, 11234/84, 11266/84.
9. See NCCL, 1991.

10. See, for example, *Human Rights in Northern Ireland*, Helsinki Watch, 1991.
11. See CAJ, *Inquests and Disputed Killings in Northern Ireland*, 1992.
12. See CAJ, *Police Accountability in Northern Ireland*, 1988.
13. See CAJ, *Life Sentence and SOSP Prisoners in Northern Ireland*, 1989.
14. See Frank Pakenham, *Peace by Ordeal*, Mercier Press, 1951.
15. See Chris Ryder, *The RUC: A Force under Fire*, Octopus, 1990.
16. See Michael Farrell, *Arming the Protestants: The Formation of the Ulster Special Constabulary and the Royal Ulster Constabulary 1920–27*, Pluto Press, 1983.
17. Gerard Hogan and Clive Walker, *Political Violence and the Law in Ireland*, Manchester University Press, 1989, at 14.
18. Civil Authorities (Special Powers) Act 1922, Section 5, Schedule 1–5 Regulations 7a, 18a, 22a, 23a, 24a. Also Regulations 18c (1923), 26a (1930), 8a (1931), 4 (1933), 22b (1933), 24c (1933).
19. Ibid., Section 1(3).
20. See *Report of the Tribunal Appointed to Inquire into the Events on Sunday 30 January 1972 which Led to the Loss of Life in Connection with the Procession in Londonderry on that day (Widgery Report)* and *Justice Denied: A Challenge to Lord Widgery's Report on Bloody Sunday*, Defence and Education Fund of the International League for the Rights of Man in association with the NCCL, 1972. 13 protesters died the day of the shootings and a 14th died later.
21. See Robbie McVeigh, *Harassment, the Security Forces and Young People in Northern Ireland*, CAJ, 1994.
22. *Andersonstown News*, 'Paratroop Peace', 19 November 1994.
23. *Disturbances in Northern Ireland: Report of the Commission appointed by the Governor of Northern Ireland (Cameron Report)*, HMSO, 1969, Cmnd 532.
24. *Report of the Advisory Committee on Police in Northern Ireland (Hunt Report)*, HMSO, 1969.
25. See Chris Ryder, *The UDR*, Methuen, 1991.
26. *Hansard*, the Army Bill, 13 February 1991, cols 1185–6. Relating to the UDR and the Royal Irish Rangers immediately before the merger.
27. *Observer*, 'Irish Special', 11 July 1993.
28. See Kader Asmal (Chairman), *Shoot to Kill? International Lawyers' Inquiry into the use of Firearms by the Security Forces in Northern Ireland*, Mercier Press, 1985, at 125.
29. See Fr Raymond Murray, *The SAS in Ireland*, Mercier Press, 1990.
30. The UK has ratified both the ECHR and the ICCPR but has not signed the Optional Protocol of the ICCPR which would allow people the right to take individual cases to the UN. However, the government must submit a report to the UN Human Rights Committee every five years outlining how it is complying with the Covenant.
31. s3(1) the Criminal Law Act 1967.
32. *R* v. *Thain* (1985) 11 NIJB 31 (CA).
33. *Guardian*, 'Where Justice Lies Bleeding for Decades', January 1995.
34. *Independent*, 'Guardsmen Get Life for Belfast Murder', 11 February 1995.
35. *Andersonstown News*, 'Pathetic', 11 February 1995.

36. See Harry Kitchin, *The Gibraltar Report*, NCCL, 1989.
37. See CAJ, *The Stalker Affair, More Questions Than Answers*, 1988 and John Stalker, *Stalker*, Harrap, 1988.
38. *Guardian*, 'Coroner Abandons 12–year "Shoot-to-kill" Inquests after Court Refuses Access to Stalker Report', 9 September 1994.
39. See *Amnesty International Concerns in Europe*, 'Killings by the Security Forces in Northern Ireland', May 1992–October 1992, at 87–90. Also *Human Rights Concerns in the UK*, Amnesty, 1991, at 34–8. See also, Murray, 1990.
40. See for example, *Hansard*, Army Bill, 13 February 1991, cols 1151–215.
41. See Cambridge Constabulary, *Summary of the Report of the Deputy Chief Constable of Cambridgeshire John Stevens, into Allegations of Collusion between Members of the Security Forces and Loyalist Paramilitaries*, Cambridgeshire Constabulary, 1990.
42. Ibid.
43. See *Shoot to Kill and Collusion*, Relatives for Justice, 1993.
44. BBC programme *Panorama*, 'Dirty War', 8 June 1992.
45. *Hansard*, Standing Committee B, 17 January 1989, col 508.
46. Ibid., col 519.
47. Ibid.
48. See *'Legal Defence in Northern Ireland, Following the Murder of Patrick Finucane on 12 February 1989'*, Report of an international delegation of lawyers, 1989.
49. Stalker, 1988, at 49.
50. *In Defence of the Defence, Fourth Report to the United Nations' Special Rapporteur on the Independence of Judges and Lawyers Concerning Attempted Intimidation of Defence Lawyers in Northern Ireland*, British Irish Rights Watch, 1994.
51. See *Strip-searching, an Inquiry into the Strip-searching of Women Remand Prisoners at Armagh Prison between 1982 and 1985*, NCCL, 1986.
52. *Hansard*, Written Answers, 29 July 1983, col 631 and 5 December 1983, col 84.
53. NCCL, 1986, at 15.
54. CAJ, *Just News*, 'Non-sense of Security', April 1992.
55. NCCL, 1986, at 6.
56. Paddy Hillyard, *Suspect Community, People's experiences of the Prevention of Terrorism Acts in Britain*, Pluto Press, 1993, at 157–9.
57. See CAJ, *Plastic Bullets and the Law*, 1990.
58. See *They Shoot Children, the Use of Rubber and Plastic Bullets in the North of Ireland*, Information on Ireland, 1987.
59. CAJ, 1990, at 13. Vote of May 1982 was 100 votes to 43 in favour of banning the use of plastic bullets in the EC.
60. See Fr Denis Faul and Fr Raymond Murray, *Plastic bullets–plastic government*, and *Rubber and plastic bullets kill and maim*, International Tribunal Against Rubber and Plastic Bullets, 1982.
61. CAJ, 1990, at 3.
62. CAJ, *Adding Insult to Injury? Allegations of Harassment and the use of Lethal Force by the Security Forces in Northern Ireland*, 1993, at 4.
63. Ibid.
64. Troops Out, 'Plastic Bullets Campaign Triumph', July 1988.

65. *Irish News*, ' "Yobs" Started Riot', 1 October 1994.
66. *Irish News*, 'Man Hit by Plastic Bullet in Hotel Disturbance', 24 October 1994.
67. *Hansard*, Prevention of Terrorism (Temporary Provisions) Bill 25 November 1974, col 882.
68. Prevention of Terrorism Act, A Liberty Briefing, NCCL, 1993, at 2.
69. Ibid., at 1–3.
70. Sir Robert Mark, *In the Office of Constable, an Autobiography*, Collins, 1978, at 174.
71. From *Statistics on the Operation of Prevention of Terrorism Legislation 1993*, Home Office Statistical Bulletin, 25 February 1994, Tables 1, 2 and 7.
72. Offenses included in calculating this table are: murder, attempted murder, conspiracy, and offenses under the Explosive Substances Act and the Firearms Act.
73. Hillyard, 1993, at 123–7.
74. Ibid., at 240.
75. Ibid., at 95–196.
76. See 'When They Come for you in the Morning', *Civil Liberty Agenda*, summer 1993.
77. Clive Walker, *The Prevention of Terrorism in British Law*, 2nd edn, Manchester University Press, 1992, at 138.
78. For example, the McNulty family and Kate Magee, leaflets issued by support groups.
79. Lord Shackleton, *Review into the operation of the Prevention of Terrorism (Temporary Provisions) Acts 1974 and 1975*, HMSO, Cmnd 7324, 1978, paras 132–3.
80. Walker, 1992, at 141–4.
81. *The Times*, 'Law report', 1 September 1992.
82. *Review of the operation of the Prevention of Terrorism (Temporary Provisions) Act 1984 by the Viscount Colville of Culross QC* (Colville Report), HMSO, 1987, at 52.
83. *R v. Richardson and Others, The Times*, 'Law report', 20 October 1989.
84. *Brogan v. UK* (1988) Series A, No 145B, at para 62.
85. *Brannigan and MacBride v. UK*, 26 May 1993, No 14552/89.
86. Schedule 8 Paragraph 6(8) Police and Criminal Evidence Act 1984.
87. Hillyard, 1993, at 95–181.
88. Walker, 1992, at 170.
89. For example, *Report to the United Kingdom government on the visit to Northern Ireland carried out by the European Committee for the Prevention of torture and inhuman and degrading treatment or punishment (CPT), from 20 to 29 July 1993*, Council of Europe, 14 March 1994.
90. David Brown, *Detention under the Prevention of Terrorism (Temporary Provisions) Act 1989: access to legal advice and outside contact*, Home Office Research and Planning Unit, Paper 75, 1993, at 8–23.
91. Ibid., at 39.
92. s15(9) Prevention of Terrorism (Temporary Provisions) Act 1989.
93. s1 Prevention of Terrorism (Temporary Provisions) Act 1989.
94. s2 Prevention of Terrorism (Temporary Provisions) Act 1989.
95. s3 Prevention of Terrorism (Temporary Provisions) Act 1989.

96. Walker, 1992, at 59.
97. *Colville Report*, 1987, at 46.
98. s8 Prevention of Terrorism (Temporary Provisions) Act 1989.
99. For example, *Hansard*, Prevention and suppression of terrorism, 9 March 1994, col 312.
100. See *Emergency Laws and the Irish in Britain, the case of John Matthews*, Britain and Ireland Human Rights Centre, 1993.
101. Complaints to Liberty's legal department.
102. Paul Sieghart, *The International Law of Human Rights*, Clarendon Press 1983, at 464. UK reservation to Article 12 of the ICCPR: 'The Government of the UK reserve the right to interpret the provisions of article 12(1) relating to the territory of a State a applying separately to each of the territories comprising the UK and its dependencies'.
103. Ibid.
104. *Guardian*, 'Exclusions Challenged', 5 March 1993.
105. *R* v. *Secretary of State for the Home Department*, ex parte *Adams, The Times*, 'Law report', 10 August 1994.
106. *R* v. *Secretary of State for the Home Department* ex parte *Gallagher*, 10 February 1994, Court of Appeal, and *R* v. *Secretary of State for the Home Department* ex parte *McQuillan*, 9 September 1994.
107. *Hansard*, Written Answer, 29 November 1994, col 552.
108. *Report of the Commission to consider legal procedures to deal with terrorist activities in Northern Ireland (Diplock Report)*, HMSO, Cmnd 5185, 1972.
109. A Briefing Paper on the Northern Ireland (Emergency Provisions) Bill, Committee on the Administration of Justice, undated, at 7.
110. Ibid.
111. *Lawless v. Ireland* App 1 No 332/56 (1961) 1 EHRR 15.
112. *Ireland v. UK* (1978) 2 EHRR 25.
113. ss16–26 Northern Ireland (Emergency Provisions) Act 1991.
114. s18 Northern Ireland (Emergency Provisions) Act 1991.
115. s28 Northern Ireland (Emergency Provisions) Act 1991. There are seven organisations proscribed under the EPA: the Irish Republican Army, Cumann na mBan, Fianna na hEireann, the Red Hand Commando, Saor Eire, the Ulster Freedom Fighters, the Ulster Volunteer Force, the Irish National Liberation Army, the Irish People's Liberation Organisation and the Ulster Defence Association.
116. There were 16 prosecutions in 1991, 15 in 1992 and 24 in 1993. *Fourth Periodic Report by the Government of the United Kingdom of Great Britain and Northern Ireland to the United Nations Human Rights Committee Under Article 40, International Covenant on Civil and Political Rights*, 1994, paras 399–400.
117. Northern Ireland Office, *Guide to the Emergency Powers*, Belfast HMSO, undated, at 50–4.
118. s10(1) and s12 Northern Ireland (Emergency Provisions) Act 1991.
119. For example see Steven Greer and Anthony White, *Abolishing the Diplock Courts*, Cobden Trust, 1986.
120. s76 Police and Criminal Evidence Act 1984.
121. *R* v. *McCormick* (1977) Northern Ireland Reports 105, cited in Kevin Boyle,

Tom Hadden and Paddy Hillyard, *Ten Years On in Northern Ireland, the Legal Control of Political Violence*, Cobden Trust, 1980, at 47.

122. See Peter Taylor, *Beating the Terrorists? Interrogations in Omagh, Gough and Castlereagh*, Penguin Books, 1980, and Dermot Walsh, *The Use and Abuse of Emergency Legislation in Northern Ireland*, Cobden Trust, 1983.

123. *Ireland v. UK* (1978) 2 EHRR 25.

124. Amnesty International, *Report of a Mission to Northern Ireland*, Amnesty, 1978.

125. *Report of the Committee of Inquiry into Police Interrogation Procedures in Northern Ireland (Bennett Report)*, HMSO Cmnd 7497, 1979.

126. Amnesty International, *United Kingdom, Human Rights Concerns*, Amnesty, 1991, at 4.

127. *Summary Record of 92nd Meeting of UN Committee on Torture*, November 1991.

128. *Report to the Government of the UK on the Visit Carried out by the European Committee for the Prevention of Torture and Inhuman or Degrading Treatment or Punishment*, Council of Europe, CPT/Inf(94) 17, 17 November 1994.

129. Anthony Jennings (ed.), *Justice Under Fire, the Abuse of Civil Liberties in Northern Ireland*, Pluto Press, 1990, at 78.

130. See Tony Gifford QC, *The Supergrasses, the Use of Accomplice Evidence in Northern Ireland*, Cobden Trust, 1984.

131. Ibid.

132. See Amnesty International, *United Kingdom, Northern Ireland: Killings by Security Forces and 'Supergrass' Trials*, 1988.

133. *Guardian*, 'King Ends Right to Silence', 21 October 1988.

134. *R v. McCann* (1991) 92 Cr App 239.

135. See for example, *New Law Journal*, 'The Case of the Winchester Three', 9 February 1990.

136. *R v. McCann* (1991) 92 Cr App 239.

137. *Hansard*, Northern Ireland, 8 November 1988, cols 182–223.

138. Ibid., col 183.

139. *Hansard*, Northern Ireland, 8 November 1988, col 182. See also, *Note by the Standing Advisory Committee on Human Rights on the Government's recent announcements affecting Northern Ireland dealing with terrorism and terrorist-related activities*, SACHR, 19 January 1989, at 3–5.

140. See James Wood and Adam Crawford, *The Right of Silence*, Civil Liberties Trust, 1989.

141. Articles 3 and 4 Criminal Evidence (Northern Ireland) Order 1988.

142. Ibid.

143. Ibid.

144. See CAJ, *The Casement Trials*, 1992.

145. *R v. Murray and Others* (CA) 7 July 1992.

146. *Murray v. UK*, 27 June 1994, App l No 18731/91.

147. Ibid.

148. See CAJ, *The Casement Trials*, 1992.

149. See Ellen Weaver, *Right of Silence Debate: the Northern Ireland Experience*, Justice, 1994.

150. Commentary on the Northern Ireland Criminal Statistics, Northern Ireland Office, 1993, at 15.

151. Weaver, 1994, at 4.
152. Ibid., summary of conclusions.
153. Ibid., at 36.
154. Ibid., at 12.
155. Hansard (HL), Royal Assent, 3 November 1994, col 921. Not all the provisions come into force immediately. Abolition of the right of silence is due to come into effect in spring 1995, once a new caution has been formalised.
156. s76(1) Criminal Justice and Public Order Act 1994.
157. s76(4) Criminal Justice and Public Order Act 1994.
158. *Policing*, 'Road Block', summer 1994.
159. Complaints received by Liberty's legal department.
160. Letter from the City of London Police, 10 January 1994, forwarded to Liberty's legal office.
161. *Operation of Certain Police Powers Under PACE, England and Wales 1993*, Home Office Statistical Bulletin, Issue 15/94 Table 1. See also, bulletins 14/91, 15/92 and 21/93.
162. Ibid.
163. s82(16) Criminal Justice and Public Order Act 1994.
164. s82(16)(1)(a) Criminal Justice and Public Order Act 1994.
165. See Laurence Lustgarten and Ian Leigh, *In From the Cold, National Security and Parliamentary Democracy*, Clarendon Press, 1994.
166. Stella Rimmington, *Security and Democracy – Is There a Conflict?*, Richard Dimbleby Lecture, 1994.
167. Ibid.
168. Ibid.
169. *Kurdistan Report*, 'MI5, Special Branch and the Criminalisation of the Kurds in Britain', Jan/Feb 1995.
170. Stella Rimmington, *James Smart Lecture*, 3 November 1994.
171. Ibid.
172. Rupert Allason, *The Branch, A History of the Metropolitan Police Special Branch 1883–1983*, Secker and Warburg, 1983, at 1–16.
173. *R v. McGonagle and Heffernan*, unreported.
174. An Phoblacht/Republican News, 'Did MI5 Let Bombs go off to Secure its Role', 27 October 1994.
175. *The Times*, 'Law report', 17 August 1994.
176. Ibid.
177. *Guardian*, 'Anonymous MI5 Witness Denies "Sight-seeing Tour",' 8 December 1994.
178. s2 Security Service Act 1989.
179. ss2 and 4 Intelligence Services Act 1994.
180. *Guardian*, 'MI5 Takeover of Whitehall Data Checks Alarms MPs', 19 October 1994.
181. *Independent*, 'Special Branch to Target Protesters', 3 November 1994.
182. Richard Norton Taylor, *In Defence of the Realm, the Case for Accountable Security Services*, Civil Liberties Trust, 1990, at 46.
183. Ibid., at 48.
184. *Guardian*, 'Big Brother's Invisible Men', 15 June 1985.
185. Norton Taylor, 1990, at 66.
186. BBC Radio, *File on Four*, 10 August 1982.

187. Norton Taylor, 1990, at 47–8.
188. *Hansard*, Written Answer, 7 March 1988, col 73.
189. *The Security Service*, HMSO July 1993, at 7–11.
190. *The Modern Law Review*, 'The Intelligence Services Act 1994', November 1994.
191. Ibid.
192. s10 Intelligence Services Act 1994.
193. See Rowthorne and Wayne, *Northern Ireland: Political Economy of the Conflict*, Polity, 1988.
194. See Bew, Gibbon and Patterson, *The State in Northern Ireland 1921–72: Political Forces and Social Classes*, Manchester University Press, 1979.
195. Wade and Bradley, *Constitutional and Administrative Law*, 11th edn (by Bradley and Ewing), Longman, 1993, at 49.
196. See for example, O'Leary, Lyne, Marshall and Rowthorn, *Northern Ireland, Sharing Authority*, IPPR, 1993.
197. See Bridgid Hadfield (ed.), *The Northern Ireland Constitution*, Open University Press, 1992, at 6–11.
198. *Fortnight*, 'Aloof in Quangoland', January 1995.
199. Joint Declaration, 15 December 1993.
200. *Frameworks for the Future*, HMSO Northern Ireland, 20 Feb 1995.
201. For example *ICCL and CAJ, The States We are In: Civil Rights in Ireland, North and South*, proceedings of a conference held in Trinity College, Dublin, 30 January 1993.
202. Interviews with author, September 1994. See also, CAJ, *A Bill of Rights for Northern Ireland*, 1993.
203. The Standing Advisory Commission on Human Rights was created by s20 of the Northern Ireland Constitution Act 1973 as a purely advisory body.

5 Women's Rights, Human Rights

1. *Third Periodic Report by the Government of the United Kingdom of Great Britain and Northern Ireland to the United Nations Human Rights Committee Under Article 40, International Covenant on Civil and Political Rights*, October 1989, para 51.
2. Ibid., para 55.
3. *Fourth Periodic Report by the Government of the United Kingdom of Great Britain and Northern Ireland to the United Nations Human Rights Committee Under Article 40, International Covenant on Civil and Political Rights*, 1994, para 60.
4. Ibid.
5. Ibid., para 63.
6. Ibid., para 67.
7. Ibid., paras 64–6.
8. Ibid., para 68.
9. Ibid., para 75.
10. Ibid., para 58.
11. *Labour Research Magazine*, 'Whose Opportunity in 2000?', March 1993.
12. Ibid.

13. *Guardian*, 'Britain Holds Poor Record for Women in Public Life', 7 September 1993.
14. Gorman, *Uncovering Discrimination: A Response to the UK Government Second Report on the United Nations Convention on the Elimination of all Forms of Discrimination Against Women*, 1993.
15. *Independent*, 'Whitehall Set to Remain Male Bastion', 10 May 1993.
16. House of Commons, *Fact Sheet No 5*, Appendix C, House of Commons Public Information Office, 1993.
17. Information from the *National Association of Local Government Women's Committees Statistics*, 12 January 1994.
18. Wade and Bradley, *Constitutional and Administrative Law*, Longman, 1993, at 157–62.
19. House of Lords Information Office. Of a total of 382 life peers, 61 are women.
20. *Guardian*, 7 September 1993. According to this article the only area where any substantial progress had been made towards improving women's participation in public life was in the trade union movement.
21. House of Commons Public Information Office.
22. Diane Abbott is Labour MP for Hackney North. Other black MPs are Paul Boateng, Bernie Grant, Piara Khabra and Keith Vaz who are all Labour. Niranjan Deva is a Conservative MP.
23. See Teresa Gorman, *The Bastards*, Pan Books, 1993. This describes the battle against ratification of the Maastricht Treaty by rebel Conservative MPs and contains illuminating insights into the sexist attitudes and institutions of those in the government and parliament.
24. ss38, 108, Broadcasting Act 1990.
25. Gorman, 1993.
26. *Guardian*, 'Do Not Adjust Your Set', 20 November 1992.
27. *Independent*, 'Sexual Harassment in Police "Serious",' 25 March 1993.
28. Ibid.
29. *Independent*, 'Women Kept Out of CID by "Quota",' 8 April 1992.
30. *Guardian*, cover feature, 'Police Story', 6 February 1993.
31. *Guardian*, 'WPC Loses Met Bias Case', 12 August 1992.
32. *Independent*, 'Policewoman's Tribunal to Hear Sex Bias Claims', 7 January 1991.
33. s1 Sex Discrimination Act 1975.
34. Ibid., s3.
35. Ibid., s4.
36. Evelyn Collins and Elizabeth Meehan, 'Women's Rights in Employment and Related Areas', in *Individual Rights and the Law in Britain*, Christopher McCrudden and Gerald Chambers (eds), Clarendon Press, 1994, at 372–407.
37. s1(1)(b) Sex Discrimination Act 1975.
38. *James v. Eastleigh Borough Council* (1990) 2 AC 751; (1990) IRLR 288 (HL).
39. s29 Sex Discrimination Act 1975.
40. Ibid., s7.
41. See Jane Straw, *Equal Opportunities, the Way Ahead*, Institute of Personnel Management, 1989, at 34–46.
42. See Stamp and Robarts, *Positive Action for Women, Changing the Workplace*, 1986, at 3. The original 1975 Act empowered the EOC to carry out formal

investigations without it needing to believe the law was being broken. This stipulation was inserted the following year.

43. Women's National Commission, *WNC Report for the World Conference on Women*, first draft, undated, at 4.
44. Ibid.
45. s1(4) Equal Pay Act 1970.
46. Ibid., s1(5).
47. Camilla Palmer and Kate Poulton, *Sex and Race Discrimination in Employment*, Legal Action Group, 1987, at 91.
48. Catherine Hakim, 'Job Segregation: Trends in the 1970s', *Employment Gazette*, December 1981.
49. Department of Employment, *New Earnings Survey 1980-7*, Part A, Tables 10 and 11, HMSO, 1987.
50. Equal Opportunities Commission, *Some Facts About Women 1993*, EOC, 1993, and *Women the Law and the Workplace*, Labour Research Department Booklets, March 1993, at 3.
51. *Bromley v. Quick* (1988) IRLR 249 (CA); *Leverton v. Clwyd County Council* (1989) IRLR 28 (HL).
52. *Bromley v. Quick* (1988) IRLR 249 (CA); and *McAuley and Others v. Eastern Health and Social Services Board* (1991) IRLR 467 (NICA).
53. *Rummler v. Dato-Druck Gmbh*, Case No 237/85 (1987) IRLR 32 (ECJ); *Handelsog Kontorfunktionaerens Forbund i Danmark v. Dansk Arbejdgiverforening (acting for Danfoss)*, Case No 109/88 (1989) IRLR 532 (ECJ).
54. Equal Opportunities Commission, *Equal Pay for Men and Women, Strengthening the Acts*, 1990, at 4. European Commission, *Third Action Programme on Equal Opportunities 1991-5*, COM (90) 449 final, 1990, at 8.
55. Equal Opportunities Commission, *Equal Treatment for Men and Women, Strengthening the Acts*, formal proposals, 1988, at 21-2.
56. See Equal Opportunities Commission, *Equal Pay, Making it Work*, EOC, 1989.
57. Case 61/81, *Commission v. UK* (6 July 1982) ECR 2601. Council Directive 75/117 on the approximation of the laws of the Member States relating to the application of the principle of equal pay for men and women.
58. *Hansard*, 20 July 1983, cols 480-99.
59. *Request to the Commission of the European Communities by the Equal Opportunities Commission for Great Britain in Relation to the Implementation of the Principle of Equal Pay*, Equal Opportunities Commission, 1993, at 47-8.
60. Ibid.
61. Ibid., at 36-40.
62. *Aldridge v. British Telecommunications plc* (1989) 1 CR 790 (1990) IRLR 10 (EAT).
63. Equal Opportunities Commission, *Request*, 1993.
64. Letters from David Hunt, Secretary of State for Employment, to Kamlesh Bahl, Chairwoman of the Equal Opportunities Commission, 19 July 1993.
65. Equal Opportunities Commission, *Request*, 1993.
66. Labour Force Survey, Quarterly Bulletin, Department of Employment and the Government Statistical Service, December 1993, at 3.

67. Equal Opportunities Commission, *Women and Men in Britain 1993*, HMSO, 1993, at 1.
68. *The Employment Gazette*, 'Employment Workforce: Great Britain: Females', 1.1, Employment Department Statistics, June 1992. The number of women in the workforce was not centrally recorded until 1978. In June 1978 there were 9.884 million women in the waged workforce. By June 1986 this had risen to 11.152 million and in June 1991 to 11.754 million.
69. *New Earnings Survey*, Department of Employment, April 1992. Average hourly pay (excluding overtime) for males was £8.10 compared with £6.38 for females. The real pay gap is wider because male workers are more likely to work overtime. Average gross weekly pay for women: £241.10 – 71% of the figure for men.
70. Equal Opportunities Commission, *Women and Men in Britain 1992*, HMSO, 1992, at 29. See also, *Narrowing the Gender Pay Gap*, Pay Equity Project, 1993.
71. Equal Opportunities Commission, *Women and Men 1993*, 9.44% of all female employees work part-time.
72. Ibid.
73. Kevin Morgan and Ellis Roberts, *The Democratic Deficit A Guide to Quangoland*, Cardiff University Papers in Planning Research No 144, October 1993, at 19.
74. Georgina Ashworth, *When Will Democracy Include Women?*, Change Thinkbook VII, Calverts Press, 1992, at 4.
75. Stamp and Robarts, 1986, at 16.
76. Ibid.
77. Equal Opportunities Commission, *The EOC Annual Report 1991, the Equality Challenge*, 1992, at 7.
78. See Institute of Manpower Studies, *Merit Pay, Performance Appraisal and Attitudes to Women's Work*, IMS Publications Office, 1992.
79. Cynthia Cockburn, *In the Way of Women: Men's Resistance to Sex Equality in Organisations*, Macmillan, 1991, at 65.
80. Labour Research Department, *Performance Appraisal and Merit Pay*, LRD Publications, 1990, at 26.
81. Ibid., at 30.
82. Equal Opportunities Commission, *The Inequality Gap*, EOC, 1993.
83. Ibid.
84. *Equality News*, 'TECs fail on Equality', Local Government Information Unit, June 1993.
85. Ibid.
86. *Older People in the United Kingdom, Some Basic Facts*, Age Concern, August 1991.
87. *Older Women, Myths and Strategies*, Women's National Commission, November 1992, at 11.
88. Equal Opportunities Commission, *The Inequality Gap*, 1993.
89. See Jay Ginn, *Why are Older Women Poorer than Older Men?*, Department of Sociology, Surrey University, 1991.
90. Ibid.
91. *Older Women*, 1992, at 18–19.
92. Ibid., at 20.

93. Labour Research Department Publications, *Tackling Sexual Harassment at Work*, January 1994, at 4.
94. Ibid.
95. See Liz Curtis, *Making Advances, What you can do about sexual harassment at work*, BBC Books, 1993.
96. *The Times*, 'EC Code to Call for Stronger Laws on Sexual Harassment', 21 October 1991.
97. Department of Employment has published leaflets and booklets for workers and employers.
98. Equal Opportunities Commission, *Women and Men*, 1993, at 9.
99. Cockburn, 1991, at 80.
100. Equal Opportunities Commission, *Women and Men*, 1993, at 11.
101. Equal Opportunities Commission, *The Inequality Gap*, 1993.
102. National Pay Equity Campaign, *Conference Report*, 1991.
103. *EOC and Another* v. *Secretary of State for Employment* (HL), *New Law Journal*, 11 March 1994, at 358.
104. *Independent*, 'Law Biased Against Part-time Workers, Lords Rules', 4 March 1994.
105. *Daily Telegraph*, 'Part-timers Win Equality Cash Battle', 4 March 1994.
106. *Bilka Kaufhaus* v. *Weber von Hartz*, 1986.
107. *Rinner Kuhn* v. *FWW Spezial Gebaudereinigung*, 1989.
108. *Kowalska* v. *Freie und Hansetadt Hamburg*, 1990.
109. s26 and sch4 of the Trade Union Reform and Employment Rights Act 1993.
110. Ibid., ss23, 24 and 25.
111. Trades Union Congress, *Trade Union Reform and Employment Rights Bill: A TUC Guide*, 1993, at 16.
112. s35 Trade Union Reform and Employment Rights Act 1993.
113. Equal Opportunities Commission, *Request*, 1993, at 60–71.
114. See *Equality News*, 'Abolition of Wages Councils – Is it Legal?', Local Government Information Unit, June 1993; and Pay Equity Project, *Narrowing the Gender Pay Gap – How Wages Councils Work for Women*, Pay Equity Project, 1993.
115. The Republic of Ireland is the only other member state not to have some form of minimum wage.
116. UN, General Comment, 4(13) para 1.
117. *Britain the Preferred Location*, Department of Trade and Industry, 1991, at 14–15. This was circulated to all British Embassies to publicise Britain's low wages relative to other countries in the European Union.
118. *Consultation Document on Wages Councils*, Department of Employment, 1988, paras 11 and 14 and Annex 1, para 1.
119. Ibid, para 17.
120. *Hansard*, Oral Answers, 3 November 1992, col 139.
121. See *Pay Equity*, The Family Wage, 1993.
122. See Equal Opportunities Commission, *Parents, Employment Rights and Child Care, Research Discussion Series No 4*, EOC, 1992.
123. *Employment Equality and Caring for Children*, European Commission Network on Childcare and Other Measures to Reconcile Employment and Family Responsibilities, Annual Report 1992, comparing the UK government's record at 71–3 with Denmark's at 35–8.

124. See Equal Opportunities Commission, *Parents, Employment Rights and Child Care*, 1992.

125. Ibid. A cost-benefit analysis of alternative models for national childcare provision carried out by the Institute for Public Policy Research shows that up to 500,000 children could be lifted out of poverty if childcare services enabled their mothers to work.

126. ss23, 24 and 25 Trade Union Reform and Employment Rights Act 1993.

127. Labour Research Department, 1993, at 26–9.

128. Ibid., at 14.

129. Ibid.

130. Bridget Anderson, *Britain's Secret Slaves: An Investigation into the Plight of Overseas Domestic Workers*, Anti-Slavery International and Kalayaan, 1993, at 42.

131. *Hansard*, Written Answer, 1 November 1990. The Home Office responded that the information was not available.

132. Anderson, 1993, at 42.

133. *Hansard*, Written Answer, 5 November 1993, col 560.

134. *Hansard*, House of Lords, 28 November 1990, col 1052, Debate on Overseas Domestic Workers.

135. Anderson, 1993, at 64–70.

136. *Hansard*, Written Answer, 6 May 1993, col 177.

137. Equal Opportunities Commission, *Formal Investigation Report: Initial Teacher Training in England and Wales*, EOC, 1989.

138. Sue Lees, *Sugar and Spice: Sexuality and Adolescent Girls*, Penguin, 1993, at 154.

139. S. Riddell, 'It's Nothing to do with Me: Teachers' Views and Gender Divisions in the Curriculum', in S. Acker (ed), *Teachers, Gender and Careers*, Falmer Press, 1989.

140. Equal Opportunities Commission, *The Inequality Gap*, EOC, 1993, at 1.

141. Equal Opportunities Commission, *Women and Men*, 1993, at 29.

142. Ibid., at 7.

143. Catherine Hakim, 'On the Margins of Europe? The Social Policy Implications of Women's Marginal Work' in *The Implications of 1992 for Social Policy: Women, Equal Opportunities and Welfare*, Cross-National Research Papers, November 1990.

144. *Hansard*, Written Answers, 15 December 1992, col 149.

145. See *Citizen's Income and Women, Basic Income Research Group Discussion Paper Number 2*, Citizen's Income, 1993.

146. Oppenheim, 1993, at 95.

147. *Guardian*, 'Doctor in Abortion Furore', 13 September 1993.

148. Ibid.

149. See for example, *Whitehouse* v. *Jordan* (1980) 1 All ER 650 at 658.

150. *Bolam* v. *Friern Hospital Management Committee* (1957) 2 All ER 118 at 122.

151. *Re T* (1992) 3 Med LR 306.

152. *S* (1993) 3 WLR 806.

153. *J* (1992) 3 Med LR 317.

154. *R* (1992) Med LR 342.

155. For example, *Re F* (1990) 2 AC 1.

156. *Positively Helpful, A Guide to Good Practice in Working with Women and AIDS*, the Association of London Authorities, 1990, at 3.
157. *Quarterly AIDS and HIV figures*, Public Health Laboratory Service, January 1994. The number of reported male AIDS cases rose from 1,341 to 1,404. The number of reported female AIDS cases rose from 142 to 215.
158. See *Working with Women and HIV*, Royal College of Physicians, Report of Conference Proceedings, Edinburgh, 1 April 1993.
159. Ibid.
160. *Weekly Journal*, 'African Babies in Controversial AIDS Experiment', 1 July 1993.
161. Efua Dorkenoo and Scilla Elworthy, *Female Genital Mutilation: Proposals for Change*, Minority Rights Group International, 1992, at 35–8.
162. See Rodney Hedley and Efua Dorkenoo, *Child Protection and Female Genital Mutilation, Advice for Health, Education and Social Work Professionals*, FORWARD, 1992.
163. See Liz Kelly, *Surviving Sexual Violence*, Polity, 1989.
164. Kelly, 1989, at 79.
165. Ibid.
166. *The Times*, 'Women Seek Halt to Male Violence', 19 January 1994.
167. *Hansard*, Written Answer, 14 June 1993, col 435. The number of offenses of rape and attempted rape reported and the numbers of men convicted is as follows – 1988: 2,855 reported, 499 men convicted; 1989: 2,305 reported, 588 men convicted; 1990: 3,391 reported, 541 men convicted; 1991: 4,045 reported, 531 men convicted; 1992: 4,142 reported, convicted figures not available.
168. Mary Baber, *Rape, Research Paper No 93/100*, House of Commons Library, 5 November 1993, at 9.
169. s1(1) Sexual Offenses (Amendment) Act 1976.
170. s142 Criminal Justice and Public Order Act 1994.
171. In 1989, in Scotland, the High Court of Justiciary held that a husband can be guilty of raping his wife even though they are living together. *Stallard* v. *HM Advocate* (1989) SCCR 248, 1989 SLT 469.
172. *R* v. *Morgan and Others* (1975) 61 Cr App R 136 (a Royal Air Force Sergeant was convicted of aiding and abetting the gang-rape of his wife by three junior aircraftsmen); *R* v. *Bourne* (1952) 36 Cr App R 125 (CCA) (a man was convicted of aiding and abetting his wife to commit buggery with a dog, although he had in fact forcibly raped her using the dog as an instrument); *R* v. *Cogan and Leak* (1976) QB 217; (1975) 2 All ER 1059; (1975) Crim LR 584 and commentary (a man was convicted of aiding and abetting a rape after he terrorised his wife into submitting to sex with another man).
173. *R* v. *R* (1991) 3 WLR 767 (HL).
174. See Law Commission, *Criminal Law: Rape Within Marriage, Report No 204*, HMSO, 1992.
175. *W* v. *UK* (14 January 1994) 20166/92 and *R* v. *UK* (14 January 1994) 20190/92.
176. See for example, Hackney Council Women's Unit, *Submission to the Royal Commission on Criminal Justice*, 1991, at 3.
177. *The Times*, 'Man Cleared of Raping Wife', 30 March 1994.

Notes

178. *Daily Telegraph*, 'Man Cleared of Raping Wife Two Days After She Said Yes', 30 March 1994.
179. *Guardian*, 'Man Beat Rape Claim Wife to Death', 9 February 1995.
180. Sharon Grace, Charles Loyd and Lorna Smith, *Rape: from recording to conviction*, Home Office Research and Planning Unit Paper 71, 1992.
181. Ibid.
182. s2 Sexual Offenses (Amendment) Act 1976.
183. Jennifer Temkin, 'Sexual History Evidence – the Ravishment of Section 2', in *The Criminal Law Review* 3–20, January 1993.
184. *R. v. Kydd*, 1 November 1993, Norwich Crown Court, reported in *Daily Telegraph*, 'CPS Defends its Policy on Rape Trials', 3 November 1993.
185. Law Commission, *Criminal Law: Corroboration of Evidence in Criminal Trials*, Law Commission, Number 202, September 1991.
186. s32 Criminal Justice and Public Order Act 1994.
187. s142 Criminal Justice and Public Order Act 1994.
188. Sue Lees, 'Lawyers' Work as Constitutive of Gender Relations', in Cain and Harrington (eds) *Lawyers in a Postmodern World*, Open University Press, 1994, at 148.
189. Lees, 1994, at 149.
190. Kennedy, 1992, at 120–1.
191. *Billam* (1986) 8 Cr App R (S) 48.
192. Research conducted for 'Rape – Attrition Rates', BBC *Panorama* programme, 28 April 1993. During 1991, about one half of all convicted rapists were sentenced to less than five years imprisonment by the courts in Newcastle, Nottingham and Manchester. Leeds Crown Court sentenced 31% of convicted rapists to less than five years imprisonment, Nottingham, 35%, while the Old Bailey in London sentenced 39% to under five years. Nottingham sentenced 20% of convicted rapists to less than three years imprisonment.
193. Baber, 1993, at 27.
194. Ibid.
195. A Home Office circular (Home Office 69/1986) issued to all Chief Police Officers in 1986, gave strict guidelines on how to treat alleged victims of rape.
196. Hackney Council Women's Unit, *Submission to the Royal Commission*, 1991, at 7–8.
197. Dobash and Dobash, *Women, Violence and Social Change*, Routledge, 1992, at 2.
198. *Gender and the Criminal Justice System*, Home Office, 1992.
199. Ibid.
200. *Domestic Violence, Report of a National Inter-Agency Working Party*, Victim Support, 1992, at 2.
201. See for example, Home Affairs Committee, *Third Report*, *Domestic Violence*, ordered by the House of Commons, HMSO, 1993.
202. Home Affairs Committee, 1993, at vi.
203. Jane Moody, *The Domestic Violence Survey*, Middlesex University and the London Borough of Islington, March 1993. The research was financed by the Department of the Environment and Middlesex University and is the most detailed and comprehensive survey to have been carried out in Britain. The survey used a sample of 1,000 people, 571 women and 429 men.

413

204. Ibid.
205. Ibid.
206. Ibid.
207. *Independent*, 'Shelter's National Housing Week Campaign', 10 June 1993.
208. *Women's Aid Federation England, Information Pack*, WAFE, undated.
209. Home Affairs Select Committee, *Domestic Violence*, Memoranda of Evidence, October 1992, at 1.
210. Ibid.
211. Quoted in Susan Edwards, *Policing 'Domestic' Violence*, Sage Publications, 1989, at 31.
212. *Domestic Violence*, 1992, at 23.
213. *Spare Rib*, 'The Murder of Vandana Patel', June 1991.
214. *Independent*, 'Woman is Killed While Police Wait Downstairs', 13 November 1991.
215. Ibid., para 55.
216. Ibid., para 131.
217. *Abuse of Women and Children, A Feminist Response*, University of North London Press, 1993, at 17.
218. Home Affairs Select Committee, 1993, para 130.
219. Southall Black Sisters, *Submission to the Royal Commission on Criminal Justice*, 1992, at 4.
220. Southall Black Sisters, *Amplification of Oral Evidence to the Home Affairs Select Committee on Domestic Violence,* 11 November 1992.
221. Home Affairs Committee, 1993, paras 33–4.
222. Southall Black Sisters, *Submission to the Royal Commission*, 1992, at 4. Direct quote taken from police officer, 1987.
223. Southall Black Sisters, *Oral Evidence*, 1992.
224. Edwards, 1989, at 49.
225. Jackie Barron, *Not Worth the Paper, The Effectiveness of Legal Protection for Women and Children Experiencing Domestic Violence*, Women's Aid Federation, 1990, at 123.
226. Ibid.
227. *Domestic Violence*, 1992, at 28–9.
228. See Liberty, 'Submission to Lord Chancellor's Office on Privacy Consultation Paper', 1993.
229. See Barron, 1990.
230. Ibid.
231. *Domestic Violence*, 1992, at 27.
232. For discussion see Edwards, 1989 at 183.
233. Correspondence between Liberty and the Home Office, 27 April 1993. 'The latest figures for the numbers of women receiving a custodial sentence for homicide for the years 1991 and 1992 are 42. The number of these cases where the relationship is spousal/lover is 17 or 40% of the total.'
234. Homicide Act 1957.
235. *R v. Duffy* (1949) 1 All ER 932 (CA).
236. *Independent*, 'Battered Wife who Killed Husband is Freed', 26 September 1992.
237. Justice for Women Campaign Newsletter, March 1993.
238. Ibid.

239. See Newham Asian Women's Project Annual Report, 1991–2, at 26–8.
240. Lees, 1994, at 133–45.
241. Ibid., at 134.
242. Ibid., at 140.
243. Ibid.
244. *Hansard*, Written Answers, 17 October 1991, no 361.
245. Sue Bandalli, 'Current Topic: Provocation from the Home Office', Criminal Law Review, October 1992, 716–20. Of 137 women and 748 men convicted of killing their partners during the period, 7% women and 4% men were indicted for manslaughter rather than murder. Of total charged with murder, 26% women and 37% men were convicted of manslaughter on grounds of diminished responsibility; 53% women and 30% men were convicted of manslaughter on other grounds. (Other grounds include provocation and also unintentional killings; figures do not differentiate between the two and do not differentiate between pleas.) The majority of these women are likely to have been victims of domestic violence and it is remarkable that few were indicted for manslaughter.
246. Ibid., para 2.
247. Ibid., para 4.
248. Ibid., para 5.
249. *One Parent Families, Key Facts 1993*, National Council for One Parent Families, 1993, at 1.
250. Ibid.
251. *Social Trends 22*, 1992, Table 2.12.
252. *Social Trends 22*, 1991, Table 2.27.
253. *Guardian,* 'Tories at Blackpool – Howard Targets Lone Mothers', 6 October 1993.
254. *Guardian*, 'Wandsworth Sets Pace', 7 October 1993.
255. *Conservative Party News*, Conservative Central Office, 6 October 1993, at 12.
256. *Guardian*, 'Major Gets Back to the Old Values', 9 October 1993.
257. See for example, *The Sunday Times*, 'Major Demands Radical Shake-up of Cabinet Policy', 7 November 1993.
258. *Daily Mail*, 'Back in the Queue', 19 January 1994.
259. Southall Black Sisters, 'Arranged Marriages', unpublished paper, April 1994.
260. Ibid.
261. See for example, Soni and Balarajan, 'Suicide and Self-burning Amongst Indians and West Indians in England and Wales', *British Journal of Psychiatry*, 1992, 161, at 365–8; Soni, Raleigh, Bulusu and Balarajan, 'Suicides Amongst Immigrants from the Indian Sub-continent', *British Journal of Psychiatry*, 1990, 156, at 46–90; Merrill and Owens, 'Ethnic Differences in Self-poisoning: A comparison of Asian and White Groups', *British Journal of Psychiatry*, 1986, 148, at 708–12; and J. Shah, 'Causes and Prevention of Suicides', *Indian Journal of Social Work*, 1960, 21, at 161–75.
262. Southall Black Sisters, April 1994.
263. Ibid.
264. Ibid.
265. Ibid.
266. Women's Aid Federation Briefing Paper on Refugees and Women's Aid Funding.

6 Sexuality and the State

1. *Daily Telegraph*, 'This Strikes the Right Balance', 22 February 1994.
2. *Independent*, 'Compromise that Retains Discrimination', 22 February 1994.
3. *Hansard*, Criminal Justice and Public Order Bill, 21 February 1994, Col 76.
4. *Independent*, 'Howard Backs Gay Sex at 18', 25 January 1994.
5. Ibid.
6. *Independent*, 'Compromise that Retains Discrimination', 22 February 1994.
7. Ibid.
8. See Peter Tatchell, *Europe in the Pink, lesbian and gay equality in the new Europe*, GMP, 1992, at 101–37. See also, Peter Tatchell, 'Age of Consent Laws in Europe Update', unpublished, May 1994.
9. Helena Jeffs, ' "Age of Consent" for Male Homosexual Acts', *Research Paper 94/12*, Home Affairs Section, House of Commons library, 20 January 1994, at 50.
10. Ibid., the others are Austria, Finland, Hungary, Bulgaria, Croatia, Gibraltar, Latvia, Lichtenstein, Lithuania, Russia and Ukraine.
11. Ibid., France, Greece, Poland, Sweden and Denmark: age 15; Italy: 14; Malta, Portugal, Spain and Holland: effectively 12; Republic of Ireland: 17; Germany announced it intends to introduce an equal age of consent of 16.
12. *Sutherland* v. *UK*, case proceeding.
13. *Gay Times*, 'Opinion Poll Shows Massive Support for Gay Law Reform', April 1992.
14. *Evening Standard* ' "Idiocy" as Head Bans Romeo and Juliet; Classic Ballet Condemned as "Heterosexual",' 20 January 1994.
15. *Independent*, 'Two Women of Hackney', 3 February 1994.
16. Ibid.
17. *Observer*, 'Plague Descends on all their Houses', 30 January 1994.
18. Robert Wintemute, 'Sexual Orientation Discrimination', in *Individual Rights and the Law in Britain*, Christopher McCrudden and Gerald Chambers (eds), Clarendon Press, 1994, at 498, cited here as Wintemute, 1994.
19. s28 Local Government Act 1988.
20. s31 Criminal Justice Act 1991.
21. s13(5) Human Fertilisation and Embryology Act 1990.
22. *R* v. *Brown and Others*, NLJ Law Reports, 19 March 1993.
23. Wintemute, 1994, at 491–535.
24. Recent scientific studies suggest that sexuality may be at least partly determined by genes or brain structure. See for example, Bailey and Pillard, 'A Genetic Study of Male Sexual Orientation', *Archives of General Psychiatry*, December 1991.
25. s1 Race Relations Act 1976 and ss1–2 Sex Discrimination Act 1975 outlaw direct or indirect direct discrimination on the grounds of race or sex.
26. See Peter Van Dijk 'The Treatment of Homosexuals under the European Convention on Human Rights', in Kees Waaldjik and Andrew Clapham (eds), *Homosexuality: A European Community Issue*, Martinus Nijhoff Publishers, 1993, at 181–219.
27. *X* v. *Federal Republic of Germany* (No 530/59) (1960), 3 YBEC 1184 at 194.
28. *Dudgeon* v. *UK* (No 7525/76) (1980) Series B, No 40, 11 at 41.
29. *Norris* v. *Ireland* (1988) Series A, No 142 (22 October 1988) at 20–1.

Notes

30. *Modinos* v. *Cyprus* (1993) Series A, No 259 (22 April 1993) at 8–9.
31. Homosexual Offenses (Northern Ireland) Order 1982.
32. Sexual Offenses (Bailiwick of Guernsey) Law 1983.
33. Sexual Offenses (Jersey) Law 1990.
34. Isle of Man Sexual Offenses Act 1992.
35. Gibraltar Criminal Offenses (Amendment) Ordinance 1993.
36. Wintemute, 1994 at 525–7 and Van Dijk, 1993 at 193–200.
37. For example *Desmond* v. *UK* (No 9721/82) (1984) 7 EHRR 145; and *X* v. *UK* (No 7215/75) (1978) 19 Dec and Rep 66.
38. *Johnson* v. *UK* (No 10389/83) (1986) 47 Dec and Rep 72.
39. *X and Y* v. *UK* (No 8710/79) (1982) 28 Dec and Rep 77 (arising from (1979) AC 617 (HL)).
40. *Morissens* v. *Belgium* (No 11389/85) 3 May 1988.
41. *Bruce* v. *UK* (No 9237/81 (1983) 34 Dec and Rep 68.
42. *Simpson* v. *UK* (No 11716/85) (1986) 47 Dec and Rep 274 (arising from (1986) 2 Fam LR 91); *ZB* v. *UK* (No 16106/90) (10 February 1990) (arising from (1989) Imm AR 595); *C and LM* v. *UK* (No 14753/89) (9 October 1989); *WJ and DP* v. *UK* (No 12513/86) (11 September 1986); and *X and Y* v. *UK* (No 9369/81) (1983) 32 Dec and Rep 220.
43. Articles 8 and 12.
44. *C and LM* v. *UK* (No 14753/89) 9 October 1989.
45. Van Dijk, 1993, at 189–99.
46. Article 8.
47. Application 14753/89, cited in Van Dijk, 1993, at 190.
48. Application 9369/81. *X and Y* v. *UK* (1983), DR 32, 220, at 221.
49. Under Articles 8 and 14 of the ECHR.
50. *Kerkhoven* v. *The Netherlands* (No 15666/89) 19 May 1992.
51. Van Dijk, 1993, at 193.
52. Ibid., at 203.
53. Wintemute, 1994, at 526.
54. *Daily Mail*, 'Let Gays Marry and Adopt, say Euro MPs', 9 February 1994.
55. *Official Journal of the European Community*, No C 61, 28 February 1994, at 40–3.
56. See Paul Crane, *Gays and the Law*, Pluto Press, 1982.
57. s3 Sex Discrimination Act 1975.
58. ss1–2 Employment Act 1990.
59. s49(1) Fair Employment Act 1989.
60. Anya Palmer, *Less Equal Than Others*, Stonewall, 1993, at 1.
61. Ibid.
62. Ibid.
63. ss16,19 Employment Protection (Consolidation) Act 1978.
64. Caroline Gooding, *Trouble with the Law?*, GMP, 1992, at 26. Constructive dismissal occurs where an employer has so altered the conditions of an employee's employment as to amount to a fundamental breach of contract.
65. *Saunders* v. *Scottish National Camps Association Ltd*, 1981 IRLR 277 (Ct Session); *Wiseman* v. *Salford City Council*, 1981 IRLR 202 (EAT).
66. *Boychuck* v. *H.J. Symons Holdings Ltd* (1977) IRLR 395.
67. *McCormack* v. *TNT Sealion Ltd* (Central London Industrial Tribunal Case),

cited in Gooding, 1992, at 32; See also, *Burman* v. *Trevor Page Ltd*, unreported, Norwich Indus. Tribunal (1977), cited in Crane, 1982, at 114.
68. For example in *Boychuck* v. *HJ Symons Holdings Ltd* (1977) IRLR 395, the NCCL, failed to persuade an EAT to overturn the dismissal of a lesbian for wearing lesbian and gay badges.
69. *McCormack* v. *TNT Sealion Ltd* (Central London Industrial Tribunal Case).
70. Crane, 1982, at 99–100.
71. *O'Rourke and Wallace* v. *BG Turnkey Services (Scotland) Ltd*, Case Nos S/457/93, S/458/93, cited in Wintemute, 1994, at 504–5.
72. Gooding, 1992, at 36.
73. Lesbian and Gay Employment Rights, *Trade Union Survey: Equal Opportunities*, LAGER, May 1989 and *Labour Research*, 'Sexuality: A Trade Union Issue?', June 1991.
74. Palmer, 1993, at 1.
75. See Dai Harris, 'AIDS and Employment', in Dai Harris and Richard Haigh (eds), *AIDS: A Guide to the Law*, Terrence Higgins Trust, 1990, at 92–3.
76. *Third Periodic Report*, 1989, at 142.
77. *Hansard*, Written Answer, 23 July 1991, Col 474.
78. Disclosed in case taken by Liberty's legal department, *R* v. *Secretary of State for the Foreign and Commonwealth Office*, ex parte *Vidler*, 22 January 1993, unreported.
79. *Pink Paper*, 'Big Ears in Sex Row', 12 November 1987.
80. Gooding, 1992, at 33.
81. s1(5) Sexual Offenses Act 1967.
82. Gooding, 1992, at 40–1.
83. *Hansard*, Armed Forces (Discipline), 17 June 1992, Col 991.
84. Ibid.
85. *British Medical Journal*, Peter McColl, 'Homosexuality and Mental Health Services', 26 February 1994, at 550–1.
86. *BMA News Review*, G. Gardner, 'Should the Age of Consent for Gays be Lowered to 16?', 19 November 1993, at 23.
87. Ibid.
88. *British Medical Journal*, 'Homosexuality and Mental Health Services', 1994.
89. Ibid.
90. *Parliamentary Briefing: Housing and Urban Development Bill*, Stonewall Group, January 1993.
91. Ibid.
92. Gooding, 1992, at 42–55.
93. *The Times*, 9 November 1990, cited in Bynoe, Barnes and Oliver, *Equal Rights for Disabled People: The case for a new law*, IPPR, 1991/2, at 26–7.
94. O'Brien, Carrier and Ward (eds), 'Housing Law and HIV Infection', in Harris and Haigh, 1990, at 59–83.
95. Gooding, 1992, at 163–4.
96. Harris and Haigh, 1990, at 145–61.
97. *AIDS – The Issue for Housing*, Resource Information Service in cooperation with the London Special Needs Group, 1987, at 43.
98. See Gooding, 1992, at 50–69.
99. *Grant* v. *Edwards* 1986.
100. *Capital Gay* 'Triumph of Tory Shits', 22 January 1993.

101. Wintemute, 1994, at 492–3.
102. Crane, 1982, at 87.
103. Indecent Display (Control) Act 1981 makes the display of 'indecent' material in public a criminal offence. Pornographic magazines may be lawfully displayed in shops, provided that they are put in a separate place marked by a warning sign. s2 Local Government (Miscellaneous Provisions) Act 1982 gives local authorities powers to control the siting of sex shops and cinemas, s42 Customs Consolidation Act 1876, s11 Post Office Act 1953, the Video Recordings Act 1984, and the Protection of Children Act 1978 all contain other restrictions. Part VII of the Criminal Justice and Public Order Bill contains regulations concerning computer pornography.
104. Gooding, 1992, at 234–41.
105. Customs Consolidation Act 1876 and Customs Excise Management Act 1979.
106. Tatchell, 1992, at 95. Wintemute, 1994, at 502.
107. *Time Out*, 'Barrier Methods', 11–18 September 1991.
108. *Knuller* v. *DPP* (1973) AC 434.
109. Gooding, 1992, at 241. Against a Birmingham-based publication in 1986.
110. Earl of Caithness, government spokesperson in the debate on the Bill. Quoted in Madeline Colvin, *Section 28: a practical guide to the law and its implications*, NCCL, 1989, at 4.
111. Wintemute, 1994, at 508.
112. Colvin, 1989, at 2. The supposed circulation of a Danish children's picture book, *Jenny Lives with Eric and Martin*, to young children in inner London was the most famous.
113. Wintemute, 1994, at 508.
114. Colvin, 1989, at 17–57; Tatchell, 1992, at 99; and Gooding, 1992, at 295–300.
115. Complaints received at Liberty's legal department 1988–94.
116. *Pink Paper*, 'Council Backs Down over Section 28', 3 February 1995.
117. K. Norrie, 'Symbolic and Meaningless Legislation', *Journal of the Law Society of Scotland*, September 1988, at 310–31.
118. Colvin, 1989, at 57.
119. Wintemute, 1994, at 509.
120. *Hansard*, Local Government Bill, 15 December 1987, Col 1009.
121. Gooding, 1992, at 300.
122. s46 Education Act 1986.
123. Circular No 11/87, 25 September 1987.
124. *Capital Gay*, ' "Drop the Clause" Outrage Urge Patten', 4 June 1993.
125. *Arrested Development?: Stonewall survey on the age of consent and sex education*, Stonewall Lobby Group, January 1994.
126. Ibid.
127. See *Sex, Education, Values, and Morality*, Health Education Authority, 1994, at 1–6.
128. *Gay Times*, 'Gay School Pupils Could be "Outed" by Teachers', June 1994.
129. Stonewall, 1994.
130. Ibid.
131. *Capital Gay*, 'Police Seize Sex Cards', 28 May 1993.
132. *Capital Gay*, 'Customs Seize Safer Sex Film', 30 October 1992.
133. Complaint received by Liberty's legal department.

134. *Capital Gay*, 'Minister Attacks Sex Education', 1 April 1994.
135. Ibid.
136. *Pink Paper*, 'Patten Pressures Students to Drop Safer Sex Sessions', 3 April 1994.
137. s11(c) Matrimonial Causes Act 1973 states that a marriage is void 'if the parties are not respectively male and female.'
138. Wintemute, 1994, at 511.
139. *Guardian*, 'Unwed Pairs' Legal Rights Under Review', 13 May 1994.
140. Crane, 1982, at 146.
141. *James v. Eastleigh Borough Council* (1990) 2 AC 751 (HL).
142. Wintemute, 1994, at 511.
143. Gooding, 1992, at 70–3.
144. Wintemute, 1994, at 511. Gooding, 1992, at 71.
145. *Harrogate Borough Council v. Simpson* (1986) 2 Fam LR 91.
146. Gooding, 1992, at 85.
147. Crane, 1982, at 144.
148. Cited in Gooding, 1992, at 82–3. *In the estate of David Thomas Nickson, deceased; Bunyan Craig v. Nickson*, 1990.
149. Gooding, 1992, at 201.
150. *United Kingdom Immigration Laws and Rules as they affect same-sex couples*, Stonewall Immigration Group Briefing Paper, April 1994.
151. Ibid.
152. Ibid.
153. *Capital Gay*, 'Prison for Gay Immigration Officer', 29 April 1994.
154. Cited in Stonewall, Immigration Group Briefing Paper, 1994.
155. Ibid.
156. Ibid.
157. Gooding, 1992, at 208. See also, Crane, 1982 at 151 which cites a case where asylum without refugee status was given to a gay man from Iran, where there had been many executions under the Khomeini regime of men convicted of homosexual offenses.
158. Tatchell, 1992, at 94–5.
159. UN General Comment to Article 24.
160. See Lesbian Custody Group, *Lesbian Mothers' Legal Handbook*, Women's Press, 1986.
161. At the time of a divorce, legal provision must be made for the custody of any daughters or sons under the age of 18. The concepts of 'custody', 'care and control' and 'access' have been replaced under ss2–5 and 8 of the Children Act 1989 by concepts of 'parental responsibility', 'residence orders' and 'contact orders.'
162. Lesbian Custody Group, 1986, at 123.
163. s1(1) Children Act 1989.
164. *C v. C* (1991) 1 FLR 223, 228 (CA).
165. *B v. B* (1991) FLR 402, 410.
166. *Re P* (1983) FLR 401, 405 (CA).
167. Wintemute, 1994, at 513.
168. *Re D* (an infant) (1977) AC 617 (HL).
169. Gooding, 1992, at 109.
170. Home Office *Sexual Offenses and Sentencing*, HMSO, 1979.

171. Lesbian Custody Group, 1986, at 62.
172. *W* v. *W* unreported Court of Appeal 17 June 1980.
173. Lesbian Custody Group, 1986, at 154–7.
174. Gooding, 1992, at 109.
175. Rutter and Golombok, London, Institute of Psychiatry, 1982, unpublished paper. See also the chapter on psycho-sexual development in M. Rutter (ed.) *Scientific Foundations of Developmental Psychiatry*, Heinemann Medical, 1980.
176. See Lorraine Trenchard and Hugh Warren, *Something to Tell You*, London Gay Teenage Group, 1984.
177. Gooding, 1992, at 104.
178. Ibid., at 131.
179. Lesbian Custody Group, 1986, at 85.
180. See *Daily Mail*, ' "Gay" Adoptions Go On', 20 October 1992. *Independent*, 'Breakthrough for Mixed Adoptions gets Go-ahead', 4 November 1993. *Guardian*, 'Bottomley Adoption Code Outlaws Ideology', 4 November 1993.
181. Paragraph 16 of the Statutory Guidance, final sentence.
182. Gooding, 1992, at 132.
183. s13(5) Human Fertilisation and Embryology Act 1990.
184. Gooding, 1992, at 126.
185. *Gay Times*, 'News in Brief', September 1990. The article cites a letter from a Home Office minister responding to complaints about a homophobic propaganda campaign by the neo-nazi British National Party.
186. *Capital Gay*, 'Reggae Star Says "Shoot Gays",' 18 September 1992.
187. *Independent,* 'Macho Man Music Puts Gays in Fear of their Lives', 4 October 1993.
188. *Independent on Sunday,* 'Is This Comparison Odious?', 31 October 1993.
189. *Pink Paper*, 'Lecturer Let off Over Leaflet', 13 May 1994.
190. Press Council, Press Release AB18521/2554, 14 May 1990.
191. *The Times*, 'Article "Was Insulting to Gays",' 7 January 1991.
192. Tatchell, 1992, at 93.
193. *Wolverhampton Express and Star*, 'Shoot all Gays Says Councillor', 17 December 1987.
194. See David Comstock, *Violence Against Lesbians and Gay Men*, Columbia University Press, 1991.
195. Burke, 1993, at 37–62.
196. GALOP, 1992, at 23.
197. Ibid., men 54%; women 68%.
198. Ibid.
199. Ibid.
200. Ibid.
201. Ibid.
202. *Gay Times*, 'Over 30 Murders of Gay Men Unsolved Since 1986', April 1994.
203. Ibid.
204. *The Response to Racial Attacks and Harassment: Guidance for the Statutory Agencies*, Report of the Inter-Departmental Racial Attacks Group, Home Office, 1989.
205. Wintemute, 1994, at 503.

206. Ibid.
207. *Capital Gay*, 'Judge Brands Victim a Sodomite', 25 March 1988.
208. *Evening Standard*, 'Caught in the Gender Trap', 18 January 1988.
209. Ibid.
210. *Corbett* v. *Corbett* (1970) 2 All ER 33.
211. *Rees* v. *UK* (17 October 1986), on issue of birth certificates, cited in Geoffrey Robertson, *Freedom, the Individual and the Law*, 6th edn, Penguin, 1989, at 383. See *Cossey* v. *UK* (27 September 1990), on the right to marry.
212. Briefing Paper, 'Gender Dysphoria 2', Press For Change, BM Network, undated.
213. Ibid.
214. Robertson, 1989, at 382.
215. The syndrome is described authoritatively by Professor John Money (Johns Hopkins University), Professor Louis Gooren and Professor Milton Diamond among other specialists in an expanding field. See Briefing Paper: 'Gender Dysphoria 1', Press for Change, BM Network, undated.

7 Human Rights and Disabled People

1. *Hansard*, Civil Rights (Disabled Persons) Bill, 6 May 1994, cols 960–1017.
2. Ibid., col 991.
3. *Hansard*, Personal Statement, 10 May 1994, col 155.
4. *Hansard*, Hon. Member for Sutton and Cheam, 25 May 1994, col 342.
5. *Hansard*, Civil Rights (Disabled Persons) Bill, 20 May 1994.
6. Ibid., 11 March 1994, col 520.
7. Ibid., col 521.
8. By convention frontbench MPs do not sign Private Member's Bills.
9. Brian Doyle, *New Directions Towards Disabled Workers Rights*, Institute for Employment Rights, 1994, at 16.
10. *Halsbury's Law of England*, Vol 34, 4th edition, 1980, para 1185.
11. Martin, Meltzer and Elliot, *The Prevalence of Disability Amongst Adults*, Office of Population Censuses and Surveys (OPCS) of Disability in Great Britain, *Report 1*, 1988, HMSO; Martin and White, *The Financial Circumstances of Disabled Adults Living in Private Households*, OPCS, *Report 2*, 1988, HMSO; Martin, White and Meltzer, *Disabled Adults: Services, Transport and Employment*, OPCS, *Report 4*, 1988, HMSO; Meltzer, Smyth and Robus, *Disabled Children: Services, Transport and Education*, OPCS, *Report 5*, 1989, HMSO.
12. See W. Wolfsenburger, 'Human Service Policies: The Rhetoric Versus the Reality' in L. Barton (ed), *Disability and Dependency*, Falmer Press, 1989.
13. *A Consultation Paper on Government Measures to Tackle Discrimination Against Disabled People*, HMSO, 16 July 1994.
14. *Hansard*, Disabled People (Consultation), 15 July 1994, col 1298.
15. *Ending Discrimination Against Disabled People*, HMSO, 1995, and Disability Discrimination Bill.
16. Disability Discrimination Bill, Part III.
17. Ibid., Part IV.
18. *Guardian*, 'Disabled Bill Gives Firms Time Limits and Costs', 13 January 1995.

Notes

19. Ibid., cols 527–8.
20. *Hansard*, Civil Rights (Disabled Persons) Bill, 11 March 1994, col 528–9, Roger Berry MP, citing the Secretary of State for Employment and Lord Henley at a meeting of the all-party parliamentary disablement group.
21. See Colin Barnes, *Disabled People in Britain and Discrimination*, Hurst and Calgary, in association with the British Council of Organisations of Disabled People, 1991.
22. See Ian Bynoe, Mike Oliver and Colin Barnes, *Equal Rights for Disabled People, The Case for a New Law*, IPPR, Social Policy Paper no 7, Welfare Series 1991/2.
23. CORAD, *Report by the Committee on Restrictions Against Disabled People*, HMSO, 1982.
24. Martin, Meltzer and Elliot, OPCS, *Report 1*, 1988; OPCS, *Report 2*, 1988; OPCS, *Report 4*, 1988; OPCS, *Report 5*, 1989.
25. Patricia Prescott-Clarke, *Employment and Handicap*, Social Community Planning Research, 1990.
26. Thompson, Buckle and Lavery, *Not the OPCS Survey: Being disabled costs more than they said*, Disablement Income Group, 1988.
27. Colin Barnes, *Disabled People in Britain and Dicrimination, A Case for Anti-discrimination Legislation*, British Council of Organisations of Disabled People, 1991.
28. Andrew Fowkes, Philip Oxley and Bryan Heiser, *Cross-sector Benefits of Accessible Public Transport*, Joseph Rowntree Foundation, undated, at 4–5.
29. OCPS, *Report 1*, 1988, at 18–21.
30. Barnes, 1991, at 8.
31. *Employment and Training for People with Disabilities: Consultative Document*, Department of Employment, 1990.
32. *Hansard*, Civil Rights (Disabled Persons) Bill, 11 March 1994, col 564.
33. Labour Research Department, *Disability and Work*, LRD, 1993, at 6.
34. *Hansard*, Civil Rights (Disabled Persons) Bill, 11 March 1994, cols 563–4.
35. Ibid.
36. OPCS, *Report 1*, 1988, at 16–26.
37. Ibid.
38. Nick Day, *The Incidence and Prevalence of AIDS and other serious HIV Diseases in England and Wales for 1982–7, using data to the end of 1992*, Communicable Disease Report and Public Health Laboratory Service, June 1993.
39. Letter from MIND, July 1993.
40. Prescott-Clarke, 1990, at 20.
41. Doyle, 1994, at 3.
42. See *OPCS Report 1*, 1988.
43. See for example, *Daily Telegraph*, 'The Disabled Have Rights but so do the Rest of Us', 24 May 1994.
44. Ibid.
45. Bynoe, Barnes and Oliver, 1991/2, at 21.
46. Barnes, 1991, at 1.
47. Bynoe, Barnes and Oliver, 1991/2, at 5.
48. Ibid.
49. Race Relations Act 1976.

50. Sex Discrimination Act 1975.
51. See Bynoe, Barnes and Oliver, 1991/2, at 61–70.
52. *Employment and Training for People with Disabilities:* 1990, para 5.14.
53. Labour Research Department, 1993, at 2.
54. Bynoe, Barnes and Oliver, 1991/2, at 25.
55. Ibid.
56. Ibid.
57. *Mail on Sunday*, 'Storm as Pub Bans Disabled Skittles Team', 25 November 1990.
58. Letter from MIND, July 1994.
59. *Personnel Management*, 'Alcohol and Drugs join HIV on Texaco's Screening Programme', May 1991.
60. Bynoe, Barnes and Oliver, 1991/2, at 25.
61. Hansard, House of Lords, Civil Rights Bill (HL), 22 June 1994, cols 391–2.
62. Barnes, 1991, at 208–26.
63. See E. Fry, *Disabled people and the 1987 general election*, Spastics Society, 1987 and 1992.
64. *The Right to Vote*, MIND (North West), 1989, at 1.
65. Ibid.
66. Barnes, 1991, at 209.
67. L. Ward, *Talking Points: The Right to Vote*, CMH, undated.
68. s18 Representation of the People Act 1983.
69. *Polls Apart: Disabled People and the 1992 General Election*, Spastics Society, July 1992.
70. Fry, 1987.
71. Barnes, 1991, at 213.
72. *The Electoral Process*, RNIB, undated.
73. Fry, 1987.
74. *Hansard*, Civil Rights (Disabled Persons) Bill, 11 March 1994, col 521–2.
75. Barnes, 1991, at 215.
76. Scott, 1994, at 27.
77. See Colin Barnes, *Disabling Imagery and the Media, An Exploration of the Principles for Media Representation of Disabled People*, British Council of Organisations of Disabled People, 1992.
78. Ibid.
79. *Pre-recorded teletext subtitles on TV*, Deaf Broadcasting Council, 1990.
80. Barnes, 1991, at 186.
81. Ibid.
82. Barnes, 1991, at 200–1.
83. Ibid.
84. *Psychiatric Bulletin*, 'Mental Illness in British Newspapers', 17, 1993, at 673–4.
85. See *Images of Disability on Television*, Broadcasting Research Unit, 1990, unfoliod.
86. Ibid.
87. Ibid.
88. Ibid.
89. Ibid.
90. Ibid.

91. Barnes, 1991, 199–201.
92. Ibid., at 202.
93. Ibid., at 202–3.
94. See J. Campbell, *Developing our Image – Who's in Control?*, paper presented to 'Cap in Hand' Conference, February 1990, cited in Barnes, 1991, at 203.
95. Barnes, 1992, at 36–8.
96. Barnes, 1991, at 203–4.
97. Ibid.
98. s9(1) Disabled Persons (Employment) Act 1944, s218 contract of Employment.
99. Prescott-Clarke, 1990, at 74.
100. Ibid., at 78.
101. LRD, 1993, at 4.
102. *Hansard*, Employment Bill, 6 June 1989, col 68.
103. Ibid.
104. *Employment and training for people with disabilities: consultative document*, Department of Employment, 1990.
105. Barnes, 1991, at 88, citing a *Review of the Organisation and Staffing of the Employment Service*, July 1989.
106. *Hansard*, Written Answer, 15 March 1994, col 564.
107. *Hansard*, Civil Rights (Disabled Persons) Bill, 11 March 1994, col 564.
108. Ibid., col 540.
109. Ibid., col 562.
110. OPCS, *Report 2*, at 12–13.
111. Barnes, 1991, at 62–97.
112. Prescott-Clarke, 1990, at 5.
113. OPCS, *Report 4*, at 68–9.
114. Ibid., at 69.
115. Ibid., at 77.
116. Ibid., at 80.
117. Ibid., at 77.
118. Ibid., at 34.
119. Ibid.
120. Barnes, 1991, at 66.
121. Prescott-Clarke, 1990, at Table 4.2.
122. OPCS, *Report 2*, at 16–19.
123. Liberty, Southall Black Sisters and Change, *Women's Rights Human Rights*, NCCL, 1994, at 21–2.
124. OPCS, *Report 2*, at 17, compares hourly earnings of disabled and non-disabled workers, 1985.
125. Renamed Scope in 1994 in recognition that 'spastic' can be used as a term of abuse.
126. E. Fry, *An Equal Chance for Disabled People: A Study of Discrimination in Employment*, Spastics Society, 1986; Graham, Jordan and Lamb, *An Equal Chance or No Chance?*, Spastics Society, 1990.
127. Graham, Jordan and Lamb, 1990, at 5.
128. Prescott-Clarke, 1990, at 99.
129. Ibid.

130. J. Morrell, *The Employment of People with Disabilities: Research into the Policies and Practices of Employers*, Department of Employment, 1990.
131. Ibid., Table 20, at 14.
132. Ibid.
133. Ibid.
134. Ibid., at 23.
135. OPCS, *Report 2*, at 19.
136. See *A Way Out of Poverty and Disability*, Disability Alliance, 1991.
137. Ibid.
138. *Hansard*, Written Answer, 6 May 1994, col 694.
139. Attendance Allowance DS2A claim form, Section 2.
140. Marylin Howard, *Disability and Invalidity Benefit Workshop Paper*, Disability Alliance, 1993.
141. Barnes, 1991, at 115.
142. OPCS, *Report 4*, 1989, at 89–101.
143. Ibid.
144. *A Way out of Poverty and Disability*, Disability Alliance, 1991.
145. Barnes, 1991, at 125.
146. Ibid., at 144.
147. *HIV and Disability: Evidence to the National AIDS Trust from Regard, National Organisation of Disabled Lesbians and Gay Men*, July 1994.
148. *Guardian*, 'Cash Urged for Mental Health Care in the Cities', 20 April 1994.
149. *Services to disabled children and their families, report of the national inspection of services to disabled children and their families*, HMSO, January 1994, para 5.1.3.
150. See Jenifer Temkin, 'Disability, Child Abuse and Criminal Justice', *Modern Law Review*, May 1994, at 402–18.
151. Barnes, 1991, at 28–61.
152. See *The School Survey, Within Reach, Access for Disabled Children to Mainstream Education*, Spastics Society and National Union of Teachers, April 1993.
153. Ibid.
154. Ibid.
155. *Disabled Young People Living Independently*, British Council of Organisations of Disabled People, 1986, at 6.
156. See *Disabled People and Institutional Discrimination*, Social Policy Research Findings, no 21, November 1991.
157. Barnes, 1991, at 45.
158. Ibid.
159. Ibid.
160. Social Policy Research, 1991, unfolioed.
161. *Hansard*, Civil Rights (Disabled Persons) Bill, 11 March 1994, col 523.
162. Ibid.
163. Incidents cited in *Hansard*, Civil Rights (Disabled Persons) Bill, 11 March 1994, col 523.
164. Day, 1993.
165. Public Health Laboratory Service *News Release*, 31 January 1994.
166. Ibid.

167. Dai Harris and Richard Haigh (eds), *AIDS: A Guide to the Law*, Terrence Higgins Trust, 1990, at 9.
168. Ibid., at 14.
169. Ibid., at 13.
170. *Pink Paper*, 'HIV Status Leak Fear', 11 March 1994.
171. *Public Transport and the Missing Six Millions: What can be learned?*, Disabled Persons Transport Environment Committee, 1989.
172. Prescott-Clarke, 1990, at 8.
173. *All change: A consumer study of transport handicap in Greater London*, Greater London Association of Disabled People (GLAD), 1986.
174. *Hansard*, Civil Rights (Disabled Persons) Bill, 11 March 1994, col 566.
175. Barnes, 1991, at 164.
176. GLAD, 1986. These specify that wheelchair users are a potential hazard 'because of difficulties of emergency evacuation'.
177. Barnes, 1991, at 166.
178. Ibid.
179. *Which*, 'No Go', June 1990.
180. Ibid.
181. Barnes, 1991, at 170.
182. Ibid.
183. Ibid., at 162.
184. Ibid.
185. Ibid.
186. Ibid., at 187.
187. Letter from Disability Awareness in Action, June 1994.
188. Crouch, Forester and Mayhew Smith, *Access in London: A guide for those who have problems getting around*, Robert Nicholson, 1989.
189. See *Arts and Disabled People: The Attenborough Report*, Carnegie UK Trust, 1985.
190. Carnegie Council Review, *After Attenborough: Arts and disabled people*, Bedford Square Press, 1988.
191. Barnes, 1991, at 190.
192. Ibid., at 130.
193. Ibid.
194. S. Brisenden, *A Charter for personal care*, HCIL, 1985, at 2.
195. *Report of the Committee of Inquiry into Complaints about Ashworth Special Hospital*, vol 1, HMSO, August 1992, at 252.
196. *Guardian*, 'Nursing Home Abuse Increases', 15 June 1994.
197. Ibid.
198. *Guardian*, 'Mentally Ill Face Care Beds Crisis in Cities', 11 December 1993.
199. Mental Health Act Commission, Fifth Biennial Report, HMSO. 1993.
200. Ibid.
201. *Mentally Incapacitated Adults and Decision Making*, Law Commission Consultation Paper, no 128, HMSO, 1993, at 13.
202. Neil Lunt and Patricia Thornton, *Employment Policies for Disabled People, A review of legislation and services in fifteen countries*, Employment Department, October 1993.
203. Ibid., at 179.
204. Ibid.

205. *Proposal for a Council Directive on Minimum Requirements to Improve the Mobility and the Safe Transport to Work of Workers with Reduced Mobility*, OJ C68/7 (16 March 1991) as amended by OJ C 15/18 (21 January 1992).
206. Doyle, 1994, at 18–22.
207. Bynoe, Barnes and Oliver, 1991/2, at 43–4.
208. See Lunt and Thornton, 1993.
209. See Chris Robson and Kieran Rose, 'Legal Equality in Ireland', unpublished.
210. *International Herald Tribune*, 'Senate Backs Bill to Protect Rights of Disabled', 10 September 1989, quoting Senator Edward Kennedy.
211. s504 Rehabilitation Act 1973.
212. Scott, 1994, at 15–23.
213. Ibid., at 7.
214. Mary K. O'Melveny, 'The Americans with Disabilities Act and collective bargaining agreements: Reasonable accommodations or irreconcilable conflicts', *Kentucky Law Journal*, vol 82, 1993–4.
215. Mary K. O'Melveny, 'The Americans with Disabilities Act and Collective Bargaining Rights: Recent developments and ongoing issues', Prepared for the AFL-CIO second annual Lanor symposium of the Americans With Disabilities Act, May 1994.
216. See Victoria Scott, *Lessons from America, A study of the Americans with Disability Act*, RADAR, 1994.
217. Ibid., at 8–9.
218. Scott, 1994, at 8.
219. Ibid., at 24–5.
220. George Bush, The White House, 26 July 1990.
221. Gwen Thayer, *Taxing Benefits: The Magic Bullet*, President's Committee on Employment of People with Disabilities Health Care Symposium, 18 May 1994.
222. *Daily Labour Report*, 'Special Report', the Bureau of National Affairs Inc, 1994.
223. Ibid.
224. *Daily Telegraph*, 25 May 1994.

8 Mental Health

1. *Report of the Committee into Complaints about Ashworth Hospital*, vol 1, HMSO, August 1992.
2. The Committee of Inquiry was commissioned in April 1991 by the Secretary of State for Health to investigate the 'allegations of improper care and treatment at Ashworth Hospital contained within the *Cutting Edge* television documentary, "A Special Hospital", transmitted on 4 March 1991 and any other relevant allegations brought to their attention'.
3. *Ashworth Report*, vol 1, at 252.
4. The needs and problems encountered by people with mental health problems are distinctly different from those of people with learning difficulties but in the context of laws applying in England and Wales it is appropriate to consider both groups together.
5. See MHAC Fifth Biennial Report, 1991–3, December 1993, HMSO, at 23.
6. A social worker considered competent in dealing with persons who are suffer-

ing from mental disorder and appointed by the local authority to carry out these functions under the Act. See ss114–15(1) of the 1983 Act. The application can also be made by the person's 'nearest relative' under s26.

7. In cases where a person should be admitted of 'urgent necessity' and there is not enough time to get a second medical recommendation, the support of one doctor is enough. The doctor providing the medical recommendation must state how long it would take to get a second doctor to assess the person and what harm might occur in the meantime. See s4 of the Act.

8. s12 of the Mental Health Act 1983.

9. s2 of the Act.

10. s1(1) of the Act.

11. L.J. Lawton in *W* v. *L* (1974) QB 711. See also B. Hoggett, *Mental Health Law*, 3rd edn, Sweet and Maxwell, 1992, 3rd edn at 48 in which she described this as 'the man must be mad test'.

12. *R* v. *South Western Hospital Managers* ex parte *M* (1994) 1 All ER 161.

13. See compulsory treatment, at 222–5.

14. ss35, 36, 37, 38 and 41, Mental Health Act 1983.

15. A Hospital Order cannot be made if the person has been convicted of murder, see s37, Mental Health Act 1983 and R. Jones, *Manual on the Mental Health Act 1983*, 3rd edn, Sweet and Maxwell, 1991, at 91.

16. B. Hoggett, 1990, at 188, section 41(3) Mental Health Act 1983.

17. *R* v. *Gardiner* (1976) 1 WLR; *R* v. *Birch* (1989) 11 Cr App R(S).

18. s132(1) Mental Health Act 1983. See Jones, 1991, at 234.

19. (1981) 4 EHRR 181.

20. Ibid.

21. *R* v. *Secretary of State for the Home Department* ex parte *K* (1990) 3 All ER 562. Despite the fact that two Mental Health Review Tribunals had held that Mr Kay was no longer suffering from any mental disorder, and in the absence of medical evidence obtained at the time or immediately afterwards, the court held the Home Secretary to be acting within his powers.

22. s58 Mental Health Act 1983.

23. P. Fennell, *Treatment Without Consent, Law, psychiatry and the treatment of mentally disordered people since 1845* (forthcoming).

24. MIND has called for a ban on compulsory ECT and on administering ECT to children and young persons. See *Policy on Physical Treatments*, MIND, 1994. Tony Baker, consultant in child and adolescent psychiatry, supported MIND's campaign concerning ECT and children and young persons, *Lancet*, Letter page, 7 January 1995.

25. Fennell (forthcoming).

26. Ibid.

27. *Health Committee, Fifth Biennial Report 1991–3*, December 1993 at 55–6.

28. Health Committee, *Fifth Report*, 'Community Supervision Orders', vol II, Minutes of Evidence, at 42.

29. Rogers, Pilgrim and Lacey, *Experiencing Psychiatry: Users' View of Services*, MIND, 1993 at 165.

30. Ibid., at 166.

31. See Fennell, *Force Feeding and the Mental Health Act 1983*, NLJ, 3 March 1995, at 319–20.

32. See MIND's briefing 'Medication and the Mental Health' (Patients in the Community) Bill, February 1995.
33. Health Committee *Fifth Report, Community Supervision Orders*, June 1992, HMSO.
34. The grounds are: the patient is suffering from mental illness, mental impairment, severe mental impairment or psychopathic disorder, and there would be a substantial risk of serious harm to the health or safety of the patient, or of others, or the patient being seriously exploited if he were not to receive after-care services under supervision and being subject to supervised after-care will help secure the after-care services, clause 25A(4).
35. *The Report of the Working Group on High Security and Related Psychiatric Provision*, Department of Health, 1994, 3.1. As at 1 January 1995, there were 1676 patients.
36. Ibid., at 3.3.
37. See *Ashworth Report*, 1992.
38. Ibid., at 86, 96–100, 148–51.
39. Ibid., at 151.
40. Ibid., at 94–101.
41. Ibid., at 73.
42. Ibid., at 253.
43. Special Hospitals Service Authority, *Big, Black and Dangerous?* 1993.
44. The Report of the Working Group on High Security and Related Psychiatric Provision, 3.21.
45. MHAC, *Fifth Biennial Report*, 25
46. *Guardian*, 'Staff Sacked over Patient Tied to Toilet', 11 December 1992.
47. J. Gunn, T. Madden and M. Swinton, *Mentally Disordered Prisoners*, Department of Forensic Psychiatry, Institute of Psychiatry, Home Office, October 1990 (revised May 1991), at 43. See the Reports of the Service Advisory Groups, 'An Overview', para 19.
48. Ibid., at 52.
49. *HM Chief Inspectors Report on HM Prison Brixton*, 1990, Home Office, *Report of the Review of Suicide and Self Harm*, HMSO, Cmd 1383. A report by a Committee of the Council of Europe in 1990 also privately informed the Home Office that the conditions for such prisoners were intolerable, leading to the closure of one of the worst prison units at Brixton, London. See Bynoe, *Treatment, Care and Security*, July 1992, MIND. See also the Torture Committee's, *Report* CPT/Int, 1991, at 15.
50. See *Report on an Efficiency Scrutiny of the Prison Medical Service*, 1990, Home Office.
51. *Knight* v. *Home Office* (1990) 3 ALL ER 237.
52. Gunn, 1990, at 46.
53. Ibid., at 65.
54. Ibid., at 64.
55. *Ashworth Report*, vol 1, at 204.
56. Ibid., at 205.
57. *Ashworth Report*, vol 2, at 1–50, see cases of Sean Michael Walton; and *Independent*, 'Broadmoor Death was Accidental', 3 April 1993, concerning the death of Orville Blackwood.
58. The only guidance is in the Code of Practice to the 1983 Mental Health Act

which is non statutory. Although the Code states that seclusion should not be used as a form of punishment, the case examined by the Ashworth Inquiry would suggest that it is used for this purpose.

59. *MHAC Fifth Biennial Report*, at 25.
60. R v. *Canons Park* MHRT ex parte A, *The Times*, 24 August 1994.
61. J. Peay, *Tribunals on Trial: A Study of Decision Making under the Mental Health Act 1983*, Clarendon Press, Oxford, 1989, at 84.
62. s72(1) Mental Health Act 1983.
63. *Independent*, 'Doctor Overrode Decision on Patient', 12 December 1992. R v. *Managers of South Western Hospital and Another, The Times*, 27 January 1993.
64. Peay, 1989 at 85
65. ss72(1)(6) and 73(1) Mental Health Act 1983. See also, *Kynaston* v. *Secretary of State for Home Affairs* (1981) 73 Cr App R 281.
66. Peay, 1989, at 84.
67. R v. *Merseyside MHRT* ex parte K, 694.
68. R v. *Secretary of State for the Home Department*, ex parte K (1990) 3 All.E.R. 562.
69. See s41(3) of the Act.
70. *Council on Tribunals Annual Report*, HMSO, December 1992.
71. Ibid.
72. *The Report of the Royal Commission on Criminal Justice*, Chairman Viscount Runciman, HMSO, Cm 2263, July 1993, at 25.
73. Code C 'The Detention, Treatment and Questioning of Persons by Police Officers', para 1.4, in the Code of Practice to the Police and Criminal Evidence Act 1984.
74. Code C, 1.7.
75. Code C, 11.16.
76. Gudjonsson, Clare, Rutter and Pearce, *Persons at Risk*, HMSO, 1993.
77. See Gudjonsson 1993 at 280–1, and J. Walker, *Police Contact with the Mentally Disordered*, Home Office Police Research Group, Police Department 1992. The predominant reason for the police assessment of mental vulnerability was the suspect exhibiting 'behavioral abnormality'. This suggests the police are failing to detect other mentally vulnerable suspects not obviously demonstrating their vulnerability.
78. Mencap, *Out of Depth and Out of Sight*, 1994.
79. R v. *Everett* (1988) Crim LR 826.
80. R v. *McKenzie* (1992) NLJ 1162.
81. The conditions were: where the prosecution evidence depends wholly upon confessions, the defendant suffers from a significant degree of mental handicap and the confessions are unconvincing to a point where a jury properly directed could not properly convict upon them then the judge, assuming that he has not excluded the confessions earlier, should withdraw the case from the jury.
82. Dell, Grounds and James, Institute of Criminology, Cambridge, and G. Robertson, Institute of Psychiatry, *Mentally Disordered Remanded Prisoners*, Report by the Home Office, London, July 1991, at 423.
83. Ibid., at 423–4.
84. *C and G Homes Ltd* v. *Secretary of State for Health, The Times*, 9 November

1990. See also, Bynoe, Oliver and Barnes *Equal Rights for Disabled People: The Case for a New Law*, IPPR, 1990, at 26–7.

85. Compare this with Mental Health (Northern Ireland) Order 1986. Article 9 of this Order permits the admission of a patient to a psychiatric hospital in Northern Ireland for up to 14 days for assessment of a possible 'mental disorder'. It is open to those responsible for the care and treatment of the patient to apply for an extension of this detention under other articles. If they do not do so by the end of their initial detention the person acquires the right, under Article 10 of the Order, not to have to disclose details of the admission assessment when being asked about their health history. Sub-paragraph 4 of Article 10 also specifically states that 'Failure to disclose that fact (a detention) shall not be a proper ground for dismissing or excluding that person from any office, profession, occupation or employment, or for prejudicing him in any way, in any occupation or employment.'

86. *Mental Health Statistics for England 1986*, HMSO, 1987.

87. See Barnes and Maple, *Women and Mental Health: Challenging the Stereotypes*, vol x, 1992, at 11. Not only do there appear to be significant diagnostic discrepancies between men and women, there are further discrepancies concerning the treatment of their mental health problems. For instance, women are twice as likely to be taking tranquillisers, two thirds of people taking antidepressants are women and women are more likely than men to receive ECT.

88. Ibid.

89. See J. Gorman, *Out of the Shadows*, MIND, 1992, *Stress on Women, Policy Paper on Women and Mental Health*, MIND, 1992 and Darton, Gorman and Sayce, *Eve Fights Back, the Successes of MIND's Stress on Women Campaign*, MIND, 1992.

90. 'Stress on Women Campaign Briefing', no 1, MIND, 1992.

91. *Stress on Women Policy Paper*, MIND, 1992

92. Ibid., at 35

93. Darton, Gorman and Sayce, 1992, at 3.

94. Ibid.

95. Mental Health Act Commission, *Fifth Biennial Report 1991–3*, December 1993, HMSO, at 19.

96. Darton, Gorman and Sayce, 1992, at 34.

97. *Review of Health and Social Services for Mentally Disordered Offenders and Services Requiring Similar Services. Report of the Official Working Group on Services for People with Special Needs*, para 8.9.

98. Ibid.

99. Ibid. para 4.22.

100. See *Ashworth Report*, vol 1, evidence given by Women in Special Hospitals, at 229.

101. Ibid., at 229, paper presented to the Ashworth Committee of Inquiry by Dr Marion Barnes; see also, *Stress of Women – Policy Paper on Women and Mental Health*, MIND, at 20.

102. *Report of the Working Group on High Security and Related Psychiatric Provision*, Chairman Dr John Reed, Department of Health, 1994, at para 3.1.

103. *Guardian*, 'Altered States', 8 August 1991.

104. Reed Committee, 1994, para 8.9.

105. *Ashworth Report* vol 1, 1992, at 229–32.
106. Ibid., at 229.
107. Ibid., evidence given by Moira Potier, principal clinical psychologist, Ashworth Hospital.
108. Ibid.
109. *The Mental Health Act Commission Fourth Biennial Report 1989–91*, HMSO, at 22.
110. *Ashworth Report,* vol I, 1992, at 232.
111. Reed Committee, 1990, para 3.5.
112. *Social Psychiatry,* vol 24, Cochrane and Ball, *Mental Health Admission Rates of Immigrants to England: A Comparison of 1971 and 1981,* 1989 in Greenslade, 'White Skins, White Masks: Mental Health Illness and the Irish in Britain', paper presented to BSA, University of Manchester, March 1991, at 5.
113. Ibid.
114. *Lesbians and Gays in Schools,* NUT, 1991; *United States Department of Health and Human Services Report by the Task Force on Youth Suicide,* 1989.
115. *Rights of Lesbians and Gay Men in Mental Health,* MIND, unpublished, 1994.
116. Lyndsey Man, *Journal of the British Association for Counselling,* vol 5, no 1, February 1994. Quoted in Angela Philips, 'Out in Mind', OPENMIND, April/May 1994.
117. *Ashworth Report,* vol 1, 1992, HMSO, at 151. See also, 'Special Hospitals'.
118. MIND, 1994.
119. Lorraine Trenchard and Hugh Warren, *Something to Tell You,* London Gay Teenage Group, 1984.
120. Ibid.
121. Gooding, 1992, at 170–90.
122. s139 Mental Health Act 1983.
123. See *Winch* v. *Jones* (1986) QB 296.
124. See *R* v. *Spencer* (1987) AC 128.
125. *Guardian,* 'Rampton Death Charge Dropped', 7 May 1993.
126. s134, Mental Health Act 1983.
127. See Harrison, 'Supervision in the Community', NLJ, 22 July 1994.
128. See MIND, press release, 14 July 1994.
129. *Psychiatric Bulletin* 18, 1994, 371.
130. Representation of the People Act 1983.
131. Ibid.
132. Ibid.

9 Migrants, Refugees and Asylum-Seekers

1. *Hansard,* Written Answer, 23 November 1994, cols 159–61.
2. Ibid.
3. *Increase in Refusals Since the Asylum Act,* Refugee Council, 22 November 1994.
4. As the numbers of people fleeing from a particular country increase, the government's response is often to impose a visa requirement on its nationals. This ensures that they will not reach the UK, because visas cannot be granted

to seek asylum. This was done for Iranians in 1980, Sri Lankans in 1985, Turks in 1989, Ugandans in 1991, people from former Yugoslavia in 1992 and Sierra Leoneans and Ivoirians in September 1994.

5. *Hansard*, Written Answer, 23 February 1993, col 496. The total number initially detained in 1992 was 6,413. In January 1993, 510 were detained (excluding those detained at ports of entry who did not claim asylum and who were detained for fewer than seven days).
6. See *Detention Report*, Asylum Rights Campaign, 19 February 1994.
7. See *United Kingdom – Cruel, inhuman or degrading treatment during forcible deportation*, Amnesty International, International Secretariat, July 1994.
8. See *Immigration Control Procedures: Report of a Formal Inquiry*, Commission for Racial Equality, 1985.
9. *M v. Home Office* (1993) 3 WLR, 433.
10. *The Times*, 'Minister may face jail for deportation', 10 July 1991.
11. *Guardian*, 'Treatment of detained refugees under scrutiny', 1994.
12. *Guardian*, 'Welcome to Britain', 8 June 1994.
13. *Guardian*, 'Asylum-seeker Commits Suicide after Husband is Refused a Visa', 9 September 1994.
14. *Guardian*, 'Inquiry Call over Injured Deportee', 28 October 1994.
15. *Voice*, 'Probe into Death Plunge of Scared Woman', 3 May 1994.
16. *Guardian*, 'Home Office Misled Gardner Lawyer', 14 August 1993.
17. See *Unlawful killing of detained asylum-seeker Omasese Lumumba*, Amnesty International British Section, 1993.
18. See Mark Ashford, *Detained without trial: a survey of Immigration Act detention*, JCWI, 1993.
19. Ibid., at 338.
20. Ann Dummett, 'Immigration and Nationality', in Christopher McCrudden and Gerald Chambers, *Individual Rights and the Law*, Clarendon, 1994, at 336, cited here as Dummett, 1994.
21. CAB 124/1191 *Working Party on Coloured People Seeking Employment in the UK*, Report 17 December 1953; and CAB 124/1191 *Report of the Working Party to Consider Certain Proposals to Restrict the Rights of British Subjects Overseas to Enter and Remain in the UK*, 1 July 1954, cited in Paul Sieghart (ed.), *Human Rights in the UK*, Pinter Publications, 1988, at 17–28.
22. *East African Asians* v. *UK* (1981) 3 EHRR 76.
23. s2 Immigration Act 1971.
24. See *Control of Immigration: Statistics United Kingdom 1993*, HMSO, Cm2637.
25. Hansard, Written Answer, 20 July 1993, col 319.
26. ss11, 23 and 26, British Nationality Act 1981.
27. *Third Periodic Report by the Government of the United Kingdom of Great Britain and Northern Ireland to the United Nations Human Rights Committee Under Article 40, International Covenant on Civil and Political Rights*, October 1989, at 73.
28. s1 Immigration Act 1988 repealed s1(5) Immigration Act 1971, which had preserved rights for 'Commonwealth citizens and their wives and children' when the Commonwealth citizen had been settled in the UK before 1 January 1973.
29. s3 Immigration Act 1988.

30. *Control of Immigration: Statistics United Kingdom 1990*, HMSO, Cm 1571, at 4.
31. See for example, *Out of sight: the new visit visa system overseas*, JCWI, 1987 and *Target Caribbean: the rise in visitor refusals from the Caribbean*, JCWI, 1990.
32. Cited in Skellington and Morris, '*Race*' *in Britain Today*, Sage Publications/ Open University Press, 1992, at 58.
33. Ibid.
34. See JCWI, 1987.
35. Richard Dunstan, *Prisoners Without a Voice: Asylum Seekers Detained in the UK*, Amnesty International, 1994, at 25.
36. s1 Immigration (Carrier's Liability) Act 1987.
37. *Hansard*, Written Answer, 21 April 1994, col 639.
38. See Sarah Spencer (ed.), *Strangers and Citizens, A Positive Approach to Migrants and Refugees*, IPPR and Rivers Oram Press, 1994, at 213–17.
39. *United Kingdom: Passing the Buck: deficient Home Office practice in 'safe third country' asylum cases*, Amnesty International British Section, 1993, at 3–4. See also, Dummett, 1994, at 350.
40. *Third Periodic Report*, 1989, at 82–3.
41. *Fourth Periodic Report by the Government of the United Kingdom of Great Britain and Northern Ireland to the United Nations Human Rights Committee Under Article 40, International Covenant on Civil and Political Rights*, 1994, para 292.
42. Ibid., para 293.
43. Ibid.
44. Ibid., para 294.
45. Ibid., paras 296–7.
46. Ibid., paras 295–8.
47. Ibid., para 189.
48. Ibid., para 190.
49. Ibid., para 192.
50. Ibid.
51. Ibid. In 1989 only 2.5% of detainees (57 people) were held for over three months. By 1993 this had risen to 7% of detainees (249 people).
52. Feldman, 1994, at 318.
53. Article 12 of the 1951 UN Convention Relating to the Status of Refugees as amended by the 1967 Protocol.
54. Dummett, 1994, at 335.
55. Ibid.
56. See Spencer (ed.), 1994.
57. See Hugo Storey, 'International Law and Human Rights Obligations', in Spencer (ed.), 1994, at 111–36.
58. *Third Periodic Report*, 1989, at 172.
59. Spencer (ed.), 1994, at 117.
60. *UK Agenda for Children*, Children's Rights Development Unit, 1994, at 245.
61. *East African Asians* v. *UK* (1981) 3 EHRR 76. The decision of the Commission was made in 1973 and communicated to the British government but was kept secret until published unofficially by JCWI in 1979.

62. *British Citizens Overseas: A report on the special voucher scheme in India*, JCWI, 1981.
63. Report of the European Commission of Human Rights, X *(Abdulaziz)*, *Cabales and Balkandali* v. *UK Cases*, March 1983, para 108, 1984 6 EHRR, 23 and (1985) 7 EHRR 471.
64. Ian Macdonald and Nicholas Blake, *Macdonald's Immigration Law and Practice*, 3rd Edn, Butterworths, 1990, at 243–5.
65. Jacqueline Bhabha and Sue Shutter, *Women's Movement: Women under Immigration, Nationality and Refugee Law*, Trentham Books, 1993, at 78–89.
66. *Vilvarajah and Others* v. *UK* (1992) 14 EHRR 248.
67. *R* v. *Secretary of State for the Home Department*, ex parte *Sivakumaran* (UN High Commission for Refugees intervening) (1988) AC 958 (1988) 1 All ER 193, HL.
68. Feldman, 1994, at 326.
69. Sarah Spencer, quoting a Home Office official in the Asylum Policy Unit in August 1993, in Spencer (ed.), 1994, at 3.
70. *Fourth Periodic Report*, 1994, paras 292–3.
71. Spencer (ed.), 1994, at 5.
72. *Fourth Periodic Report*, 1994, para 292.
73. Spencer (ed.), 1994, at 8.
74. Chris Randall, 'An Asylum Policy for the UK', in Spencer (ed.), 1994, at 206.
75. *Hansard*, Written Answer, 21 April 1994, col 639.
76. Increase in refusals since the Asylum and Immigration Appeals Act, Information and Policy Division, Refugee Council, September 1994.
77. Ibid.
78. Ibid.
79. *Hansard*, Written Answer, 21 July 1994, col 412.
80. Ibid., cols 412–13.
81. *Hansard*, Written Answer, 5 July 1993, col 10.
82. *Guardian*, 'Dutch return Kurds deported under "third country" rule', 1 November 1993.
83. Amnesty International British Section, 1993, at 2–3.
84. *United Kingdom: Deficient policy and practice for the protection of asylum-seekers*, Amnesty International, May 1991.
85. Ibid.
86. *Fourth Periodic Report*, 1994, paras 295–8.
87. Hansard (HL) The Rt Hon Earl Ferrers, Minister of State, 11 February 1993, col 877.
88. Immigration Rules, HC 395, para 345.
89. Ex parte *Mehari* (1194) 2 All ER 494.
90. UNHCR's observations to the Asylum Bill and related rules, the UN High Commission on Refugees, London Office, November 1992.
91. *Fourth Periodic Report*, 1994, para 292.
92. Hansard, Written Answers, 18 May 1993, cols 97–8.
93. Family reunion, Refugee Council factfile number 17, June 1994.
94. Spencer (ed.), 1994, at 209.
95. Refugee status can also be withdrawn in strictly defined circumstances, but those with ELR are more vulnerable to losing their status.
96. Spencer (ed.), 1994, at 211.

97. *Hansard*, Written Answer, 19 July 1994, cols 162–4.
98. s3 Immigration Act 1971.
99. s15(3) Immigration Act 1971.
100. See Ken Follett, *Three Blind Mice, Deportations Without Justice*, Charter 88, 1992, and 'National Insecurity', *JCWI Bulletin*, May 1991, *JCWI Annual Report 1990–1*.
101. See Dummett, 1994, at 352–3.
102. *JCWI Bulletin*, May 1991.
103. Mr Sadi, UN Human Rights Committee, 41st session, 2 April 1991, CCPR/C/SR.1047, at 10.
104. *The Times*, 'Britain to Deport Kurdish Leader', 28 October 1994.
105. *Guardian*, ' "Error" let Banned Kurd Enter UK', 8 November 1994.
106. Letter from the Home Secretary, Michael Howard, to Jack Straw MP, 6 November 1994.
107. Kurdistan Information Centre, Press Release, 10 November 1994.
108. *R v. Secretary of State for the Home Department*, ex parte *Chahal, The Times*, 'Law report', 12 March 1993.
109. *Chahal Family v. UK* Application No 22414/93.
110. See *Urgent Action, Fear of refoulement, Karamjit Singh Chahal*, Amnesty International, 30 July 1993.
111. *Hansard*, Written Answer, 12 December 1993, cols 237–8.
112. s5 Immigration Act 1988.
113. *Third Periodic Report*, 1989, at 73. The exclusion of immigration law is confirmed in the *Fourth Periodic Report*, 1994, at para 42.
114. Ibid., at 81.
115. *Fourth Periodic Report*, 1994, para 289.
116. *Third Periodic Report*, 1989, at 81.
117. Ibid.
118. Ibid., at 83; *Fourth Periodic Report*, 1994, para 290.
119. s16(2), Immigration Act 1971.
120. *Third Periodic Report*, 1989, at 83.
121. *Fourth Periodic Report*, 1994, para 290.
122. Briefing Paper on the Death of Mrs Joy Gardner on or between 28 July and 1 August 1993, The 1990 Trust, August 1993.
123. *Guardian*, 'Home Office Misled Gardner Lawyer', 14 August 1993.
124. See also, *Deportations and Amnesty*, Churches Commission for Racial Justice, the Council of Churches for Britain and Ireland, December 1993.
125. Ibid.
126. See *United Kingdom – Cruel, inhuman or degrading treatment during forcible deportation*, Amnesty International, International Secretariat, July 1994.
127. Ibid., Report summary.
128. Ibid., at 14.
129. Ibid., at 10–11.
130. Ibid., at 12.
131. CRE, 1985, at 133.
132. Geoff Wilkins, *An Immigration Watchdog: Proposals for an immigration control review body*, JCWI, 1986.
133. *Hansard*, Written Answer, 31 March 1993, col 226.
134. Ibid., 29 June 1994, col 624. In 1993, 10,530 people were detained overnight

or longer under powers contained in the Immigration Act 1971. These records do not distinguish between asylum-seekers and others.

135. Immigration (Places of Detention) Direction 1993, made under s2, para 18(1) to the Immigration Act 1971.

136. See Dummett, 1994, at 352, citing *R* v. *Secretary of State for the Home Department*, ex parte *Phansopkar* (1976) QB 606 (1975) 3 All ER 497 (CA); *Re Wajid Hassan* (1976) 2 All ER 123. See also, Feldman, 1993, at 342.

137. Sch 2, para 29 and Sch 3, para 3 to the Immigration Act 1971.

138. Cited in Dunstan, 1994, at 31–2.

139. Sue Shutter, *Immigration and nationality law handbook*, JCWI, 1992 edn, at 197.

140. *Gurinder Singh Dhillon* v. *Home Secretary* (1987) Immigration Appeals Reports, 222.

141. Article 9(4) ICCPR.

142. *Hansard*, Written Answer, 23 November 1994, cols 159–61.

143. Ibid.

144. Letter to Amnesty International from Home Office Minister Charles Wardle, 14 April 1994.

145. See Dunstan, 1994.

146. Ibid., at 17. Of the 17 unresolved cases, four are still awaiting an initial decision on their claim, seven are appealing to the IAA against rejections of their claims, one is awaiting a reconsideration of a rejection by the Home Office, one is awaiting the outcome of a judicial review and four are awaiting removal from the country. One of the 17 has been released on bail by the IAA, 13 have been released on temporary admission by the Immigration Service and three remain in detention.

147. Ibid., at 17–18.

148. Ibid., at 18.

149. Ibid., at 19.

150. *Hansard*, Written Answer, 19 July 1994, col 173.

151. *Detentions of Asylum Seekers*, Refugee Council fact file number 4, October 1994.

152. Home Office Statistical Bulletin 19/93.

153. Dunstan, 1994, at 21.

154. Article 9(2) ICCPR.

155. Dunstan, 1994, at 23.

156. Ibid., at 28.

157. Ibid., at 29.

158. Ibid., at 32.

159. Ibid., at 29–30.

160. *Hansard*, Written Answer, 21 July 1994, cols 489–90. This listed the following prisons where detainees were held on 19 July: Aberdeen, Armley, Bedford, Belfast, Belmarsh, Blakenhurst, Bristol, Brinsford, Brixton, Bullingdon, Cardiff, Chelmsford, Cookham Wood, Dorchester, Durham, Edinburgh, Elmley, Erlestoke, Exeter, Feltham, Gloucester, Greenock, Haslar, Highdown, Holloway, Hull, Lewes, Liverpool, Manchester, Norwich, Pentonville, Reading, Rochester, Shrewsbury, Swaleside, Swansea, Wandsworth, Winchester, Winson Green, the Wolds and Wormwood Scrubs. The government had also

announced an intention in the future to concentrate immigration detainees in five prisons: Doncaster, Haslar, Holloway, Rochester and Winson Green.

161. *Fourth Periodic Report*, 1994, para 282.
162. 'Detention of asylum seekers in the UK', Refugee Council fact sheet number 4, March 1994.
163. Quoted in Ashford, 1993, at 60–1.
164. Dunstan, 1994, at 46.
165. *A Betrayal of Hope and Trust*, Medical Foundation for Care of Victims of Torture, 1994, at 5.
166. Dunstan, 1994, at 45.
167. Ibid., at 46.
168. *Hansard*, Written Answer, 27 June 1994, col 426.
169. *Hansard*, Written Answer, 19 April 1994, cols 453–4.
170. See *Repatriation of Tamil asylum seekers*, Tamil Refugee Action Group, 1989.
171. Ashford, 1993, at 63–71.
172. Steve Cohen, *From the Jews to the Tamils, Britain's Mistreatment of Refugees*, Manchester Law Centre, 1988, at 24.
173. Ibid.
174. Dunstan, 1994, at 40.
175. Ibid., at 44–5.
176. Ashford, 1993, at 27.
177. UNHCR ExCom Conclusion 44, cited in Dunstan, 1994, at 46.
178. Agreement on the European Economic Area, signed at Oporto on 2 May 1992, as adjusted by a protocol signed at Brussels on 17 March 1993. Incorporated into British law by the Immigration (European Economic Area) Order 1994, para 3.
179. s2 Immigration Act 1971.
180. *Statement of Changes in Immigration Rules, laid before parliament on 23 May 1994 under section 3(2) of the Immigration Act 1971*, HMSO, 1994.
181. *Control of Immigration: Statistics United Kingdom 1993*, HMSO, Cm2367.
182. s11 Asylum and Immigration Appeals Act 1993.
183. See CRE, 1985.
184. *Independent*, 'Jamaican immigration rules "racist" ' 24 January 1994. The article also cited examples from other countries.
185. Ibid.
186. Ibid.
187. See for example, *Police and Immigration Activity in the London Area*, JCWI, 1990.
188. *Hansard*, Written Answer, 1 December 1994, cols 842–3.
189. *Daily Mail*, 'Never Again', 13 January 1994.
190. 'Family Reunion', Refugee Council factfile no 17, June 1994.
191. *Guardian*, 'Home Office "Shamefully Lax" Over Asylum Seekers', 14 November 1994.
192. Refugee Council, 1994, quoting letter from the Home Office 16 May 1994.
193. Dummett, 1994, at 345.
194. Ibid.
195. Quoted in JCWI, *The entry clearance queue and procedures, Memorandum to the House of Commons Home Affairs Committee Sub-Committee on Race Relations and Immigration*, 1982.

196. Dummett, 1994, at 345–7.
197. *Guardian*, 'Refugee Kurd Sets Himself Alight', 13 March 1993.
198. Immigration Rules, HC 251, para 50 (now HC 395 para 281 (ii)).
199. Dummett, 1994, at 345.
200. Bhabha and Shutter, 1994 at 79.
201. Ibid., at 82.
202. *Hansard*, Written Answer, 30 June 1992, cols 523–4.
203. Immigration Rules, HC 251, paras 51, 131 and 132 (now HC 395 paras 287–8, 363–4).
204. See Bhabha and Shutter, 1994.
205. Since the mid-1980s, people with a time limit on their stay and who had to show under the immigration rules that they could support and accommodate themselves in the UK have not been entitled to income support. After a change in the income support regulations with effect from 1 August 1993, the only people applying to the Home Office for a variation of leave who are eligible to receive income support are asylum-seekers. These restrictions were extended to housing benefit and council tax benefit from 1 April 1994.
206. See, for example, JCWI Annual Reports of almost any year; the refusal rate for children in Dhaka reached nearly 50% in 1985 and 1986.
207. For example, Mohammed Akram and Sarah Leigh, *Where do you keep your string beds?*, Runnymede Trust, 1978, Ranjit Sondhi, *Divided Families*, Runnymede Trust, 1987, Amrit Wilson and Sushma Lal, *But My Cows Aren't Going to England*, Manchester Law Centre, 1986.
208. *JCWI Annual Report 1991–2*, at 9.
209. Immigration Rules, HC251, para 56 (now HC 395, para 317).
210. *JCWI Annual Report 1991–2*, at 9.
211. s5 Immigration Act 1971. Immigration Rules 1990, at 169–71.
212. *Uppal v. UK* (No 2) (1981) 3 EHRR 399.
213. Home Office instruction DP/2/93, publicised by JCWI and ILPA in early 1993, mentioned in *Amankwah*, Divisional Court, 10 December 93.
214. *Guardian*, 'Expulsion will Leave Six Children Alone', 17 August 1993.
215. *Guardian*, 'Contempt Case', 11 November 1993.
216. *Guardian*, 'Home Secretaries Accused of Contempt', 16 May 1994.

10 Freedom of Expression and Human Rights

1. 'Streets of Sorrow', Terry Woods/Unchained Melodies. 'Birmingham Six', Shane MacGowan/Stiff Music Ltd. From the Pogues, *If I should fall from Grace With God*, Pogue Mahone Records, 1988.
2. *R v. Callaghan and Others* (1992) 2 All ER 417.
3. *R v. Richardson and Others, The Times*, 20 October 1989.
4. Liz Curtis and Mike Jempson, *Interference on the Airwaves, Ireland, the Media and the Broadcasting Ban*, Campaign For Press and Broadcasting Freedom, 1993, at 68.
5. *Irish News*, 'IBA Lifts Broadcasting Ban on Song for Birmingham Six', 21 March 1991.
6. *Hansard*, Broadcasting and terrorism, 19 October 1988, col 885. The text of the order forbids the broadcast of:
   1. any words spoken whether in the course of an interview or otherwise by

a person who appears, or is heard, on the programme in which the matter is broadcast where: (a) the person speaking the words represents, or purports to represent, an organisation specified in paragraph 2 below; or (b) the words support, or solicit, or invite support for, such an organisation other than any matter specified in paragraph 3 below.

2. the organisations referred to in paragraph 1 above are: (a) any organisation which is for the time being a proscribed organisation for the purposes of the Prevention of Terrorism (Temporary Provisions) Act 1984 or the Northern Ireland (Emergency Provisions) Act 1978; (b) Sinn Fein, Republican Sinn Fein and the Ulster Defence Association.

3. the matter excluded from paragraph 1 above is any words spoken: (a) in the course of the proceedings in parliament; or (b) by, or in support of, a candidate at a parliamentary or local election pending that election.

Proscribed organisations in 1988 were: the Irish Republican Army, the Irish National Liberation Army, Cumann na mBan, Fianna na Heireann, the Red Hand Commando Force, Saor Eire, the Ulster Volunteer Force and the Ulster Freedom Fighters. The Irish People's Liberation Organisation was proscribed in March 1990 and added to the list. The Ulster Defence Association was proscribed in 1992 under the Northern Ireland (Emergency Provisions) Act 1991.

7. s29(3) Broadcasting Act 1981.
8. Clause 13(4) Licence and Agreement April 1981.
9. See Patrick Twomey, *Denying Terrorists the Oxygen of Publicity: Broadcasting Restrictions in the UK and the Republic of Ireland*, W.G. Hart legal workshop 1994, *Understanding Human Rights*, Institute of Advanced Legal Studies, 1994. The Secretary of State may from time to time by notice in writing require the (BBC/IBA) to refrain at any specified time or at all times from sending any matter or matter of any class specified in such a notice. Following the introduction of the Broadcasting Act 1990 equivalent notices are now issued to the Independent Television Commission (which replaced the IBA), the Welsh Fourth Channel Authority and the Radio Authority.
10. *Hansard*, Broadcasting and terrorism, 19 October 1988, col 885.
11. *The Times*, 'Leader Aims for Fourth Term', 26 October 1988.
12. *Independent*, 'A Gag that Chokes Freedom', 12 September 1994. Taken from Tony Hall, *The Broadcasting Ban*, Violations Paper, Charter 88, 1994.
13. *Index on Censorship*, October 1990, at 34.
14. Twomey, 1994, at 14. For example, Bernadette McAliskey, the civil rights activist, was invited onto 'Black on Black', a BBC discussion programme on conflicts and colonialism, specifically because she was not a member or supporter of a proscribed organisation but could describe what motivated people to resort to violence in Northern Ireland. Her words were subsequently subtitled and the High Court rejected her attempt to challenge the decision.
15. Ex parte *Brind* 2 WLR (1991) 58.
16. *Brind* v. *UK* App No 18714/91, 12 May 1994.
17. Report of the UN Human Rights Committee, 48th session, 1993, at para 607.
18. *Dail Eireann Official Record*, Broadcasting Authority, 1 February 1994, col 232.
19. *Hansard*, Oral Answers, 7 February 1994, col 17.

20. *Public expenditure: the Pergau hydro-electric project, Malaysia, the aid and trade provision and related matters*, HMSO, July 1994, para 44.
21. *Hansard*, Oral Answers, 31 January 1991, col 1102.
22. *R* v. *Henderson, Allen and Abraham*, unreported. See *Public Law*, 'Matrix Churchill, Supergun and the Scott Inquiry', Winter 1993, at 630–49.
23. See Tony Tant, *Constitutional aspects of official secrecy and freedom of information*, Essex Papers in Politics and Government, Essex University, 1988.
24. Prior restraint means that a publication is prevented from publishing material by a court injunction.
25. Sandra Coliver (ed.), *Striking a Balance, hate speech, freedom of expression and non-discrimination*, Article XIX, 1992.
26. *Third Periodic Report by the Government of the United Kingdom of Great Britain and Northern Ireland to the United Nations Human Rights Committee Under Article 40, International Covenant on Civil and Political Rights*, October 1989, at 107.
27. *Fourth Periodic Report by the Government of the United Kingdom of Great Britain and Northern Ireland to the United Nations Human Rights Committee Under Article 40, International Covenant on Civil and Political Rights*, 1994, paras 372–9.
28. *Third Periodic Report*, 1989.
29. Ibid., at 109.
30. Ibid., at 109–10.
31. Ibid., at 111.
32. Ibid., at 110–11.
33. Ibid., at 113.
34. *Fourth Periodic Report*, 1994.
35. Ibid., para 371.
36. Geoffrey Robertson, *Freedom, the Individual and the Law*, Penguin, 1989, at 141.
37. *R* v. *Aitken* (1971), unreported, documented in John Gardner, 'Freedom of Expression', in Christopher McCrudden and Gerald Chambers (eds), *Individual Rights and the Law in Britain*, Clarendon Press, 1994, at 225.
38. *R* v. *Ponting* (1985) Crim LR 318. Ponting was prosecuted and acquitted under Section 2 although he had leaked information on the sinking of the Argentine battleship *Belgrano*, which undermined the truth of the official version. The jury's acquittal of Ponting, reflected a view that he had been morally correct to have breached the Act in this instance. In 1985 Cathy Massiter, an MI5 officer, revealed the security services were carrying out operations against trade unionists, peace activists and leading officials in the NCCL. She was not prosecuted, presumably because the authorities did not believe a jury would convict her.
39. The government used pre-trial injunctions to stifle the publication of the *Spycatcher* allegations. These injunctions were upheld by the courts in 1986 and 1987, despite the widespread publication of *Spycatcher* internationally. *Attorney General* v. *Observer Ltd and Others* and *Attorney General* v. *Times Newspapers Ltd and Another*, both in *The Times*, 'Law report', 22 December 1987. They were eventually overturned by the House of Lords in 1988, *Attorney General* v. *Guardian Newspapers Ltd* (No 2) (1988), 3 All ER 545.
40. *Observer and the Guardian* v. *UK* (1991) EHRR 153, Series A, No 216, App

No 13585/88; and *Sunday Times* v. *UK* (No 2) (1991) EHRR 229, Series No 217, App No 13166/87.
41. s5 Official Secrets Act 1989.
42. Peter Thornton, *Decade of Decline, Civil Liberties in the Thatcher Years*, NCCL, 1989, at 7–9.
43. Ibid., at 9–11.
44. Ibid.
45. Robertson, 1989, at 265.
46. See Ian Cram, 'When the "Interests of Justice" Outweigh Freedom of Expression', *Modern Law Review*, vol 55, no 3, 1992, at 400.
47. *Independent*, 'Journalist Fined £5,000 for Refusing to Reveal Sources', 11 April 1990.
48. *X Ltd* v. *Morgan-Grampian Ltd and Others* (1991) 1 AC 1.
49. *Sunday Times* v. *UK*, App No 6538/74 (1979) EHRR 245.
50. *Goodwin* v. *UK*, App No 17488/90 (7 September 1993).
51. s9, s1, Police and Criminal Evidence Act, 1984.
52. For example, *Class War*, 'No Ceasefire in the Class War', Nov/Dec 1994, in its coverage of a riot in London in October 1994 encouraged rioters to attack the press and seize their film.
53. See chapter 4 of this book on broadcasting and the Northern Ireland conflict.
54. See *No Comment: Censorship, Secrecy and the Irish Troubles*, Article 19, 1989, at 44.
55. For example *Hansard*, Right-to-Know Bill, 2 July 1993, col 1268.
56. Robertson, 1989, at 163.
57. Ibid., at 164.
58. *Open Government, Code of Practice on Access to Government Information*, Citizen's Charter, 1994.
59. See *Testing the Open Government Code of Practice*, Freedom of Information Campaign, May 1994.
60. Cited in Robertson, 1989, at 163.
61. Ibid.
62. *Hansard*, Bills Presented, Pardon for Soldiers of the Great War, 3 November 1993, col 368.
63. See *Civil Liberty Agenda*, 'The Same Old Story', No 7, Summer 1993.
64. Richard Norton Taylor, *In Defence of the Realm, The Case for Accountable Security Services*, Civil Liberties Trust, 1990, at 81–98.
65. See *Some Examples of Moves Towards Open Government*, Cabinet Office, Whitehall, October 1993.
66. *Open Government*, HMSO, Cm 2290, 4 April 1994.
67. Patrick Birkinshaw, *Reforming the Secret State*, Open University Press, 1990, at 47.
68. Ibid., at 46–9.
69. *Conway* v. *Rimmer* (1968) AC 910 HL and *Burmah Oil* v. *Bank of England* (1980) AC 1090.
70. *R* v. *Henderson, Allen and Abraham*, unreported. See *Public Law*, 'Matrix Churchill, Supergun and the Scott Inquiry', Winter 1993, at 630–49.
71. *The Times*, letters page, 13 November 1992.
72. *Hansard*, Matrix Churchill, 10 November 1992, col 743.
73. *Telegraph*, 'Downing Street Clashes with Legal Experts Over Immunity', 12

November 1992. *The Times*, 'Lord Taylor Attacks Abuse of Justice in Arms Trial', 29 July 1994.
74. Ex parte *Wiley* (HL) *The Times*, 15 July 1994.
75. Adam Tomkins, 'Public Interest Immunity after Matrix Churchill', *Public Law*, Winter 1993, at 665.
76. *Council for Civil Service Unions* v. *Minister for the Civil Service* (1985) AC 374 during which Lord Diplock asserted that national security issues were non-justiciable.
77. *Balfour* v. *Foreign and Commonwealth Office* (1994) 2 All ER 588.
78. *The Times*, 'Law report', 1 September 1992.
79. *Independent*, 'Court Backs Channel 4 over Sinn Fein Film', 11 August 1994.
80. *The Times*, 'Law report', 1 September 1992.
81. Paragraph 3, Schedule 7, Prevention of Terrorism Act 1989.
82. *The Times*, 'Law report', 1 September 1992.
83. *Independent*, 'Contempt Claim over RUC Collusion Story', 6 October 1992.
84. *Independent*, 'Charges over Documentary on the RUC are Dropped', 24 November 1992.
85. *Guardian*, 'Death Squad Inquiry Call as TV Case Falls', 24 November 1994.
86. *Hansard*, Prevention of Terrorism (Temporary Provisions) Bill, 25 November 1975, col 451. In introducing the Bill the then Home Secretary, Roy Jenkins, described its powers as so draconian as to be unprecedented in peace time and predicted that it would only remain in force for about six months.
87. s4(1) Prevention of Terrorism Act 1989.
88. Twomey, 1994, at 16.
89. Ibid.
90. Curtis and Jempson, 1993, at 42–91.
91. See Liz Curtis, *Ireland, the Propaganda War*, Pluto Press, 1984.
92. Robertson, 1989, at 266.
93. *Hansard*, Oral Answers, 5 December 1991, cols 392–3. See also, *Mirror*, 'The Lie', 6 December 1991.
94. s8 The Courts and Legal Services Act 1990. For example, in March 1993 the Court of Appeal reduced damages from £250,000 to £110,000 in the case of *Rantzen* v. *Mirror Group Newspapers*.
95. *Steel and Morris* v. *UK*, App No 21325/93, admissibility decision of European Commission of Human Rights, 5 May 1993.
96. *The Times*, 'Law report', 14 April 1994.
97. Proceedings in court or parliament are protected by 'absolute privilege', which means that libel cases cannot be brought in respect of statements made in these proceedings. Information given to the police and employment references are protected by 'qualified privilege'.
98. Robertson, 1989, at 269.
99. *Duchess of Argyll* v. *Duke of Argyll* (1965) 1 All ER 611.
100. *BSC* v. *Granada Television Ltd* (1981) 1 All ER 484.
101. *Attorney General* v. *Jonathan Cape Ltd* (1975) 3 All ER 282.
102. Robertson, 1989, at 262.
103. See for example, John Gardner in McCrudden and Chambers, 1994, at 212.
104. See Ronald Dworkin, *A Matter of Principle*, Clarendon Press, 1986.
105. See Nadine Strossen, 'A Feminist Critique of "the" Feminist Critique of Pornography', *Virginia Law Review*, vol 79, August 1993, no 5.

106. See Avedon Carol, *Nudes, Prudes and Attitudes: Pornography and Censorship*, New Clarion Press, 1994.
107. Ibid.
108. For these arguments, see Coliver, 1992.
109. Article 20 ICCPR.
110. Article 24 ICCPR.
111. Article 3 ICCPR.
112. Article 26 ICCPR.
113. Article 19 ICCPR.
114. See Joanna Oyediran, 'The United Kingdom's Compliance with Article 4 of the International Convention on the Elimination of all Forms of Racial Discrimination', in Coliver, 1992, at 251.
115. Ibid.
116. *Hansard*, Written Answers, 18 January 1993, col 4. There was one prosecution in 1990, four in 1991 and one in 1992. Two cases were pending. The government's third report to the UN stated that since 1979 there have been 44 prosecutions for incitement to racial hatred. Although the law on incitement was strengthened by amendments to the Public Order Act 1986, there have been only 18 prosecutions in England and Wales since that date.
117. *R v. Read* (1978) *The Times*, 7 January C Cr Ct. Two men who made speeches referring to 'coons', 'wogs', etc., were acquitted after arguing that their language was so extreme it was more likely to arouse sympathy.
118. *R v. Hancock* (1969) *The Times*, 29 Mar, C Cr Ct.
119. Oyediran, in Coliver 1992, at 248.
120. *Guardian*, 'MPs told Race Attacks May Top 130,000 a Year', 15 July 1993.
121. s13, Sch 4 Criminal Law Act 1967.
122. David Edwards, 'Toleration and the Blasphemy Laws', in Horton and Mendus, *Aspects of Toleration*, Methuen, 1985, at 75–97.
123. Tanya Callman, *To What Extent Can and Should the Law Restrict Freedom of Expression to Protect Religious Sensibilities*, Institute of Advanced Legal Studies, July 1994, at 3.
124. Law Commission Working Paper no 145, *Offenses Against Religion and Public Worship*, 1985, at para 2.1.
125. *Whitehouse v. Gay News Ltd and Lemon* (1979) 68 Crim App R 381.
126. *Gay News Ltd and Lemon v. UK*, App No 8710/79 (1982) 5 EHRR 123.
127. *Daily Telegraph*, 'Euro Ruling Questions Law on Blasphemy', 9 April 1994.
128. Salman Rushdie, *The Satanic Verses*, Viking, 1988.
129. *R v. Chief Metropolitan Stipendiary Magistrate,* ex parte *Choudhury* (1991) 1 All ER 306, DC.
130. Tariq Modood, 'Establishment, Multiculturalism and British Citizenship', *Political Quarterly*, vol 65, no 1, 1994, at 56.
131. Ibid.
132. *Mandla v. Dowell Lee* (1983) 2 WLR 620.
133. Lee, *Law, Respect for Religious Identity and the Multi-faith Society, Report of a Seminar organised by Inter-faith Network and the Commission for Racial Equality*, October 1990, at 11, cited in Callman, 1994, at 34.
134. Sebastian Poulter, 'Towards Legislative Reform of the Blasphemy and Racial Hatred Laws', *Public Law*, Autumn 1991, at 371–85.
135. For example Andrea Dworkin, *Pornography: Men Possessing Women*,

Women's Press, 1981; Catherine Itzin (ed.), *Pornography: Women, Violence and Civil Liberties*, Oxford University Press, 1992.

136. Itzin, 1992, at 423–5.
137. Ibid., at 422–3.
138. For example, Catherine MacKinnon, *Only Words*, HarperCollins, 1994 and Sheena McMurtrie, *Pornography and Rights: The Theory and Practice of Control*, Institute of Advanced Legal Studies, 1994.
139. CEDAW, General Recommendation no 19, GAOR, 47th Session, Supp no 38, 1992, comment on Articles 2(f), 5 and 10(c), para 12.
140. For example Alison Assiter and Avedon Carrol (eds), *Bad Girls and Dirty Pictures: the Challenge to Reclaim Feminism*, Pluto Press, 1993.
141. Strossen, 1993, at 1109.
142. Ibid., at 1186–7.
143. Ibid.
144. Dennis Howitt and Guy Cumberbatch, *Pornography: Impacts and Influences, A Review of Available Research Evidence on the Effects of Pornography*, Home Office Research and Planning Unit, 1990.
145. For contrasting views see Itzin, 1992, at 201–399 and Strossen, 1993, at 1173–85. See also, Bill Thompson, *Soft Core*, Cassell, 1994.
146. Obscene Publications Act 1959, amended in 1964.
147. s1 Obscene Publications Act 1959.
148. Raymond Williams, *Report of the Committee on Obscenity and Film Censorship*, HMSO, 1979, at 175.
149. s2 Local Government (Miscellaneous Provisions) Act 1982.
150. s42 Customs Consolidation Act 1876.
151. ss11 and 68 Post Office Act 1953.
152. s1 Protection of Children Act 1978.
153. s1 Children and Young Persons (Harmful Publications) Act 1955.
154. ss4 and 9 Video Recordings Act 1984.
155. Williams, 1979, at 183.
156. Paul Crane, *Gays and the Law*, Pluto Press, 1982, at 87.
157. Robertson, 1989, at 193.
158. Ibid.
159. Gavin McFarlane, 'The Limits of Obscenity', *New Law Journal*, 24 January 1992, at 85–93.
160. s42 Customs Consolidation Act 1876 and s170 Customs and Excise Management Act 1979.
161. s49 Customs and Excise Management Act 1979.
162. *Conegate Ltd* v. *HM Customs and Excise* (1986) 2 All ER 688.
163. *Report of the Commissioner of the Police of the Metropolis 1992/3*, the Metropolitan Police, 1993, at 38.
164. *HM Customs and Excise 1990/1 Report*, HMSO, October 1991, at 23.
165. For example *Pink Paper*, 'Customs in Confusion', 3 January 1993.
166. *Hansard*, Oral Answer, 22 July 1993, col 493. A Home Office minister stated that 'it is essentially the same test as we have had since 1868. It was regarded by many people as over-effective for 100 years, but now people say that it is under-effective.'
167. Robertson, 1989, at 190–4.

Notes

168. A.W.B. Simpson, *Pornography and Politics, the Williams Committee in Retrospect*, Waterlow Publishers, 1983, foreword.
169. *A Code of Practice*, Broadcasting Standards Council, undated, at 35–41.
170. For details of the BBFC screen and video guidelines see Simpson, 1983, Appendices B and C.
171. Robertson, 1989, at 190.
172. *Everywoman*, August 1994.
173. *City Limits*, 13–20 June 1991, reporting that a number of shops refused to stock *Love Bites*, a lesbian book of erotica, for fear of prosecution.
174. *Time Out*, 'Clean Sweep', 9–16 October 1991.
175. *Independent*, 'The Only Way to Talk to Smackheads', 20 August 1991.
176. See Assiter and Carrol (eds), 1993.
177. See Williams, 1979.
178. Howitt and Cumberbatch, 1990.
179. Itzin, 1992, at 560–4.
180. Williams, 1979, at 102.
181. Ibid., at 131.
182. Ibid.
183. Ibid., at 127–8.
184. Indecent Display (Controls) Act 1981 and Local Government (Miscellaneous Provisions) Act 1982.
185. Simpson, 1983, at 41–57.
186. Ibid., at 82–96.
187. R v. *Butler* (1992) 1 SCR 452 505.
188. *Pornography and Prostitution in Canada*, Canadian Government Publishing Centre, 1985.
189. s163 Criminal Code RSC 1985. 'Any publication a dominant characteristic of which is the undue exploitation of sex, or of sex and any one or more of the following subjects, namely, crime horror, cruelty or violence shall be deemed obscene.'
190. Catherine Itzin, *Pornography as Hate Speech: Inciting Hatred and Violence Against Women*, Seminar on Women's Human Rights, Department of Law, SOAS, May 1994, at 9.
191. Strossen, 1993, at 1103–85.
192. Itzin, 1992, at 423–5.
193. For example, *Campaign Against Pornography Newsletter*, Winter 1993/4, reported the case of a woman whose photograph appeared in a pornographic magazine, accompanied by offensive and inaccurate text, with her real name used.
194. See Carol Avedon, *Nudes, Prudes and Attitudes*, New Clarion Press, 1994.
195. Williams, 1979, at 131.
196. *Infringements of Privacy*, the Lord Chancellor's Department and the Scottish Office, July 1993.
197. *Kaye v. Robertson* (1991) FSR 62.
198. *Media Freedom and Megia Regulation, An Alternative White Paper*, Association of British Editors, Guild of Editors, International Press Institute, 1994.
199. See for example, Patrick Milmo QC, 'The New Law of Privacy', *New Law Journal*, 13 August 1993.

200. Legal Opinion of Lord Lester QC to The Times Newspapers Ltd, 13 November 1993, para 20.
201. Wade and Bradley, *Constitutional and Administrative Law*, Longman, 11th edn, 1993, at 246–7.
202. Campaign for Press and Broadcasting Freedom, Submission to the Calcutt Committee, 1991.
203. See the *Report of Special Parliamentary Hearings on Freedom and Responsibility of the Press*, Crantock Communications, 1993.
204. Press Wise, established in 1993.
205. See *A Right to be Left Alone? Liberty's Response to the Government's Consultation Paper, Infringement of Privacy*, October 1993.
206. John O'Neill, 'Journalism in the Market Place', in Andrew Belsey and Ruth Chadwick (eds), *Ethical Issues in Journalism and the Media*, Routledge, 1992, at 15.
207. See *Report of the Committee on Civil Liberties and Internal Affairs on Freedom of Expression, Press Freedom and Freedom of Information*, European Parliament, DOC EN\RR\237\237310, PE 200.619/fin, 13 October 1993; and the *Declaration on Freedom of Expression and Information*, adopted by the Council of Europe, 29 April 1982.
208. *Resolution of the European Parliament*, 15 January 1994. It calls on the Commission to submit a proposal for a directive that would harmonise national restrictions on media concentration and enable the Community to intervene in the event of media concentration which endangers pluralism on a European scale.
209. *Report of the Committee on Civil Liberties and Internal Affairs on Freedom of Expression, Press Freedom and Freedom of Information*, European Parliament, 1993, 8.
210. Published in 1949, 1962 and 1977.
211. Cited in CPBF, *Britain's Media – How They are Related*, 1994, at 40.
212. Eric Barendt, *Broadcasting Law*, Clarendon Press, 1993, at 124.
213. See James Curran and Jean Seaton, *Power Without Responsibility: the Press and Broadcasting in Britain*, Routledge, 1988, at 92.
214. CPBF, 1994, at 46. See also, Bob Franklin and David Murray, *What News? The Market, Politics and the Local Press*, Routledge, 1991.
215. See Curran and Seaton, 1988, at 102–3. For example, between 1946 and 1976, public affairs news coverage fell from 18% to 9% of total editorial space in the *Daily Mirror*, while advertising went up from 16 to 42% of total editorial space. The same trend occurred in the 'quality' press. Similarly, television financed by competitive advertising tends to compete for the 'centre ground' of taste, because the television companies need to maximise audiences.
216. CPBF, 1994, at 44. See also, Franklin and Murray, 1991.
217. Ibid., 1994, at 44.
218. This excludes the *Morning Star*, which is not distributed nationally.
219. In Italy Silvio Berlusconi, owner of Finivest, used his media power to launch a political movement and secure the Premiership of Italy. Berlusconi owns three commercial TV stations, with 45% of national viewers, the largest publishing house and the highest circulation news weekly, *Panorama*.
220. Broadcasting Research Unit analysis of opinion data collected by the IBA,

cited in *Submission to the National Heritage Cross-Media Ownership Review*, Campaign for Press and Broadcasting Freedom, 1994.

221. Opinion polls over the weekend before the election suggested a Labour victory. The *Sun* then carried a 9–page article, 'Nightmare on Kinnock Street'; the *Express* and *Mail* both warned of the 'threat of massive immigration under Labour', and the *Mail* carried a front page 'WARNING' of higher mortgage rates. According to a poll by MORI, the week before the election 64% of *Daily Express* readers and 62% of *Daily Mail* readers intended to vote Conservative. They actually voted Conservative by 67% and 65%. Only 15% of *Express* readers voted Labour, compared with the 19% who intended to vote Labour the week before. This assault on Labour by the pro-Conservative press coincided with a late swing to the Conservatives, of about 3% among *Sun* readers and 9% among *Express* readers. See CPBF, 1994, at 60–7.

222. Martin Linton, *Money and Votes*, IPPR, 1994, at 30–1.

223. *Sunday Telegraph*, 12 April 1992. Quoted in CPBF, 1994, at 61.

224. CPBF, 1994, at 36.

225. Curran and Seaton, 1988, at 108.

226. Fifth object of the Press Council. See Geoffrey Robertson, *People Against the Press*, Quartet, 1983, at 117.

227. Ibid., at 120–1.

228. Ibid., at 124–31.

229. Ibid.

230. Keane, 1991, at 77.

231. 1988 White Paper on Broadcasting, quoted in CPBF, 1994, at 40–1.

232. Barendt, 1993, at 129.

233. Central merged with Carlton, Meridian acquired Anglia and, following a hostile bid, Granada took over LWT. Carlton has the biggest share of the ITV network in terms of audience and advertising. It now has a 15% share in GMTV, 50% stake in London News Network and a 36% share in ITN.

234. Radio Clyde controls every major commercial station in Scotland, except for West Sound in Ayr and Dumfries. Metro Radio controls virtually all stations in the North East, while Capital, the largest radio company, has created an alliance with GWR to give the group control of almost all the commercial stations in the Midlands.

235. See *Submission to the Department of National Heritage Cross Media Ownership Review*, National Union of Journalists, 1994, at 9.

236. Ibid., at 41. See also, Barendt, 1993, at 131–2.

237. 1988 Home Affairs Select Committee, quoted by NUJ.

238. *Guardian*, 'Dependency Threat to TV Journalism', 27 August 1994.

239. Ibid.

240. Thames Television came under a concerted attach from Conservative politicians and a number of newspapers after it broadcast a documentary, *Death on the Rock*, which questioned the government's version of the circumstances surrounding the shooting dead of three unarmed IRA members by the Special Air Services in Gibraltar.

241. *Guardian*, 27 August 1994.

11 Human Rights in the Workplace

1. John Hendy QC, *A Law unto Themselves, Conservative Employment Laws: A National and International Assessment*, Institute of Employment Rights, third edn, 1994, at 43–4.
2. *Fourth Periodic Report by the Government of the United Kingdom of Great Britain and Northern Ireland to the United Nations Human Rights Committee under Article 40, International Covenant on Civil and Political Rights*, 1994, para 388.
3. See Keith Ewing, *Britain and the ILO*, the Institute of Employment Rights, second edn, 1994.
4. Article 3, ILO constitution.
5. Article 19(2), ILO constitution.
6. Article 19(5)(b), ILO constitution.
7. Article 19(5)(c), ILO constitution.
8. Article 22, ILO constitution.
9. See Breen Creighton, 'The ILO and the Protection of Freedom of Association in the United Kingdom', in Ewing, Gearty and Hepple, *Human Rights and Labour Law*, Mansell, 1994, at 3.
10. Ewing, 1994, at 18.
11. Creighton, 1994, at 3. They were ratified in 1949, 1950 and 1980 respectively.
12. Ewing, 1994, at 19.
13. See Julia Lourie, *Employment and Trade Union Legislation Since 1979*, House of Commons Library, Research Paper 94/111, 10 November 1994.
14. *Fourth Periodic Report*, 1994, para 389.
15. Ibid., para 30.
16. *Third Periodic Report by the Government of the United Kingdom of Great Britain and Northern Ireland to the United Nations Human Rights Committee Under Article 40 of the International Covenant on Civil and Political Rights*, October 1989, at 119–20.
17. Creighton, 1994, at 4–5, one complaint in relation to Britain during the 1970s; nine during the 1980s.
18. Ewing, 1994, at 30.
19. Cited in Hendy, 1994, at 79.
20. Ewing, 1994, at 41.
21. Case No 1618 283rd Report of the Freedom of Association Committee (interim conclusions) and 287th Report.
22. Ibid.
23. See Mark Hollingworth and Charles Tremayne, *The Economic League, the Silent McCarthyism*, NCCL, 1989.
24. *Statewatch*, 'Economic League Relaunched', May-June 1994.
25. ILO 81st Session, Report of the Committee of Experts on the Application of Conventions and Recommendations, Report III (Part 4A) (1994), at 292–3.
26. Case No 1619 284th Report of the Freedom of Association Committee (Convention 151).
27. Case No 1391 256th Report of the Freedom of Association Committee.
28. Ewing, 1994, at 32–4.
29. *Hansard*, GCHQ (Employment Protection Act), 25 January 1984, col 917.
30. s138 Employment Protection (Consolidation) Act 1978.

31. Case No 1261 (234th Report of the Freedom of Association Committee).
32. *Council of Civil Service Unions* v. *Minister for the Civil Service* (1985) AC 374 (HL).
33. *Council of Civil Service Unions* v. *UK* (1988) 10 EHRR 269.
34. Case No 1261 (234th Report of the Freedom of Association Committee).
35. Ibid., para 371.
36. ILO 71st Session, Report of the Committee of Experts on the Application of Conventions and Recommendations, Report III (Part 4A) 1985, at 194.
37. ILO 76th Session, Report III (Part 4A) (1989), at 234.
38. Ibid., at 26–54.
39. Ewing, 1994, at 28.
40. *Hansard*, House of Lords, 13 January 1994, col 263.
41. *Hansard*, Written Answer, 13 January 1994, col 254.
42. Ibid.
43. Ewing, 1994, at 24–5.
44. *Guardian*, 'Union Ban on MoD Guards' , 29 July 1992.
45. *Fourth Periodic Report*, 1994, para 394. The court accepted that under Section 8 of the Prison Act 1952, prison officers have the power of police officers and were therefore in 'police service' for the purposes of employment protection and trade union legislation. It was therefore unlawful for the Prison Officers' Association to induce its members to breach their employment contracts. Sections 126–8 of the Criminal Justice and Public Order Act 1993 restored the immunities of a trade union to the Prison Officers' Association but nevertheless maintained that it was unlawful for it to induce prison officers to engage in industrial action.
46. s219 Trade Union and Labour Relations (Consolidation) Act 1992.
47. Hendy, 1994, at 59.
48. ss15–16 Employment Act 1982, now ss20–22 Trade Union and Labour Relations (Consolidation) Act 1992.
49. *Taff Vale Railway Company* v. *Amalgamated Society of Railway Servants* (1901) AC 426.
50. *Quinn* v. *Leatham*, 1901, AC 495.
51. *Amalgamated Society of Railway Servants* v. *Osborne* (1910) AC 87, 79 LJ Ch 87, HL.
52. *Rooks* v. *Barnard*, 1964, AC 1129.
53. Hendy, 1994, at 15–16.
54. Ibid.
55. Creighton, 1994, at 4.
56. Simon Deakin, *The Utility of 'Rights Talk': Employees' Personal Rights*, W.G. Hart legal workshop, 1994, Institute of Advanced Legal Studies, 1994, at 9.
57. *Royal Commission on Trade Unions and Employers' Associations* (chairman Lord Donovan), 1968, HMSO, Cmnd 3623, at 14.
58. Keith Ewing, *A Bill of Rights for Britain?*, Institute of Employment Rights, 1990, at 5–6.
59. See Liberty and Charter 88, *Democracy and Human Rights in the UK*, NCCL, 1994. See also, People's Charter, NCCL, 1991, which discusses different models of entrenchment.
60. s137 Trade Union and Labour Relations (Consolidation) Act 1992.

61. Richard Painter and Keith Puttick, *Employment Rights*, Pluto Press, 1993, at 7.
62. Ibid.
63. See Seumas Milne, *The Enemy Within*, Verso, 1994.
64. Tony Judge, *The Force of Persuasion, the Story of the Police Federation*, Police Federation, 1994, at 405–6.
65. ILO 76th Session, Report III (Part 4A (1989), 238.
66. Cited in Hendy, 1994, at 48.
67. Ibid.
68. Ibid.
69. s22 Trade Union Reform and Employment Rights Act 1993.
70. Ibid.
71. Nigel Giffin and Elizabeth Slade, *Tolley's Employment Handbook*, Tolley Publishing Company, eighth edn, 1993, at 338.
72. s224 Trade Union and Labour Relations (Consolidation) Act 1992.
73. Except in workplaces employing fewer than 50 people.
74. ss226–34 Trade Union and Labour Relations (Consolidation) Act 1992. The Code of Practice on Trade Union Ballots on Industrial Action was last revised in February 1991. The latest draft revision is currently out for consultation. See *Department of Employment Press Release on New Code of Practice*, 20 October 1994.
75. s229 Trade Union and Labour Relations (Consolidation) Act 1992.
76. John Hendy QC, Damian Brown and Steve Gibbons, *Taking Industrial Action, a Guide to Workers' Rights*, Labour Research Department, July 1993, at 7.
77. s21 Trade Union Reform and Employment Rights Act 1993.
78. *Blackpool and the Fylde College v. NATFHE*, CA, 25 February 1994 (unreported).
79. *Financial Times*, 'Appeal Court Upholds College Strike Ruling', 27 February 1994.
80. *Hansard*, Standing Committee F, 15 December 1992, col 236.
81. *Financial Times*, 'Strike by Lecturers Ruled Unlawful', 25 February 1994.
82. s16 Employment Act 1980, now s224 of Trade Union and Labour Relations (Consolidation) Act.
83. *Code of Practice, Picketing*, Department of Employment, undated but came into effect 1 May 1992.
84. *Piddington v. Bates* (1961) 1 WLR 162.
85. *Thomas v. National Union of Mineworkers* (1985) 2 WLR 1081.
86. s14 (1)(a) and (b) Public Order Act 1986.
87. s68 Criminal Justice and Public Order Act 1994.
88. Ibid., at s69 (1)(b).
89. Article 3, *Freedom of Association and Protection of the Right to Organise Convention*, 1948 (Convention No 87).
90. Part I Trade Union Act 1984; ss12, 14 and 15 Employment Act 1988, (now ss226–35 Trade Union and Labour Relations (Consolidation) Act 1992; ss1–5 Trade Union Reform and Employment Rights Act 1993.
91. ss5–9 Trade Union and Labour Relations (Consolidation) Act 1992.
92. Ibid., Part VII.
93. s12 Employment Act 1984, now s73 (3) Trade Union and Labour Relations (Consolidation) Act 1992.

94. Ibid., s77 (4)(a) and (b).
95. s3, s1, Trade Union Reform and Employment Rights Act 1993.
96. s72 Trade Union and Labour Relations (Consolidation) Act 1992.
97. Painter and Puttick, 1993, at 298.
98. *Young, James and Webster* v. *UK* (1981) IRLR 408.
99. s137 Trade Union and Labour Relations (Consolidation) Act 1992.
100. *Cheall* v. *APEX* (1983) AC 180 (HL) ((1983) CLJ 207).
101. s14 Trade Union Reform and Employment Rights Act 1993.
102. *Lee* v. *Showmen's Guild of GB* (1952) 1 All ER 1175 CA.
103. *Roebuck* v. *NUM (Yorkshire Area)* (No 2) (1978) ICR 676.
104. s3 Employment Act 1988, now s64 Trade Union and Labour Relations (Consolidation) Act 1992 and s16 Trade Union Reform and Employment Rights Act 1993.
105. See for example, *Bradley* v. *NALGO* (1991) IRLR 159 (EAT).
106. s65 Trade Union and Labour Relations (Consolidation) Act 1992.
107. *The Law at Work*, Labour Research Department, 1994, at 5.
108. ss24 and 26 Trade Union Reform and Employment Rights Act 1993.
109. ss28–9 Trade Union Reform and Employment Rights Act 1993.
110. s2 Trade Union Reform and Employment Rights Act 1993.
111. Hendy, 1994, at 18.
112. Unfair Dismissal (Variation of Qualifying Period) Order 1979 SI No 959.
113. Ibid., 1985 SI No 782.
114. ss6 and 8 Employment Act 1980, now ss116 (4)-(7) Trade Union and Labour Relations (Consolidation) Act 1992.
115. s20 Employment Act 1989.
116. *Labour Research*, November 1994.
117. *Hansard*, Written Answer, 8 July 1994, col 332.
118. *Resolving Employment Rights Disputes, Options for Reform*, Employment Department, HMSO Cm 2707, 1994, at 4.
119. Ibid., at 20–34.
120. s42 Trade Union Reform and Employment Rights Act 1993.
121. Lourie, 1994, at 6.
122. *Hansard*, Resolution of the House of Commons, 16 December 1982, col 499–575.
123. ss12 and 16 Wages Act 1986.
124. s35 Trade Union Reform and Employment Rights Act 1993. Wages Councils for agricultural workers were retained.
125. *Equalities News*, 'Abolition of Wages Councils – Is it Legal?', Local Government Information Unit, June 1993; and Pay Equity Project, *Narrowing the Gender Pay Gap – How Wages Councils Work for Women*, Pay Equity Project, 1993. The Republic of Ireland is the only other member state not to have some form of minimum wage.
126. ss10 and 13 Employment Act 1989.
127. ss23–5 Trade Union Reform and Employment Rights Act 1993.
128. Ibid., s28
129. Ibid., s33.
130. Ibid., s43.
131. Ibid., s36.
132. Hendy, 1994, at 59.

133. Ibid.
134. *Guardian*, 'Equality Rules Dropped in Sell-off Push', 24 May 1993.
135. *Fourth Periodic Report*, 1994, para 390.
136. *Wilson* v. *Associated Newspapers Ltd* (1993) IRLR 63.
137. ss23–6 Employment Protection (Consolidation) Act 1978, now ss146–67 Trade Union and Labour Relations (Consolidation) Act 1992.
138. s1 Employment Act 1990, now ss137–8 Trade Union and Labour (Consolidation) Act 1992.
139. ILO 81st Session, Report of the Committee of Experts on the Application of Conventions and Recommendations, Report III (Part 4A) (1991), at 289.
140. s1 Employment Act 1990.
141. s238 Trade Union and Labour Relations (Consolidation) Act 1992.
142. s9 Employment Act 1990, now s223 Trade Union and Labour Relations (Consolidation) Act 1992.
143. Simon Deakin and Frank Wilkinson, *The Economics of Employment Rights*, Institute of Employment Rights, 1991, at 25.
144. For example, the *Directive on the Protection at Work of Pregnant Women or Women who have Recently Given Birth*, Dir 92/85/EEC.
145. ss23–5 Trade Union Reform and Employment Rights Act 1993.
146. Unfair Dismissal (Variation of Qualifying Period) Order 1979 SI No 959 and Order 1985 SI No 782.
147. s12 Employment Act 1980.
148. *Labour Force Survey*, Department of Employment, Spring 1993.
149. Gorman, *Uncovering Discrimination: A Response to the UK Government's Second Report on the United Nations Convention on the Elimination of all forms of Discrimination Against Women*, 1993.
150. See Chapter 5.
151. *Request to the Commission of the European Communities by the Equal Opportunities Commission for Great Britain in relation to the Implementation of the Principle of Equal Pay*, Equal Opportunities Commission, 1993, at 60–71.
152. See Reena Bhavorani, *Black Women in the Labour Market*, Equal Opportunities Commission, 1994, and David Owen, *Ethnic Minority Women and the Labour Market*, Equal Opportunities Commission, 1994.
153. Caroline Gooding, *Trouble With the Law?*, GMP, 1992, at 26. Constructive dismissal occurs where an employer has so altered the conditions of an employee's employment as to amount to a fundamental breach of contract.
154. See Roy Lewis and Jon Clark, *Employment Rights, Industrial Tribunals and Arbitration: the Case of Alternative Dispute Resolution*, the Institute for Employment Rights, 1993.
155. See *Class Action and Equal Pay*, Labour Research Department, Public Law Project and the Pay Equity Campaign, January 1991.
156. See *Civil Rights for Civil Servants*, NCCL, 1984, and *The Purging of the Civil Service*, NCCL, 1985.
157. Paddy Hillyard and Janie Percy-Smith, *The Coercive State: the Decline of Democracy in Britain*, Fontana, 1988, at 115.
158. s2 Official Secrets Act 1989.
159. *Third Periodic Report*, 1989, at 140–2.
160. Ibid.

Notes

161. ss1–2 Local Government and Housing Act 1989.
162. *Restrictions on Public Political Activity by Senior Local Government Staff*, Consultation Paper by the Department of the Environment, the Scottish Office and the Welsh Office, undated.
163. *The Times*, 'Is Whitehall Turning Tory?', 22 December 1992.
164. *Hansard*, Written Answer, 3 April 1985, col 621.
165. Ibid., 24 July 1990, col 159–61.
166. Disclosed in case taken by Liberty's legal department, R v. *Secretary of State for the Foreign and Commonwealth Office*, ex parte, 22 January 1993, unreported.
167. See Lucy Vickers, *'Whistleblowing'*, Institute of Employment Rights, forthcoming.
168. *First Annual Report*, Public Concern at Work, 1994.
169. Ibid., at 11.
170. See *The Public Inquiry into the Piper Alpha Disaster*, Department of Energy, HMSO Cm 1310, 1990; and *Court Inquiry*, Department of Transport, Ct No 8074, HMSO, 1987.
171. *Inquiry into the Supervision of the Bank of Credit and Commerce International*, HMSO, 22 October 1992.
172. Graham Pink, *Whistleblowing, For Whom the Truth Hurts*, Charter 88, 1992; and *Labour Research*, February 1995.
173. See *Freedom of Speech in the NHS: A Guide for Negotiators*, Manufacturing, Science and Finance, July 1993.
174. *Labour Research*, February 1995.
175. Ibid.
176. Vickers, forthcoming.
177. *Guardian*, 'Health Service Gags Doctors', 16 December 1994.
178. *Britain the preferred location*, Department of Trade and Industry, 1991, at 14–15.
179. *Hansard*, Written Answer, 10 January 1995, col 33.
180. Ibid., 31 March 1994, col 928.
181. *Labour Research*, 'Boardroom Bonanza Continues', August 1994.
182. *The New Review*, Low Pay Unit, Nov/Dec 1994, at 9.
183. See Carey Oppenheim, *Poverty the Facts*, Child Poverty Action Group, 1993.
184. Philip Pearson and Matilda Quiney, *Poor Britain: Poverty, Inequality and Low Pay in the Nineties*, Low Pay Unit, undated, at 2.
185. Hendy, 1994, at 68–9.
186. *Hansard*, Written Answer, 9 May 1994, col 37–8. There were 1,018,000 part-time male employees and 4,624,000 part-time female employees in 1984. By 1993 this had grown to 1,451,000 and 5,206,000 respectively. During the same period the overall size of the workforce increased from 23,833,000 to 24,603,000.
187. Ibid., 16 March 1994, col 714.
188. Ibid., 8 December 1994, col 341.
189. Hendy, 1994, at 98.
190. s8 Finance Act 1980.
191. Hendy, 1994, at 68.
192. *Slaughter on Britain's Building Sites*, Connolly Publications, 1990, at 5–6.
193. For example, *Guardian* 'Fears for 600 Jobs in East Midlands Power Shakeup',

22 December 1993; *Guardian* ' "Lives at Risk" in Pit Safety Deregulation', 24 August 1993; and *Guardian* 'Unions Raise Fears of More Job Losses', 22 December 1993.
194. Hendy, 1994, at 58.
195. Painter and Puttick, 1993, at 263.
196. Ibid.
197. Ibid., at 264.
198. *Hansard*, Written Answer, 3 November 1994, col 1355.
199. See *Blackspot Construction*, Health and Safety Executive, 1988.
200. *Hansard*, Written Answer, 30 March 1994, col 814.
201. See David Bergman, *The Perfect Crime?*, West Midlands Health and Safety Advice Centre, 1994.
202. *Health and Safety Commission Annual Report 1993/4*, HSE Books, 1994, at 106–9 for the most recent figures; and *Health and Safety Commission Annual Report 1992/3*, HSE Books, 1993, at 96–7 which gives the number of fatal injuries and the injury rate per worker for each industry over the last 10 years.
203. See Roger Moore *The Price of Safety: the Market, Workers' Rights and the Law*, Institute for Employment Rights, 1991.
204. Ibid., at 20.
205. Health and Safety Executive, 1988.
206. *Slaughter on Britain's Building Sites*, 1990, at 13.
207. *Health and Safety Commission Annual Report 1992/3*, HSE Books, 1993, at 96–9.
208. Ibid., at 110.
209. Hendy, 1994, at 72.
210. Ibid., at 18.
211. *Blowout*, The Off-shore Liaison Committee, January 1995.
212. Ibid.
213. Department of Energy, HMSO, 1990.
214. Hendy, 1994, at 55.
215. *New Statesman and Society*, David Bergman, 'A Killing in the Boardroom', 15 June 1990.
216. Ibid.
217. Moore, 1991, at 12.
218. See *TUC Consultative Report: Representation at Work*, TUC, 1995.
219. Ibid.

INDEX